The Collected Courses of the Academy of European Law
Series Editors: Professor Marise Cremona,
                Professor Bruno de Witte, and
                Professor Francesco Francioni,
                European University Institute,
                Florence
Assistant Editor: Anny Bremner, *European University*
                Institute, Florence

VOLUME XVIII/1
The Access of Individuals to International Justice

The Collected Courses of the Academy of European Law
Edited by Professor Marise Cremona,
Professor Bruno de Witte, and Professor Francesco Francioni
Assistant Editor: Anny Bremner

This series brings together the Collected Courses of the
Academy of European Law in Florence. The Academy's mission is to
produce scholarly analyses which are at the cutting edge of the two
fields in which it works: European Union law and human rights law.
A 'general course' is given each year in each field, by a
distinguished scholar and/or practitioner, who either examines the
field as a whole through a particular thematic, conceptual, or
philosophical lens, or who looks at a particular theme in the context
of the overall body of law in the field. The Academy also publishes
each year a volume of collected essays with a specific theme in each
of the two fields.

The Access of Individuals to International Justice

ANTÔNIO AUGUSTO
CANÇADO TRINDADE

Former President of the Inter-American Court of Human Rights;
Judge of the International Court of Justice;
Emeritus Professor of International Law at the University of Brasilia
Member of the *Institut de Droit International*, and of the *Curatorium* of The Hague
Academy of International Law

OXFORD
UNIVERSITY PRESS

OXFORD
UNIVERSITY PRESS

Great Clarendon Street, Oxford OX2 6DP
United Kingdom

Oxford University Press is a department of the University of Oxford.
It furthers the University's objective of excellence in research, scholarship,
and education by publishing worldwide. Oxford is a registered trade mark of
Oxford University Press in the UK and in certain other countries

First published 2011
Reprinted 2012

British Library Cataloguing in Publication Data
Data available

Library of Congress Cataloging in Publication Data
Data available

ISBN 978-0-19-958096-5

À memória de minha mãe
Maria Antonieta,
e à Carmela,
em reconhecimento do testemunho do raro
amor incondicional.

– 'A meio do caminho desta vida
achei-me a errar por uma selva escura,
longe da boa via, então perdida. (. . .)
Nada pôde abater o meu pendor
de ir pelo mundo, em longo aprendizado,
dos homens perquirindo o erro e o valor. (. . .)
Relembrai vossa origem, vossa essência:
criados não fostes como os animais,
mas donos de vontade e consciência (. . .).
Vós, os viventes, com simplicidade,
julgais estar aos céus tudo imputado,
por força de fatal necessidade.
Mas com isto se vira erradicado
o livre-arbítrio, e senso não faria
haver-se o mal punido e o bem premiado. (. . .)
Quem contra o mal, seguro, se enrijece,
e a luta adentra, de consciência digna,
acaba por vencer e não perece'.

Dante Alighieri, *A Divina Comédia*, book I-1, verses 1–3;
book I-26, verses 97–99 and 118–20; book II-16,
verses 67–72 and 76–8 (1308–1321, Brazilian reed. of 1991).

– 'Caminante, son tus huellas
el camino, y nada más;
caminante, no hay camino,
se hace camino al andar.
Al andar se hace camino,
y al volver la vista atrás
se ve la senda que nunca
se ha de volver a pisar'.

Antonio Machado, 'Proverbios y Cantares',
in *Poesías Completas* (1912–1913, Spanish reed. of 2003).

–'Y la vida es misterio; la luz ciega
y la verdad inaccesible asombra;
la adusta perfección jamás se entrega,
Y el secreto Ideal duerme en la sombra.
Por eso ser sincero es ser potente.
De desnuda que está, brilla la estrella;
el agua dice el alma de la fuente
en la voz de cristal que fluye d'ella. (. . .)
La virtud está en ser tranquilo y fuerte;
con el fuego interior todo se abrasa;
se triunfa del rencor y de la muerte,
y hacia Belen . . . la caravana pasa!'.

Rubén Darío, *Cantos de Vida y Esperanza* (1905, Spanish
reed. of 2004).

Contents

Tables of Cases   xiii
Table of International Treaties, Conventions, and Instruments   xx
Table of Statutes of International Courts   xxiv
Table of National Legislation   xxv
Introduction   xxvii

I   The Historical Recovery of the Human Person as Subject
    of the Law of Nations   1

    I.   Introduction: The Legacy of the Individual's Subjectivity in the
         Emerging Law of Nations   1
    II. The Individual's Presence and Participation in the International
         Legal Order   3
    III. The Rescue of the Individual as a Subject of International Law   6
    IV. Personality and Capacity: the Individual's Access to Justice at
         International Level   13
    V.   Concluding Observations: The Historical Significance of the
         International Subjectivity of the Individual   15

II The Exercise of the Right of Access to International
    Justice: The Right of International Individual Petition   17

    I.   Evolution and Juridical Nature of the Right of Individual Petition   17
    II. Consolidation and Scope of the Right of Individual Petition   20
    III. The Titularity of the Right of Individual Petition: Distinct
         Formulations   22
    IV. The Significance and Overriding Importance of the Right of
         Individual Petition   27
    V.   The Right of Direct Access of Individuals to International
         Human Rights Tribunals   32
         1. Developments in the European System of Protection   32
         2. Developments in the Inter-American System of Protection   37
         3. Developments in the African System of Protection   46
    VI. Concluding Observations   47

III Access to Justice at International Level and the
    Right to an Effective Domestic Remedy   50

    I.   Access to International Justice and Admissibility of Petitions   50
    II. The Right to an Effective Domestic Remedy as a Basic Pillar
         of the Rule of Law in a Democratic Society   51
    III. The Intangibility of Judicial Guarantees in All Circumstances   56
    IV. The Right to Recognition of Juridical Personality   58

V. The Converging Case-Law of the European and Inter-American
Courts of Human Rights on the Rights of Access to Justice
and to a Fair Trial 59

IV The Interrelation between the Access to Justice (Right to an
Effective Remedy) and the Guarantees of the Due Process of Law 63

I. Introduction 63
II. The Interrelation between the Access to Justice (Right to an
Effective Remedy) and the Guarantees of the Due Process
of Law in the Case-Law of the IACtHR 64
III. The Overcoming of Vicissitudes as to the Right to an Effective
Remedy in the Jurisprudential Construction of the ECtHR 66
IV. The Right of Access to Justice *Lato Sensu* 71
V. Concluding Observations 74

V Access to International Justice in Relation to the Interaction
between International Law and Domestic Law 76

I. Access to International Justice of Victims of Human Rights
Violations: General Considerations 76
II. The Interaction between International Law and Domestic
Law in Human Rights Protection 82
III. The Needed Revision or Control of Reservations to Human
Rights Treaties 89
IV. The Interaction between International Law and Domestic
Law and the Rule of Exhaustion of the Local Remedies 98
1. Human Rights Treaties and the Role of National Courts 98
2. The State's Duty to Provide Effective Local Remedies and
the Individual's Duty to Have Recourse to Them:
The Emphasis on Redress or the Realization of Justice 99
3. The *Rationale* of the Local Remedies Rule in Human
Rights Protection 100
V. The Principle of Complementarity in International Criminal Law 107
VI. Beyond Subsidiarity: State Responsibility, Substantive Law, and
the Interaction between International Law and Domestic Law
in the Present Domain of Protection 110

VI Access to Justice: The Safeguard and Preservation of the
Integrity of International Jurisdiction 113

I. The Intangibility of International Jurisdiction 113
II. The Position of International Human Rights Tribunals 114
1. Developments in the European Human Rights System 114
2. Developments in the Inter-American Human Rights System 115
3. General Assessment 118

III. Direct Access of Individuals in Provisional Measures of
     Protection   119
IV. Access to Justice: The Realization of the Right to Justice   120
 V. The Prevalence of the Guarantees of the Due Process of Law   122
VI. Concluding Observations   123

VII New Developments in the Notion of 'Potential Victim':
     The Preventive Dimension of Protection   125

  I. Introduction   125
 II. Origins and Development of the Notion of Victim   125
III. The Continuing Evolution of the Notion of 'Potential Victim'   127
IV. New Developments of the Notion of 'Potential Victim'   129
    1. Autonomous Configuration of the Notion of Victim in its
       Preventive Dimension   130
    2. Condition of Victim and *Legitimatio ad Causam*:
       A Precision   130
 V. Concluding Observations   131

VIII The Protection of Victims in Situations of Great Adversity
     or Defencelessness – I   132

  I. Introduction: International Protection of Victims in Distress   132
 II. The Drama of Uprootedness and the Growing Need of
     Protection of Migrants   133
III. The Protection of Migrants in International Case-Law   142
    1. European Human Rights System   142
    2. Inter-American Human Rights System   144
       a The Advisory Opinion on the *Right to Information on
         Consular Assistance in the Framework of the Guarantees
         of the Due Process of Law* (1999)   145
       b The Advisory Opinion on the *Juridical Condition and
         Rights of Undocumented Migrants* (2003)   147
IV. Concluding Observations   149

 IX The Protection of Victims in Situations of Great Adversity
     or Defencelessness – II   151

  I. Introduction: The Centrality of the Suffering of the Victims   151
 II. The Protection of Abandoned or 'Street Children'   152
III. The Protection of Members of Peace Communities and Other
     Civilians in Situations of Armed Conflict   157
IV. The Protection of Internally Displaced Persons   163
 V. The Protection of Persons under Sub-human Conditions
    of Detention   171
VI. Concluding Observations: The Prevalence of Human Rights
    of Persons in Situations of Vulnerability   174

X   Access to Justice of Victims of Massacres and Crimes
    of State   179

    I. Massacres and Crimes of State: Introductory Observations   179
    II. Victims of Massacres   182
    III. The Determination of the Aggravated Responsibility
        of the State   183
    IV. The Determination of the Condition of Victim   186
        1. Identified and Identifiable Victims: Identification of
            Victims at Distinct Stages of the Procedure   186
        2. Classification or Categorization of Victims   187
        3. Centrality and Expansion of the Notion of Direct Victim   188
    V. The Victims' Right to Redress   189
    VI. Concluding Observations   190

XI The Overcoming of Obstacles to Direct Access to Justice   192

    I. Introduction   192
    II. The Proper Role of International Human Rights Tribunals   193
    III. Towards the End of Self-Amnesties   194
    IV. The Right to the Law (*droit au Droit/Derecho al Derecho*)
        as an Imperative of *Jus Cogens*   196
    V. The Expansion of the Material Content of *Jus Cogens*   198
    VI. The Evolving Presence of Victims in International
        Criminal Jurisdictions   201
    VII. Concluding Observations: The Protection of the Human
        Person in the Light of Considerations of International
        Ordre Public   205

Conclusions   209

Select Bibliography   213
    I. Books   213
    II. Courses, Collections, Contributions to Books   218
    III. Monographs and Reports   224
    IV. Articles   225
Index   231

Tables of Cases

ADVISORY OPINIONS

Advisory Opinion No 8, 30 January 1987, IACtHR 56
Advisory Opinion No 9, 06 October 1987, IACtHR. 57
Effect of Reservations on the Entry into Force of the American Convention on
Human Rights, Advisory Opinion, 24 September 1982, IACtHR 26, 93
Juridical Condition and Human Rights of the Child, Advisory Opinion
No 17, 28 August 2002, IACtHR. 12, 14, 41, 156
Juridical Condition and Rights of Undocumented Migrants, Advisory Opinion
No. 18, 17 September 2003, IACtHR. 15, 134, 139, 145, 147, 148, 159, 165,
196, 197, 199
Reparations for Damages, Advisory Opinion, 1949, ICJ. 16
Reservations to the Convention against Genocide, Advisory
Opinion, 1951, ICJ 89, 91, 96, 97
Restrictions to the Death Penalty, Third Advisory Opinion, (1983), IACtHR 93
Right to Information on Consular Assistance in the Framework of the
Guarantees of the Due Process of Law, Advisory Opinion OC-16/99, Series A,
n.16, IACtHR 11, 64, 65, 139, 145, 146, 149, 152, 165

AFRICAN COMMISSION ON HUMAN AND PEOPLES' RIGHTS

African Institute for Human Rights and Development (on Behalf of Sierra
Leonean Refugees in Guinea) v Guinea (2004). 107
Alhassan Abubakar v Gana (1996) 57
Bissangou v Republic of Congo (2006) 73, 106
Commission Nationale des Droits de l'homme et des Libertés v
Chad (n. 74/92). 106
Constitutional Rights Project (in relation to Akamu, Adega et alii) v Nigeria
(n. 69/91), 10 Interights Bulletin (1996) p.18 . . . . .57, 106
Constitutional Rights Project (in respect of Z. Lekwot and 6 Others)
v Nigeria (n. 87/93) 106
Civil Liberties Organisation in Respect of the Nigerian Bar Association v Nigeria. 106
Democratic Republic of Congo v Burundi, Rwanda and Uganda, Communication
227/99, Decision of May 2003 162
Jawara v Gambia case (2000) 106
Lawyers' Committee for Human Rights v Zaire (n. 47/90). 105
Lawyers for Human Rights v Swaziland (2005) 107
Les Témoins de Jehovah v Zaire (n. 56/91) 105
Media Rights Agenda and Others v Nigeria (1998) 106
Purohit and Another v Gambia (2003) 106
'Rencontre Africaine pour la Defense des Droits de l'Homme' v Zambia (1996) 57, 106
Social and Economic Rights Action Centre (SERAC) and Another v Nigeria (2001) 106
Union Interafricaine des Droits de l'Homme v Zaire (n. 100/93) 105
World Organisation against Torture v Zaire (n. 25/89) 105
Zimbabwe Human Rights NGO Forum v Zimbabwe (2006). 74, 106

EUROPEAN COMMISSION OF HUMAN RIGHTS CASES

Abdulaziz, Cabales and Balkandali v United Kingdom (1983). 142
Association of Air Pilots of the Republic, J. Mata el Al. versus Spain, Appl. n. 10733/84,
        decision of 11 March 1985, 41 Decisions and Reports (1985) p. 222, ECommHR 24
East African Asians cases. 142
Greek Federation of Customs Officials, N. Gialouris, G. Christopoulos and 3333
        Other Customs Officials v Greece, Appl. n. 24581/94, decision of 6 April 1995, 81-B
        Decisions and Reports (1995) p. 127, EComHR 24
K. Sygounis, I. Kotsis and Police Union v Greece, Appl. n. 18598/91, decision
        of 18 May 1994, 78 Decisions and Reports (1994) p. 77, EComHR. 24
North Ireland case (1976) 172
N.N.Tauira and 18 Others v France, Appl. n. 28204/95, decision of 04 December
        1995, 83-A Decisions and Reports (1995) p. 130, EComHR 24
Scientology Kirche Deutschland e.V. v Germany, Appl. n. 34614/96, decision of
        7 April 1997, 89 Decisions and Reports (1997) p. 170, EComHR 24
Vietnamese Orphans (H. Becker v Denmark case, 1975) 128, 129
Zentralrat Deutscher Sinti und Roma y R. Rose v Germany, Appl. n. 35208/97),
        decision of 27 May 1997, p. 4 (unpublished), EComHR 24

EUROPEAN COURT OF HUMAN RIGHTS CASES

Abdulaziz, Cabales and Balkandali v United Kingdom, Judgment,
        28 May 1985. . . . . .54, 66, 142, 143
Airey v Ireland (1979) 60
Akdeniz and Others v Turkey (1999) 160
Akdivar and Others v Turkey, Judgment, 16 September 1996 . . . . .66, 67, 104, 160
Akkoc v Turkey (2000) 160
Aksoy v Turkey, Judgment, 18 December 1996. . . . . .54, 66, 104, 160
Alikhadzhiyeva v Russia, Judgment, 05 July 2007 . . . . 31, 70
Barbera, Messegué and Jabardo v Spain (1988) 60
Baysayeva v Russia, Judgment, 05 April 2007 . . . . .31, 105
Bazorkina v Russia, Judgment, 27 July 2006 28
Beldjoudi v France, Judgment, 26 March 1992 144
Belilos v Switzerland (1988) 92, 114, 119
Bitiyeva and X v Russia, Judgment, 21 June 2007 31
Cakici v Turkey (1999) 160
Campbell and Fell v United Kingdom, Judgment, 28 June 1984 172
Cruz Varas and Others v Sweden, Merits, Series A, vol. 201. 23
Cyprus v Turkey, Judgment, 10 May 2001 . . . . .170, 176
De Jong, Baljet and van den Brink v The Netherlands (1984). 128
Delcourt v Belgium (1970). 60
Donnelly and Others v United Kingdom (1973) 78
Dudgeon v United Kingdom (1981). 78, 128
Ergi v Turkey (1998). 160
Ertak v Turkey (2000). 160
Gaskin v United Kingdom (1989). 60
Golder v United Kingdom (1975). 60, 70
Gul v Turkey (2000) 160
H. Becker v Denmark (1975). 78, 128
Holy Monasteries v Greece, Judgment, 09 December 1994 26
Hornsby v Greece, Judgment, 19 March 1997, Series A, n.33 . . . . .72, 121

Hornsby v Greece, Reparations Judgment, 10 April 1998 121
Iatridis v Greece, Judgment, 25 March 1999 69
Ilascu, Lesco, Ivantoc and Petrov-Popa v Moldova and the Russian Federation,
    Preliminary Objections, Judgment, 4 July 2001 . . . . 27, 115, 119
Ilascu and Others v Moldova and Russia, 8 July 2004 30
Imakayeva v Russia, Judgment, 09 November 2006 31
Ireland v United Kingdom, Merits Judgment, 18 January 1978, Series A, n.25, p. 62 193
Isayeva, Yusupova and Bazayeva v Russia, Judgment, 24 February 2005 . . . . 69, 105
Issa and Others v Turkey, Judgment, 16 November 2004 159
Jelicic v Bosnia and Herzegovina, Judgment, 31 October 2006 72
Johnson and Others v Ireland (1986) 128
Kaya v Turkey (2000) 160
Khashiyev and Akayeva v Russia, Judgment, 24 February 2005 . . . . 69, 70, 105
Kilic v Turkey (2000) 160
Kjeldsen v Denmark (1972) 78
Klass and Others v Federal Republic of Germany, Judgment,
    6 September 1978 . . . . 22, 54, 66, 78, 128
Klyakhin v Russia, Judgment, 6 June 2005 30
Kudla v Poland, Judgment, 18 October 2000 68
Kurt v Turkey, Judgment 25 May 1998 . . . . 25, 70, 104, 123, 160
Lamguindaz v United Kingdom case (1992) 144
Lawless v Ireland, 1960 . . . . 32, 33
Loizidou et alii v Turkey, Preliminary Objections, Judgment,
    23 March 1995 . . . . 25, 27, 93, 114, 115, 119, 206
Mamatkulov v Turkey, Judgment, 04 February 2005 36
Marckx (P. and A.) v Belgium (1979) 78, 128
Markovic and Others v Italy, Judgment, 14 December 2006 . . . . 70, 71
Matznetter case (1969) 99
Mentes and Others v Turkey, Judgment, 28 November 1997 . . . . 67, 68
Moustaquim v Belgium, Judgment, 18 February 1991 144
Norris v Ireland, Judgment, 26 October 1988, Series A, vol 142 24
Nurmagomedov v Russia, 07 June 2007 30
Petra v Romania, Judgment, 23 September 1998 . . . . 171, 172
Plattform 'Ärzte für das Leben' v Austria (1988) 60
Poleshchuk v Russia, Judgment, 07 October 2004 31
Popov v Russia 30
Russian cases 30–1
Selmouni v France, Merits Judgment, 28 July 1999 . . . . 153, 172
Shamayev and Others v Georgia and Russia, Judgment, 12 April 2005 . . . . 31, 70
Silver and Others v United Kingdom (1983) 54, 66
Soering (J.) v United Kingdom (1989) 78, 129
Tanrikulu v Turkey, Judgment, 08 July 1999 . . . . 29, 69, 104, 160
Tas v Turkey (2000) 160
Timurtas v Turkey (2000) 160
Tomasi v France, Judgment, 27 August 1992 172
Trubnikov v Russia, Judgment, 05 July 2005 31
Turkish cases 29, 160
Uner v Netherlands, Judgment, 18 October 2006 144
Vagrancy cases (1970) 32
Weber (1990) 92
Yasa v Turkey (1998) 160

INTER-AMERICAN COURT OF HUMAN RIGHTS CASES

19 Tradesmen v Colombia, Judgment, 05 July 2004 . . . . .52, 65, 180, 183
Acevedo Jaramillo and Others, Judgment, 07 February 2006 . . . . .187, 189
Acosta Calderón v Ecuador, Judgment, 24 June 2005 . . . . .52, 199
Aloeboetoe and Others, Reparations, 1991 187
Almonacid Arellano v Chile, Judgment, 26 September 2006. . . . . 110, 181, 182, 195,
196, 200, 201
Baena Ricardo and Others v Panama, Judgment on the Merits,
02 February 2001. . . . . .62, 65, 120, 204
Baena Ricardo and Others v Panama, Judgment on Jurisdiction, 28 November 2003. 120
Baldeón García v Peru, Judgment, 06 April 2006. . . . . .189, 199
Bámaca Velásquez v Guatemala, Merits, Judgment, 25 November 2000 . . . . .52, 65, 151
Bámaca Velásquez v Guatemala, Reparations Judgment, 22 February 2002 . . . . .142, 151
Bámaca Velásquez v Guatemala, Request for Measures of Protection, Resolution,
20 December 2002. 119
Blake v Guatemala, Merits, Judgment, 24 January 1998. . . . . 52, 62, 116, 151, 159, 204
Blake v Guatemala, Preliminary Objections (1996) 116
Blake v Guatemala, Reparations Judgment, 22 January 1999 . . . . .89, 116, 151
Brothers Gómez Paquiyauri v Peru, Judgment, 08 July 2004 . . . . .65, 111, 198, 199
Caballero Delgado and Santana v Colombia (1995) 51
Caballero Delgado and Santana v Colombia, Reparations, Judgment, 29 January
1997, Dissenting Opinion of Judge A.A. Cançado Trindade 51, 55, 85, 86, 123, 187
Caesar v Trinidad and Tobago, Judgment, 11 March 2005. . . . . 65, 89, 95, 198, 199
Cantoral Benavides v Peru, Merits Judgment, 18 August 2000 .52, 153
Cantos v Argentina, Judgment, 28 November 2002. . . . . 52, 62, 65
Cardot v France, Judgment, 19 March 1991 104
Castillo Paez, Preliminary Objections, 30 January 1996 . . . . 39, 40, 43, 45, 51, 52, 103
Castillo Paez v Peru, Merits, Judgment, 03 November 1997. .61, 64, 206
Castillo Petruzzi and Others v Peru (Preliminary Objections), Judgment,
04 September 1998, Series C, n. 41. . . . . .13, 21, 26, 27, 39, 43, 45,
50, 62, 117, 131
Castillo Petruzzi and Others v Peru, Judgment, 30 May 1999. .52, 115
Cesti Hurtado v Peru, Judgment, 29 September 1999, par. 121 52
Children and Adolescents Deprived of Freedom in the Premises of Tatuapé
of FEBEM v Brazil, Provisional Measures of Protection, Resolutions,
17 and 29 November 2005. 173
Children and Adolescents Deprived of Freedom in the Premises of Tatuapé
of FEBEM v Brazil, Provisional Measures of Protection, Resolution,
30 November 2005 . . . . .40–1, 122
Children Yean and Bosico v Dominican Republic, Judgment, 08 September 2005. . . . . . . .65, 155
Communities of Jiguamiandó and Curbaradó, Provisional Measures of
Protection, 06 March 2003. . . . . .157, 158
Communities Yakye Axa v Peru *see* Indigenous Communities Yakye Axa v Peru
Community Mayagna (Sumo) Awas Tingni v Nicaragua, Judgment, 31 August 2001. 52
Community Moiwana v Suriname, Judgment *see* Moiwana Community v Suriname
Community of Peace of San José of Apartadó v Colombia, Provisional Measures
of Protection, Resolution 18 June 2002. . . . . .157, 158
Constitutional Tribunal v Peru, Judgment on Jurisdiction, 24 September 1999 . . . . 29, 49, 62,
115, 116, 117, 211
Constitutional Tribunal v Peru, Request for Interim Measures of Protection (2000). 119, 120

Durand and Ugarte v Peru, Judgment, 16 August 2000 . . . . .52, 65
El Amparo, Verbatim Records of the Public Hearing Held before the Court on
   27 January 1996 on Reparations 38
El Amparo v Venezuela, Reparations Judgment, 14 September 1996 . . . . . . 86, 122, 187, 193, 204
El Amparo v Venezuela, Resolution on interpretation of judgement, 16 April 1997 123
Fermín Ramírez v Guatemala, Judgment, 20 June 2005 65
Five Pensioners v Peru, Judgment, 28 February 2003 . . . . 40, 43, 62, 121, 122
Gangaram Panday v Suriname, Preliminary Objections, 04 December 1991 . . . . .51, 103
Genie Lacayo v Nicaragua, Appeal for Revision of Judgment, Resolution of
   13 September 1997 . . . . .51, 52, 53, 55, 123
Godinez Cruz, Compensatory Damages, Judgment 21 July 1989 38
Godinez Cruz, Preliminary Objections 50
Goiburú and Others v Paraguay, Judgment, 22 September 2006 . . . . . . .110, 181, 182, 185, 187,
                                         189, 191, 199, 200, 201, 202, 203
Gómez Palomino v Peru, Judgment, 22 November 2005 65
Gutiérrez Soler v Colombia, Judgment, 12 September 2005 184
Haitians and Dominicans of Haitian Origin in the Dominican Republic,
   Provisional Measures of Protection, Order, 18 August 2000 . . . . .141, 144, 145
Hermanas Serrano Cruz v El Salvador, Judgment, 01 March 2005 65
Hilaire, Benjamin,and Constantine v Trinidad and Tobago, Preliminary Objections,
   01 September 2001 . . . . .29, 117, 119, 211
Hilaire, Constantine y Benjamin y Otros v Trinidad y Tobago, Judgment,
   21 June 2002 . . . . .52, 65
Indigenous Community Yakye Axa v Peru, Judgment, 17 June 2005 . . . . .41, 65, 168, 170
'Institute of Rehabilitation of Minors' v Paraguay, Judgment, 02 September
   2004 . . . . .154, 155, 173, 187
Ivcher Bronstein v Peru, Judgment on Jurisdiction,
   24 September 1999 . . . . 29, 49, 62, 115, 116, 117, 119, 211
Juan Humberto Sánchez v Honduras, Judgment, 07 June 2003 . . . . .52, 65
La Cantuta v Peru, Judgment, 29 November 2006 . . . . .185, 196, 200
Las Palmeras v Colombia, Judgment, 06 December 2001 . . . . .62, 65
'Last Temptation of Christ' *see* Olmedo Bustos and Others v Chile
Loayza Tamayo v Peru, Preliminary Objections, 31 January 1996 . . . . . 39, 40, 43, 45, 51, 62, 103
Loayza Tamayo v Peru, Judgment, 17 September 1997 122
Loayza Tamayo v Peru, Request for Interim Measures of Protection (2000) 119, 120
López Álvarez v Honduras, Judgment, 01 February 2006 199
Maritza Urrutia v Guatemala, Judgment, 27 November 2003 . . . . .52, 65
Massacre of Barrios Altos (Chumbipuma Aguirre and Others) v Peru,
   Judgment 14 March 2001 . . . . 62, 65, 180, 183, 185, 194, 195, 196, 200, 212
Massacre of Caracazo v Venezuela, Reparations, 29 August 2002 . . . . .180, 187, 188
Massacre of Mapiripán v Colombia, Judgment,
   15 September 2005 . . . . .64, 65, 170, 180, 183, 185, 186, 187, 189
Massacre of Plan de Sánchez v Guatemala, Merits, Judgment,
   29 April 2004 . . . . .110, 180, 183, 184, 185, 187, 191, 199
Massacre of Plan de Sánchez v Guatemala, Reparations Judgment, 19 November 2004 . . .185, 199
Massacre of Pueblo Bello v Colombia, Judgment,
   31 January 2006 . . . . .52, 64, 65, 71, 83, 158, 180, 197, 199
Massacres of Ituango v Colombia, Judgment, 01 July 2006 . . . . 110, 170, 183, 185,
                                                 186, 187, 189, 199
Moiwana Community v Suriname, Merits, Judgment,
   15 June 2005 . . . . .65, 141, 142, 144, 168, 169, 170, 180, 183, 186
Moiwana Community v Suriname, Interpretation of Sentence, 8 February 2006 145

Montero Aranguren and Others (Detention Centre of Catia) v Venezuela, Judgment,
05 July 2006 . . . . 173, 180, 182, 182, 188, 189
Myrna Mack Chang v Guatemala, Judgment, 25 November 2003 . . . . 65, 66, 180, 184
Neira Alegría v Peru (1996) 204
Olmedo Bustos and Others v Chile, Judgment, 05 February 2001 . . . . 111, 193, 194
Operation Condor *see* Goiburú and Others v Paraguay
Palamara Iribarne v Chile, Judgment, 22 November 2005 . . . . .52, 65
Paniagua Morales and Others v Guatemala, Judgment, 08 March 1998. . . . . .52, 62
Paniagua Morales and Others v Guatemala (2001). 204
Prison Castro Castro v Peru, Judgment, 25 November 2006. . . . . 173, 180, 182, 183
Prison 'Urso Branco' v Brazil, Resolutions, 18 June and 29 August 2002. 173
Prison 'Urso Branco' v Brazil, Provisional Measures of Protection, Resolutions,
22 April and 07 July 2004 173
Prisons of Mendoza v Argentina, Resolutions, 22 November 2004 and 18 June 2005 173
Sarayaku Indigenous People v Ecuador, Resolutions, 06 July 2004 and 17 June 2005 158
Sawhoyamaxa Indigenous Community v Paraguay, Judgment,
28 March 2006 . . . . 41, 58, 59, 168, 169, 170
Servellón and Others v Honduras, Merits and Reparations, Judgment,
1 September 2006 156–8
Sisters Serrano Cruz v El Salvador, Preliminary Objections, Judgment,
23 November 2004 29–30
Sisters Serrano Cruz v El Salvador, Merits and Reparations, Judgment,
01 March 2005 . . . . .52, 155
'Street Children' case *see* Villagrán Morales and Others v Guatemala
Suárez Rosero v Ecuador, Judgment, 12 November 1997. . . . . .52, 61, 129, 130
Tibi v Ecuador, Judgment, 07 September 2004 . . . . .52, 198, 199
Trujillo Oroza v Bolivia (2002). 62
Vargas Areco, Judgment, 26 September 2006 189
Velásquez Rodríguez v Honduras, Compensatory Damages, Judgment 21 July 1989 38
Velásquez Rodríguez v Honduras, Preliminary Objections 50
Villagrán Morales and Others v Guatemala ('Street Children' case), Merits Judgment,
19 November 1999, Series C, n. 63, Joint Concurring Opinion 14, 41, 52, 66,
152, 153, 154, 155, 156, 169, 204
Villagrán Morales and Others v Guatemala ('Street Children' case), Judgment on
Reparations, 26 May 2001 . . . . 41, 152, 153, 154, 155, 156, 169, 187, 188, 189
Ximenes Lopes v Brazil, Judgment, 04 July 2006. 189
Yatama v Nicaragua, Judgment, 23 June 2005. . . . . .52, 65, 199

INTERNATIONAL CRIMINAL COURT

Situation in the Democratic Republic of Congo. 204
Thomas Lubanga Dyilo 204

INTERNATIONAL COURT OF JUSTICE

Applicability of the Obligation to Arbitrate under the Headquarters Agreement of the
United Nations (case of the PLO Mission), ICJ Reports (1988) 83
Avena and Other Mexican Nationals (2004) 165
LaGrand (2001). 165

PERMANENT COURT OF INTERNATIONAL JUSTICE

Administration of the Prince von Pless case (1933)................................. 99
Free Zones (1932), Series A/B, n. 46.. 83
Greek-Bulgarian Communities (1930), Series B, n. 17 83
Polish Nationals in Danzig (1931), Series A/B, n. 44 83

Table of International Treaties, Conventions, and Instruments

African Charter on Human and Peoples' Rights (ACHPR) 46, 47, 73, 74, 125
Art.1 85
Art.2 163
Art.4 163
Art.7 74
Art.7(1) 57, 74
Art.12(1) 163
Art.12(2) 163
Art.18(1) 163
Art.21–2 163
Art.55–6 23
Art.55–8 22
Art.60 163
Art.61 163
Burkina Faso Protocol (1998) 46, 47
Art.5(1) 46
Art.5(3) 46
Art.34(6) 47
American Convention on Human
  Rights 1948 . . . . 7, 13, 19, 23, 25,
                26, 28, 32, 37, 40, 42,
           44, 45, 46, 47, 50, 51, 52,
      54, 55, 56, 57, 62, 71, 74, 75, 86,
    90, 93, 99, 111, 113, 115, 116, 117,
    118, 119, 122, 125, 129, 130, 131,
        142, 146, 149, 154, 156, 157,
        158, 159, 170, 174, 184, 186,
      187, 193, 195, 201, 206, 207
Art.1(1) 52, 54, 55, 56, 58, 61,
             62, 64, 85, 86, 121, 142, 155,
                159, 184, 195
Art.2 . . . . 55, 56, 83, 85, 86, 121,
               129, 155, 193, 195
Art.3 58
Art.4 . . . . .146, 152, 155, 198
Art.5 . . . . .155, 184, 198
Art.7 198
Art.7(5) 129
Art.8 . . . . 11, 54, 55, 57, 62, 64, 65,
              66, 67, 71, 74, 169, 188,
                195, 197, 199
Art.8(1) 55, 64, 65, 129, 184
Art.8(2) 129
Art.8(4) 122
Art.11 184
Art.12 184
Art.13 . . . . 184, 193
Art.16 184
Art.19 . . . . 154, 155
Art.21 . . . . 121, 184
Art.22 142
Art.22(8) 145
Art.24 184
Art.25 . . . . 51, 52, 54, 55, 56, 57, 61,
              64, 65, 66, 67, 71, 74, 121,
               169, 184, 188, 195, 197,
                199, 206
Art.25(1) 57
Art.27 79
Art.27(1) 56
Art.27(2) 56, 57
Art.29(b) 88
Art.29(c) 57
Art.44 . . . . 17, 18, 22, 23, 25, 28,
               39, 45, 50, 130, 131
Art.45 25
Art.50(2) 44
Art.51(1) 44
Art.57 37
Art.59 44
Art.61(1) 37
Art.62 . . . . .29, 39, 44, 45, 117
Art.62(2) 117
Art.63(1) 37, 153
Art.63(2) 119
Art.65 . . . . 44, 120
Art.68 44
Art.75 . . . . 44, 90, 93
Art.77 44
Art.77(1) 44
Additional Protocol in the matter of
  Economic, Social and Cultural Rights (1988)
Art.2 85
Art.4 88
American Declaration on the Rights and
  Duties of Man 1948 . . . . 53, 67
Art.XVIII 53, 54

Antarctica Treaty 1959. 5
  Madrid Protocol on Environmental
    Protection in the Antarctic (1991). 5
Convention on the Elimination of All Forms of
    Racial Discrimination 1966 . . . . . 21, 22,
                                    92, 94, 139
  Art.XIV. 21
  Art.XIV(1). 22
  Art.XIV(2). 22
  Art.XXII 94
Convention for the Prevention and Punishment
    of the Crime of Genocide 1948. . . 78, 96
  Art.8. 78
Convention of the Reduction of Statelessness
    1961 140
Convention Relating to the Status of Stateless
    Persons 1954 140
Declaration and Programme of Action in Vienna
    1993 27
Declaration of Basic Principles of Justice for
    Victims of Crime and Abuse of Power
    1985 . . . . 189, 190
Declaration of Cartagena on Refugees
    1984 . . . . 165, 166
Declaration of San José on Refugees and
    Displaced Persons 1994 . . . . . . 165, 166
European Convention on Human
    Rights 1950 . . . . . 9, 20, 22, 23, 25, 26,
              28, 30, 32, 33, 34, 36, 37, 47, 54,
              60, 61, 67, 68, 71, 72, 73, 75, 78,
              82, 93, 99, 100, 104, 113, 114, 118,
              119, 122, 125, 129, 131, 142, 160,
              170, 171, 172, 174, 183, 206
  Title I 23
  Art.1 . . . . 54, 69, 115, 160, 161, 176
  Art.2 . . . . 69, 70, 176
  Art.3 . . . . 69, 70, 129, 142, 176,
                                    177, 182, 183
  Art.5 . . . . .59, 123, 171, 182
  Art.5(1). 123
  Art.6 . . . . 55, 59, 61, 67, 68, 69, 70,
                                    71, 72, 73, 74
  Art.6(1). 60, 61, 67, 68, 72, 121
  Art.6(2). 60
  Art.8 . . . . 128, 142, 143, 144, 171
  Art.8(2). 170
  Art.13 . . . . 36, 54, 55, 61, 66, 67, 68,
              69, 70, 74, 99, 100, 143, 161, 171
  Art.14 143
  Art.15 79
  Art.25 . . . . 61, 62,114, 115, 172
  Art.25(1). 172
  Art.26 99

Art.32 30
Art.33 (former Art.24) 26
Art.34 (former Art.25) 17, 18,
              19, 22, 23, 24, 25, 26, 27, 29,
              30, 31, 32, 127, 128
Art.34(1) (former Art.25(1) 23
Art.35(1). 104, 105
Art.38 31
Art.38(1)(a) 31, 32
Art.41 81
Art.44 37
Art.46 . . . . .30, 114, 115
Art.52 182
Art.60 88
Art.64 . . . . 93, 114
Protocol 1
  Art.1 171
Protocol 4 (1963). 142
  Art.4 143
Protocol 9 . . . . 33, 35, 127
Protocol 11 (1994). 23, 28, 30, 33,
              34, 35, 93, 104, 114, 127
Protocol 14 (2004). 35, 36, 37, 100
European Convention for the Prevention
    of Torture and Inhuman or Degrading
    Treatment or Punishment 1987 78
  Art.1 78
  Art.17(1). 88
European Convention on Recognition
    of the Legal Personality of International
    Non-Governmental Organizations
    1986 5
  Art.1 5
  Art.2 5
European Social Charter
  Art.32 88
Framework Convention for the Protection
    of National Minorities of the Council of
    Europe 1994 9
Geneva Convention I
  Art.6 4
Geneva Convention II
  Art.6 4
Geneva Convention III 163
  Art.6 4
  Art.14 3
  Art.78 3
Geneva Convention IV
  Art.7 4
  Art.27 3
Geneva Conventions on International
    Humanitarian Law 1949. . . 3, 4, 85, 163
  Art.1 85

Additional Protocol I, 1977
  Art.1(1) 8
  Art.34 163
  Art.75 197
Additional Protocol II, 1977 163
ILO Constitution
  Art.24 175
  Art.26 175
ILO Convention No 169 1991 9
Inter-American Convention to Prevent
  and Punish Torture 1985 62
  Art.1 78
  Art.6 78
International Convention on the
  Protection of the Rights of
  All Migrant Workers and Members
  of their Families 1990 . . . . .138, 140, 141
  Pt III 138
  Pt IV 138
  Pt V 138
  Art.2(1) 138
  Art.2(2) 138
  Art.7 138
  Arts 8–35 138
  Art.22(1) 141
  Arts 36–56 138
  Arts 57–63 138
  Art.72 138
  Arts 73–4 138
  Arts 76–7 138
Mexico Declaration and Plan of Action
  to Strengthen the International Protection
  of Refugees in Latin America
  2004 . . . . .165, 166, 167
Ottawa Convention on the Prohibition of
  Anti-Personnel Mines and on Their
  Destruction 1997 5
Pact of San José 1969 28
UN Convention on the Elimination
  of All Forms of Discrimination against
  Women (CEDAW) 92, 139
  Art.23 88
  Optional Protocol 1999 . . . . 21, 27
UN Convention on the Rights of the
  Child 1989 . . . . .5, 12, 92, 156
  Art.2(1) 85
  Art.38(1) 85
  Art.41 88
UN Convention against Torture and
  Other Cruel, Inhuman or Degrading
  Treatment or Punishment
  1984 . . . . 5, 78, 92
  Art.1 182

  Art.2(1) 78, 85
  Art.16 78
  Art.22 . . . . 21, 22
  Optional Protocol 2002 . . . . 5, 78
UN Convention against
  Transnational Organized Crime 165
Protocol to Prevent, Suppress and Punish
  Trafficking in Persons, Especially Women
  and Children 165
Protocol against Smuggling of Migrants by
  Land, Sea and Air 165
UN Covenant on Civil and Political
  Rights 1966 . . . . 77, 78, 79, 92,
                                        93, 99, 141
  Art.2(1) 54, 85
  Art.2(2) 83, 85
  Art.2(3) 54
  Art.4 79
  Art.5(2) 88
  Art.6 146
  Art.26 93
  First Optional Protocol 77, 78, 99
    Art.1 93
    Art.1–3 21
    Art.2 22
    Art.5 21
UN Covenant on Economic, Social and
  Cultural Rights 1966 77
  Optional Protocol 27
UN Declaration on Basic Principles of
  Justice for Victims of Crime and Abuse
  of Power 1985 . . . . 126, 127
UN Millennium Declaration 2000 150
UNESCO Convention on the Protection
  and Promotion of the Diversity of
  Cultural Expressions 2005 5
Universal Declaration of Human
  Rights 1948 . . . . 5, 7, 10, 19, 20, 52, 53,
                                   56, 76, 139, 206
  Art.8 . . . . 53, 54
  Art.71 5
Vienna Convention on Consular
  Relations 1963 . . . . .12, 139, 147
  Art.36 . . . . 11, 12, 146
  Art.36(1) 12
  Art.36(1)(b) 139, 146, 147
Vienna Convention on the Law of
  Treaties 1969 . . . . 18, 89, 90, 91, 93,
                                        94, 97, 116
  Arts 19–20 91
  Arts 19–23 89
  Art.20 89
  Art.20(4) 93

Art.27 83
Arts 31–3 . . . . 18, 85
Vienna Convention on the Law of Treaties
    between States and International
    Organizations or between International
    Organizations 1986 . . . . . 18, 89, 90, 91,
                                    93, 94, 97

Arts 19–23 89
Art.20 89
Art.27 83
Arts 31–3 . . . . 18, 85
Vienna Declaration and Programme of Action
    1993 164

Table of Statutes of International Courts

International Court of Justice 114
   Art.34(1) 113
   Art.36 . . . . .114, 115
International Criminal Tribunal for Rwanda 108
   Art.8 108
International Criminal Tribunal for the Former Yugoslavia 108
   Art.9 108
Permanent Court of International Justice 113, 114
Rome Statute of the International Criminal Court 1998 .5, 108, 109
   Preamble 108
   Arts 12–14 108
   Arts 13–14 202
   Art.15(3) 204
   Art.17 . . . . .108, 109
   Art.19(3) 204
   Art.43(6) 202
   Art.68 . . . . .203, 204
   Art.75 . . . . .203, 204
   Art.79 . . . . .202, 204

Table of National Legislation

Belgium

Civil Code. 128

Chile

Chilean Constitution 1980
   Art.19(12) 193
Decree Law No 2191 of 1978 . . . . .195, 201

Ecuador

Penal Code 129
   Art.114 *bis*. 129

Introduction

May I devote these brief words of Introduction to the contents and purpose of this book are derived from the General Course on International Human Rights Law, that I delivered at the Academy of European Law of the European University Institute, in Florence, in June 2007. The *Leitmotiv* which permeates the present work – the direct access of the human person to international justice – is one which I have been cultivating for a great many years. It is, in particular, ineluctably permeated by my recollections, still fresh in my memory, of the jurisprudential construction of the Inter-American Court of Human Rights during the years I served the Court as its Judge and President. This book presents and develops the basic message of my General Course of Florence, throughout which attention was focused largely on the direct access of individuals to international human rights tribunals (such as, mainly though not exclusively,[1] the European and Inter-American Courts) in operation, for four compelling reasons.

First, because such access represents the essence of the international protection of human rights, the counterposition of individual petitioners to respondent States; secondly, because that access further represents the culmination of a long evolution, namely, that of the gradual consolidation of the international legal capacity of individuals as subjects of International Law; thirdly, because the direct access of individuals to international justice ultimately permeates the whole *corpus juris* of the International Law of Human Rights; and fourthly, because the judicial solution is, in my view, the most perfected and advanced means of vindication of rights and settlement of disputes, in the present domain of protection, at intra-State level.

Thus, the case-law examined herein is drawn essentially – but not exclusively – from that of international human rights tribunals. It is only too natural that I devoted special regard to the case-law of the Inter-American Court of Human Rights, as its former President: in 12 one-hour lectures delivered in my General Course at the Academy of European Law, I purported *inter alia* to summarize my 12 years of endeavours within that international Court to consolidate the direct access of individuals to it. The subject is here retaken in a larger perspective, focusing on the individual's international subjectivity mostly in its active dimension, but without overlooking its passive dimension (e.g., in the framework of the International Criminal Court). In so far as contemporary international tribunals are concerned, reference is at times made to the case-law of international criminal

---

[1] Attention is also turned to the recently-established African Court on Human and Peoples' Rights.

tribunals,[2] or else to decisions of other international human rights organs (e.g., at United Nations level) – though attention is concentrated on the case-law of the international tribunals (mainly Inter-American and European Courts) of human rights, in operation for a much longer time.

The consideration of such case-law does not intend to be exhaustive, but rather illustrative, of the position taken by those international tribunals, and their contribution to the issues dealt with, and examined herein, pertaining to the *Leitmotiv* of the General Course. Such issues are distributed in the eleven chapters that compose the present book, in such a way as to cover, in logical sequence, the following aspects of the central theme:

a the historical recovery of the human person as subject of the law of nations (*droit des gens*);

b the exercise of the right of access to international justice: the right of international individual petition;

c access to justice at international level and the right to an effective domestic remedy;

d access to justice: the safeguard and preservation of the integrity of international jurisdiction;

e access to international justice in relation to the interaction between international law and domestic law;

f the interrelation between the access to justice (right to an effective remedy) and the guarantees of the due process of law;

g new developments in the notion of 'potential victim': the preventive dimension of protection;

h the protection of victims in situations of great adversity or defencelessness (including cases of massacres); and

i the overcoming of obstacles to direct access to justice.

The way will then be paved for the presentation of my conclusions. The approach pursued in the present book ineluctably purports to dedicate special attention to the consolidation of the position of the human person before international tribunals, in particular those of human rights, in pursuance or vindication of the rights inherent to her. I believe my approach is fully justified – as evidenced by some remarkable jurisprudential advances in recent years – at a time when, moreover, a growing importance is attributed to the role reserved to contemporary international tribunals, disclosing the phenomenon which is currently being called the 'jurisdictionalization' or 'judicialization' of the international legal order.[3]

---

[2] Besides the International Criminal Court, the *ad hoc* International Criminal Tribunals for the Former Yugoslavia and for Rwanda.

[3] Cf., e.g., [Various Authors,] *La juridictionnalisation du Droit international* (Colloque de Lille de la Société Française de Droit International), Paris, Pédone, 2003, pp. 7–545; A.A. Cançado Trindade, "International Law for Humankind: Towards a New *Jus Gentium* – General Course on Public International Law – Part II", 317 *Recueil des Cours de l'Académie de Droit International de la Haye* (2005), ch. XXV, pp. 217–45.

In the course of my study, I shall also refer – whenever relevant for the aforementioned basic purpose of this book, namely, the demonstration of the consolidation of the direct access of the human person to international justice – to my own experience as a former long-standing Judge (1991–2006) and President (1999–2004) of one of those two international tribunals, the Inter-American Court of Human Rights. As, throughout all those years of exercise of my judicial functions, I was all the time attentive to the central issue of the direct access of individuals to the international jurisdiction for the vindication of their rights,[4] it is only too natural that I have chosen this fundamental issue – which, in my understanding, best reflects the essence and transcendence of the International Law of Human Rights – as the *idée-force* or *Leitmotiv* of my General Course delivered in the summer of 2007 at the Academy of European Law at Florence.

Last but not least, I would like to leave on record my appreciation for the fruitful and open dialogue sustained with the students and participants in the course of my 12 one-hour lectures at the Academy of European Law. In addition, my recognition is extended to two distinguished colleagues for several years: Professor Francesco Francioni, for the invitation, and to him and to Professor Pierre-Marie Dupuy, for the warm hospitality in Florence, as well as to Ms Anny Bremner, for the attention and care during my academic visit to the Academy of European Law of the European University Institute.

The Hague, 4 February 2009.

A.A.C.T.

---

[4] Which constitutes the essential key-point of the bases for a *Draft Protocol to the American Convention on Human Rigths to Strengthen Its Mechanism of Protection*, which I elaborated, as *rapporteur* of the IACtHR, and presented, on behalf of the Court, as its President, to the General Assembly of the Organization of American States (OAS) in 2001, and which remains in its agenda until now (mid-2007); cf. A.A. Cançado Trindade, *Bases para un Proyecto de Protocolo a la Convención Americana sobre Derechos Humanos, para Fortalecer Su Mecanismo de Protección*, vol. II, 1st. ed., San José of Costa Rica, IACtHR, 2001, pp. 1–668, esp. pp. 1–64; and vol. II, 2nd. ed., 2003, pp. 1–1015.

I

The Historical Recovery of the Human Person as Subject of the Law of Nations

I. Introduction: The Legacy of the Individual's Subjectivity in the Emerging Law of Nations   1

II. The Individual's Presence and Participation in the International Legal Order   3

III. The Rescue of the Individual as a Subject of International Law   6

IV. Personality and Capacity: the Individual's Access to Justice at International Level   13

V. Concluding Observations: The Historical Significance of the International Subjectivity of the Individual   15

I. Introduction: The Legacy of the Individual's Subjectivity in the Emerging Law of Nations

For some years I have argued the necessity of the *legitimatio ad causam* of individuals in International Law[1] – in its doctrinal aspects as well as its procedural implications. The considerable importance attributed to the matter by the so-called 'founding fathers' of the discipline should not be forgotten. Throughout the XVIth century, the conception of Francisco de Vitoria (author of the renowned *Relecciones Teológicas*, 1538–1539) flourished, in which the law of nations regulates an international community (*totus orbis*) constituted of human beings organized socially in States and coexistent with humanity itself; the reparation of breaches of (human) rights reflects an international necessity fulfilled by the law of nations,

---

[1] A.A. Cançado Trindade, *El Acceso Directo del Individuo a los Tribunales Internacionales de Derechos Humanos*, Bilbao, Universidad de Deusto, 2001, pp. 17–96; A.A. Cançado Trindade, 'The Procedural Capacity of the Individual as Subject of International Human Rights Law: Recent Developments', in *K. Vasak Amicorum Liber – Les droits de l'homme à l'aube du XXIe siècle*, Bruxelles, Bruylant, 1999, pp. 521–44; A.A. Cançado Trindade, 'Vers la consolidation de la capacité juridique internationale des pétitionnaires dans le système interaméricain des droits de la personne', 14 *Revue québécoise de droit international* (2001) pp. 207–39; A.A. Cançado Trindade, 'El Nuevo Reglamento de la Corte Interamericana de Derechos Humanos (2000): La Emancipación del Ser Humano como Sujeto del Derecho Internacional de los Derechos Humanos', 30/31 *Revista del Instituto Interamericano de Derechos Humanos* (2001) pp. 45–71.

with the same principles of justice applying both to States and to individuals and peoples who form them. In turn, Alberico Gentili (author of *De Jure Belli*, 1598) maintained, at the end of the XVIth century, that law governs the relationships between the members of the universal *societas gentium*.[2]   *ise*

In the XVIIth century Francisco Suárez (author of the treaty *De Legibus ac Deo Legislatore*, 1612) said the law of nations discloses the unity and universality of humankind, and regulates the States in their relations as members of the universal society. Shortly afterwards, the conception elaborated by Hugo Grotius (*De Jure Belli ac Pacis*, 1625) maintained that *societas gentium* comprises the whole of humankind, and the international community cannot pretend to base itself on the *voluntas* of each State individually; human beings – occupying a central position in international relations – have rights vis-à-vis the sovereign State, which cannot demand obedience of their citizens in an absolute way (the imperative of the common good), as the so-called '*raison d'État*' has its limits, and cannot prescind from Law.[3]

In this line of reasoning, in the XVIIth century, Samuel Pufendorf (*De Jure Naturae et Gentium*, 1672) maintained the subjection of the legislator to reason, while Christian Wolff (*Jus Gentium Methodo Scientifica Pertractatum*, 1749), pondered that, just as individuals ought – in their association with the State – to promote the common good, the State in turn has the correlative duty to seek its perfection. Also in the same century, Cornelius van Bynkershoek (*De Foro Legatorum*, 1721; *Questiones Juris Publici – Libri Duo*, 1737) continued to uphold a multiplicity of subjects of *jus gentium* (nations, peoples, persons).[4]

The subsequent personification of the all-powerful State, inspired mainly by Hegelian legal philosophy, had a harmful influence in the evolution of International Law by the end of the XIXth century and in the first decades of the XXth century. This doctrinal trend resisted as much as it could the ideal of emancipation of the human being from the absolute control of the State, and the recognition of the individual as subject to International Law. But the individual's submission to the 'will' of the State was never convincing to all, and it soon became openly challenged by the more lucid doctrine. The idea of absolute State sovereignty – which led to the irresponsibility and the alleged omnipotence of the State, not impeding the successive atrocities committed by it (or in its name) against human beings – appeared with the passing of time entirely unfounded. The State – it is nowadays acknowledged – is responsible for all its acts – both *jure gestionis* and *jure imperii* – as well as for all its omissions.[5] In the case of a violation of human rights, the *direct*

---

[2] A.A. Cançado Trindade, 'International Law for Humankind: Towards a New *Jus Gentium* – General Course on Public International Law – Part I', 316 *Recueil des Cours de l'Académie de Droit International de la Haye* (2005), ch. IX, pp. 252–7.

[3] Ibid., pp. 252–7.

[4] Ibid., pp. 252–7; and cf. also A.A. Cançado Trindade, 'A Consolidação da Personalidade e da Capacidade Jurídicas do Indivíduo como Sujeito do Direito Internacional', 16 *Anuario del Instituto Hispano-Luso-Americano de Derecho Internacional* – Madrid (2003) pp. 240–47.

[5] A.A. Cançado Trindade, 'International Law for Humankind: Towards a New *Jus Gentium*...', *op. cit. supra* n. (2), pp. 256–7.

access of the individual to international jurisdiction is thus fully justified, to vindicate such rights, even against his own State.[6]

II. The Individual's Presence and Participation in the International Legal Order

The individual is thus subject of both domestic and international law.[7] In fact, he has always remained in contact, directly or indirectly, with the international legal order. In the inter-war period, the experiments of the *minorities*[8] and *mandates*[9] *systems* under the League of Nations, for example, bear witness to this.[10] They were followed by the *trusteeship system*[11] in the United Nations era, parallel to the development under the latter, throughout the years, of the multiple mechanisms – conventional and extraconventional – of international protection of human rights. Those early experiments in the XXth century were of relevance for subsequent developments in the international safeguard of the rights of the human person.[12]

The considerable evolution in the last decades not only of the International Law of Human Rights but likewise of International Humanitarian Law has contributed decisively to the evidencing and reassertion of the constant contact of the individual with the international legal order. International Humanitarian Law likewise considers protected persons not only as the simple object of the regulation that it establishes, but rather as true subjects of International Law.[13] This is what clearly

[6] S. Glaser, 'Les droits de l'homme à la lumière du droit international positif', *Mélanges offerts à H. Rolin – Problèmes de droit des gens*, Paris, Pédone, 1964, pp. 117–18, and cf. pp. 105–6 and 114–16.

[7] On the historical evolution of legal personality in the law of nations, cf. H. Mosler, 'Réflexions sur la personnalité juridique en Droit international public', in *Mélanges offerts à H. Rolin – Problèmes de droit des gens*, Paris, Pédone, 1964, pp. 228–51; G. Arangio-Ruiz, *Diritto Internazionale e Personalità Giuridica*, Bologna, Coop. Libr. Univ., 1972, pp. 9–268; G. Scelle, 'Some Reflections on Juridical Personality in International Law', in *Law and Politics in the World Community* (ed. G.A. Lipsky), Berkeley/L.A., University of California Press, 1953, pp. 49–58 and 336; J.A. Barberis, 'Nouvelles questions concernant la personnalité juridique internationale', 179 *Recueil des Cours de l'Académie de Droit International de La Haye [RCADI]* (1983) pp. 157–238.

[8] Cf., e.g., P. de Azcárate, *League of Nations and National Minorities: An Experiment*, Washington, Carnegie Endowment for International Peace, 1945, pp. 123–30; J. Stone, *International Guarantees of Minorities Rights*, Oxford, University Press, 1932, p. 56; A.N. Mandelstam, 'La protection des minorités', 1 *RCADI* (1923) pp. 363–519.

[9] Cf., e.g., G. Diena, 'Les mandats internationaux', 5 *RCADI* (1924) pp. 246–61; N. Bentwich, *The Mandates System*, London, Longmans, 1930, p. 114; Quincy Wright, *Mandates under the League of Nations*, Chicago, University Press, 1930, pp. 169–72.

[10] C.A. Norgaard, *The Position of the Individual in International Law*, Copenhagen, Munksgaard, 1962, pp. 109–31; A.A. Cançado Trindade, 'Exhaustion of Local Remedies in International Law Experiments Granting Procedural Status to Individuals in the First Half of the Twentieth Century', 24 *Netherlands International Law Review/Nederlands Tijdschrift voor international Recht* (1977) pp. 373–92.

[11] Cf., e.g., C.E. Toussaint, *The Trusteeship System of the United Nations*, London, Stevens, 1956, pp. 39, 47 and 249–50; J. Beauté, Le droit de pétition dans les territoires sous tutelle, Paris, LGDJ, 1962, pp. 48–136; G. Vedovato, 'Les accords de tutelle', 76 *RCADI* (1950) pp. 613–94.

[12] Cf., e.g., C.Th. Eustathiades, 'Une nouvelle expérience en Droit international – Les recours individuels à la Commission des droits de l'homme', in *Grundprobleme des internationalen Rechts – Festschrift für J. Spiropoulos*, Bonn, Schimmlebusch, 1957, pp. 111–37, esp. pp. 77 and 121 n. 32.

[13] This ensues from, e.g., the position of the four Geneva Conventions on International Humanitarian Law of 1949, on the rights of protected persons (e.g., III Convention, Articles 14 and 78; IV Convention, Article 27).

ensues from the fact that the four Geneva Conventions plainly prohibit the States Parties from derogating – by special agreements – from the rules enunciated in them and in particular to restrict the rights of the protected persons set forth in them.[14] In effect, the impact of the norms of the International Law of Human Rights has, in turn, already been having repercussions in the *corpus juris* and the application of International Humanitarian Law for a long time. Thus, International Humanitarian Law gradually frees itself from an obsolete purely inter-State outlook, giving increasingly greater emphasis – in the light of the principle of humanity – to protected persons and to responsibility for the violation of their rights.[15]

The attempts of the past to deny individuals the status of subjects of International Law as a result of their lack of some State capacities (such as, e.g., that of treaty-making), are definitively devoid of any meaning. Similarly, at the domestic law level, not all individuals participate, directly or indirectly, in the law-making process, and yet they do not thereby cease to be subjects of law. This doctrinal trend, attempting to insist on a rigid definition of international subjectivity, making the latter conditional upon the very formation of international norms and compliance with them, simply does not sustain itself, not even at the level of domestic law, in which it is not required – and never has been – that all individuals participate in the creation and application of legal norms in order to be the subjects (*titulaires*) of rights, and to be bound by the duties emanating from such norms.

Besides being unsustainable, that conception appears contaminated by an ominous ideological dogmatism, the main consequence of which is the alienation of the individual from the international legal order. It is surprising – if not astonishing – not to mention regrettable, to see that conception repeated mechanically and *ad nauseam* by a doctrinal trend, apparently trying to make believe that the State, as intermediary between individuals and the international legal order, would be something inevitable and permanent. Nothing could be more fallacious. In the brief historical period in which that Statist conception prevailed, in the light – or, more precisely, in the darkness – of legal positivism, successive atrocities were committed against human beings, on a scale without precedent.

The result is quite clear today; there is nothing intrinsic to International Law that impedes or renders it impossible for non-State actors to enjoy international legal personality. No one in sane conscience would today dare to deny that individuals effectively possess rights and obligations which emanate directly from International Law, with which they find themselves, therefore, in direct contact. And it is perfectly possible to conceptualize any person or entity as a subject of International

[14] I, II and III Geneva Conventions, Article 6; and IV Geneva Convention, Article 7. In fact, as early as the passage from the XIXth to the XXth century, the first Conventions on International Humanitarian Law expressed concern for the fate of human beings in armed conflicts, thus recognizing the individual as a direct beneficiary of obligations in international conventions.

[15] Th. Meron, 'The Humanization of Humanitarian Law', 94 *American Journal of International Law [AJIL]* (2000) pp. 239–78. On the historical roots of this development, cf. E.W. Petit de Gabriel, *Las Exigencias de Humanidad en el Derecho Internacional Tradicional (1789–1939)*, Madrid, Tecnos, 2003, pp. 149, 171 and 210.

Law, *titulaire* of rights and obligations which emanate directly from the norms of International Law. This is the case of individuals, who now have strengthened direct contact – without intermediaries – with the international legal order. The international movement in favour of human rights, launched by the Universal Declaration of Human Rights of 1948, disavowed the aforementioned false analogies, and overcame traditional distinctions (e.g., on the basis of nationality); subjects of law are thus all human beings as members of the 'universal society'.[16]

Moreover, individuals and non-governmental organizations (NGOs) nowadays assume an increasingly relevant role in the actual formation of *opinio juris communis*.[17] NGOs have gained considerable visibility throughout the recent cycle of U.N. World Conferences (1992–2001), by their presence and lobbying in the Conferences themselves[18] or by articulation in their own forums parallel to such Conferences.[19] In recent years, they have been entitled to present on a regular basis their *amici curiae* before international tribunals such as the Inter-American and the European Courts of Human Rights, and the ad hoc International Criminal Tribunals for the Former Yugoslavia and for Rwanda.

The very process of formation and application of the norms of International Law has ceased to be a monopoly of the States.[20] Furthermore, beyond the individual's

[16] R. Cassin, 'L'homme, sujet de droit international et la protection des droits de l'homme dans la société universelle', in *La technique et les principes du Droit public – Études en l'honneur de G. Scelle*, vol. I, Paris, LGDJ, 1950, pp. 81–2.

[17] At global level, Article 71 of the U.N. Charter has served as basis to the advisory *status* of NGOs acting in the ambit of the U.N., and resolution 1996/31, of 26 July 1996, of the U.N. Economic and Social Council (ECOSOC) regulates in detail the relations between the U.N. and NGOs with advisory status (providing the framework for accreditation of these latter). At regional level, the Permanent Council of the Organization of American States (OAS) has issued directives (on 15 December 1999) governing the participation of NGOs and other entities of civil society in OAS activities; ever since they have appeared regularly before the Council and other OAS organs. And the European Convention on Recognition of the Legal Personality of International Non-Governmental Organizations (of 24 April 1986), in its turn, provides for the constitutive elements of the NGOs (Article 1) and for the *ratio legis* of their legal personality and capacity (Article 2).

[18] The Rules of Procedure of the Preparatory Committee to the U.N. World Conference against Racism, Racial Discrimination, Xenophobia and Related Intolerance (Durban, 2001), e.g., contained a provision (Rule 66) which regulated the participation of NGOs directly in its own work (as from May 2000).

[19] For my personal recollections of the World NGO Forum parallel to the U.N. II World Conference on Human Rights (Vienna, 1993), cf. A.A. Cançado Trindade, *Tratado de Direito Internacional dos Direitos Humanos*, vol. I, 2nd. ed., Porto Alegre/Brazil, S.A. Fabris Ed., 2003, pp. 220–31; and cf. also M. Nowak (ed.), *World Conference on Human Rights (Vienna, June 1993) – The Contribution of NGOs, Reports and Documents*, Wien, Manzsche Verlags- und Universitätsbuchhandlung, 1994, pp. 1–231.

[20] In recent years, individuals and NGOs have effectively participated in the *travaux préparatoires* of certain international treaties, or influenced them (e.g., the 1984 U.N. Convention against Torture and its 2002 Optional Protocol, the 1989 U.N. Convention on the Rights of the Child, the 1991 Madrid Protocol (to the 1959 Antarctica Treaty) on Environmental Protection in the Antarctica, the 1997 Ottawa Convention on the Prohibition of Anti-Personnel Mines and on Their Destruction, the 1998 Rome Statute of the International Criminal Court, and the 2005 UNESCO Convention on the Protection and Promotion of the Diversity of Cultural Expressions), and, subsequently, in the monitoring of their implementation. The growing performance, at international level, of NGOs and other entities of civil society has had an inevitable impact on the theory of subjects of International Law, contributing to render individuals not only direct beneficiaries (without intermediaries) of the international norms, but also true subjects of International Law, and to put an end to the purely

presence and participation in the international legal order, the recognition of his rights, as a subject of International Law, ought to correspond to the procedural capacity to vindicate them at international level. It is by means of the consolidation of the full international procedural capacity of individuals that the international protection of human rights becomes reality.[21] Even if, by the circumstances of life, certain individuals (e.g., children, the mentally ill, aged persons, among others) cannot fully exercise their capacity (e.g., in civil law), this does not mean that they cease to be *titulaires* of rights, opposable even to the State. Irrespective of the circumstances, the individual is subject *jure suo* of international law, as sustained by the more lucid doctrine since the writings of the so-called founding-fathers of the discipline.[22] Human rights were conceived as *inherent* to every human being, independently of any circumstances.

III. The Rescue of the Individual as a Subject of International Law

Although one cannot deny that the contemporary international scenario is entirely distinct from that of the era of the so-called 'founding fathers' of international law, who propounded a *civitas maxima* ruled by the law of nations, there is a recurrent human aspiration, transmitted from one generation to another, throughout recent centuries, to construct an international legal order applicable both to States (and international organizations) and to individuals, pursuant to certain universal standards of justice. Hence the importance which, in this new *corpus juris* of protection, the international legal personality of the individual assumes, as subject of both domestic and international law.

The individual, as a subject of International Law in his own right, was certainly distinguishable from his own State, and a wrong done to him was a breach of classical *jus gentium*, as universal minimal law.[23] The whole new *corpus juris* of the International Law of Human Rights has been constructed on the basis of the imperatives of protection and the superior interests of the human being, irrespective of nationality or political standing or any other situation or circumstance. Thus, in this new law

---

inter-State anachronistic dimension of the latter. Moreover, their activities have contributed to the prevalence of superior common values in the ambit of International Law; R. Ranjeva, 'Les organisations non-gouvernementales et la mise-en-oeuvre du Droit international', 270 *RCADI* (1997) pp. 22, 50, 67–8, 74 and 101–2. Individuals, NGOs and other entities of civil society come, thus, to act in the process of formation as well as application of international norms; M. Bettati and P.-M. Dupuy, *Les O.N.G. et le Droit international*, Paris, Economica, 1986, pp. 1, 16, 19–20, 252–61 and 263–5.

[21] Cf. A.A. Cançado Trindade, *El Acceso Directo del Individuo a los Tribunales Internacionales . . .*, *op. cit. supra* n. (1), pp. 17–96; A.A. Cançado Trindade, 'Vers la consolidation de la capacité juridique internationale des pétitionnaires dans le système interaméricain des droits de la personne', 14 *Revue québécoise de Droit international* (2001) n. 2, pp. 207–39.

[22] P.N. Drost, *Human Rights as Legal Rights*, Leyden, Sijthoff, 1965, pp. 226–7, and cf. pp. 223 and 215.

[23] C. Parry, 'Some Considerations upon the Protection of Individuals in International Law', 90 *RCADI* (1956) pp. 686–8 and 697–8.

of protection, the legal personality of the individual, as subject of both domestic and international law, is of great importance. The application and expansion of the International Law of Human Rights, in turn, not surprisingly, has repercussions with an appreciable impact on the trends of contemporary Public International Law.[24]

In fact, in the first decades of the XXth century one already recognized the manifest inconveniences of the protection of the individuals based on their respective nation States, by the exercise of discretionary diplomatic protection, which rendered the 'complaining' States at the same time 'judges and parties'. One started, as a consequence, to nourish the idea of the *direct access* of the individuals to the international jurisdiction, under certain conditions, to vindicate their rights against States – a theme which came to be considered by the *Institut de Droit International* in its sessions of 1927 and 1929.

In a monograph published in 1931, the Russian jurist André Mandelstam argued the necessity of a *juridical minimum* – with the primacy of international law and of human rights over the State legal order – below which the international community should not allow the State to fall. In his vision, the 'horrible experience of our time' demonstrated the urgent need for acknowledgement of this *juridical minimum*, to put an end to the 'unlimited power' of the State over the life and the freedom of its citizens, and to the 'complete impunity' of the State in breach of the 'most sacred rights of the individual'.[25]

In his celebrated *Précis du Droit des Gens* (1932–1934), Georges Scelle criticized the fiction of the contraposition of an 'inter-State society' to a (national) society of individuals: both – he pondered – are formed by individuals, subjects of domestic law and of international law, whether they are individuals moved by private interests, or else endowed with public functions (rulers and public officials) in charge of looking after the interests of national and international collectivities.[26] G. Scelle then identified 'the movement of extension of the legal personality of individuals', by means of the emergence of the right of individual petition at international level, which led him to conclude that:

Les individus sont à la fois sujets de droit des collectivités nationales et de la collectivité internationale globale: ils sont *directement* sujets de droit des gens.[27]

Also in the American continent, in the XXth century, even before the adoption of the American and Universal Declarations of Human Rights of 1948, doctrinal

---

[24] Cf. A.A. Cançado Trindade, *Tratado de Direito Internacional dos Direitos Humanos*, vol. I, 2nd. ed., Porto Alegre/Brazil, S.A. Fabris Ed., 2003, pp. 33–50, and vol. II, 1999, pp. 23 194; A.A. Cançado Trindade, *O Direito Internacional em um Mundo em Transformação*, Rio de Janeiro, Ed. Renovar, 2002, pp. 1048–109; A.A. Cançado Trindade, *El Derecho Internacional de los Derechos Humanos en el Siglo XXI*, Santiago, Editorial Jurídica de Chile, 2001, pp. 15–58 and 375–427.

[25] A.N. Mandelstam, *Les droits internationaux de l'homme*, Paris, Éds. Internationales, 1931, pp. 95–6 and 138, and cf. p. 103.

[26] G. Scelle, *Précis de Droit des Gens – Principes et systématique*, part I, Paris, Libr. Rec. Sirey, 1932 (CNRS reprint, 1984), pp. 42–4.

[27] Ibid., p. 48. Also singling out the importance of the attribution to individuals of remedies for the protection of their rights, cf. Lord McNair, *Selected Papers and Bibliography*, Leiden/N.Y., Sijthoff/Oceana, 1974, pp. 329 and 249.

manifestations flourished in favour of the international juridical personality of the individuals, such as those which are found, for example, in the writings of Alejandro Álvarez[28] and Hildebrando Accioly.[29] Philip Jessup, in 1948, pondered that the old conception of State sovereignty was not consistent with the higher interests of the international community and the *status* of the individual as subject of International Law.[30]

In Europe, Hersch Lauterpacht, in a substantial work published in 1950, did not hesitate to assert that 'the individual is the final subject of all law', there being nothing inherent in international law impeding him from becoming a subject of the law of nations and a party in proceedings before international tribunals.[31] In turn, in a perspicacious essay also published in 1950, Maurice Bourquin pondered that the growing concern of International Law with the problems directly affecting the human being revealed the overcoming of the exclusively inter-State vision of the international legal order.[32]

In his course delivered at the Hague Academy of International Law three years later, in 1953, Constantin Eustathiades linked the international subjectivity of the individual to the broad theme of international responsibility (of the individual, parallel to that of States). The recognition of the rights and duties of the individual at international level, and his capacity to act in order to defend his rights, are linked to his capacity to commit an international delict. International responsibility thus comprises, in his vision, both the protection of human rights as well as the punishment of war criminals (forming a whole).[33] This development heralded the emancipation of the individual from the tutelage of his own State; thus, one could clearly see the individual's status as a subject of International Law.[34]

The same conclusion was reached by Paul Guggenheim, in a course delivered also at the Hague Academy, one year earlier, in 1952: since the individual is the 'subject of duties' at the international legal level, one cannot deny his international

---

[28] A. Álvarez, *La Reconstrucción del Derecho de Gentes – El Nuevo Orden y la Renovación Social*, Santiago de Chile, Ed. Nascimento, 1944, pp. 46–7 and 457–63, and cf. pp. 81, 91 and 499–500.

[29] H. Accioly, *Tratado de Direito Internacional Público*, vol. I, 1st. ed., Rio de Janeiro, Imprensa Nacional, 1933, pp. 71–5.

[30] Ph. C. Jessup, *A Modern Law of Nations – An Introduction*, New York, MacMillan Co., 1948, p. 41.

[31] H. Lauterpacht, *International Law and Human Rights*, London, Stevens, 1950, pp. 69, 61 and 51, and cf. p. 70. Such recognition of the individual as a subject of rights also at international law level brings about a clear rejection of the old positivist dogmas, discredited and unsustainable, of the dualism of subjects in the domestic and international orders, and of the 'will' of States as the exclusive 'source' of International Law; cf. ibid., pp. 8–9. On the 'natural right' of petition of individuals, exercised also in the general interest, cf. ibid., pp. 247–51, and cf. pp. 286–91 and 337.

[32] M. Bourquin, 'L'humanisation du droit des gens', in *La technique et les principes du Droit public...*, *op. cit. supra* n. (16), vol. I, pp. 21–54.

[33] C.Th. Eustathiades, 'Les sujets du Droit international et la responsabilité internationale – Nouvelles tendances', 84 *RCADI* (1953) pp. 402, 412–13, 424, 586–9, 601 and 612.

[34] C.Th. Eustathiades, 'Les sujets du Droit international...', *op. cit. supra* n. (33), pp. 426–7, 547, 586–7, 608 and 610–11. Although not endorsing the theory of Duguit and Scelle (of individuals as the sole subjects of International Law), regarded as expression of the 'sociological school' of International Law in France, Eustathiades recognized in it the great merit of reacting to the traditional doctrine which visualized States as the sole subjects of International Law; the recognition of individuals as international subjects, parallel to States, came to transform the structure of International Law and to foster the spirit of international solidarity; ibid., pp. 604–10.

legal personality, recognized also in fact by *customary* International Law itself.[35] Still in the mid-XXth century, in the first years of application of the European Convention on Human Rights, there was support for the view that the individuals had become '*titulaires* of legitimate international interests', as, in International Law, a process of emancipation of individuals from the 'exclusive tutelage of the State agents' had already started.[36] In the legal doctrine of that time the recognition of the expansion of the protection of individuals in the international legal order became evident.[37] In the lucid words of B.V.A. Röling, the overcoming of legal positivism was reassuring, as the individual, bearer of international rights and duties, was no longer at the mercy of his State, and:

Humanity of today instinctively turns to this natural law, for the function of law is to serve the well-being of man, whereas present positive international law tends to his destruction.[38]

|This view was in keeping with the posture upheld by the Japanese jurist Kotaro Tanaka, in his Opinions in cases before the ICJ at The Hague during this period, that is, an International Law transcending the limitations of legal positivism,[39] and thus capable of responding effectively to the needs and aspirations of the international community as a whole.[40] In the late 1960s, the pressing need for international protection of the human person both individually and *in groups* was pointed out,[41] for unless such international protection was secured, 'the fate of the individual'

---

[35] P. Guggenheim, 'Les principes de Droit international public', 80 *RCADI* (1952) pp. 116, and cf. pp. 117–18.

[36] G. Sperduti, 'L'individu et le droit international', 90 *RCADI* (1956) pp. 824, 821 and 764. The juridical experience of the epoch itself contradicted categorically the unfounded theory according to which individuals were simple *objects* of the international legal order, and destructed other prejudices of State positivism; ibid., pp. 821–2; and cf. also G. Sperduti, *L'Individuo nel Diritto Internazionale*, Milano, Giuffrè Ed., 1950, pp. 104–7.

[37] C. Parry, 'Some Considerations upon the Protection of Individuals in International Law', 90 *RCADI* (1956) p. 722; B.V.A. Röling, *International Law in an Expanded World*, Amsterdam, Djambatan, 1960, pp. XXII and 1–2.

[38] B.V.A. Röling, *op. cit. supra* n. (37), p. 2.

[39] Cf. Y. Saito, 'Judge Tanaka, Natural Law and the Principle of Equality', in *The Living Law of Nations – Essays in Memory of A. Grahl-Madsen* (eds. G. Alfredsson and P. Macalister-Smith), Kehl/Strasbourg, N.P. Engel Publ., 1996, pp. 401–2 and 405–8; K. Tanaka wanted Law to be wholly liberated from both the State ('as asserted by Hegel and his followers') and from the nation (*Völk*, as asserted by Savigny and Puchta, and other jurists of the 'historical school'); ibid., p. 402.

[40] Cf. V. Gowlland-Debbas, 'Judicial Insights into Fundamental Values and Interests of the International Community', in *The International Court of Justice: Its Future Role after Fifty Years* (eds. A.S. Muller *et alii*), The Hague, Kluwer, 1997, pp. 344–6.

[41] As acknowledged, e.g., by the 1994 Framework Convention for the Protection of National Minorities of the Council of Europe (in force as from February 1998). For earlier general studies, cf., e.g., P. Thornberry, *International Law and the Rights of Minorities*, Oxford, Clarendon Press, 1992 [reprint], pp. 38–54; F. Ermacora, 'The Protection of Minorities before the United Nations', 182 *Recueil des Cours de l'Académie de Droit International de La Haye* (1983) pp. 257–347. Cf. also the 1989 ILO Convention concerning Indigenous and Tribal Peoples in Independent Countries (ILO Convention n. 169, in force as from 05 September 1991). Furthermore, endeavours undertaken in both the United Nations and the OAS, throughout the nineties, to bring about the recognition of indigenous peoples' rights through their projected and respective Declarations, pursuant to certain basic principles (such as, e.g., that of equality and non-discrimination), have emanated from human conscience. Those endeavours, it has been suggested, recognize the debt that humankind owes to indigenous peoples, due to 'historical misdeeds against them', and a corresponding sense of duty to 'undo the wrongs' done to

would be 'at the mercy of some *Staatsrecht*'.[42] In an essay published in 1967, René Cassin, who had participated in the preparatory process of the elaboration of the Universal Declaration of Human Rights of 1948,[43] stressed with eloquence the advance represented by the access of individuals to international instances of protection, secured by many human rights treaties.[44]

To Paul Reuter, individuals become subjects of International Law when two basic conditions are fulfilled, namely, when they are *titulaires* of rights established directly by International Law, which they can exercise, and are bearers of obligations sanctioned directly by International Law'.[45] A similar view was upheld by Eduardo Jiménez de Aréchaga, to whom 'there is nothing inherent to the structure of the international legal order' which impedes the recognition of rights for individuals emanating directly from International Law, as well as international remedies for the protection of those rights.[46] Also in this line of reasoning, J. Barberis pondered in 1983 that, for individuals to be subjects of law, it is necessary that the legal order at issue attributes rights or obligations to them (as is the case in international law).[47]

In fact, successive studies of instruments of international protection came to emphasize precisely the historical importance of the recognition of international legal personality of individuals as a complaining party before international organs.[48] In my own lectures delivered at the Hague Academy of International Law in 1987, I pondered that the continuous expansion of International Law is also reflected in

---

them; A. Meijknecht, *Towards International Personality: The Position of Minorities and Indigenous Peoples in International Law*, Antwerpen/Groningen, Intersentia, 2001, pp. 228 and 233.

[42] J.J. Lador-Lederer, *International Group Protection*, Leyden, Sijthoff, 1968, p. 19.

[43] As *rapporteur* of the Working Group of the United Nations Commission on Human Rights, entrusted with the preparation of the Draft Declaration (May 1947 to June 1948).

[44] R. Cassin, 'Vingt ans après la Déclaration Universelle', 8 *Revue de la Commission Internationale de Juristes* (1967) n. 2, pp. 9–10, and cf. pp. 11–17.

[45] Thus, as from the moment when the individual is granted a remedy before an organ of international protection (access to international jurisdiction) and can thus initiate the procedure of protection, he becomes subject of International Law; P. Reuter, *Droit international public*, 7th. ed., Paris, PUF, 1993, pp. 235 and 238, and cf. p. 106.

[46] E. Jiménez de Aréchaga, *El Derecho Internacional Contemporáneo*, Madrid, Tecnos, 1980, pp. 207–8; and cf. A. Cassese, *International Law*, Oxford, OUP, 2001, pp. 79–85.

[47] Subjects of law are, thus, heterogeneous, he added, and theoreticians who beheld only States as such to be subjects simply distorted reality, failing to take into account the transformations undergone by the international community, which came to admit that non-State actors also possess international legal personality; J. Barberis, 'Nouvelles questions concernant la personnalité juridique internationale', 179 *RCADI* (1983) pp. 161, 169, 171–2, 178 and 181.

[48] Cf., e.g., A.A. Cançado Trindade, *The Application of the Rule of Exhaustion of Local Remedies in International Law*, Cambridge, University Press, 1983, pp. 1–445; A.Z. Drzemczewski, *European Human Rights Convention in Domestic Law*, Oxford, Clarendon Press, 1983, pp. 20–34 and 341; F. Matscher, 'La Posizione Processuale dell'Individuo come Ricorrente dinanzi agli Organi della Convenzione Europea dei Diritti dell'Uomo', in *Studi in Onore di Giuseppe Sperduti*, Milano, Giuffrè, 1984, pp. 601–20; J.A. Carrillo Salcedo, *Dignidad frente a Barbarie – La Declaración Universal de Derechos Humanos, Cincuenta Años Después*, Madrid, Ed. Trotta, 1999, pp. 27–145; E.-I.A. Daes (rapporteur spécial), *La condition de l'individu et le Droit international contemporain*, U.N. doc. E/CN.4/Sub.2/1988/33, of 18 July 1988, pp. 1–92; R.A. Mullerson, 'Human Rights and the Individual as Subject of International Law: A Soviet View', 1 *European Journal of International Law* (1990) pp. 33–43.

the multiple contemporary mechanisms of international protection of human rights, the operation of which cannot be dissociated from the new values acknowledged by the international community.[49] At last individuals were enabled 'to exercise rights emanating directly from International Law (*droit des gens*)'. And I added:

In this connection, the insight and conception of Vitoria developed in his manuscripts of 1532 (made public in 1538–1539), can be properly recalled in 1987, four-and-a-half centuries later: it was a conception of a universal law of nations, of individuals socially organized in States and also composing humanity (...); redress of violations of (human) rights, in fulfilment of an international need, owed its existence to the law of nations, with the same principles of justice applying to both States and individuals or peoples forming them.

(...) There is a growing and generalized acknowledgement that human rights, rather than deriving from the State (or from the will of individuals composing the State), all inhere in the human person, in whom they find their ultimate point of convergence. (...) The non-observance of human rights entails the international responsibility of States for treatment of the human person.[50]

Almost two decades later, I have had occasion to reassert the same point, to a greater depth, in my recent *General Course on Public International Law*, delivered likewise at the Hague Academy of International Law, in 2005.[51] The international subjectivity of the human being (whether a child, an elderly person, a person with disability, a stateless person, or any other) erupted indeed with vigour in the legal science of the XXth century, as a reaction of the universal juridical conscience against the successive atrocities committed against humankind. An eloquent testimony of the erosion of the purely inter-State dimension of the international legal order is found in the historical and pioneering Advisory Opinion n. 16 of the Inter-American Court of Human Rights (IACtHR), on the *Right to Information on Consular Assistance in the Framework of the Guarantees of the Due Process of Law* (of 01 October 1999),[52] which has served as orientation to other international tribunals and has inspired the evolution *in statu nascendi* of the international case-law on the matter.

The IACtHR recognized, in the light of the impact of the *corpus juris* of the International Law of Human Rights on the international legal order itself, the crystallization of a true individual subjective right to information on consular assistance,[53] of which every human being deprived of his freedom in another

---

[49] A.A. Cançado Trindade, 'Co-existence and Co-ordination of Mechanisms of International Protection of Human Rights (At Global and Regional Levels', 202 *RCADI* (1987) pp. 32–3.

[50] Ibid., pp. 411–12.

[51] A.A. Cançado Trindade, 'International Law for Humankind: Towards a New *Jus Gentium* ...', *op. cit. supra* n. (2), ch. IX-X, pp. 252–317.

[52] Inter-American Court of Human Rights, Advisory Opinion OC-16/99, Series A, n. 16, pp. 3–123, pars. 1–141, and resolutory points 1–8.

[53] Set forth in Article 36 of the 1963 Vienna Convention on Consular Relations and linked to the guarantees of the due process of law under Article 8 of the American Convention on Human Rights.

country is *titulaire*;[54] furthermore, it broke away from the traditional purely inter-State outlook of the matter,[55] bringing support to numerous individuals victimized by poverty, discrimination, and deprived of freedom abroad. The subsequent Advisory Opinion n. 17 of the IACtHR, on the *Juridical Condition and Human Rights of the Child* (of 28 August 2002), fits into the same line of assertion of the juridical emancipation of the human being, in stressing the consolidation of the juridical personality of the child, as a true subject of law and not simply an object of protection, and irrespective of the extent of his legal capacity to exercise his rights for himself (capacity of exercise).

In this respect, the 1989 U.N. Convention on the Rights of the Child recognizes the subjective rights of the child as a subject of law, and further reckons that, given his vulnerability, the child needs special protection and legal representation, whilst remaining a *titulaire* of rights; this is in accordance with the Kantian conception of every human person being ultimately an end in herself.[56] The juridical category of international legal personality has not shown itself insensible to the *necessities* of the international community, such as providing protection to human beings, in particular those who find themselves in a situation of special vulnerability.

To the legal doctrine of the second half of the XXth century it did not pass unnoticed that individuals, besides being *titulaires* of rights at the international level, also have duties which are attributed to them by international law itself. And – more significantly – a grave violation of those duties, reflected in crimes against humanity, engages *international* individual penal responsibility, *independently* from what *domestic* law provides on the matter.[57] Contemporary developments in international criminal law have, in fact, a direct influence on the crystallization of both the international individual penal responsibility (the individual subject, both active and passive, of international law, *titulaire* of rights as well as bearer of duties emanating directly from the law of nations (*droit des gens*)), as well as the principle of universal jurisdiction.

The consolidation of the international legal personality of individuals as active as well as passive subjects of international law, enhances accountability in international

---

[54] In that Opinion, the Inter-America n Court lucidly pointed out that the rights set forth in Article 36(1) of the Vienna Convention on Consular Relations of 1963 'have the characteristic that their *titulaire is the individual*. In effect, this provision is unequivocal in stating that the rights to consular information and notification are 'accorded' to the interested person. In this respect, Article 36 is a notable exception to the essentially Statist nature of the rights and obligations set forth elsewhere in the Vienna Convention on Consular Relations; as interpreted by this Court in the present Advisory Opinion, it represents a notable advance in respect of the traditional conceptions of International Law on the matter' (par. 82, emphasis added).

[55] This Opinion, pioneering in international case-law, has had a remarkable impact in the countries of the region, which have sought to harmonize their practice with it, aiming to put an end to abuses on the part of the police and to discrimination against poor and illiterate foreigners (mainly migrants), often victimized by all sorts of discrimination (also *de jure*) and injustice. The Inter-American Court thus gave a considerable contribution to the evolution itself of the Law in this respect.

[56] D. Youf, *Penser les droits de l'enfant*, Paris, PUF, 2002, pp. 93–6, 100 and 118–19; and cf. F. Dekeuwer-Défossez, *Les droits de l'enfant*, 5th. ed., Paris, PUF, 2001, pp. 4–5, 22 and 74.

[57] M.Ch. Bassiouni, *Crimes against Humanity in International Criminal Law*, 2nd. rev. ed., The Hague, Kluwer, 1999, pp. 106 and 118.

law for abuses perpetrated against human beings. Thus, individuals are also bearers of duties under international law, and this reflects the consolidation of their international legal personality.[58] Developments in international legal personality and international accountability go hand in hand, and this whole evolution bears witness to the formation of the *opinio juris communis* to the effect that the gravity of certain violations of fundamental rights of the human person directly affects the basic values of the international community as a whole.[59]

IV. Personality and Capacity: the Individual's Access to Justice at International Level

Ultimately, all Law exists for the human being, and the law of nations is no exception to that, guaranteeing his rights and respect for his personality to the individual.[60] The respect for the individual's personality at international level is instrumentalized by the international right of individual petition. It is for this reason that, in my Concurring Opinion in the case of *Castillo Petruzzi and Others versus Peru* (Preliminary Objections, Judgment of 04 September 1998) before the Inter-American Court of Human Rights, urged by the circumstances of the *cas d'espèce*, I saw it fit to characterize the international right of individual petition as a *fundamental clause* (*cláusula pétrea*) of the human rights treaties which provide for it,[61] adding that:

The right of individual petition shelters, in fact, the last hope of those who did not find justice at national level. I would not refrain myself nor hesitate to add, – allowing myself the metaphor, – that the right of individual petition is undoubtedly the most luminous star in the universe of human rights.[62]

---

[58] H.-H. Jescheck, 'The General Principles of International Criminal Law Set Out in Nuremberg, as Mirrored in the ICC Statute', 2 *Journal of International Criminal Justice* (2004) p. 43.

[59] Cf., e.g., A. Cassese, 'Y a-t-il un conflit insurmontable entre souveraineté des États et justice pénale internationale?', in *Crimes internationaux et juridictions internationales* (eds. A. Cassese and M. Delmas-Marty), Paris, PUF, 2002, pp. 15–29; and cf., generally, [Various Authors], *La Criminalización de la Barbarie: La Corte Penal Internacional* (ed. J.A. Carrillo Salcedo), Madrid, Consejo General del Poder Judicial, 2000, pp. 17–504.

[60] F.A. von der Heydte, 'L'individu et les tribunaux internationaux', 107 *Recueil des Cours de l'Académie de Droit International de La Haye* (1962) p. 301; cf. also, in this respect, e.g., E.M. Borchard, 'The Access of Individuals to International Courts', 24 *American Journal of International Law* (1930) pp. 359–65.

[61] To which one can add, insofar as the American Convention on Human Rights is concerned, the other *fundamental clause* (*cláusula pétrea*) of the recognition of the competence of the Inter-American Court of Human Rights in contentious matters; for a study, cf. A.A. Cançado Trindade, 'Las Cláusulas Pétreas de la Protección Internacional del Ser Humano: El Acceso Directo de los Individuos a la Justicia a Nivel Internacional y la Intangibilidad de la Jurisdicción Obligatoria de los Tribunales Internacionales de Derechos Humanos', *El Sistema Interamericano de Protección de los Derechos Humanos en el Umbral del Siglo XXI – Memoria del Seminario* (November 1999), San José de Costa Rica, CtIADH, 2001, pp. 3–68.

[62] IACtHR, case *Castillo Petruzzi and Others versus Peru* (Preliminary Objections), Judgment of 04 September 1998, Series C, n. 41, Concurring Opinion of Judge A.A. Cançado Trindade, p. 62, par. 35.

Human rights assert themselves against all forms of domination or arbitrary power.[63] In the public hearings before the Inter-American Court of Human Rights (mainly those pertaining to reparations), a point which has particularly drawn my attention has been the remark, increasingly more frequent, on the part of the victims or their relatives, to the effect that, were it not for their access to the international instance, justice would never have been done in their specific cases. Without the right of individual petition, and the consequent access to justice at international level, the rights set forth in human rights treaties would be reduced to little more than dead letter.

The human being emerges, at last, even in the most adverse conditions, as the ultimate subject of Law, domestic as well as international. The case of the '*Street Children*' (case *Villagrán Morales and Others versus Guatemala*, 1999–2001), decided by the Inter-American Court, the first in which the cause of children abandoned in the streets was brought before an international human rights tribunal,[64] and in which some of those marginalized and forgotten by this world succeeded in resorting to an international tribunal to vindicate their rights as human beings,[65] is truly paradigmatic, and gives a clear and unequivocal testimony that the International Law of Human Rights has now achieved maturity. As can be inferred from this historic case, the international juridical subjectivity of individuals is now an irreversible reality, and the violation of their fundamental rights, emanating directly from the international legal order, brings about juridical consequences.

As I have seen it fit to sum up in my Concurring Opinion in the aforementioned Advisory Opinion of the Inter-American Court on the *Juridical Condition and Human Rights of the Child* (2002):

every human person is endowed with juridical personality, which imposes limits to State power. The juridical capacity varies in virtue of the juridical condition of each one to undertake certain acts. Yet, although such capacity of exercise varies, all individuals are endowed with juridical personality. Human rights reinforce the universal attribute of the human person, given that to all human beings correspond likewise the juridical personality and the protection of the Law, independently of her existential or juridical condition (par. 34).

---

[63] A.A. Cançado Trindade, 'The Future of the International Protection of Human Rights', *B. Boutros-Ghali Amicorum Discipulorumque Liber – Paix, Développement, Démocratie*, vol. II, Bruxelles, Bruylant, 1998, pp. 961–86. On the need to overcome the current challenges and obstacles to the prevalence of human rights, cf. A.A. Cançado Trindade, 'L'interdépendance de tous les droits de l'homme et leur mise-en-oeuvre: obstacles et enjeux', 158 *Revue internationale des sciences sociales* – Paris/UNESCO (1998) pp. 571–82.

[64] IACtHR, case *Villagrán Morales and Others versus Guatemala*, Judgment (merits) of 19 November 1999, Series C, n. 63, pars. 1–253, and Joint Concurring Opinion of Judges A.A. Cançado Trindade and A. Abreu Burelli, pars. 1–11.

[65] In fact, in that case of the killing of the '*Street Children*', the mothers of the murdered children (and the grandmother of one of them), as poor and abandoned as their sons (and grandson), had access to the international jurisdiction, appeared before the Court (public hearings of 28/29 January 1999 and of 12 March 2001), and, due to the judgments of the Inter-American Court (as to the merits, of 19 November 1999, and reparations, of 26 May 2001), which brought them redress, could at least recover their faith in human justice.

In respect of the human rights of individuals belonging to groups or human collectivities, reference is to be made to the important recent Advisory Opinion n. 18, on the *Juridical Condition and Rights of Undocumented Migrants* (of 17 September 2003), of the Inter-American Court of Human Rights. The Court stressed that migratory status cannot serve as a justification for depriving a person of the enjoyment and exercise of their human rights, including labour rights. The Court added that States cannot discriminate, or tolerate discriminatory situations concerning migrants, and ought to guarantee the due process of law to any person, irrespective of her migratory status. The Court further warned that States cannot subordinate or condition the observance of the fundamental principle of non-discrimination and equality before the law to the aims of their migratory or other policies. In my Concurring Opinion I maintained that this fundamental principle belonged to the domain of *jus cogens*, and stressed the importance of the *erga omnes* obligations (encompassing also inter-individual relations) vis-à-vis the rights of undocumented migrants. The Advisory Opinion of the Court thus benefitted a considerable number of persons, including those belonging to numerous groups of undocumented migrants, exposed to all sorts of abuses in numerous countries nowadays.

V. Concluding Observations: The Historical Significance of the International Subjectivity of the Individual

The international juridical subjectivity of the human being, as foreseen by the so-called founders of international law (the *droit des gens*), is now a reality. At the beginning of the XXIst century, this highly significant conquest can be appreciated within the framework of the historical process of *humanization* of international law – to which it is a privilege to be able to contribute – which, always attentive to fundamental values, occupies itself more directly with the realization of common goals. In the ambit of the International Law of Human Rights, in the European, inter-American, and African systems of protection – endowed with international tribunals – parallel to legal personality, the international procedural capacity (*locus standi in judicio*) of the individual is also acknowledged today.

This is a logical development, as it does not seem reasonable to conceive of rights at international level without the corresponding procedural capacity to vindicate them; individuals are the true complainants in the international *contentieux* of human rights. The right of individual petition is the juridical mechanism for the emancipation of the human being vis-à-vis his own State in terms of his ability to enforce his rights under the International Law of Human Rights[66] – an emancipation

---

[66] If the aforementioned right of petition had not been originally conceived and consistently understood in this way, the international protection of human rights would have advanced very little in this half a century of evolution. With the consolidation of the right of individual petition before international tribunals – the European and Inter-American Courts – of human rights, it is the international protection that attains its maturity.

which constitutes, in our days, a true juridical revolution, at last giving an ethical content to the norms of both domestic public law and international law.

The recognition of the direct access of individuals to international justice reveals, at the beginning of the XXIst century, the new primacy of the *raison d'humanité* over the *raison d'État*, inspiring the process of *humanization* of international law.[67] The subjects of international law are no longer only territorial entities.[68] It appears quite clear nowadays that there is nothing intrinsic to international law that would impede, or render impossible, the endowment of non-State 'actors' with international legal personality and capacity. Yet contemporary legal doctrine continues to refer to individuals as 'actors' (rather than subjects) in the international legal order. This is not a juridical term, it is rather a term of art, to which no specific juridical contents and consequences are necessarily attached. To call individuals 'actors' in international law is nothing but a platitude. They are true subjects of international law, bearers of rights and duties which emanate from international law.

No one in sane conscience would deny that individuals effectively possess rights and have duties which derive directly from international law, with which they thus are in direct contact. And it is perfectly possible to conceptualize as a subject of international law, any person or entity, *titulaire* of rights and bearer of obligations which emanate directly from norms of international law. This evolution is to be appreciated in a wider dimension: the expansion of international legal personality, encompassing the idea of individuals as active and passive subjects of international law, goes *pari passu* with the acknowledgment of accountability in international law.

This contributes ultimately to the international rule of law, and also to the realization of justice at the international level, thus fulfilling a long-standing aspiration of humankind. In reaction to the successive atrocities which, throughout the XXth century, have harmed millions of human beings, on an unprecedented scale, the universal juridical conscience – as the ultimate *material source* of all Law[69] – has restored to the human being his condition of subject of both domestic and international law, and final addressee of all legal norms, of national as well as international origin. Human beings were to benefit from that, and international law itself was thereby enriched and justified. International law thus liberated itself from the chains of statism, and again has met with the conception of a true, and new, *jus gentium*.

---

[67] A.A. Cançado Trindade, *A Humanização do Direito Internacional*, Belo Horizonte/Brazil, Edit. Del Rey, 2006, pp. 3–409; A.A. Cançado Trindade, 'The Emancipation of the Individual from His Own State: The Historical Recovery of the Human Person as Subject of the Law of Nations', in *Human Rights, Democracy and the Rule of Law – Liber Amicorum L. Wildhaber* (eds. S. Breitenmoser *et alii*), Zürich/Baden-Baden, Dike/Nomos, 2007, pp. 151–71.

[68] More than half a century ago, as acknowledged in the celebrated Advisory Opinion of the International Court of Justice on *Reparations for Damages* (1949), the advent of international organizations had put an end to the States' monopoly of international legal personality and capacity, with all the juridical consequences which ensued therefrom; cf., for a general study on the matter, A.A. Cançado Trindade, *Direito das Organizações Internacionais*, 3rd. ed., Belo Horizonte/Brazil, Edit. Del Rey, 2003, pp. 9–853.

[69] A.A. Cançado Trindade, 'International Law for Humankind: Towards a New *Jus Gentium* . . .', *op. cit. supra* n. (2), ch. VI, pp. 177–202.

II

The Exercise of the Right of Access to International Justice: The Right of International Individual Petition

I.	Evolution and Juridical Nature of the Right of Individual Petition	17
II.	Consolidation and Scope of the Right of Individual Petition	20
III.	The Titularity of the Right of Individual Petition: Distinct Formulations	22
IV.	The Significance and Overriding Importance of the Right of Individual Petition	27
V.	The Right of Direct Access of Individuals to International Human Rights Tribunals	32
	1. Developments in the European System of Protection	32
	2. Developments in the Inter-American System of Protection	37
	3. Developments in the African System of Protection	46
VI.	Concluding Observations	47

I. Evolution and Juridical Nature of the Right of Individual Petition

One of the most significant developments in international human rights law in the last six decades has undoubtedly been the consolidation of the procedural capacity of the individual as a subject of International Law in the domain of human rights protection. This can be illustrated in particular by his standing before the international tribunals (namely, the European and the Inter-American Courts) of human rights. It may thus be worth recalling the significant developments of the right of individual petition under the European and American Conventions on Human Rights (Article 34 [former Article 25] and Article 44, respectively).

The importance of the right of individual petition does not appear to have been sufficiently stressed to date, or not as much as it deserves; the attention which has been devoted to the matter has not been commensurate to its importance. It should be kept in mind that, ultimately, it is by the free and full exercise of the right of individual petition that the direct access of the individual to justice at international level is guaranteed.

The question of the *legitimatio ad causam* of the petitioners has occupied a central position in international human rights law. The provisions on the right of individual petition (such as Article 34 [former Article 25] of the ECHR and Article 44 of the ACHR) cannot be analyzed in the same way as other provisions of those Conventions because they are related to the obligation of the States Parties not to create obstacles or difficulties to the free and full exercise of the right of individual petition, and they are not rights of equal hierarchy with other procedural provisions. The right of individual petition constitutes, in sum, the cornerstone of the access of the individuals to the whole mechanism of protection of those Human Rights Conventions.

This right is a definitive conquest of the International Law of Human Rights. It was precisely by the exercise of such right of petition that the *historical rescue* of the position of the human being as a subject of international human rights law, endowed with full international procedural capacity, took place.[1] At the international level, for some time States assumed a monopoly on being a subject of rights;[2] individuals were left entirely at the mercy of the discretionary intermediation of their nation-States for their protection. The international legal order excluded the ultimate addressee of juridical norms: the human being – which the excesses of legal positivism attempted in vain to justify.

The international legal order thus marked by the prevalence of sovereign States and the temporary exclusion of individuals was incapable of avoiding massive violations of human rights, perpetrated in all regions of the world, and successive atrocities in the XXth century,[3] and early XXIst century. Such atrocities awoke the *universal juridical conscience* to the necessity of reconceptualizing the foundations themselves of the international legal order, restoring the human being to the central position from which he had been displaced.

The reconstruction of these foundations over the last six decades has taken distinct conceptual bases, such as those of the realization of superior common values, of the human being as a subject of rights emanating directly from international law, of the collective guarantee of the realization of these latter, and of the objective character of the obligations of protection.[4] The international order of sovereign States yielded to solidarity.

---

[1] Cf. chapter I, *supra*.   [2] Cf. chapter I, *supra*.

[3] Such as the holocaust, the *gulag*, followed by new acts of genocide, e.g., in South-East Asia, in central Europe (former Yugoslavia), in Africa (Rwanda). Cf., for general studies, e.g., A.J. Toynbee, *Civilization on Trial*, Oxford, University Press, 1948, pp. 3–263; A.J. Toynbee, *Guerra e Civilização*, Lisbon, Ed. Presença, 1963, pp. 11–207; Stefan Zweig, *O Mundo que Eu Vi* (*Die Welt von Gestern*), Rio de Janeiro, Ed. Record, 1999 [reed.], pp. 7–519; Primo Levi, *Oeuvres*, Paris, Ed. R. Laffont, 2005, pp. 1–1118; B. Bruneteau, *Le siècle des génocides*, Paris, A. Colin, 2004, pp. 5–233; E. Staub, *The Roots of Evil – The Origins of Genocide and Other Group Violence*, Cambridge, University Press, 2005 [reprint], pp. 1–283; B.A. Valentino, *Final Solutions – Mass Killing and Genocide in the 20th Century*, Ithaca/London, Cornell University Press, 2004, pp. 1–253; G. Bensoussan, *Europe, une passion génocidaire – Essai d'histoire culturelle*, Paris, Ed. Mille et une nuits/Libr. A. Fayard, 2006, pp. 7–460.

[4] With a direct incidence of those canons in the methods of interpretation of the international norms of protection, without necessarily departing from the general rules of interpretation of treaties set forth in Articles 31–3 of the two Vienna Conventions on the Law of Treaties (of 1969 and 1986).

This profound transformation of the international legal order, precipitated as from the Universal and American Declarations of Human Rights of 1948, six decades ago, has not taken place without difficulties, precisely because it requires a different mentality. From the beginning it has been stressed that, although motivated by the search for individual redress, the right of individual petition contributes also to securing respect for obligations of objective character which are incumbent upon States Parties to human rights treaties.[5] On several occasions the exercise of the right of individual petition has gone even further, generating changes in the domestic legal order and in the practice of the public organs of the State. The significance of the right of individual petition can only be appropriately appreciated in the light of past developments.[6]

In fact, the *historia juris* of some countries discloses that the old *right to petition*, at domestic level, gradually developed into a legal remedy to be used for the reparation for damages.[7] Only in a more recent era has the *right of petition* (no longer *right to petition*) formed within the ambit of international organizations. The first classic distinctions appeared, such as that elaborated by N. Feinberg[8] and endorsed by P.N. Drost,[9] between *pétition plainte*, based upon a violation of an individual private right (e.g., a civil right) and in search of reparation on the part of the authorities, and *pétition voeu*, pertaining to the general interests of a group (e.g., a political right) and in search of public measures on the part of the authorities.

The *pétition voeu* evolved into what came to be called 'communication'; examples, in turn, of *pétitions plaintes* – or 'petitions' *stricto sensu* – are found, for example, in the systems of minorities and mandates under the League of Nations and in the trusteeship system under the United Nations.[10] Those were some of the first international experiments to grant procedural capacity directly to individuals

---

[5] For example, under the former Article 25 (nowadays Article 34) of the ECHR; cf. H. Rolin, 'Le rôle du requérant dans la procédure prévue par la Commission européenne des droits de l'homme', 9 *Revue hellénique de droit international* (1956) pp. 3–14, esp. p. 9; C.Th. Eustathiades, 'Les recours individuels à la Commission européenne des droits de l'homme', in *Grundprobleme des internationalen Rechts – Festschrift für Jean Spiropoulos*, Bonn, Schimmelbusch & Co., 1957, p. 121; F. Durante, *Ricorsi Individuali ad Organi Internazionali*, Milano, Giuffrè, 1958, pp. 125–52, esp. pp. 129–30; K. Vasak, *La Convention européenne des droits de l'homme*, Paris, LGDJ, 1964, pp. 96–8; M. Virally, 'L'accès des particuliers à une instance internationale: la protection des droits de l'homme dans le cadre européen', 20 *Mémoires Publiés par la Faculté de Droit de Genève* (1964) pp. 67–89; H. Mosler, 'The Protection of Human Rights by International Legal Procedure', 52 *Georgetown Law Journal* (1964) pp. 818–19.

[6] As pointed out in A.A. Cançado Trindade, *Tratado de Direito Internacional dos Direitos Humanos*, vol. I, 2nd. rev. ed., Porto Alegre/Brazil, S.A. Fabris Ed., 2003, pp. 100–21.

[7] J. Humphrey, 'The Right of Petition in the United Nations', 4 *Revue des droits de l'homme/Human Rights Journal* (1971) p. 463.

[8] N. Feinberg, 'La pétition en droit international', 40 *Recueil des Cours de l'Académie de Droit International de La Haye* (1932) pp. 576–639.

[9] P.N. Drost, *Human Rights as Legal Rights*, Leyden, Sijthoff, 1965, pp. 67–75, and cf. pp. 91–6 and 101.

[10] Cf., e.g., J. Stone, 'The Legal Nature of Minorities Petition', 12 *British Year Book of International Law* (1931) pp. 76–94; M. Sibert, 'Sur la procédure en matière de pétition dans les pays sous mandat et quelques-unes de ses insuffissances', 40 *Revue générale de Droit international public* (1933) pp. 257–72; Jean Beauté, *Le droit de pétition dans les territoires sous tutelle*, Paris, LGDJ, 1962, pp. 1–256.

and private groups.[11] Those antecedents, throughout the first half of the twentieth century, paved the way to the development, within the ambit of the United Nations and under human rights treaties at global and regional levels, of the contemporary mechanisms of petitions or communications pertaining to violations of human rights.[12]

II. Consolidation and Scope of the Right of Individual Petition

With the consolidation of mechanisms granting direct access of individuals to international tribunals, the recognition also occurred at procedural level, that human rights, inherent to the human person, precede and stand above the State and any other forms of political organization, and the human being emancipated himself from the domination of the State whenever the latter appeared arbitrary. The individual recovered his presence, for the vindication of his rights, at international level, presence which had been denied to him in the historical process of formation of the modern State but which had originally manifested itself in the immediate concern with the human being in the original manuscripts of the so-called founding fathers of international law.[13]

That transformation, such a product of our time, corresponds to the recognition of the necessity that all States, in order to avoid new violations of human rights, are made responsible for the way they treat human beings who are under their jurisdiction. This would simply not have been possible without the consolidation of the right of individual petition, amidst the recognition of the objective character of the obligations of protection and the undertaking of the collective guarantee of

---

[11] To them, one ought to add other petitioning systems (such as those of Upper Silesia, of the Aaland Islands, of the Saar and of Danzig), the system of navigation of the river Rhine, the experience of the Central-American Court of Justice (1907–1917), the case-law of the Mixed Arbitral Tribunals and of the Mixed Claims Commissions, besides the International Prize Court proposed at the II Peace Conference of the Hague of 1907. Cf. C.A. Norgaard, *The Position of the Individual in International Law*, Copenhagen, Munksgaard, 1962, pp. 99–172; A.A. Cançado Trindade, 'Exhaustion of Local Remedies in International Law Experiments Granting Procedural Status to Individuals in the First Half of the Twentieth Century', 24 *Netherlands International Law Review* (1977) pp. 373–92; and, earlier on, J.-C. Witenberg, 'La recevabilité des réclamations devant les juridictions internationales', 41 *Recueil des Cours de l'Académie de Droit International de La Haye* (1932) pp. 5–135; C.Th. Eustathiades, 'Les sujets du Droit international et la responsabilité internationale – nouvelles tendances', 84 *Recueil des Cours de l'Académie de Droit International de La Haye* (1953) pp. 401–614.

[12] Cf. M.E. Tardu, *Human Rights – The International Petition System*, binders 1–3, Dobbs Ferry N.Y., Oceana, 1979–1985; Tom Zwart, *The Admissibility of Human Rights Petitions*, Dordrecht, Nijhoff, 1994, pp. 1–237.

[13] Cf. A.A. Cançado Trindade, 'International Law for Humankind: Towards a New *Jus Gentium* – General Course on Public International Law' – Part I, 316 *Recueil des Cours de l'Académie de Droit International de la Haye* (2005) pp. 252–57; A.A. Cançado Trindade, 'The International Law of Human Rights at the Dawn of the XXIst Century', 3 *Cursos Euromediterráneos Bancaja de Derecho Internacional* – Castellón/Spain (1999) pp. 186–207.

compliance with them. This is the real meaning of the *historical rescue* of the individual as subject of international human rights law.[14]

Yet, at global level, it was necessary to wait until the first half of the 1970s for the right of petition to be crystallized at conventional level (with the entry into force of human rights treaties and conventions)[15] as well as in extra-conventional mechanisms (established by resolutions) in the ambit of the United Nations. Parallel to that, at European regional level, the right of individual petition, together with the notion of collective guarantee, came to constitute one of the most remarkable features of the new system of protection inaugurated by the 1950 European Convention on Human Rights, and, *a fortiori*, of international human rights law as a whole.

Four decades ago, on the occasion of the twentieth anniversary of the Universal Declaration of Human Rights of 1948, René Cassin, who had participated in the preparatory process of its elaboration,[16] stated that:

(. . .) If there still subsist on earth great zones where millions of men and women, resigned to their destiny, do not dare to utter the least complaint nor even to conceive that any remedy whatsoever is made possible, those territories diminish day after day. The awakening of conscience that an emancipation is possible, becomes increasingly more general. (. . .) The first condition of all justice, namely, the possibility of cornering the powerful so as to subject them to (. . .) public control, is nowadays fulfilled much more often than in the past. (. . .) The Conventions and Covenants [of human rights] in their majority, (. . .) urge the States Parties to create in them the instances of remedies and foresee certain measures of international protection or control. (. . .) The fact that the resignation without hope, that the wall of silence and that the absence of any remedy are in the process of reduction or disappearance, opens to moving humanity encouraging perspectives (. . .).[17]

The assessment of the right of individual petition as a method of international implementation of human rights has necessarily to take into account the basic point of the *legitimatio ad causam* of the petitioners and of the conditions of the use and the admissibility of the petitions (set forth in the distinct instruments of human rights which foresee them).[18] In this respect, the human rights treaties which provide for the right of individual petition[19] generally condition the exercise of

---

[14] A.A. Cançado Trindade, 'El Derecho de Petición Individual ante la Jurisdicción Internacional', 48 *Revista de la Facultad de Derecho de México* – UNAM (1998) pp. 131–51; A.A. Cançado Trindade, 'The Emancipation of the Individual from His Own State – The Historical Recovery of the Human Person as Subject of the Law of Nations', in *Human Rights, Democracy and the Rule of Law – Liber Amicorum L. Wildhaber* (eds. S. Breitenmoser *et alii*), Zürich/Baden-Baden, Dike/Nomos, 2007, pp. 151–71.

[15] Cf. n. (17), *infra*.

[16] As *rapporteur* of the Working Group of the United Nations Commission on Human Rights, entrusted with the preparation of the Draft Declaration (May 1947 to June 1948).

[17] Cassin, 'Vingt ans après la Déclaration Universelle', 8 *Revue de la Commission Internationale de Juristes* (1967) n. 2, pp. 9–10 (my own translation).

[18] This was, precisely, the central aspect of the legal questions raised in the case of *Castillo Petruzzi and Others versus Peru* (Preliminary Objections, 1998), before the Inter-American Court of Human Rights.

[19] At global level, the right of individual petition is provided for, e.g., in the [first] Optional Protocol to the Covenant on Civil and Political Rights (Articles 1–3 and 5), in the Convention on the Elimination of All Forms of Racial Discrimination (Article XIV), in the U.N. Convention against Torture (Article 22), in the Optional Protocol to the Convention on the Elimination of All Forms of Discrimination against Women (*infra*). At regional level, the right of individual petition is set forth both in the European

this right upon the author of the complaint or communication being – or claiming to be – a *victim* of a human rights violation (e.g., ECHR, Article 34 [former Article 25]; [first] Optional Protocol to the Covenant on Civil and Political Rights, Article 2; Convention on the Elimination of All Forms of Racial Discrimination, Article XIV (1) and (2); United Nations Convention against Torture, Article 22).

III. The Titularity of the Right of Individual Petition: Distinct Formulations

A striking difference in the petitioning systems under the European and American Conventions on Human Rights is the presence of the 'victim' requirement in the former (Article 34, former Article 25 of the ECHR), and its absence in the latter (Article 44 of the ACHR), opening access to international justice widely, to 'any person or group of persons, or any nongovernmental entity legally recognized in one or more member States' of the OAS, all being entitled to exercise the right of petition.

In the European system, the presence of the 'victim' requirement in the provision on the right of individual petition has led to a jurisprudential construction aimed at securing access to international justice. It is generally assumed that the applicants ought to be personally affected by the alleged wrongs complained of; moreover, it was soon reckoned that, when the direct victim cannot act by himself, recourse can be made to the 'indirect' victim'.[20] The notion of 'victim' under Article 34 – former Article 25 – of the ECHR has thus not been, and cannot be, strictly construed. On the contrary, it has been construed bearing in mind the imperative of access to justice.

From the start, the ECtHR accorded 'favourable treatment' to individual applicants, having expressly regarded it (e.g., in its Judgment of 06 September 1978 in the case of *Klass and Others versus Federal Republic of Germany*) as 'one of the keystones in the machinery for the enforcement' of the protected rights under the Convention.[21] The petitioner can thus even claim to be a 'potential' victim of a breach of the Convention.[22] This has, again, fostered the individual's access to justice under the European Convention.

The notion of victim has, significantly, experienced considerable expansion through the jurisprudential construction of the international supervisory organs, under such human rights treaties as the ECHR and the ACHR, in coming to comprise direct and indirect victims, as well as 'potential' victims, that is, those who sustain an admittedly valid potential personal interest in the vindication of their

---

Convention on Human Rights (Article 25) as well as in the American Convention on Human Rights (Article 44) and in the African Charter on Human and Peoples' Rights (Articles 55–8).

[20] K. Rogge, 'The "Victim" Requirement in Article 25 of the European Convention on Human Rights', in *Protecting Human Rights: The European Dimension – Studies in Honour of G.J. Wiarda* (eds. F. Matscher and H. Petzold), Köln/Berlin, C. Heymanns Verlag, 1988, pp. 539–45.

[21] H. Delvaux, 'The Notion of Victim under Article 25 of the European Convention on Human Rights', in *Protection of Human Rights in Europe – Limits and Effects* (ed. I. Maier), Heidelberg, C.F. Müller Juristischer Verlag, 1982, p. 41.

[22] Ibid., pp. 52 and 64. And cf. further, on this issue, chapter VII, *infra*.

rights.[23] The ACHR (Article 44) and the African Charter on Human and Peoples' Rights (Articles 55–56) adopt, however, a more liberal solution on this particular point, as they do not impose upon the petitioners the requisite of the condition of victim.

In any case, the solutions given by human rights treaties and instruments to the *jus standi* of the complainant (with variations, namely, alleged victim and 'author of communication', 'reasonably presumed' victim, special qualifications of the complainants, right of petition widely conferred) appear to be linked to the nature of the procedures at issue (right of petition or communication or [individual] representation).[24] Differences in the legal nature of those procedures, however, significantly have not hindered the development, by the distinct international supervisory organs, of a converging case-law on more effective protection of the alleged victims.

It has been under the ECHR that a vast case-law on the right of individual petition has evolved. It is certain that the former Article 25 (today Article 34) (prior to Protocol n. 11) was originally conceived as an optional clause; nowadays, however, with the entry into force of Protocol n. 11 in November 1998, the right of petition before the new ECtHR (as the sole jurisdictional organ under the amended Convention) is mandatory to all States Parties (as it has been under the ACHR since its adoption in 1969).

Two additional observations appear to me necessary, at this stage. In the first place, over half a century ago, in conceiving Article 25 originally as an optional clause, the draftsmen of the European Convention were, however, careful enough to determine, in the first paragraph *in fine* of the clause, the obligation of the States Parties which accepted it of not interposing any impediment or obstacle to the exercise of the right of individual petition. In the case of *Cruz Varas and Other versus Sweden* (1990–1991), the European Court and, to a larger extent, the old European Commission, recognized the right of a procedural nature which Article 25(1) conferred upon the individual complainants, by virtue of which these latter could take the initiative of freely resorting to the Commission, without any impediment or difficulty having been raised by the State Party at issue.[25]

The right of individual petition is, thus, endowed with autonomy, distinct as it is from the substantive rights listed in title I of the ECHR. Any obstacle interposed by the State Party to its free exercise would bring about, therefore, an *additional*

---

[23] On the evolution of the notion of 'victim' (including the potential victim) in the International Law of Human Rights, cf. A.A. Cançado Trindade, 'Co-existence and Co-ordination . . .', *op. cit. infra* n. (31), pp. 243–99, esp. pp. 262–83.

[24] Ibid., pp. 248–61.

[25] Compare the Judgment, of 20 March 1991, of the European Court of Human Rights in the case *Cruz Varas and Others versus Sweden* (Merits, Series A, vol. 201), pp. 33–4 and 36, pars. 92–3 and 99, with the Opinion, of 07 June 1990, of the European Commission of Human Rights in the same case (Annex, in ibid.), pp. 50–2, pars. 118, 122 and 125–6. The Commission went further than the Court, arguing, moreover, that, in failing to comply with a request of not deporting the individual complainant (H. Cruz Varas, Chilean), Sweden violated the obligation provided for in Article 25 *in fine* of the European Convention of not impeding the efficacy of the right of individual petition; the European Court, in a decision adopted by 10 votes to 9, did not agree with the Commission – in a less persuasive form than this latter – on this point in particular.

violation of the Convention, parallel to other violations which become proved of the substantive rights enshrined in this latter. Its autonomy was in no way affected by the fact of having been originally foreseen in an optional clause of the Convention (former Article 25).

Secondly, reinforcing this point, both the old European Commission and the Court of Human Rights have understood that the concept itself of victim (in the light of Article 25 of the Convention) ought to be interpreted *autonomously*. This understanding today finds solid support in the *jurisprudence constante* under the Convention. Thus, in several decisions throughout the years, the old European Commission consistently and invariably warned that the concept of 'victim' utilized in the former Article 25 (nowadays in Article 34) of the Convention ought to be interpreted *in an autonomous way* and *independently of concepts of domestic law* such as those of the interest or quality to interpose a judicial action or to participate in a legal process.[26]

The ECtHR, in its turn, in the *Norris versus Ireland* case (1988), said that the conditions which governed individual petitions under Article 25 'are not necessarily the same as national criteria relating to *locus standi*', which may even serve purposes distinct from those contemplated in Article 25.[27] The autonomy of the right of individual petition at international level vis-à-vis provisions of domestic law is thus clearly defined. The elements singled out in this case-law of protection apply equally under procedures of other human rights treaties which require the condition of 'victim' for the exercise of the right of individual petition.

It seems rather odd to find, from time to time, in part of the European legal writing on the matter,[28] the suggestion that the right of individual petition would perhaps not be effective in relation to massive and systematic violations of human rights. This suggestion does not stand, and is not corroborated by the facts. That has not been the case, at least in recent years, when the ECtHR has indeed come to pronounce on systematic violations of human rights under the ECHR.

---

[26] Cf. in this sense: European Commission of Human Rights (EComHR), case *Scientology Kirche Deutschland e.V. versus Germany* (appl. n. 34614/96), decision of 07 April 1997, 89 *Decisions and Reports* (1997) p. 170; EComHR, case *Zentralrat Deutscher Sinti und Roma y R. Rose versus Germany* (appl. n. 35208/97), decision of 27 May 1997, p. 4 (unpublished); EComHR, case *Greek Federation of Customs Officials, N. Gialouris, G. Christopoulos and 3333 Other Customs Officials versus Greece* (appl. n. 24581/94), decision of 06 April 1995, 81-B *Decisions and Reports* (1995) p. 127; EComHR, case *N.N. Tauira and 18 Others versus France* (appl. n. 28204/95), decision of 04 December 1995, 83-A *Decisions and Reports* (1995) p. 130 (petitions against the French nuclear tests in the atoll of Mururoa and in that of Fangataufa, in French Polinesia); EComHR, case *K. Sygounis, I. Kotsis and Police Union versus Greece* (appl. n. 18598/91), decision of 18 May 1994, 78 *Decisions and Reports* (1994) p. 77; EComHR, case *Association of Air Pilots of the Republic, J. Mata el Al. versus Spain* (appl. n. 10733/84), decision of 11 March 1985, 41 *Decisions and Reports* (1985) p. 222. According to this same case-law, to fulfil the condition of 'victim' (under Article 25 of the Convention) there ought to be a 'sufficiently direct link' between the individual complainant and the alleged damage, resulting from the alleged violation of the Convention.

[27] European Court of Human Rights, case *Norris versus Ireland*, Judgment of 26 October 1988, Series A, vol. 142, p. 15, par. 31.

[28] Cf. R. Müllerson, 'The Efficiency of the Individual Complaint Procedures: The Experience of CCPR, CERD, CAT and ECHR', *Monitoring Human Rights in Europe – Comparing International Procedures and Mechanisms* (ed. A. Bloed *et alii*), Dordrecht, Nijhoff, 1993, pp. 25–43, esp. p. 32.

Thus, the emphasis given by the ECtHR, for example, in the case of *Loizidou et alii versus Turkey* (Preliminary Objections, 1995), on the effectiveness of domestic remedies and the rights guaranteed by the ECHR, has been regarded as a turning point in the ECtHR's case-law on the matter:

la Cour adhère à l'option selon laquelle le traitement judiciaire est *aussi* particulièrement nécessaire pour les violations structurelles.[29]

The ECtHR came to display a preparedness – like its counterpart the IACtHR – to resolve, by means of the examination of individual petitions, systematic violations of human rights,[30] affecting a plurality of victims. This is illustrated by several Judgments in recent years forming the cycle of the *south-east Turkey complaints*, and its more recent and successive Judgments concerning Russia and pertaining to the situation in *Chechnya*.

In upholding the right of individual petition in such adverse circumstances affecting a plurality of victims, the ECtHR has kept in mind the situation of vulnerability of these latter. Thus, in the *Kurt versus Turkey* case (Judgment of 25 May 1998), for example, the ECtHR expressly warned that:

regard must be had to the vulnerability of the complainant and his or her susceptibility to influence exerted by the authorities. In this connection, the Court, having regard to the vulnerable position of applicant villagers and the reality that in south-east Turkey complaints against the authorities might well give rise to a legitimate fear of reprisals, has found that the questioning of applicants about their applications to the [former] Commission amounts to a form of illicit and unacceptable pressure, which hinders the exercise of the right of individual petition, in breach of Article 25 of the Convention (par. 160).

This is but one example in illustration of the point at issue. Further decisions of the Court, taken in the last decade, to the same effect (e.g., concerning the situation in *Chechnya* – *infra*) could also be recalled in this connection.

The ECHR only accepted the right of individual petition originally enshrined in an optional clause by requiring demonstration of the condition of *victim* by the individual complainant – which, in its turn, generated a remarkable jurisprudential development of the notion of 'victim'.[31] The ACHR, in a distinct way, rendered the right of individual petition (Article 44) mandatory, of automatic acceptance by the ratifying States, extending it, as already pointed out, to 'any person or group of persons, or non-governmental entity legally recognized in one or more member States of the Organization' of American States– which discloses the great importance attributed to it.[32]

---

[29] J.-F. Flauss, 'La Cour de Strasbourg face aux violations systématiques des droits de l'homme', in *Les droits de l'homme au seuil du troisième millénaire – Mélanges en hommage à P. Lambert*, Bruxelles, Bruylant, 2000, pp. 346–7.

[30] Cf. ibid., pp. 356–61.

[31] Cf. A.A. Cançado Trindade, 'Co-existence and Co-ordination of Mechanisms of International Protection of Human Rights (At Global and Regional Levels)', 202 *Recueil des Cours de l'Académie de Droit International de La Haye* (1987), pp. 243–99.

[32] The other type of petition, the inter-State one, was only provided for on an optional basis (Article 45 of the American Convention, contrary to the scheme of the European Convention – former Article

This was one of the great advances achieved by the ACHR, at conceptual and normative, as well as operational, levels.[33] One has to bear in mind always the autonomy of the right of individual petition vis-à-vis the domestic law of the States. Its relevance cannot be minimized, as it may occur that, in a given internal legal order, an individual becomes unable, by the circumstances of a legal situation, to take judicial measures by himself. This does not mean that he would be deprived of doing so in the exercise of the right of individual petition under the ACHR, or another human rights treaty.

But the ACHR goes further than that: the *legitimatio ad causam*, which it extends to every and any petitioner, can even do without a manifestation on the part of the victim himself or herself. The right of individual petition, thus widely conceived, has, as an immediate effect, the enlargement of the scope of protection, above all in cases in which the victims (e.g., those detained *incommunicado*, disappeared persons, among other situations) find themselves unable to act *motu propio*, and stand in need of the initiative of a third party as petitioner on their behalf. The right of individual petition under the ACHR is, in sum, widely open to *any person* or *group of persons*.

Just like the right itself of individual petition per se the requisite of legality of a petitioning non-governmental entity in particular is also *denationalized*.[34] The protection of human rights set in operation by the exercise of the right of individual petition takes place in the light of the notion of *collective guarantee*, underlying human rights treaties which provide for the petitioning system. It is in this context that one should assess the wide scope of the *legitimatio ad causam* under those treaties (providing for the right of individual petition).

The ECtHR, in its judgment of 09 December 1994 in the case of the *Holy Monasteries versus Greece*, decided to dismiss an attempt to impose restrictions (other than that of the condition of 'victim') to the non-governmental organization at issue. The respondent State argued that, given the links which it maintained with the Greek Orthodox Church and the 'considerable influence' of the latter in the

---

24, today Article 33 – in this particular), which stresses the relevance attributed to the right of individual petition. This point did not pass unnoticed from the IACtHR, which, in its second Advisory Opinion, on the *Effect of Reservations on the Entry into Force of the American Convention on Human Rights* (of 24 September 1982), invoked this particularity as illustrative of the 'overriding importance' attributed by the American Convention to the obligations of the States Parties vis-à-vis the individuals, vindicated by these latter without the intermediation of another State (par. 32).

[33] The matter is examined in detail in my Concurring Opinion in the case *Castillo Petruzzi and Others versus Peru* (Preliminary Objections, Judgment of 04 September 1998), pars. 1–46 of the Concurring Opinion.

[34] Under the European Convention of Human Rights, for example, the requisite of legal recognition of a petitioning non-governmental entity (under original Article 25) does not even exist. The practice of the former European Commission of Human Rights endorsed the interpretation that the reference of original Article 25 of the Convention to 'non-governmental organization' *tout court*, without conditionings or qualifications, had the purpose of impeding the exclusion of any persons, other than physical persons, enabled to resort to the European Commission; cf. *Les droits de l'homme et les personnes morales* (1969 Louvain Colloquy), Brussels, Bruylant, 1970, p. 20 (intervention of H. Golsong); and cf. *Actes du Cinquième Colloque International sur la Convention Européenne des Droits de l'Homme* (1980 Frankfurt Colloquy), Paris, Pédone, 1982, pp. 35–78 (report by H. Delvaux).

State activities and in public administration, the complainant Monasteries were not non-governmental organizations in the sense of Article 25 of the ECHR (par. 48). The Court dismissed this argument, in finding that the Monasteries referred to did not exercise governmental powers. Their classification as entities of public law was intended only to extend to them legal protection vis-à-vis third parties. As the Holy Monasteries were under the 'spiritual supervision' of the local archbishop and not under the supervision of the State, they were distinct from this latter, from which they were 'completely independent'. Accordingly, the ECtHR concluded, the complainant Monasteries were non-governmental organizations in the sense of former Article 25 (par. 49).

Each of the procedures which regulate the right of individual petition under international human rights treaties and instruments, despite differences in their legal nature, has contributed, in its own way, to the gradual strengthening of the procedural capacity of the complainant at international level. In an express recognition of the relevance of the right of individual petition, the Declaration and Programme of Action of Vienna, the main document adopted by the Second World Conference on Human Rights (1993), urged its adoption, as an additional method of protection, by means of Optional Protocols to the Convention on the Elimination of All Forms of Discrimination against Women [CEDAW] and to the Covenant on Economic, Social and Cultural Rights.[35] That document recommended, moreover, to the States Parties in human rights treaties, the acceptance of all the available optional procedures of individual petitions or communications.[36]

IV. The Significance and Overriding Importance of the Right of Individual Petition

Of all the mechanisms of international protection of human rights, the right of individual petition is, in fact, the most dynamic one, in even granting the initiative of action to the individual himself (the ostensibly weaker party vis-à-vis the public power), distinctly from the exercise *ex officio* of other methods (such as those of fact-finding and reports) on the part of the international supervisory organs. It is the one which best reflects the specificity of international human rights law, in comparison with other solutions proper to Public International Law – as it can be inferred from the case-law of both the ECtHR and the IACtHR.[37]

---

[35] Declaration and Programme of Action of Vienna of 1993, part II, pars. 40 and 75, respectively. The Optional Protocol to CEDAW was adopted on 10 December 1999, having entered into force on 22 December 2000.

[36] Declaration and Programme of Action of Vienna of 1993, part II, par. 90.

[37] Cf., e.g., the Judgment of the ECtHR in the case of *Loizidou versus Turkey* (Preliminary Objections, 1995), and the Judgment of its Grand Chamber in the case of *I. Ilascu, A. Lesco, A. Ivantoc and T. Petrov-Popa versus Moldova and the Russian Federation* (Preliminary Objections, 2001), as well as the Judgments of the IACtHR in the cases of *Castillo Petruzzi and Others versus Peru* (Preliminary Objections, 1998), of the *Constitutional Tribunal* and of *Ivcher Bronstein versus Peru* (Competence, 1999), and of *Hilaire, Benjamin, and Constantine versus Trinidad and Tobago* (Preliminary Objections, 2001). Cf. chapter V, *infra*.

Moreover, the *denationalization* of the protection and of the requisites of the international action of safeguard of human rights,[38] besides sensibly enlarging the circle of protected persons, rendered it possible to individuals to exercise rights emanating directly from international law, implemented in the light of collective guarantee, and no longer simply 'granted' by the State. With the access of individuals to justice at international level, by means of the exercise of the right of individual petition, concrete expression has at last been given to the recognition that the human rights to be protected are inherent to the human person and do not derive from the State. Accordingly, the action in their protection does not exhaust – cannot exhaust – itself in the action of the State.

In the inter-American system of protection of human rights, the right of individual petition has constituted an effective way of facing not only individual cases but also massive and systematic violations of human rights, even before the entry into force of the ACHR (i.e., in the initial practice of the Inter-American Commission on Human Rights, in the period 1959–1969, prior to the adoption of the ACHR). Its importance has been fundamental, and could never be minimized. The consolidation of the right of individual petition under Article 44 of the ACHR was endowed with special significance. Not only was its importance for the mechanism of the Convention as a whole duly emphasized in the *travaux préparatoires* of that provision of the Convention,[39] it also represented an advance in relation to what, until the adoption of the Pact of San José in 1969, had been achieved in that respect, in the ambit of international human rights law.

In almost three decades of application of the ACHR (since its entry into force in 1978), and in more than half a century of application of the ECHR (since its entry into force in 1953), the right of individual petition has proven to be the mechanism *par excellence* of the emancipation of the individual vis-à-vis his own State.[40] In the public hearings before the IACtHR in distinct cases – above all in those pertaining to reparations – a point which has particularly drawn my attention has been the observation, increasingly more frequent, on the part of the victims or their relatives, to the effect that, had it not been for their access to the international instance, justice would never have been done in their concrete cases.

Again in the period subsequent to the entry into force of Protocol n. 11 to the ECHR, the ECtHR has seen it fit to warn, in the *Bazorkina versus Russia* case (Judgment of 27 July 2006), that 'it is of the utmost importance for the effective

---

[38] In the present domain of protection, nationality disappears as a *vinculum juris* for the exercise of protection (differently from the discretionary diplomatic protection in the inter-State *contentieux*, based upon fundamentally distinct premises), sufficing that the individual complainant – irrespective of nationality or domicile – is (even though temporarily) under the jurisdiction of one of the States Parties to the human rights treaty at issue.

[39] Cf. OAS, *Conferencia Especializada Interamericana sobre Derechos Humanos – Actas y Documentos* (San José of Costa Rica, 07–22 November 1969), doc. OAS/Ser.K/XVI/1.2, Washington D.C., General Secretariat of the OAS, 1978, pp. 43, 47 and 373.

[40] A.A. Cançado Trindade, 'A Emancipação do Ser Humano como Sujeito do Direito Internacional e os Limites da Razão de Estado', 6/7 *Revista da Faculdade de Direito da Universidade do Estado do Rio de Janeiro* (1998–1999) pp. 425–34; A.A. Cançado Trindade, 'The Emancipation of the Individual from His Own State...', *op. cit. supra* n. (14), pp. 158–71.

operation of the system of individual petition instituted under Article 34 of the Convention that States should furnish all necessary facilities to make possible a proper and effective examination of applications' (par. 170). Besides that, the Court added in the *Tanrikulu versus Turkey* case (Judgment of 08 July 1999), under Article 34 (former Article 25) of the Convention, 'applicants or potential applicants should be able to communicate freely with the Convention organs without being subject to any form of pressure from the authorities', so as 'to withdraw or modify their complaints' (pars. 70 and 130).

This becomes more evident in cases of extreme vulnerability, if not defencelessness, of the victims.[41] In recent years the ECtHR has expressed this concern, for example, in the cycle of so-called *Turkish cases*, involving reiterated complaints of violations of the right to personal integrity by brutalities perpetrated by security forces, of curtailment of political rights and freedoms, and of breaches of the right to property of members of minorities, in the Kurdish region. The concern was expressly singled out by the Court, *inter alia*, in its Judgment on the *Tanrikulu* case, where it stated that:

(...) In previous cases the Court has had regard to the vulnerable position of applicant villagers and the reality that in south-east Turkey complaints against the authorities might well give rise to a legitimate fear of reprisals, and it has found that the questioning of applicants about their applications to the [old] Commission amounts to a form of illicit and unacceptable pressure, which hinders the exercise of the right of individual petition in breach of former Article 25 of the Convention (par. 130).

In fact, it is difficult to escape the conclusion that, without the right of individual petition, freely and fully guaranteed and exercised, and the consequent access to justice at international level, the rights enshrined into the human rights treaties which set up international human rights tribunals would be reduced to a little more than dead letter. It is by the free and full exercise of the right of individual petition that the rights set forth in those treaties become *effective*. The right of individual petition shelters, in fact, the last hope of those who did not find justice at national level. I would not hesitate to add – allowing myself the metaphor – that the right of individual petition is undoubtedly the most luminous star in the universe of human rights.

The right of individual petition – upon which is erected the judicial mechanism of the emancipation of the human being vis-à-vis his own State – is a fundamental clause of the human rights treaties that provide for it, as is the submission of States Parties to the contentious jurisdiction of the international human rights tribunal at issue.

In the case of the IACtHR, this is done by acceptance of the optional clause of Article 62 of the ACHR; yet that clause does not admit limitations other than those expressly contained in that Article, as clarified by the IACtHR in its *jurisprudence constante*.[42] Thus, the fact that it is provided for in an optional clause does not deprive it of its character of fundamental clause. In the case of ECtHR, this has

---

[41] On the protection of victims in cases of great adversity or defencelessness, cf. chapter VII, *infra*.

[42] Cf. its Judgments on competence in the cases of *Ivcher Bronstein* and *Constitutional Tribunal* (of 24 September 1999), concerning Peru, and on preliminary objections in the cases of *Hilaire, Benjamin*, and *Constantine versus Trinidad and Tobago* (of 01 September 2001). There has been, however, an unfortunate set-back recently, in the case of the *Sisters Serrano Cruz versus El Salvador* (Preliminary

become a point of only historical interest, as the former optional clause of the old Article 46 of the ECHR has now been appropriately replaced by its *automatic* jurisdiction in contentious matter, pursuant to the new Article 32, as amended by Protocol n. 11.[43]

The right of individual petition under the ECHR reads:

The Court may receive applications from any person, non-governmental organisation or group of individuals claiming to be the victim of a violation by one of the High Contracting Parties of the rights set forth in the Convention or the Protocols thereto. The High Contracting Parties undertake not to hinder in any way the effective exercise of this right.

This provision has been the object, recently, of significant case-law of the ECtHR, in the new cycle of *Russian cases*, with the effect of drawing attention to the overriding importance of the right of individual petition.

Thus, in its Judgment (of 06 June 2005) in *Klyakhin versus Russia*, the ECtHR recalled that it was:

of the utmost importance for the effective operation of the system of individual application instituted by Article 34 that applicants should be able to communicate freely with the Court without being subjected to any form of pressure from the authorities to withdraw or modify their complaints. In this context, 'pressure' includes not only direct coercion and flagrant acts of intimidation, but also other improper indirect acts or contacts designed to dissuade or discourage applicants from using a Convention remedy (par. 119).

The ECtHR further indicated that 'unacceptable practices' (e.g., in the exercise by authorities of the domestic investigative function, or else the interception of letters by prison authorities, among others) from the standpoint of Article 34 were to be determined in the light of the circumstances of the case; in the *Klyakhin* case, the ECtHR found that there had been a violation of Article 34 (par. 123). In *Ilascu and Others versus Moldova and Russia* (of 08 July 2004) and *Nurmagomedov versus Russia* (of 07 June 2007), the ECtHR also concluded that there had been a breach of Article 34 in view of the hindrance to the applicants' right of individual petition.

The ECtHR reached the same conclusion in its Judgment (of 13 July 2006) in the case of *Popov versus Russia* (par. 251), where attention was drawn to the aggravating circumstance of the vulnerability of the applicant:

whether or not contacts between the authorities and an applicant are tantamount to unacceptable practices from the standpoint of Article 34 must be determined in the light of the particular circumstances of the case. In this respect, regard must be had to the

---

Objections, Judgment of 23 November 2004); cf. Dissenting Opinion of Judge A.A. Cançado Trindade, pars. 1–49.

[43] For a plea in favour of the *automatic* jurisdiction also of the Inter-American Court in contentious matters, cf. A.A. Cançado Trindade, 'Las Cláusulas Pétreas de la Protección Internacional del Ser Humano: El Acceso Directo de los Individuos a la Justicia a Nivel Internacional y la Intangibilidad de la Jurisdicción Obligatoria de los Tribunales Internacionales de Derechos Humanos', in *El Sistema Interamericano de Protección de los Derechos Humanos en el Umbral del Siglo XXI – Memoria del Seminario* (November 1999), vol. I, 1st. ed., San José of Costa Rica, Inter-American Court of Human Rights, 2001, pp. 3–68.

vulnerability of the complainant and his or her susceptibility to influence exerted by the authorities (...). The applicant's position might be particularly vulnerable when he is held in custody with limited contacts with his family or the outside world (par. 247).

In Judgment (07 October 2004) in the *Poleshchuk versus Russia* case, the ECtHR again found a breach of Article 34 (par. 28), and clarified that:

Article 34 of the Convention imposes an obligation on a Contracting State not to hinder the right of individual petition. While the obligation imposed is of a procedural nature, distinguishable from the substantive rights set out in the Convention and Protocols, it flows from the very essence of this procedural right that it is open to individuals to complain of its alleged infringements in Convention proceedings (...). The Court also recalls that the undertaking not to hinder the effective exercise of the right of individual application precludes any interference with the individual's right to present and pursue his complaint before the Court effectively (...) (par. 27).

In the *Baysayeva versus Russia* case (05 April 2007) and *Bitiyeva and X versus Russia* case (21 June 2007), the ECtHR again stressed the importance of Article 34 (pars. 163, of both Judgments); although it did not find a breach of Article 34 in those two cases, yet the ECtHR proceeded to a separate finding of a breach of Article 38(1)(a) of the Convention. This last provision (on examination of a case) provides that, if need be, the Court will 'undertake an investigation, for the effective conduct of which the States concerned shall furnish all necessary facilities'. In the *Baysayeva* case, the ECtHR stated that 'a failure to submit information which is crucial to the establishment of facts' may give rise – as it did – to a separate finding of a breach of Article 38(1)(a) of the Convention (par. 164).

In *Trubnikov versus Russia* (Judgment of 05 July 2005), and *Imakayeva versus Russia* (Judgment of 09 November 2006), the ECtHR again found a separate failure to fulfil the obligation under Article 38(1)(a). In the recent case *Alikhadzhiyeva versus Russia* case (Judgment of 05 July 2007), the ECtHR, though finding no violation under this provision nor under Article 38 (par. 106), saw it fit to clarify its case-law: it reiterated the utmost importance of the right of individual petition under Article 34 (par. 100), and added that 'delays in submitting information which is crucial to the establishment of facts may give rise to a separate finding under Article 38 of the Convention' (par. 101). The Court concluded that Article 38 'is applicable to cases which have been declared admissible' (par. 104), while the main objective of Article 34 is 'to ensure the effective operation of the right of individual petition' (par. 105).

In *Shamayev and Others versus Georgia and Russia* (Judgment of 12 April 2005), the ECtHR found a breach of Article 34 as well as non-compliance with the obligation under Article 38(1)(a) of the Convention. The Court warned that, given the 'utmost importance' of 'the system of individual petition', States Parties should 'furnish all necessary facilities to make possible a proper and effective examination of applications' (par. 508). It added:

This obligation requires the Contracting States to furnish all facilities necessary to the Court for it to conduct an on-site investigation or to carry out the general tasks which are incumbent on it when examining applications. The failure by a Government, as has been the situation in the present case, to enable the Court to hear witnesses and to ascertain the facts without a satisfactory explanation may reflect negatively on the level of compliance by a respondent State with its obligations under Articles 34 and 38(1)(a) of the Convention (par. 509).

V. The Right of Direct Access of Individuals to International Human Rights Tribunals

Surely one of the greatest historical achievements of the international protection of human rights is the access of individuals to the international judicial organs of protection and the recognition of their international procedural capacity in cases of violations of human rights. As the systems of protection of the European and American Conventions were conceived, the mechanisms finally adopted did not originally provide for the direct representation of individuals in the proceedings before the ECtHR and the IACtHR – these two tribunals have now been joined by a new international human rights tribunal, the African Court on Human and Peoples' Rights (elected and set up on 22 January 2006).

Some resistance to the establishment of a new international jurisdiction for the safeguard of human rights became clear, and led to the attempt, by the intermediation of the old European and Inter-American Commissions of Human Rights, to avoid the direct access of individuals to the ECtHR and the IACtHR. Such resistances have now been definitively overcome by the ECtHR (with the recognition of the *jus standi* of individuals), and has likewise been largely overcome by the IACtHR (with the setting forth of the *locus standi in judicio* for petitioners at all stages of the procedure before it), and has also been circumvented by the newly-created African Court (in foreseeing the individuals' *jus standi in judicio* on an optional basis).

1. Developments in the European System of Protection

Already in the examination of their *first* contentious cases, both the European and the Inter-American Courts of Human Rights rebelled against the artificiality of the intermediation of the respective Commissions. It may be recalled that, as early as the *Lawless versus Ireland* case (1960), the ECtHR began to receive, through the delegates of the European Commission, written arguments of the complainants themselves, which often appeared quite critical vis-à-vis the Commission itself. This measure was regarded as normal, as the arguments of the alleged victims did not have to coincide entirely with those of the delegates of the Commission. One decade later, during the proceedings in the *Vagrancy* cases, pertaining to Belgium (1970), the ECtHR accepted the request of the Commission to give the floor to a lawyer of the three complainants; in taking the floor, that lawyer criticized the opinion expressed by the Commission in its report.[44]

---

[44] Cf. M.-A. Eissen, *El Tribunal Europeo de Derechos Humanos*, Madrid, Civitas, 1985, pp. 28–36.

The developments which followed are known: the granting of *locus standi* to the legal representatives of the individual complainants before the Court (by means of the reform of the Regulations of 1982, in force as from 01 January 1983) in cases submitted to the Court by the Commission or the States Parties, followed by the adoption of Protocol n. 9 (of 1990) to the ECHR, which paved the way for further steps. As the *Explanatory Report* of the Council of Europe on the matter stressed, Protocol n. 9 granted 'a type of *locus standi*' to the individuals before the Court, undoubtedly an advance, but which did not yet secure to them an '*equality of arms/ égalité des armes*' with the respondent States and the full benefit of utilizing the mechanism of the ECHR for the vindication of their rights.[45]

In any case, relations of the ECtHR with the individual complainants became direct, without necessarily requiring an intermediation from delegates of the Commission. This follows a certain logic, as the roles or functions of the complainants and of the Commission are distinct; as the ECtHR pointed out in its *first* case (*Lawless*), the Commission appears rather as an organ which assists the Court. There were frequent diverging opinions between the delegates of the Commission and the representatives of the victims, and this was considered as normal, and even as inevitable. States had become used to the practice of the delegates of the Commission to resort almost always to the assistance of a representative of the victims, or at least not to object to it.

It should not pass unnoticed that this whole evolution has taken place, in the European system of protection, gradually, through the reform of the Rules of Court and the adoption of Protocol n. 9 to the Convention. The ECtHR determined the scope of its own powers through the reform of its *interna corporis*, affecting even the condition of the parties before itself. Some cases were in fact settled under Protocol n. 9, in relation to States Parties to the ECHR which ratified the latter: hence the co-existence of Rules of Court A and B of the European Court.[46] It is certain that, as from the day of entry into force (01 November 1998) of Protocol n. 11 (of 1994) (on the reform of the mechanism of this Convention and the establishment of a new European Court as the sole jurisdictional organ of supervision of the Convention).[47] Protocol n. 9 became anachronistic, of only historical interest.

---

[45] Council of Europe, *Protocol n. 9 to the Convention for the Protection of Human Rights and Fundamental Freedoms – Explanatory Report*, Strasbourg, C.E., 1992, pp. 8–9, and cf. pp. 3–18; for other comments, cf. J.-F. Flauss, 'Le droit de recours individuel devant la Cour européenne des droits de l'homme – Le Protocole n. 9 à la Convention Européenne des Droits de l'Homme', 36 *Annuaire français de droit international* (1990) pp. 507–19; G. Janssen-Pevtschin, 'Le Protocole Additionnel n. 9 à la Convention Européenne des Droits de l'Homme', 2 *Revue trimestrielle des droits de l'homme* (1991) n. 6, pp. 199–202; M. de Salvia, 'Il Nono Protocollo alla Convenzione Europea dei Diritti dell'Uomo: Punto di Arrivo o Punto di Partenza?', 3 *Rivista Internazionale dei Diritti dell'Uomo* (1990) pp. 474–82; and cf. also R. Ryssdall, 'The Coming of Age of the European Convention on Human Rights', 1 *European Human Rights Law Review* (1996) pp. 18–29.

[46] Rules of Court A applicable to cases pertaining to States Parties to the European Convention which did not ratify Protocol n. 9, and Rules of Court B applicable to cases pertaining to States Parties to the Convention which ratified Protocol n. 9.

[47] Cf. Council of Europe, *Protocol n. 11 to the Convention for the Protection of Human Rights and Fundamental Freedoms and Explanatory Report*, Strasbourg, C.E., 1994, pp. 3–52; and cf. also A. Drzemczewski, 'A Major Overhaul of the European Human Rights Convention Control

Contrary to what sceptics used to predict, in a relatively short time all the States Parties to the ECHR, in an unequivocal demonstration of maturity, became Parties also to Protocol n. 11, thus enabling also it to enter into force in 1998. This event represented a highly gratifying step to all those who labour in favour of the strengthening of the international protection of human rights. The individual is thus endowed, at last, with *direct access* to an international tribunal (*jus standi*), as a true subject – and with full legal capacity – of the international law of human rights.

I well remember the ceremony of the commemoration of the entry into force of Protocol n. 11 and the establishment of the new ECtHR – which I attended as the representative of the IACtHR. There was a sense of accomplishment in the *Palais des Droits de l'Homme* in Strasbourg, of achievement of a culmination in the emancipation of the individual vis-à-vis his own State, after almost half a century of evolution to this end. Shortly afterwards, in my message to the 2000 Rome Conference in commemoration of the fiftieth anniversary of the ECHR, I pointed out that:

Both the European and Inter-American Courts have rightly set limits to State voluntarism, have safeguarded the integrity of the respective human rights Conventions and the primacy of considerations of *ordre public* over the will of individual States, have set higher standards of State behaviour and established some degree of control over the interposition of undue restrictions by States, and have reassuringly enhanced the position of individuals as subjects of the International Law of Human Rights, with full procedural capacity. (. . .)

Last year we celebrated, in San José of Costa Rica, the 30th anniversary of the adoption of the American Convention on Human Rights and the 20th anniversary of the establishment of the Inter-American Court of Human Rights. This year we celebrate, in Rome, the 50th anniversary of the adoption of the European Convention on Human Rights. The evolving case-law of the European and Inter-American Courts of Human Rights is nowadays the juridical patrimony of all States and peoples of our continents.[48]

This remarkable achievement was made possible above all by a new mentality towards the protection of human rights at international and national levels. Even at the time of the adoption of Protocol n. 9 to the ECHR, paving the way for Protocol n. 11, it was

Mechanism: Protocol n. 11', 6 *Collected Courses of the Academy of European Law* (1997)-II, pp. 121–244. Cf. also: S. Marcus Helmons, 'Le Onzième Protocole Additionnel à la Convention Europénne des Droits de l'Homme', 113 *Journal des Tribunaux* – Bruxelles (1994) n. 5725, pp. 545–7; R. Bernhardt, 'Reform of the Control Machinery under the European Convention on Human Rights: Protocol n. 11', 89 *American Journal of International Law* (1995) pp. 145–54; J.A. Carrillo Salcedo, 'Vers la réforme du système européen de protection des droits de l'homme', in *Présence du droit public et des droits de l'homme – Mélanges offerts à Jacques Velu*, vol. II, Bruxelles, Bruylant, 1992, pp. 1319–25; H. Golsong, 'On the Reform of the Supervisory System of the European Convention on Human Rights', 13 *Human Rights Law Journal* (1992) pp. 265–9; K. de V. Mestdagh, 'Reform of the European Convention on Human Rights in a Changing Europe', in *The Dynamics of the Protection of Human Rights in Europe – Essays in Honour of H.G. Schermers* (eds. R. Lawson and M. de Blois), vol. III, Dordrecht, Nijhoff, 1994, pp. 337–60.

[48] A.A. Cançado Trindade, 'The Trans-Atlantic Perspective: The Contribution of the Work of the International Human Rights Tribunals to the Development of Public International Law/La perspective trans-atlantique: La contribution de l'oeuvre des cours internationales des droits de l'homme au développement du droit public international', in: *The European Convention on Human Rights at 50 – Human Rights Information Bulletin on Human Rights/La Convention européenne des droits de l'homme à 50 ans – Bulletin d'information sur les droits de l'homme*, n. 50 (special issue), Strasbourg, Council of Europe, 2000, p. 9, and cf. pp. 8–9.

pointed out that granting the individual the right of participation in international legal procedure, 'en lui attribuant une action autonome devant la Cour, est l'aboutissement d'un long mûrissement au sein du Conseil de l'Europe', a reform which 'se situait (. . .) dans la perspective évolutive, indiquée dans le Préambule de la Convention'.[49]

Shortly afterwards, the changes introduced by Protocol n. 9 had been overcome by the sweeping amendments – granting unrestricted *jus standi* to individual petitioners before the ECtHR – to the ECHR introduced by Protocol n. 11. In its turn, Protocol n. 9 retained its utility for the consideration of the aforementioned *jus standi* of individuals in historical perspective, which culminated in the adoption of Protocol n. 11. With the entry into force, of Protocol n. 11, the individual was at last endowed with *direct access* to an international tribunal (*jus standi*), as a true subject – with full juridical capacity – of International Law in the present domain of protection of his rights.

However, the entry into force of Protocol n. 11 was accompanied, not surprisingly, by a prompt, constant and considerable increase in the total number of cases brought before the ECtHR.[50] Due to the sharp increase in the number of cases, which has been growing considerably ever since, it was not surprising that, shortly after the adoption and entry into force of Protocol n. 11, a 'reform of the reform' was already being contemplated in the European human rights system to face the overload of cases.[51] Such 'reform of the reform' was soon to see the light of day, with the adoption, on 13 May 2004, of Protocol n. 14 to the European Convention. The Protocol – which will come into force in June 2010 – aims at enhancing the ECtHR's 'filtering' methods, foreseeing 'clearly inadmissible cases', 'repetitive cases' and creating a new admissibility criterion of applications disclosing that petitioners have not suffered a 'significant disadvantage'.[52]

---

[49]   G. Janssen-Pevtschin, 'Le Protocole n. 9 de la Convention Européenne des Droits de l'Homme', in *Présence du Droit public et des droits de l'homme – Mélanges offerts à J. Velu*, vol. II, Bruxelles, Bruylant, 1992, pp. 1274 and 1276.

[50]   From the end of 1998 (year of the entry into force of Protocol n. 11) to the end of the year 2000, the number of individual applications lodged with the Court raised from 18,164 to 30,069; by the year 2004, that total kept on sharply increasing up to 40943. In the same period, the Court delivered 105 judgments in 1998, a total which raised up to 695 judgments in 2000 and 718 in 2004. Council of Europe/ECtHR, *Survey of Activities 2004*, Strasbourg, ECtHR, 2004, p. 35. And, for an assessment of the first months of application of Protocol n. 11, cf. J.-F. Flauss (ed.), *La mise en oeuvre du Protocole n. 11: le nouveau Règlement de la Cour Européenne des Droits de l'Homme*, Bruxelles, Bruylant, 2000, pp. 101–35; A. Drzemczewski, 'Le Protocole n. 11 à la Convention Européenne des Droits de l'Homme – Entrée en vigueur et première année d'application', 11 *Revue universelle des droits de l'homme* (1999) pp. 377–93.

[51]   Cf., on this point, e.g., L. Wildhaber, 'Some Reflections on the First Year of Operation of the "New" European Court of Human Rights', in *Millennium Lectures – The Coming Together of the Common Law and the Civil Law* (ed. B.S. Markesinis), Oxford, Hart Publ., 2000, pp. 215–24; H. Petzold, 'Epilogue: la réforme continue', in *Protection des droits de l'homme: la perspective européenne – Mélanges à la mémoire de R. Ryssdal* (eds. P. Mahoney *et alii*), Köln/Berlin, C. Heymanns Verlag, 2000, pp. 1571–87; J.A. Pastor Ridruejo, 'El Tribunal Europeo de Derechos Humanos: La Reforma de la Reforma', in *El Sistema Interamericano de Protección de los Derechos Humanos en el Umbral del Siglo XXI* (Proceedings of the Seminar of San José of Costa Rica, of November 1999), vol. I, 2nd. ed., San José of Costa Rica, IACtHR, 2003, pp. 673–5.

[52]   Cf., for details, Council of Europe/Steering Committee for Human Rights, *Collection of Texts on the Reform of the Human Rights Protection System and in Particular the Protocol n. 14 and Other Texts Adopted at the 114th Session of the Committee of Ministers* (12–13 May 2004), C.E. document CDDH (2004)015 of 03 June 2004, Strasbourg, C.E., 2004, pp. 3–66; and, for a recent assessment, cf. G. Cohen-Jonathan and J.-F. Flauss (eds.), *La réforme du système de contrôle contentieux de la Convention*

In the course of the *travaux préparatoires* of Protocol n. 14, it was warned that the preservation of the individual right of petition to the ECtHR was necessary in order for individuals to obtain redress, this being linked to securing full access to justice; it was also recalled that the case-law of the ECtHR had carefully developed the right of individual petition over the past 40 years, and it lay at the heart of the mechanism of protection of the Convention, which contributed to transforming Public International Law itself.[53] The right of individual petition therefore ought not to be undermined, as its free exercise is essential for the realization of justice under the European Convention.

Shortly after the adoption of Protocol n. 14, it was pointed out that, while, on the one hand, its reform of the ECHR was meant to improve the efficacy of Article 13 (the right to an effective domestic remedy), which came out of it enhanced, on the other hand the new condition of admissibility of petitions was to be regretted, precisely for undermining – with the subjectivity of the expression 'significant disadvantage' – the right of individual petition, which remains a basic pillar of the system of protection under the ECHR.[54] Legal representatives of the victims promptly complained that the new condition of admissibility – with the aggravation that it could be decided by one sole judge, thus defying the collegiality of the Court – was contrary to the spirit of the ECHR and its jurisprudential evolution, and argued that it amounted to an unacceptable and undue restriction to the right of individual petition.[55]

There is thus now a concern that the controversial new admissibility requirement established by Protocol n. 14 may undermine the *pro victima* approach followed thus far by the ECtHR, precisely at a time when the ECtHR has again stressed, in the *Mamatkulov versus Turkey* case (Judgment of 04 February 2005), the considerable importance of the right of individual petition; the fear has thus been expressed that the new admissibility condition of Protocol n. 14 is bound to have a negative impact on the victim's right of access to international justice.[56]

It is therefore not surprising that the new admissibility condition of Protocol n. 14 has met with strong opposition, especially from those who take a *principled*, rather than a *pragmatic*, approach, sustaining, contrary to the 'constitutional justice' outlook, that the right to individual petition, consonant with the 'individual rights'

Européenne des Droits de l'Homme (Le Protocole n. 14 et les Recommandations et Résolutions du Comité des Ministres), Bruxelles, Bruylant/Nemesis, 2005, pp. 9–182; M. Eaton and J. Schokkenbroek, 'Reforming the Human Rights Protection System Established by the European Convention on Human Rights: A New Protocol n. 14 to the Convention and Other Measures to Guarantee the Long-Term Effectiveness of the Convention System', 26 *Human Rights Law Journal* (2005) pp. 1–17. For criticisms of that new admissibility criterion of applications, cf. G. Cohen-Jonathan and J.-F. Flauss (eds.), *La réforme du système...*, cit. supra (this footnote), pp. 42–4, 59, 73, 113, 122–5, 129 and 189; P. Lemmens and W. Vandenhole (eds.), *Protocol n. 14 and the Reform of the European Court of Human Rights*, Antwerpen/ Oxford, Intersentia, 2005, pp. 45, 50, 52–4, 59, 62, 64, 68–76 and 78–84.

[53] J. Wadham and T. Said, 'What Price the Right of Individual Petition: Report of the Evaluation Group to the Committee of Ministers on the European Court of Human Rights', 2 *European Human Rights Law Review* (2002) pp. 170–2.

[54] G. Cohen-Jonathan and J.-F. Flauss (eds. Various Authors), *La réforme du système de contrôle contentieux de la Convention Européenne des droits de l'homme* (Le Protocole n. 14 et les Recommandations et Résolutions du Comité de Ministres), Bruxelles, Bruylant/Nemesis, 2005, pp. 19, 42–4, 57–8, 77, 123 and 155.

[55] Ibid., pp. 42 and 122–5.

[56] P. Lemmens and W. Vandenhole (eds. Various Authors), *Protocol n. 14 and the Reform of the European Court of Human Rights*, Antwerpen/Oxford, Intersentia, 2005, pp. 45, 49–50 and 52.

outlook, appears as an end in itself to the extent that it contributes to the realization of justice.[57] Protocol n. 14 ruptures the integrity of the unrestricted right of individual petition, safeguarded thus far, and which has characterized the evolution of the European human rights system, which remains crucially important to the victims and should thus be preserved.[58]

The new admissibility criterion of Protocol n. 14 may negatively affect the very notion of "victim" under the ECHR; it unduly suggests that some human rights violations may appear "more important" than others. In so doing, it leads to an abandonment of the generalized right to an international remedy, undermining the right to individual petition and the access of all human rights victims to international justice.[59]

2. Developments in the Inter-American System of Protection

A recurring central question in the inter-American system is the condition of the *parties* in human rights cases under the ACHR, and, in particular, to the legal representation or the *locus standi in judicio* of the alleged victims (or their legal representatives) *directly* before the IACtHR, in cases already submitted to it by the Inter-American Commission. It is certain that the ACHR determines that only the States Parties and the Commission have the right 'to submit a case' to the Court (Article 61(1)); but the Convention, for example, in providing for reparations, also refers to 'the injured party' (Article 63(1)), i.e., the victims and not the Commission. In fact, to recognize the *locus standi in judicio* of the victims (or their representatives) before the Court contributes to the 'jurisdictionalization' of protection (on which all emphasis is to be placed), putting an end to the ambiguity of the function of the Commission, which is not a 'party' in the process, but rather a guardian of the correct application of the Convention.

The ACHR (Articles 61(1) and 57) in this regard followed the corresponding original provision of the ECHR (Article 44); despite the latter, in the system under the ECHR individual applicants, as already seen, were only gradually granted direct legal representation before the ECtHR; and like the experience accumulated by the ECtHR as from its very first case, the IACtHR, also in its *first* contentious cases, concerning Honduras, faced the artificiality of the initial scheme, and reacted against it.

In the procedure before the IACtHR, for example, the legal representatives of the victims had been in the past integrated to the delegation of the Commission with the euphemistic designation of 'assistants' to the latter: this 'pragmatic' solution counted on the endorsement, with all good intentions, of the decision taken in a joint meeting of the Inter-American Commission and Court, held in Miami in January 1994.[60] Instead of solving the problem, it created, however, ambiguities. The need to clarify the situation was apparent given that the roles of the Commission

---

[57] Ibid., pp. 53–4, and cf. pp. 59 and 62.
[58] Ibid., 68–70, 72–6 and 84.
[59] Ibid., pp. 79–84.
[60] The same had occurred in the European system of protection until 1982, when the fiction of the 'assistants' to the European Commission was at last overcome by the reform in that year of the Rules of Court of the European Court; cf. P. Mahoney and S. Prebensen, 'The European Court of Human

(as guardian of the Convention assisting the Court) and of individuals (as the true complainant party) are clearly distinct. The evolution in the sense of the final recognition of these distinct roles was to take place *pari passu* with the gradual jurisdictionalization of the mechanism of protection.

The Rules of Court of the IACtHR of 1991 foresaw, in rather oblique terms, a timid participation of the victims or their representatives in the procedure before the Court, above all in the stage of reparations and when requested by the latter.[61] Relatively quickly, in the *Godínez Cruz* and *Velásquez Rodríguez* cases (reparations, 1989), concerning Honduras, the Court received briefs from the relatives and lawyers of the victims, and took note of them.[62] However, the really significant step was taken subsequently in the *El Amparo* case (reparations, 1996), concerning Venezuela, a landmark case in this respect. In the public hearing on this case on 27 January 1996, one of the Judges, in expressing his understanding that at least at that stage of the proceedings there could be no doubt that the representatives of the victims were '*the true complainant party before the Court*', began to address questions to those representatives of the victims (rather than to the delegates of the Commission or to the agents of the State), who presented their answers.[63]

Shortly after that memorable public hearing in the *El Amparo* case, the representatives of the victims presented two briefs to the Court (of 13 May 1996 and 29 May 1996). Parallel to that, with regard to compliance with the judgment of interpretation of the previous sentence on compensatory damages in the earlier cases of *Godínez Cruz* and *Velásquez Rodríguez*, the representatives of the victims presented likewise a further two briefs to the Court (dated 29 March 1996 and 02 May 1996). The Court, with its composition of September 1996, only decided to close those two cases after having verified the compliance, on the part of Honduras, with the sentences on compensatory damages and on interpretation of this latter, and after having taken note of the points of view not only of the Commission and the respondent State, but also of the petitioners and the legal representatives of the families of the victims.[64]

The way was paved for the modification of the pertinent provisions of the Rules of Court by the developments in the proceedings in the *El Amparo* case. The decisive next step was taken by the third Rules of Court, adopted on 16 September 1996 and in force as from 01 January 1997 – the original draft of which I had the honour to be *rapporteur* of, by designation of the Court, – Article 23 of which

---

Rights', *The European System for the Protection of Human Rights* (eds. R.StJ. Macdonald, F. Matscher and H. Petzold), Dordrecht, Nijhoff, 1993, p. 630.

[61] Cf. the previous Rules of Court of the Inter-American Court, of 1991, Articles 44(2) and 22(2), and cf. also Articles 34(1) and 43(1) and (2).

[62] IACtHR, *Godínez Cruz* and *Velásquez Rodríguez* cases (Compensatory Damages), Judgments of 21 July 1989.

[63] Cf. the intervention of Judge A.A. Cançado Trindade, and the answers of Mr W. Márquez and of Ms L. Bolívar, as representatives of the victims, in: IACtHR, *Verbatim Records of the Public Hearing Held before the Court on 27 January 1996 on Reparations – El Amparo Case* [original in Spanish], pp. 72–6 (internal circulation).

[64] Cf. the two resolutions of the Court, of 10 September 1996, on the *Velásquez Rodríguez* and *Godínez Cruz* cases, respectively, in: Corte I.D.H., *Informe Anual de la Corte Interamericana de Derechos Humanos 1996*, pp. 207–13.

provided that 'at the stage of reparations, the representatives of the victims or of their next of kin may independently submit their own arguments and evidence'.

Shortly before, in the Judgments of the Court on preliminary objections, of 30 and 31 January 1996, in the cases *Castillo Páez* and *Loayza Tamayo* respectively, pertaining to Peru, I advanced, in my Separate Opinions, the following considerations, which were followed by the changes introduced into the third and fourth Rules of Court, which now – as I have always maintained – grant *locus standi in judicio* to the petitioners in *all* the stages of the contentious proceedings before the Court:

(...) Without the *locus standi in judicio* of both parties any system of protection finds itself irremediably mitigated, as it is not reasonable to conceive rights without the procedural capacity to vindicate them directly.

In the universe of the international law of human rights, it is the individual who alleges violations of his human rights, who alleges having suffered damages, who has to comply with the requirement of prior exhaustion of domestic remedies, who actively participates in an eventual friendly settlement, and who is the beneficiary (he or his relatives) of eventual reparations and indemnities. (...)

In the inter-American system of protection, *de lege ferenda* one gradually ought to overcome the paternalistic and anachronistic conception of the total intermediation of the Commission between the individual (the true complaining party) and the Court, according to clear and precise criteria and rules, previously and carefully defined. In the present domain of protection, every international jurist, faithful to the historical origins of his discipline, will know to contribute to the rescue of the position of the human being as a subject of international law (*droit des gens*), endowed with international legal personality and full capacity (pars. 14–17).

By the time the third Rules of Court (of 1996) were already in force, in the Judgment of the IACtHR (on preliminary objections) in the case of *Castillo Petruzzi and Others versus Peru*, of 04 September 1998, in a long Concurring Opinion I saw fit to single out the *fundamental* character of the right of individual petition (Article 44 of the ACHR) as 'the cornerstone of the access of the individuals to the whole mechanism of protection of the American Convention' (pars. 3 and 36–38). By means of such right of petition – a 'definitive conquest of the International Law of Human Rights' – the '*historical rescue* of the position of the human being as subject of the International Law of Human Rights, endowed with full international procedural capacity', took place (pars. 5 and 12).

After examining the history of the right of petition (pars. 9–15), I referred to the expansion of the notion of 'victim' in the international case-law under human rights treaties (pars. 16–19), as well as to the *autonomy* of the right of individual petition vis-à-vis the domestic law of the States (pars. 21, 27 and 29). I added that 'it is by the free and full exercise of the right of individual petition that the rights set forth in the Convention become *effective*. The right of individual petition shelters, in fact, the last hope of those who did not find justice at national level' (pars. 33 and 35). The jurisdictional solution being the 'most perfected and evolved' means of international protection of human rights, I maintained in that Concurring Opinion that individuals should have 'the right of direct access [to the Court] independently of the acceptance of an optional clause', such as that of Article 62 of the ACHR, by the respective States (par. 40). That is, in my understanding, both the right of individual petition and the jurisdiction of the IACtHR (in contentious matters) should be *automatically mandatory* for all the States Parties to the ACHR (par. 41). I pondered, in addition, that:

This means to seek to secure, not only the direct representation of the victims or their relatives (*locus standi*) in the procedure before the Inter-American Court in cases already forwarded to it by the Commission (in all stages of the proceedings and not only in that of reparations),[65] but rather the right of direct access of individuals before the Court itself (*jus standi*), so as to bring a case directly before it, as the sole future jurisdictional organ for the settlement of concrete cases under the American Convention. To that end, individuals would do without the Inter-American Commission, which would, nevertheless, retain functions other than the contentious one,[66] prerogative of the future permanent Inter-American Court.[67]

(...) Above all, this qualitative advance would fulfill, in my understanding, an imperative of justice. The *jus standi* – no longer only *locus standi in judicio*, – without restrictions, of individuals, before the Inter-American Court itself, represents, – as I have indicated in my Opinions in other cases before the Court,[68] – the logical consequence of the conception and formulation of rights to be protected under the American Convention at international level, to which it ought to correspond necessarily the full juridical capacity of the individual petitioners to vindicate them.

The jurisdictionalization of the mechanism of protection becomes an imperative as from the recognition of the essentially distinct roles of the individual petitioners – the true complainant party – and of the Commission (organ of supervision of the Convention which assists the Court). Under the American Convention, the individuals mark presence at the *beginning* of the process, in exercising the right of petition in view of the alleged damages, as well as at the *end* of it, as beneficiaries of the reparations, in cases of proven violations of their rights; there is no sense in denying them presence *during* the process. The right of access to justice at international level ought in fact to be accompanied by the guarantee of procedural equality (*equality of arms/égalité des armes*) in the proceedings before the judicial organ, an element essential to any jurisdictional mechanism of protection of human rights, without which such mechanism will be irremediably mitigated (pars. 42–46).

Subsequently, in my Concurring Opinion in the first contentious case entirely heard under the new, fourth Rules of Court, (*Five Pensioners versus Peru* (Judgment of 28 February 2003)), in the same line of thinking, I pondered that:

In fact, the assertion of those juridical personality and capacity constitutes the truly revolutionary legacy of the evolution of the international legal doctrine in the second half of the XXth century. The time has come to overcome the classic limitations of the *legitimatio ad causam* in International Law, which have so much hindered its progressive development towards the construction of a new *jus gentium* (...) (par. 24).[69]

---

[65] As occurs under the Regulations of the Court, Article 23.

[66] Like those of the undertaking of missions of *in loco* observation and the elaboration of reports.

[67] Enlarged, functioning in chambers, and with considerably larger human and material resources.

[68] Cf., in this sense, my Separate Opinions in cases *Castillo Páez* (Preliminary Objections, Judgment of 30 January 1996), pars. 14–17, and *Loayza Tamayo* (Preliminary Objections, Judgment of 31 January 1996), pars. 14–17, respectively (cf. *supra*).

[69] More recently, I recalled this discussion in my Concurring Opinion (par. 7) in the Provisional Measures of Protection in the case of the *Children and Adolescents Deprived of Freedom in the Premises of*

Manifestations of this are found in the recent case-law of the IACtHR not only in *contentious*, but also in *advisory* matters, as exemplified by Advisory Opinion n. 17, on the *Juridical Condition and Human Rights of the Child* (of 28 August 2002), which followed the same argument regarding the juridical emancipation of the human being, in emphasizing the consolidation of the legal personality of the child as a true subject of rights and not a simple object of protection; this was the *Leitmotiv* which permeated the whole Advisory Opinion n. 17 of the Court.[70]

Article 23 of the 1996 (third) Rules of Court was a significant step to pave the way for the subsequent developments in the same direction, which took place in the year 2000, to the effect of securing *locus standi* for individuals in the proceedings before the Court not only at the reparations stage but also in preliminary objections as well as the merits of the cases submitted to it by the Commission, that is, ultimately, in *all* phases of the proceedings before the IACtHR (a long-held goal of mine). This was achieved by the adoption of the new and current (fourth) Rules of Court, on 24 November 2000, which entered into force on 01 June 2001.[71] Article 23 of the Rules of Court (on the 'Participation of the Alleged Victims') significantly provided that

   a When the application has been admitted, the alleged victims, their next of kin or their duly accredited representatives may submit their requests, arguments and evidence, autonomously, throughout the proceedings.

   b When there are several alleged victims, next of kin or duly accredited representatives, they shall designate a common intervenor who shall be the only person authorized to present requests, arguments and evidence during the proceedings, including the public hearings.

   c In case of disagreement, the Court shall make the appropriate ruling.

The arguments which militated in favour of the recognition of the *locus standi* of the alleged victims in the proceedings before the IACtHR in cases already referred to it by the Commission were, in my understanding, solid,[72] and can be summed

---

Tatuapé of FEBEM versus Brazil (Resolution of 30 November 2005). Moreover, seven years after the Judgment on the merits of the Inter-American Court in the paradigmatic case of the '*Street Children*' (*Villagrán Morales and Others versus Guatemala*, Judgment of 19 November 1999, and the Judgment on reparations in the same case, of 26 May 2001), the abandoned and forgotten of the world again reach an international tribunal of human rights in search of justice, in the cases of the members of the *Communities Yakye Axa* (Judgment of 17 June 2005) and *Sawhoyamaxa* (Judgment of 28 March 2006). In these recent cases, those forcefully displaced from their homes and ancestral lands, and socially marginalized and excluded, have effectively reached an international jurisdiction, before which they have at last found justice.

[70] And eloquently asserted in its pars. 41 and 28.

[71] For a study of these new Rules of Court, cf. A.A. Cançado Trindade, 'El Nuevo Reglamento de la Corte Interamericana de Derechos Humanos (2000) y Su Proyección Hacia el Futuro: La Emancipación del Ser Humano como Sujeto del Derecho Internacional', in: *XXVIII Curso de Derecho Internacional Organizado por el Comité Jurídico Interamericano* – OAS (2001) pp. 33–92.

[72] Such arguments were developed in my course at the External Session (for Central America) of the Hague Academy of International Law, held in Costa Rica in April–May 1995; cf. A.A. Cançado Trindade, 'El Sistema Interamericano de Protección de los Derechos Humanos (1948–1995): Evolución, Estado Actual y Perspectivas', in *Derecho Internacional y Derechos Humanos/Droit international et*

up as follows. To the acknowledgment of rights, at national as well as international levels, corresponds the procedural capacity to vindicate or exercise them. The protection of rights ought to be endowed with the *locus standi in judicio* of the alleged victims (or their legal representatives), which contributes to a better hearing of the cases at issue, without which the hearings would be lacking an essential element (in the search for truth and justice), besides being ineluctably mitigated and in flagrant procedural imbalance. The jurisdictionalization of the procedure greatly contributes to remedy and put an end to those deficiencies which can no longer find any justification.

The contraposition of the victims of violations and the respondent States is the very essence of the international *contentieux* of human rights. Such *locus standi* of the individuals concerned is the logical consequence, at the procedural level, of a system of protection purported to guarantee individual rights at international level, as it is not reasonable to conceive of rights without the procedural capacity to vindicate them. Moreover, the right of freedom of expression of the alleged victims is an element which integrates the due process of law, at both national and international levels. The equity and transparency of the procedure, which are equally applicable to the international supervisory organs, are beneficial to all, including the individual complainants and the respondent States.

The right of access to justice at international level ought to be accompanied by the guarantee of procedural equality (*equality of arms/égalité des armes*) in the proceedings before the Court, essential to any jurisdictional mechanism of protection of human rights, without which such mechanism will be mitigated. These advances help to put an end to the current ambiguities as to the Commission's role,[73] and enable the latter to concentrate on its proper function of guardian of the correct and just application of the ACHR (no longer with the additional function of 'intermediary' between the individuals and the Court). The advances in the sense of the direct representation of the individuals before the Court – already consolidated in the European system of protection – require other measures to render them fully effective, e.g., the foreseeing of *ex officio* legal assistance to individual complainants on the part of the Commission, whenever they are not able to count on the professional services of a legal representative.

This improvement of the inter-American system of protection represents an additional guarantee to the parties – the individual complainants as well as the respondent States – in contentious cases of human rights. As I pointed two decades ago in a course delivered at the Hague Academy of International Law, it is proper that every international lawyer, faithful to the historical origins of the discipline, endeavours to secure the rescue of the position of the human being in the law of

droits de l'homme (eds. D. Bardonnet and A.A. Cançado Trindade), The Hague/San José of Costa Rica, The Hague Academy of International Law/IIHR, 1996, pp. 47–95, esp. pp. 81–9.

[73] In contentious cases, while in the prior stage before the Commission the parties are the individual complainants and the respondent States, subsequently, before the Court, it is the Commission and the respondent States that appear. The Commission thus finds itself in the ambiguous role of at a time defending the interests of the alleged victims and defending likewise the 'public interests' as a *Ministère Public* of the inter-American system of protection. This ambiguity is to be avoided.

nations (*droit des gens*), and to sustain the recognition and crystallization of his international personality and full legal capacity.[74]

A significant qualitative advance was achieved by the fourth Rules of Court, whereby the active legitimation or direct participation (*locus standi in judicio*) was granted (Article 23) to the individual petitioners (the alleged victims, their relatives or their duly accredited representatives) in *all* the stages of the procedure before the Tribunal.[75] Viewed in historical perspective, this constitutes the most transcendental modification of the fourth Rules of Court, besides being a true turning-point in the evolution of the inter-American system of protection of human rights in particular, within the framework of international human rights law in general.

In fact, with the Rules of 2000 of the IACtHR, the alleged victims, their relatives or legal representatives were enabled to present requests, arguments and evidence in an autonomous way during the *whole* process before the Tribunal, and thus became endowed with all the faculties and obligations in procedural matters, which, until the Rules of Court of 1996, were previously attributed only to the Inter-American Commission and the respondent State (except in the stage of reparations).

By the time the new Rules of Court had been in force for three years, more than 20 contentious cases had been lodged with the Court thereunder. The first case decided by the Court and entirely processed under those Rules was *Five Pensioners versus Peru* (Judgment of 28 February 2003), wherein the Court correctly held that, in their arguments, the alleged victims could invoke additional rights that they considered to have been violated, even if they had not been mentioned by the Inter-American Commission in the complaint lodged with the Court.

In all these cases the Tribunal – to my great personal satisfaction – has counted on the effective participation of the alleged victims, or their relatives, or their legal representatives. It has adopted the practice whereby, once it has received the brief of requests, arguments and evidence of these latter, it is forwarded both to the Commission and the respondent State, so that they may present their observations thereon, thus securing, throughout the whole procedure, the faithful observance of the *principe du contradictoire*.

---

[74] A.A. Cançado Trindade, 'Co-existence and Co-ordination . . . ', *op. cit. supra* n. (31), pp. 410–12. I again made the same warning, subsequently, in Separate Opinions in cases *Castillo Páez* and *Loayza Tamayo* (Preliminary Objections, January 1996), and in case *Castillo Petruzzi* (Preliminary Objections, September 1998), pertaining to Peru, in the sense of the need to overcome the *capitis diminutio* which individual petitioners suffer in the inter-American system of protection, as a result of dogmatic considerations proper of another historical epoch which sought to avoid their direct access to the international judicial organ. Such considerations, I added, appear entirely meaningless, even more in so far as an international tribunal *of human rights* is concerned. I propounded, in our aforementioned Opinions, the overcoming of the paternalist and anachronistic conception of the total intermediation of the Inter-American Commission between the individual petitioners (the true complainant party) and the Court, so as to grant to them *direct* access (*jus standi*) to the Court. Cf. IACtHR, *Castillo Páez versus Peru* case (Preliminary Objections, Judgment of 30 January 1996), Separate Opinion of Judge A.A. Cançado Trindade, pars. 16–17; IACtHR, *Loayza Tamayo versus Peru* case (Preliminary Objections, Judgment of 31 January 1996), Separate Opinion of Judge A.A. Cançado Trindade, pars. 16–17; IACtHR, *Castillo Petruzzi versus Peru* case (Preliminary Objections, Judgment of 04 September 1998), Concurring Opinion of Judge A.A. Cançado Trindade, pars. 39–46.

[75] The previous (third) Rules of Court of 1996 had given the first step in that direction (at the stage of reparations).

In these six years of the application of its new Rules of Court (2001–2007), individual petitioners have been incorporated as a true complaining procedural party in the procedure before the Court. The human person has thus been erected, in an unequivocal way, as a subject of international human rights law, endowed with juridico-procedural capacity in the proceedings before the IACtHR. This has undoubtedly been a development of transcendental importance; as I saw it fit to mention in my intervention of 10 June 2003 at the plenary of the General Assembly of the Organization of American States (OAS) in Santiago of Chile, the IACtHR, in the evolution of its procedures and of its case-law, has contributed to:

the consolidation of the new paradigm of International Law, the new *jus gentium* of the XXIst century, which recognizes the human being as subject of rights.[76]

The new Rules of Court forms part of a *process* of improvement and strengthening of the system of protection under the ACHR as a whole. The next step of this evolution ought to consist, as I have been maintaining for a long time, in a *Protocol of Reforms to the American Convention on Human Rights,*[77] preceded by ample consultations with the States Parties to the Convention, the entities of civil society and the beneficiaries of the system in general. The future Protocol ought initially to *incorporate the advances of the Rules of Court* already achieved,[78] but, in my view, it ought to go beyond that. The substantive part of the ACHR (pertaining to the protected rights) ought to be duly preserved, without alterations, as a growing and rich case-law of the Court is already developed thereon. The part of the Convention concerning the mechanism of protection and corresponding procedures, however, certainly requires reforms to strengthen these mechanisms.[79] To this end I prepared, and presented to the OAS in May 2001, my Report titled *Basis for a Draft Protocol to the American Convention on Human Rights, to Strengthen Its Mechanism of Protection.*[80]

In this Report I recommended amendments to Articles 50(2), 51(1), 59, 65, 68, 75 and 77 of the ACHR. Moreover, I recommended that Article 62 should be amended so as to render the jurisdiction of the Court *automatically* compulsory for all States Parties, not admitting any type of restrictions, without the need of an additional manifestation of consent, subsequent to the ratification of the

---

[76] Cf. 'Discurso [del Presidente de la Corte Interamericana de Derechos Humanos, Juez Antônio Augusto Cançado Trindade, en el Plenario de la Asamblea General de la OEA]', in: OEA, *Asamblea General, XXXIII Período Ordinario de Sesiones (Santiago de Chile, Junio de 2003) – Actas y Documentos,* vol. II, Washington D.C., Secretaría General de la OEA, pp. 168–71.

[77] Pursuant to Article 77(1) of the American Convention.

[78] A Protocol, once it comes into force, constitutes the safest way to obtain real commitments on the part of the States, without major risks of steps backwards, as to a more effective mechanism of protection of human rights.

[79] Cf., in this respect, A.A. Cançado Trindade, *El Acceso Directo del Individuo a los Tribunales Internacionales de Derechos Humanos,* Bilbao, University of Deusto, 2001, pp. 9–104.

[80] A.A. Cançado Trindade, *Bases para un Proyecto de Protocolo a la Convención Americana sobre Derechos Humanos, para Fortalecer Su Mecanismo de Protección,* vol. II, 2nd. ed., San José of Costa Rica, IACtHR, 2003, pp. 1–1015, esp. pp. 3–64.

Convention.[81] The compulsory jurisdiction of the IACtHR constitutes the indispensable complement of the right of individual petition under the ACHR: both constitute the basic pillars of international protection, of the mechanism of emancipation of the human being vis-à-vis his own State.[82] I have accordingly seen it fit to characterize Articles 44 and 62 of the ACHR, which provide for both of them, as true *fundamental clauses* (*cláusulas pétreas*) of the protection of the human person under that Convention.[83]

Ever since my aforementioned presentation of 2001 to the OAS, this Report (containing the basis for the Draft Protocol) has been continued to be present in the agenda of the General Assembly of the OAS from 2001 to 2007 (as found in pertinent documents of the Assemblies of San José of Costa Rica in 2001, of Bridgetown/Barbados in 2002, of Santiago of Chile in 2003, of Quito in 2004, and also remaining present in those of the General Assemblies the OAS in 2005–2006[84] and 2007). The Report nourishes the hope that the *jus standi* of individuals directly before the Court[85] may be achieved in the future. Such *jus standi* – no longer only *locus standi in judicio* – without restrictions, of individuals before the IACtHR itself represents – as I have indicated in my Individual Opinions in successive cases before the Court[86] – the logical consequence of the conception and formulation of rights to be protected under the ACHR at international level, to which the full juridical capacity to vindicate them necessarily corresponds.

---

[81] Earlier on, I had sustained the need for compulsory jurisdiction of the Inter-American Court in my Concurring Opinion in the case of *Castillo Petruzzi and Others versus Peru* (Judgment on preliminary objections, of 04 September 1998), pars. 40–6. It is likewise to be hoped that all the States of the region, juridically equal as they are, become Parties to the American Convention, and accordingly accept the contentious jurisdiction of the Inter-American Court.

[82] As foreseen by the so-called 'founding fathers' of the law of nations; cf. A.A. Cançado Trindade, 'The Emancipation of the Individual from His Own State – The Historical Recovery of the Human Person as Subject of the Law of Nations', in *Human Rights, Democracy and the Rule of Law – Liber Amicorum Luzius Wildhaber* (eds. S. Breitenmoser *et alii*), Zürich/Baden-Baden, Dike/Nomos, 2007, pp. 151–71.

[83] Cf. IACtHR, *Castillo Petruzzi and Others versus Peru* case (Preliminary Objections, Judgment of 04 September 1998), Concurring Opinion of Judge A.A. Cançado Trindade, pars. 36–8; and IACtHR, Advisory Opinion n. 16, on *The Right to Information on Consular Assistance in the Framework of the Guarantees of the Due Process of Law* (of 01 October 1999), Concurring Opinion of Judge A.A. Cançado Trindade, par. 30. And cf. A.A. Cançado Trindade, 'Las Cláusulas Pétreas de la Protección Internacional del Ser Humano: El Acceso Directo de los Individuos a la Justicia a Nivel Internacional y la Intangibilidad de la Jurisdicción Obligatoria de los Tribunales Internacionales de Derechos Humanos', in *El Sistema Interamericano de Protección de los Derechos Humanos en el Umbral del Siglo XXI – Memoria del Seminario* (November 1999), vol. I, 2nd. ed., San José of Costa Rica, IACtHR, 2003, pp. 3–68.

[84] OAS, doc. AG/RES.2129 (XXXV-0/050), of 07 June 2005, pp. 1–3; OAS, doc. CP/CAJP-2311/05/Rev.2, of 27 February 2006, pp. 1–3. Cf., in this respect, A.A. Cançado Trindade, *El Derecho Internacional de los Derechos Humanos en el Siglo XXI*, 2nd. ed., Santiago, Editorial Jurídica de Chile, 2006, pp. 9–10 and 515–24.

[85] As the sole jurisdictional organ under the Convention, endowed with a possible first instance for the consideration of the admissibility of the petitions, and without prejudice to the preservation of the non-contentious functions of the Inter-American Commission.

[86] Cf., in this sense, my Separate Opinions in cases *Castillo Páez* (Preliminary Objections, Judgment of 30 January 1996), pars. 14–17, and *Loayza Tamayo* (Preliminary Objections, Judgment of 31 January 1996), pars. 14–17; and my Concurring Opinion in the *Castillo Petruzzi versus Peru* case (Preliminary Objections, Judgment of 04 September 1998), pars. 39–46.

3. Developments in the African System of Protection

Individuals have, as already pointed out, attained *jus standi* before the ECtHR, and *locus standi in judicio* in all stages of the procedure before the IACtHR. The African system of human rights protection has also experienced lately the process of 'jurisdictionalization', with the decision of the Burkina Faso Protocol to the African Charter of Human and Peoples' Rights, adopted on 10 June 1998 and entered into force on 25 January 2004, to set up an African Court of Human and Peoples' Rights[87] (elected on 22 January 2006), in pursuance of the old ideal of realization of international justice.

Before the African Court, the question of the *legitimatio ad causam* is governed by Article 5 of the 1998 Burkina Faso Protocol, paragraph 1 of which enables the African Commission on Human and Peoples' Rights as well as States Parties to the African Charter to submit cases to the consideration of the Court (in addition to African intergovernmental organizations, for issues concerning them). Paragraph 3 of Article 5, drafted in the form of an optional clause, acknowledges a true *jus standi in judicio*, securing the direct access to the Court of individuals and certain non-governmental organizations[88] to lodge cases with it.

In the account of a former President of the African Commission, this was 'one of the most complex questions' considered during the *travaux préparatoires* of the Protocol to the African Charter.[89] The provision of Article 5(3) of the Burkina Faso Protocol represents an advance in the African system of human rights protection, erecting the individual as the true complaining party directly before the new African Court. Presumably this direct access on an optional basis renders obsolete the prior procedure before the African Commission, and its acceptance (apparently without restrictions) can be effected at the moment of the ratification of the Protocol referred to.[90]

In any case, new perspectives have lately been opened as to the individual's right of access to international justice in the African system of human rights protection.

---

[87] For an account of the *travaux préparatoires* and adoption of the 1998 Protocol to the African Charter on Human and Peoples Rights, cf. A.A. Cançado Trindade, *Tratado de Direito Internacional dos Direitos Humanos*, vol. III, Porto Alegre/Brazil, S.A. Fabris Ed., 2003, pp. 214–20; and cf., e.g., 'Government Legal Experts Meeting on the Question of the Establishment of an African Court on Human and Peoples' Rights' (Cape Town, South Africa, September 1995), 8 *African Journal of International and Comparative Law* (1996) pp. 493–500. Cf., further, Ben Kioko, *The Process Leading to the Establishment of the African Court on Human and Peoples' Rights*, Addis Abeba, African Society of International and Comparative Law (X Annual Conference), 1998, pp. 5–6 (internal circulation); I.A. Badawi El-Sheikh, 'Draft Protocol to the African Charter on Human and Peoples' Rights on the Establishment of an African Court on Human and Peoples' Rights – Introductory Note', 9 *African Journal of International and Comparative Law* (1997) pp. 943–52; and cf. M. Mubiala, 'La Cour Africaine des Droits de l'Homme et des Peuples: mimetisme institutionnel ou avancée judiciaire?', 102 *Revue générale de Droit international public* (1998) pp. 765–80, esp. p. 768.

[88] Endowed with the status of observers before the African Commission.

[89] I.A. Badawi El-Sheikh, 'Draft Protocol... – Introductory Note', *op. cit. supra* n. (87), p. 947.

[90] F. Quilleré-Majzoub, 'L'option juridictionnelle de la protection des droits de l'homme en Afrique – Étude comparée autour de la création de la Cour Africaine des Droits de l'Homme et des Peuples', 44 *Revue trimestrielle des droits de l'homme* (2000) pp. 758–9.

The judicialization operated by the Protocol is a turning point in the evolution of the African human rights system.[91] The African Court is bound to supplement, and to enhance, the procedure of individual communications of the African Commission. For the individual's right to petition or resort directly to the new African Court (*jus standi*) (Article 5(3) of the Protocol) to be truly effective, the Protocol still needs to come into force, and States Parties have to accept the Court's jurisdiction under the optional clause of Article 34(6) of the Protocol to the Charter.[92] The African Court, for its part, has also much to contribute, in the near future, in addressing the right of access to justice (also at domestic law level), particularly in view of the difficulties faced in this respect by the African Commission to date.[93]

It has not passed unnoticed that the advance achieved by the 1998 Protocol to the African Charter would have been more considerable if its draftsmen had gone beyond the *optional* clause, and secured the direct access of individuals to the African Court automatically,[94] upon ratification of the Protocol itself (not providing for it on an optional basis). It remains to be seen how the African Commission and the Court will achieve in practice, by their coordinated action, the consolidation of the *jus standi* of individuals and non-governmental organizations before the African Court on Human and Peoples' Rights.

VI. Concluding Observations

Human rights treaties acknowledge and guarantee individual subjective rights, inherent to the human person, and set forth obligations of the States vis-à-vis the individuals under their respective jurisdictions. The configuration of victims calls promptly for the *redress* owed to them under those treaties.[95] The right of individual petition[96] appears as a true right of (legal) action on the part of the individual as opposed to the respondent State, as subjects, or (legal) persons of

---

[91] F. Ouguergouz, *The African Charter on Human and Peoples' Rights*, The Hague, Nijhoff, 2003, pp. 723–4 and 755–6; the Protocol to the African Charter, like the American Convention (and distinctly from the European Convention), does not require the individual petitioner to be the victim of the alleged violations of human rights.

[92] Cf. F. Viljoen, *International Human Rights Law in Africa*, Oxford, Univ. Press, 2007, pp. 424, 435 and 438–51; M. Mubiala, 'L'accès de l'individu à la Cour africaine des droits de l'homme et des peuples', in *La promotion de la justice, des droits de l'homme et du règlement des conflits par le Droit international – Liber amicorum L. Caflisch* (ed. M.G. Kohen), Leiden, Nijhoff, 2007, pp. 369–78.

[93] E.g., given the regretted absence of an express provision, under the African Charter, specifically on the right to an effective remedy; cf., on this issue, G.M. Musila, 'The Right to an Effective Remedy under the African Charter on Human and Peoples' Rights', 6 *African Human Rights Law Journal* (2006) pp. 442–64.

[94] Association for the Prevention of Torture (APT), *The African Court on Human and Peoples' Rights – Presentation, Analysis and Commentary: The Protocol to the African Charter on Human and Peoples' Rights, Establishing the Court* (Occasional Paper), Geneva, APT, January 2000, p. 4.

[95] J.A. Frowein, 'La notion de victime dans la Convention Européenne des Droits de l'Homme', in *Studi in Onore di G. Sperduti*, Milano, Giuffrè, 1984, pp. 589, 593 and 598.

[96] Under the human rights treaties which provide for it before international tribunals, that is, the European and the American Conventions on Human Rights, and the African Charter on Human and Peoples' Rights (together with the 1998 Burkina Faso Protocol).

international law.[97] From its very conception, and insertion, in human rights treaties, such as the European and American Conventions on Human Rights, it was well understood that States Parties committed themselves to avoid creating obstacles to the free and full exercise of the right of individual petition.[98]

The petitioning system was created in pursuance of certain fundamental values shared by all States Parties. An express reference to such values can normally be found in the preambles of human rights treaties[99] providing for the petitioning system. The gradual consolidation and strengthening of the right of individual petition over the years is not so surprising: after all, that right implies, and calls for, the increasing participation of the individual complainants in international procedures, as subjects of international law.[100] As I stated almost a decade ago:

> The right of individual petition is a cornerstone of the international protection of human rights: the counterposition between the individual complainants and the respondent States in cases of alleged violations of the protected rights is indeed of the essence of such protection. It is by the exercise of the right of individual petition that direct access is granted to the individual to justice at international level, and that the individual asserts his position as subject of International Human Rights Law. (. . .)
>
> Of all the mechanisms of international protection of human rights, the right of individual petition is, in fact, the most dynamic one, in even granting the initiative of action to the individual himself (the ostensibly weaker party vis-à-vis the public authorities), distinctly from the exercise *ex officio* of other methods (such as those of fact-finding and reports) on the part of the international supervisory organs. (. . .)
>
> The right of individual petition is a fundamental clause of the human rights treaties that provide for it, (. . .) upon which is erected the juridical mechanism of the emancipation of the human being vis-à-vis his own State for the protection of his rights in the ambit of the International Law of Human Rights. (. . .).[101]

In fact, the *jus standi* of individuals before international human rights tribunals benefits not only the petitioners but also States Parties to the respective human rights treaties (those which become respondent States), as well as the mechanism of protection as a whole; such jurisdictionalization provides an additional guarantee of the prevalence of the *rule of law* in the whole *contentieux* of human rights under those treaties. The free and full exercise of the right of individual petition directly before international human rights tribunals (such as the European, Inter-American

[97] F. Matscher, 'La Posizione Processuale dell'Individuo come Ricorrente Dinanzi agli Organi della Convenzione Europea dei Diritti dell'Uomo', in *Studi in Onore di G. Sperduti*, Milano, Giuffrè, 1984, pp. 607–9 and 620.

[98] A. Debricon, 'L'exercice efficace du droit de recours individuel', in *The Birth of European Human Rights Law – Liber Amicorum C.A. Norgaard* (eds. M. de Salvia and M.E. Villiger), Baden-Baden, Nomos Verlagsgesellschaft, 1998, pp. 237–42.

[99] Cf., e.g., N. Bobbio, 'Il Preambolo della Convenzione Europea dei Diritti dell'Uomo', 57 *Rivista di Diritto Internazionale* (1974) pp. 437–45.

[100] N. Valticos, 'L'émergence progressive de l'individu comme sujet du droit international', in *El Derecho Internacional en un Mundo en Transformación – Liber Amicorum en Homenaje al Prof. E. Jiménez de Aréchaga*, vol. I, Montevideo, Fundación de Cultura Universitaria, 1994, pp. 283–4 and 297.

[101] A.A. Cançado Trindade, 'The Procedural Capacity of the Individual as Subject of International Human Rights Law: Recent Developments', in *Les droits de l'homme à l'aube du XXIe. siècle – K. Vasak Amicorum Liber*, Bruxelles, Bruylant, 1999, pp. 521 and 542–3.

and, more recently, African Courts) bears witness to the fact that the *jurisdictional* solution constitutes the most perfected and evolved means of international protection of human rights.

The right of individual petition and the compulsory jurisdiction of the European and Inter-American Courts of Human Rights in contentious cases are fundamental clauses (*cláusulas pétreas*), and constitute a matter of international *ordre public*, which could not be at the mercy of limitations not provided for in the treaties, invoked by the States Parties for reasons or vicissitudes of domestic law.[102] If the right of individual petition had not been originally conceived and consistently understood in this way, the international protection of human rights would have advanced very little in this half-century of evolution.

With the consolidation of the right of individual petition before international tribunals of human rights, international protection has attained its maturity. The human being nowadays occupies the central position which he merits, as *subject of both domestic and international law*, amidst the process of *humanization* of international law, which is becoming more directly attentive to the identification and realization of common superior values and goals. The international legal titularity of the human being is now an undeniable reality, calling now for the consolidation, in distinct human rights systems, and within the framework of the universality of human rights, of his full juridico-procedural capacity at the international level.[103]

---

[102] Cf. IACtHR, case of the *Constitutional Tribunal* concerning Peru (Judgment on Jurisdiction, of 24 September 1999), pars. 31–55; IACtHR, case *Ivtcher Bronstein versus Peru* (Judgment on Jurisdiction, of 24 September 1999), pars. 32–56. And cf. A.A. Cançado Trindade, 'Las Cláusulas Pétreas de la Protección Internacional del Ser Humano: El Acceso Directo de los Individuos a la Justicia a Nivel Internacional y la Intangibilidad de la Jurisdicción Obligatoria de los Tribunales Internacionales de Derechos Humanos', in *El Sistema Interamericano de Protección de los Derechos Humanos en el Umbral del Siglo XXI – Memoria del Seminario* (November 1999), vol. I, 2nd. ed., San José of Costa Rica, Inter-American Court of Human Rights, 2003, pp. 3–68.

[103] A.A. Cançado Trindade, 'International Law for Humankind: Towards a New *Jus Gentium* – General Course on Public International Law', 316 *Recueil des Cours de l'Académie de Droit International de La Haye* (2005), ch. IX–X, pp. 252–317.

III

Access to Justice at International Level and the Right to an Effective Domestic Remedy

I. Access to International Justice and Admissibility of Petitions   50

II. The Right to an Effective Domestic Remedy as a Basic Pillar of the
Rule of Law in a Democratic Society   51

III. The Intangibility of Judicial Guarantees in All Circumstances   56

IV. The Right to Recognition of Juridical Personality   58

V. The Converging Case-Law of the European and Inter-American
Courts of Human Rights on the Rights of Access to Justice and
to a Fair Trial   59

I. Access to International Justice and Admissibility of Petitions

The central question of the individual's access to justice at international level has been discussed by the IACtHR, with regard both to the right of individual petition under the American Convention as well as the conditions of admissibility of individual complaints. In the case of *Castillo Petruzzi and Others versus Peru* (Preliminary Objections, 1998), the Court upheld the right of individual petition (challenged by the respondent State) under the American Convention (Article 44). It drew attention to the importance of that right, observing that the broad faculty 'to make a complaint is a characteristic feature of the system for the international protection of human rights' (par. 77). In my Concurring Opinion, I pondered that the right of individual petition rendered the protected rights effective, and thus constituted 'a fundamental clause (*cláusula pétrea*)' upon which was erected 'the juridical mechanism of emancipation of the human being vis-à-vis his own State for the protection of his rights in the ambit of the International Law of Human Rights'.[1]

As to the conditions of admissibility of individual complaints, in its earlier case-law,[2] the IACtHR used to allow the reopening and reexamination by the Court of an objection of pure admissibility, favouring the respondent party, which should have been definitively resolved by the Inter-American Commission (IAComHR).

---

[1] Concurring Opinion of Judge A.A. Cançado Trindade, pars. 35–6.
[2] Cf. preliminary objections decisions in the cases *Velásquez Rodríguez* and *Godínez Cruz versus Honduras* (1987).

Just as the Commission's decisions of inadmissibility were final, so should its decisions of admissibility be: either all decisions – of admissibility or otherwise – were allowed to be reopened before the Court, or they were all to be kept exclusive to the Commission. To allow for a reopening or review by the Court of a decision on admissibility by the IAComHR[3] created an imbalance between the parties, favouring the respondent States.

In the case *Gangaram Panday versus Suriname* (Preliminary Objections, 1991) the Court came to admit that, if an objection of non-exhaustion of local remedies is not raised *in limine litis*, it is tacitly waived. But it was necessary to go further than that, since, if the respondent State waived the objection of non-exhaustion of local remedies by not raising it *in limine litis* in the prior procedure before the IA-ComHR, it would be inconceivable that it could withdraw that waiver in the subsequent procedure before the IACtHR by raising the objection again. This is precisely what happened in the *Loayza Tamayo* and *Castillo Páez* cases (Preliminary Objections, 1996), concerning Peru, where the Court, reorienting its case-law, took the important step of rightly determining that, if the respondent State failed to invoke the preliminary objection of non-exhaustion of local remedies in the proceedings on admissibility before the Commission, it was precluded by estoppel from invoking it subsequently before the Court.[4] This has become *jurisprudence constante* of the IACtHR on the issue to date. In this way, the Court corrected the earlier detrimental imbalance against complainants and fostered the procedural position of individuals in proceedings under the ACHR.

II. The Right to an Effective Domestic Remedy as a Basic Pillar of the Rule of Law in a Democratic Society

In its Judgment in the *Castillo Páez versus Peru* case (1997), the IACtHR, in contrast with its earlier approach to the right to an effective remedy under the ACHR,[5] for the first time elaborated on the right set forth under Article 25. In its own words, Article 25 on the right to an effective remedy before the competent

---

[3] As the Court upheld in the aforementioned *Honduran* cases.

[4] Cf., on this point, in both cases, the Separate Opinions of Judge A.A. Cançado Trindade.

[5] In other early cases, such as its Judgments on the merits in the cases *Caballero Delgado and Santana versus Colombia* (1995) and *Genie Lacayo versus Nicaragua* (1997), the Court had summarily disposed of the matter, on the basis of the test of the *availability*, rather than of the *adequacy* and *effectiveness*, of domestic remedies. In this way, no violation was established in those earlier cases of the State's duty to provide effective local remedies under Article 25 of the Convention. This view, however, did not pass unchallenged. A Dissenting Opinion was expressed to the effect that Article 25 was a provision far more important than one might *prima facie* assume, as the right to an effective remedy before competent national tribunals constituted a basic pillar not only of the Convention but of the rule of law itself in a democratic society, and its correct application had the sense of improving the administration of justice at national level. The dissent further recalled the Latin American origin of that provision (cf. *infra*). IACtHR, case *Genie Lacayo versus Nicaragua* (revision of sentence, 1997), Dissenting Opinion of Judge A.A. Cançado Trindade (pars. 18–21); and cf. case *Caballero Delgado and Santana versus Colombia* (reparations, 1997), Dissenting Opinion of Judge A.A. Cançado Trindade (pars. 2–3).

national judges or tribunals, 'constitutes one of the basic pillars, not only of the American Convention, but of the rule of law (*État de Droit, Estado de Derecho*) itself in a democratic society in the sense of the Convention' (par. 82).[6] The Court added, in the *Castillo Páez* case, that Article 25 is closely linked with the general obligation of Article 1(1) of the Convention, in conferring functions of protection upon the domestic law of States Parties.[7]

This conception of Article 25 and its link to Article 1(1) now constitutes *jurisprudence constante*.[8] The IACtHR has likewise insisted, e.g., *inter alia*, in its Judgment (of 31 January 2006) in the case of the *Massacre of Pueblo Bello*, concerning Colombia, on the wide scope of the general duty of guarantee of Article 1(1) of the American Convention, in the light of which – it stated – 'the action or omission of any public authority constitutes a fact imputable to the State, which engages its international responsibility in the terms foreseen by the Convention itself and in accordance with general international law' (par. 112).[9]

Given the importance ascribed to Article 25 on the right to an effective domestic remedy, it is worth examining its legislative history. To start with, the *travaux préparatoires* of the Universal Declaration of Human Rights followed distinct stages. The U.N. Commission on Human Rights decided in favour of the elaboration of a project in April/May 1946, when it designated a 'nuclear commission' to undertake the initial studies. UNESCO conducted parallel consultations (in 1947) to thinkers of the epoch on the foundations of a future Universal Declaration.[10] The draft

---

[6] For the antecedent of this significant *obiter dictum* of the Court, cf. the Dissenting Opinion (paragraph 18) of Judge Cançado Trindade in the *Genie Lacayo versus Nicaragua* case, Resolution (on appeal for revision of judgement) of 13 September 1997.

[7] On the interrelationship between Articles 25 and 1(1) of the American Convention, cf., again, the antecedent of my Dissenting Opinion (pars. 20–1) in the *Genie Lacayo versus Nicaragua* case, Resolution (on appeal for revision of judgement) of 13 September 1997.

[8] E.g., its Judgments on the merits in the cases *Suárez Rosero versus Ecuador* (Judgment of 12 November 1997, par. 65), of *Paniagua Morales and Others versus Guatemala* (Judgment of 08 March 1998, par. 164), of *Blake versus Guatemala* (Judgment of 24 January 1998, par. 102), of *Castillo Petruzzi and Others versus Peru* (Judgment of 30 May 1999, par. 184), of *Cesti Hurtado versus Peru* (Judgment of 29 September 1999, par. 121), of *'Street Children' (Villagrán Morales and Others versus Guatemala* (Judgment of 19 November 1999, par. 234), of *Durand and Ugarte versus Peru* (Judment of 16 August 2000, par. 101), of *Cantoral Benavides versus Peru* (Judgment of 18 August 2000, par. 163), of *Bámaca Velásquez versus Guatemala* (Judgment of 25 November 2000, par. 191), *Community Mayagna (Sumo) Awas Tingni versus Nicaragua* (Judgment of 31 August 2001, par. 112), of *Hilaire, Constantine y Benjamin y Otros versus Trinidad y Tobago* (Judgment of 21 June 2002, par. 150), of *Cantos versus Argentina* (Judgment of 28 November 2002, par. 52), of *Juan Humberto Sánchez versus Honduras* (Judgment of 07 June 2003), of *Maritza Urrutia versus Guatemala* (Judgment of 27 November 2003, par. 117), of *19 Tradesmen versus Colombia* (Judgment of 05 July 2004, par. 193), of *Tibi versus Ecuador* (Judgment of 07 September 2004, par. 131), of *Sisters Serrano Cruz versus El Salvador* (Judgment of 01 March 2005, par. 75), of *Yatama versus Paraguay* (Judgment of 23 June 2005, par. 169), of *Acosta Calderón versus Ecuador* (Judgment of 24 June 2005, par. 93), of *Palamara Iribarne versus Chile* (Judgment of 22 November 2005, par. 184).

[9] Cf., on this specific point, A.A. Cançado Trindade, 'La Convention Américaine relative aux Droits de l'Homme et le droit international général', in *Droit international, droits de l'homme et juridictions internationales* (eds. G. Cohen-Jonathan and J.-F. Flauss), Bruxelles, Bruylant, 2004, pp. 59–71.

[10] UNESCO, *Los Derechos del Hombre – Estudios y Comentarios en torno a la Nueva Declaración Universal*, Mexico/Buenos Aires, Fondo de Cultura Económica, 1949, pp. 233–46.

Declaration itself was prepared in the ambit of the U.N. Commission on Human Rights, by a Working Group (whose *rapporteur* was René Cassin) between May 1947 and June 1948. As from September 1948, the draft Declaration was examined by the Third Committee of the U.N. General Assembly, and approved on 10 December of that year by the Assembly itself.[11] One of the key provisions of the Universal Declaration of 1948 is found in its Article 8, whereby every person has the right to an effective remedy before competent national tribunals against acts which violate the fundamental rights granted to her by the Constitution or by the law.

Article 8 of the Universal Declaration sets forth, ultimately, the *right of access to justice* (at the domestic law level), an essential element in every democratic society. The draft Article which became Article 8, despite its relevance, was only inserted into the text at the final stage of the *travaux préparatoires* of the Universal Declaration, when the subject at issue was already under examination in the Third Committee of the U.N. General Assembly. Nevertheless, significantly it found no objection at all, having been approved at the Third Committee by 46 votes to none and three abstentions, and at the plenary of the General Assembly by unanimity. This late, but successful initiative, came from the Delegations of the Latin-American States.[12]

The provision of Article 8 of the 1948 Universal Declaration was inspired, in fact, in the equivalent provision of Article XVIII of the American Declaration on the Rights and Duties of Man of eight months before (April 1948);[13] its origin[14] – almost forgotten in our days – is Latin American.[15] The basic argument for the insertion of that provision in the American and Universal Declarations of 1948 filled a gap in both: protecting the rights of the individual against abuses of public power and submitting each and every abuse of individual rights to the Judiciary at domestic law level.[16]

---

[11] For an account, cf. A.A. Cançado Trindade, *Tratado de Direito Internacional dos Direitos Humanos*, vol. I, 2nd. ed., Porto Alegre/Brazil, S.A. Fabris Ed., 2003, ch. I, pp. 51–77.

[12] One may even consider that Article 8 (on the right to an effective remedy) represents the Latin-American contribution par excellence to the Universal Declaration.

[13] Such Latin-American initiative was strongly influenced in the principles that govern the remedy of *amparo*, already set forth by then in the national legislations of many countries of the region. Such was the case that, at the Bogotá Conference of April 1948, the aforementioned American Declaration had its Article XVIII adopted by unanimity of the 21 Delegations present. On the legacy of the 1948 American Declaration, cf. A.A. Cançado Trindade, 'O Legado da Declaração Universal de 1948 e o Futuro da Proteção Internacional dos Direitos Humanos', 14 *Anuario Hispano-Luso-Americano de Derecho Internacional* (1999) pp. 197–238.

[14] As I recalled in my Dissenting Opinion (cf. *supra*) in the case of *Genie Lacayo versus Nicaragua* (resolution on appeal for revision of judgment, of 13 September 1997), pars. 18–21.

[15] At a moment when, in parallel, the Commission on Human Rights of the United Nations was still preparing the Draft Universal Declaration (from May 1947 until June 1948), as recalled, in a fragment of memory, by the *rapporteur* of the Commission (René Cassin); the insertion of the provision on the right to an effective remedy before national jurisdictions in the Universal Declaration (Article 8), inspired in the corresponding provision of the American Declaration (Article XVIII), took place in the subsequent debates (of 1948) of the III Committee of the General Assembly of the United Nations. Cf. R. Cassin, 'Quelques souvenirs sur la Déclaration Universelle...', *op. cit. infra* n. (16) n. 1, p. 10.

[16] Cf. A. Verdoodt, *Naissance et signification de la Déclaration Universelle des Droits de l'Homme*, Louvain, Nauwelaerts, [1963], pp. 116–19; Eide et alii, *The Universal Declaration of Human Rights – A Commentary*, Oslo, Scandinavian University Press, 1992, pp. 124–6 e 143–4; R. Cassin, 'Quelques souvenirs sur la Déclaration Universelle de 1948', 15 *Revue de droit contemporain* (1968) n. 1, p. 10;

In sum, the original acknowledgement of the right to an effective remedy before competent national judges or tribunals in the American Declaration (Article XVIII) was transplanted to the Universal Declaration of Human Rights (of December 1948, Article 8), and from this latter to the European and American Conventions on Human Rights (Articles 13 and 25, respectively), as well as to the U.N. Covenant on Civil and Political Rights (Article 2(3)). Under the ECHR, in particular, it promptly generated considerable case-law,[17] as well as doctrinal debate. Article 8 of the Universal Declaration, and the corresponding provisions in human rights treaties in force, establish the duty of the State to provide adequate and effective domestic remedies; such duty constitutes – as I have always maintained – in effect a basic pillar not only of the mechanisms of protection of those treaties, but of the rule of law itself in a democratic society, and its correct application is to the effect of improving administration of justice (material and not only formal) at national level.

Moreover, this key provision is closely linked to the general obligation of States, set forth in human rights treaties, to *respect* the rights set forth therein, and to *ensure respect* for their free and full exercise by all persons subject to their respective jurisdictions.[18] It is, furthermore, linked to the guarantees of due process (Article 8 of the ACHR),[19] to the extent that it secures access to justice. In this way, by acknowledging the right to an effective remedy before competent national tribunals, the guarantees of due process, and general obligations to *guarantee* the protected rights, the ACHR (Articles 25, 8 and 1(1)), and other human rights treaties, confer the function of protection to the domestic law of the States Parties.

It is axiomatic that the rights protected under human rights treaties each have a material content of their own, from which its distinct formulations emanate – as is the case of Articles 25 and 8 of the ACHR. We are here at an essentially *ontological* level. Although they are endowed with a material content of their own, some rights have had a long jurisprudential evolution to reach autonomy, for example, the right

---

R. Cassin, 'La Déclaration Universelle et la mise en oeuvre des droits de l'homme', 79 *Recueil des Cours de l'Académie de Droit International de La Haye* (1951) pp. 328–9.

[17] At its beginnings, such case-law sustained the 'accessory' character of Article 13 of the European Convention, seen – as from the eighties – as guaranteeing a subjective individual substantive right. Gradually, in its judgments in the cases of *Klass versus Germany* (1978), *Silver and Others versus United Kingdom* (1983), and *Abdulaziz, Cabales and Balkandali versus United Kingdom* (1985), the European Court of Human Rights began to recognize the autonomous character of Article 13. Finally, after years of hesitation and wavering, the European Court, in its Judgment of 18 December 1996, in the case of *Aksoy versus Turkey* (paragraphs 95–100), determined the occurrence of an 'autonomous' violation of Article 13 of the European Convention.

[18] American Convention on Human Rights, Article 1(1); European Convention of Human Rights, Article 1; U.N. Covenant on Civil and Political Rights, Article 2(1).

[19] On judicial protection and the guarantees of the due process of law under the American Convention, cf. A.A. Cançado Trindade, 'The Right to a Fair Trial under the American Convention on Human Rights', in *The Right to Fair Trial in International and Comparative Perspective* (ed. A. Byrnes), Hong Kong, University of Hong Kong, 1997, pp. 4–11; A.A. Cançado Trindade, 'Judicial Protection and Guarantees in the Recent Case-Law of the Inter-American Court of Human Rights', in *Liber Amicorum in Memoriam of Judge J.M. Ruda*, The Hague, Kluwer, 2000, pp. 527–35.

to an effective remedy, under Article 25 of the ACHR and Article 13 of the ECHR. It is likewise the case for Article 8 of the ACHR and Article 6 of the ECHR.

The jurisprudential interpretation by the two Courts has attributed a proper meaning to those provisions, to be understood, in the light of the principle of intertemporal law, as construed in their case-law to date. The fact that the protected rights are endowed with a material content of their own does not mean that they cannot, or should not, be related to each other, by virtue of the circumstances of the specific case. On the contrary, such interrelatedness is, in my understanding, the one which propitiates a more effective protection, given the indivisibility of all human rights. We move here from the ontological to the *hermeneutic* level.

One decade ago, in my Dissenting Opinion (pars. 18–23) in the case of *Genie Lacayo versus Nicaragua* (Appeal for Revision of Judgment, Resolution of 13 September 1997),[20] I proceeded to an analysis of the material content and scope of Article 25, in relation to Article 8(1) (judicial guarantees) of the Convention, as well as the general duties (of guarantee of the exercise of the protected rights and of harmonization of the domestic law with international conventional law) set forth, respectively, in Articles 1(1) and 2 of the Convention. Contrary to what the IACtHR held in that case – which approached those conventional provisions from the perspective of formal, rather than material, justice – I concluded that there had occurred a violation, by the respondent State, of Articles 25, 8(1), 1(1) and 2 of the Convention 'taken altogether' (par. 28).

In the same line of reasoning, in my previous Dissenting Opinion in the case *Caballero Delgado and Santana versus Colombia* (Reparations, Judgment of 29 January 1997),[21] I propounded an integrating hermeneutics of Articles 8, 25, 1 (1) and 2 of the American Convention, again taking them jointly,[22] and sustaining, contrary to the position then adopted by the Court on this point, the violation by the respondent State of those four conventional provisions *inter se*. On the right to an effective remedy under Article 25 I allowed myself to formulate, in my afore-mentioned Dissenting Opinion in the case *Genie Lacayo versus Nicaragua*, the following observation:

The right to a simple, prompt and effective remedy before the competent national judges or tribunals, enshrined in Article 25 of the Convention, is a fundamental judicial guarantee far more important than one would *prima facie* assume,[23] and which can never be minimized. It constitutes, ultimately, one of the basic pillars not only of the American Convention on Human Rights, but of the rule of law (*État de Droit*) itself in a democratic society (in the sense of the Convention). Its correct application has the sense of improving the administration of justice at national level, with the legislative changes necessary to the attainment of that purpose. (. . .)

---

[20] IACtHR, Resolution of 13 September 1997 (Appeal for Revision of Judgment), pp. 3–25.
[21] CtIADH, Judgment of 29 January 1997 (Reparations), Series C, n. 31, pp. 3–43.
[22] Paragraphs 2–4 and 7–9 of the aforementioned Opinion.
[23] Its importance was pointed out, for example, in the *Report of the Commission of Jurists of the OAS for Nicaragua*, of 04 February 1994, pp. 100 and 106–7, paragraphs 143 and 160 (unpublished to date).

Articles 25 and 1(1) of the Convention are mutually reinforcing, in the sense of securing the compliance with one and the other in the ambit of domestic law. Articles 25 and 1(1) require, jointly, the *direct* application of the American Convention in the domestic law of the States Parties. In the hypothesis of alleged obstacles of domestic law, Article 2 of the Convention comes into operation, requiring the *harmonization* with the Convention of the domestic law of the States Parties. These latter are obliged, by Articles 25 and 1(1) of the Convention, to establish a system of simple and prompt local remedies, and to give them *effective* application.[24] If *de facto* they do not do so, due to alleged lacunae or insufficiencies of domestic law, they incur into a violation of Articles 25, 1(1) and 2 of the Convention (pars. 18–21).

It is important that the jurisprudential advances on this particular issue, achieved to date,[25] be preserved and further developed in the future, to the benefit of the protected persons. The relevance of the duty of States to provide adequate and effective domestic remedies should never be understated. The right to an effective remedy, before competent national judges or tribunals, of all persons subject to the jurisdiction of the State – to which the 1948 Universal Declaration gave projection at world level – is far more relevant than one would *prima facie* assume.[26] The right to a simple, prompt and effective remedy before the competent national tribunals or judges, enshrined in Article 25 of the ACHR, is a fundamental provision: it constitutes, ultimately, one of the basic pillars not only of the ACHR, but of the rule of law (*État de Droit*) itself in a democratic society (in the sense of the Convention). Its correct application has the sense of improving the administration of justice at national level, with the legislative changes necessary for the attainment of that purpose.

III. The Intangibility of Judicial Guarantees in All Circumstances

In addressing the question of limitations and derogations in emergency situations – which was the object of attention of its Advisory Opinion n. 8, of 30 January 1987 – the IACtHR upheld the intangibility and prevalence of *habeas corpus* in those situations. The Court warned in this regard that clearly no right guaranteed in the ACHR may be suspended unless 'very strict' conditions (set forth in Article 27(1)) are met. Moreover:

even when these conditions are satisfied, Article 27(2) provides that certain categories of rights may not be suspended under any circumstances. Hence, rather than adopting a

---

[24] The question of the effectiveness of local remedies is intimately linked to the administration of justice itself and to the operation of the competent national organs to redress the violations of the protected rights.

[25] Cf. chapter III, *infra*.

[26] The duty of States Parties to provide those remedies in the ambit of their domestic law and to secure to all persons under their jurisdictions the guarantee of the free and full exercise of all the rights set out in human rights treaties, as well as all the guarantees of the due process of law, assume an even greater importance, in a continent such as the American, marked by casuisms which not seldom deprive individuals of the protection of the Law.

philosophy that favours the suspension of rights, the Convention establishes the contrary principle, namely, that all rights are to be guaranteed and enforced unless very special circumstances justify the suspension of some, and that some rights may never be suspended, however serious the emergency (par. 21).

The American Convention includes, among the rights that may not be suspended (Article 27(2) *in fine*), the judicial guarantees which are essential for the protection of such rights, in a clear indication that, even in emergency situations, there is no suspension of the rule of law and its inseparable bond with the principle of legality and the democratic institutions.[27] The Court concluded that, as the writs of *habeas corpus* and *amparo* are among those judicial remedies that are essential for the protection of non-derogable rights and for the preservation of legality in a democratic society, any attempt by the Constitutions and legal systems of States Parties to suspend them would be incompatible with the obligations imposed on those States by the American Convention (pars. 43–44).

Shortly afterwards, in its Advisory Opinion n. 9, of 06 October 1987, the Court added that 'essential' judicial guarantees, not subject to derogation (Article 27(2)), include, besides *habeas corpus* and *amparo*, any other effective remedy before judges or competent tribunals (Article 25(1)), designed to guarantee respect of the rights whose suspension is not permitted by the ACHR. 'Essential' judicial guarantees, not subject to suspension, include judicial procedures inherent to representative democracy as a form of government (Article 29(c)), designed to guarantee the full exercise of non-derogable rights, whose suppression or restriction entails the lack of protection of such rights. Those judicial guarantees, the Court concluded, should be exercised within the framework and the principles of the due process of law, laid down in Article 8 of the Convention (par. 41). The IACtHR thus considered the provisions of Articles 25 and 8 to be interrelated.

The African Commission on Human and Peoples' Rights has also pronounced, on some occasions, on the intangibility of judicial guarantees.[28] The African Commission established violations of judicial guarantees (in breach of Article 7 (1) of the African Charter on Human and Peoples' Rights) in '*Rencontre Africaine pour la Defense des Droits de l'Homme' versus Zambia* (1996),[29] '*Constitutional Rights Project' (in relation to Akamu, Adega et alii) versus Nigeria* (1995),[30] and *Alhassan Abubakar versus Gana* (1996).[31] In a resolution adopted in its session of March 1992 (in Tunis, Tunisia), the African Commission formulated an appeal to the States Parties to the African Charter to give effect, at their domestic law level, to the *right of access to justice*, which comprised, in its view, four elements, namely:

---

[27] Paragraphs 36, 24 and 26–7.

[28] For an account, cf. A.A. Cançado Trindade, *Tratado de Direito Internacional dos Direitos Humanos*, vol. III, Porto Alegre/Brazil, S.A. Fabris Ed., 2003, pp. 208–13.

[29] Communication n. 71/92, case reported in: AComHPR, *Decisions of the African Commission on Human and Peoples' Rights*, vol. I (1986–1997), Series A, Banjul, 1997, pp. 77–82.

[30] Case reported in: 10 *Interights Bulletin* (1996) p. 18; and in: 18 *Human Rights Law Journal* (1997) pp. 28 and 30.

[31] Comunication n. 103/93, case reported in: AComHPR, *Decisions of the African Commission on Human and Peoples' Rights*, vol. I (1986–1997), Series A, Banjul, 1997, pp. 116–19.

a the right of access to competent national jurisdictions;

b the right to presumption of innocence;

c the right to defence;

d the right to be judged within a reasonable time by an impartial jurisdiction.[32]

Over a decade ago, in a study which I presented in an International Seminar of the International Committee of the Red Cross (ICRC) on the right to a fair trial, held in Hong Kong, China, I pondered:

In a wider horizon, whether we have in mind the component elements of the right to a fair trial, as developed in the countries of common law, or those which conform the fundamental guarantees (*garanties fondamentales*), as developed in countries of civil law (*droit civil*), in the present domain we find ourselves before general principles of law, universally acknowledged. With the advent of international instruments of human rights (. . .), the concepts of fair trial and fundamental guarantees, enshrined therein, acquire an autonomous meaning. The principles they incorporate are universal; they are general principles of law (e.g., presumption of innocence, *nullum crimen sine lege previa*, fair hearing, equality of arms, among others), found in different legal systems. They are (. . .) a reflection of the juridical conscience of humankind. As such, they find expression in different parts of the world (. . .).

In respect of the right to a fair trial and fundamental guarantees, it could hardly be denied that there are some minimum standards of protection of the human person below which no country can allow itself to fall. (. . .) The basic principles of the due process of law (. . .) correspond to certain elementary notions of justice, found in all States and all legal systems. (. . .).[33]

IV. The Right to Recognition of Juridical Personality

There is a further point which cannot pass unnoticed in the present chapter. It can occur that the acknowledgement of the individual's international legal personality comes to reinforce its legal personality at domestic level. This has in fact already occurred, as illustrated, e.g., by a case pertaining to the members of an internally displaced indigenous community. Thus, in its Judgment (of 29 March 2006) in the case of the *Sawhoyamaxa Indigenous Community versus Paraguay*, the IACtHR, *sponte sua*, decided, in application of the principle *jura novit curia*, to examine for the first time the right of recognition of legal personality (Article 3 of the ACHR), in the light of the circumstances of the specific case.

Bearing in mind that children of the aforementioned Community did not have birth certificates, or any other document of identification (par. 72.73), the Court established a violation of Article 3 – in connection with Article 1(1) – of the Convention in that case. The relevance of the juridical personality of the human

---

[32] Cf. CAfDHP, *Communiqué Final de la 11ème Session Ordinaire de la Commission Africaine des Droits de l'Homme et des Peuples* (Tunis, Tunisia, 1992), doc. ACHPR/FIN.COM/XI/REV.1, of 1992, pp. 5–6 (restricted circulation).

[33] Cf. A.A. Cançado Trindade, 'The Right to a Fair Trial . . . ', *op. cit. supra* n. (19), pp. 10–11, and cf. pp. 4–11.

person at both domestic and international law needs hardly be stressed.[34] As I pointed out in my Separate Opinion in the *Sawhoyamaxa Indigenous Community* case:

even if the State fails to recognize the juridical personality of the human being as subject of law, apt to exercise his subjective rights in the domestic legal order, the human being is not thereby deprived of his juridical personality, as the right to such personality is a right inherent to the human being. Here, once again, the impact of the International Law of Human Rights on the domestic or national legal orders is evident. In the face of the shortcomings of these latter, the International Law of Human Rights comes to protect the individuals, to secure the enforcement of their basic right to the juridical personality, which no one can be deprived of. The individual, – as I have been sustaining in the last four decades, – is *subject of both domestic as well as international law*, endowed in both legal orders with juridical personality, and with the corresponding juridico-procedural capacity to vindicate the rights which are inherent to him (par. 75).

V. The Converging Case-Law of the European and Inter-American Courts of Human Rights on the Rights of Access to Justice and to a Fair Trial

Last but not least, it may be observed that there is a converging case-law of the European and Inter-American Courts of Human Rights[35] on the right of access to justice and the right to a fair trial. In fact, Articles 5 and 6 of the ECHR have, not surprisingly, generated a vast and rich case-law on this matter, encompassing issues

[34] Of my own writings, cf. A.A. Cançado Trindade, 'A Personalidade e Capacidade Jurídicas do Indivíduo como Sujeito do Direito Internacional', in *Jornadas de Direito Internacional* (Cidade do México, dez. de 2001), Washington D.C., Subsecretaría de Asuntos Jurídicos de la OEA, 2002, pp. 311–47; A.A. Cançado Trindade, 'Vers la consolidation de la capacité juridique internationale des pétitionnaires dans le système interaméricain des droits de la personne', 14 *Revue québécoise de droit international* (2001) n. 2, pp. 207–39; A.A. Cançado Trindade, 'A Consolidação da Personalidade e da Capacidade Jurídicas do Indivíduo como Sujeito do Direito Internacional', 16 *Anuario del Instituto Hispano-Luso-Americano de Derecho Internacional* – Madrid (2003) pp. 237–88; A.A. Cançado Trindade, 'Hacia la Consolidación de la Capacidad Jurídica Internacional de los Peticionarios en el Sistema Interamericano de Protección de los Derechos Humanos', 37 *Revista del Instituto Interamericano de Derechos Humanos* (2003) pp. 13–52; A.A. Cançado Trindade, 'El Derecho de Acceso a la Justicia Internacional y las Condiciones para Su Realización en el Sistema Interamericano de Protección de los Derechos Humanos', 37 *Revista del Instituto Interamericano de Derechos Humanos* (2003) pp. 53–83; A.A. Cançado Trindade, 'Le nouveau Règlement de la Cour Interaméricaine des Droits de l'Homme: quelques réflexions sur la condition de l'individu comme sujet du Droit international', in *Libertés, justice, tolérance – Mélanges en hommage au Doyen G. Cohen-Jonathan*, vol. 1, Bruxelles, Bruylant, 2004, pp. 351–65; A.A. Cançado Trindade, 'The Procedural Capacity of the Individual as Subject of International Human Rights Law: Recent Developments', in *Les droits de l'homme à l'aube du XXIe siècle – K. Vasak Amicorum Liber*, Bruxelles, Bruylant, 1999, pp. 521–44; A.A. Cançado Trindade, 'A Emancipação do Ser Humano como Sujeito do Direito Internacional e os Limites da Razão de Estado', 6/7 *Revista da Faculdade de Direito da Universidade do Estado do Rio de Janeiro* (1998–1999) pp. 425–34.

[35] Cf., in general, A.A. Cançado Trindade, 'Approximations and Convergences in the Case-Law of the European and Inter-American Courts of Human Rights', in *Le rayonnement international de la jurisprudence de la Cour européenne des droits de l'homme* (eds. G. Cohen-Jonathan and J.-F. Flauss), Bruxelles, Nemesis/Bruylant, 2005, pp. 101–38.

of the utmost relevance, such as access to justice, judicial guarantees of the accused and of persons deprived of freedom, the correct administration of justice, and fair trial (*procès équitable*)[36] – all essential to the prevalence of the rule of law. Some aspects of that case-law can be pointed out here, in so far as they relate to the evolving case-law on the matter of the IACtHR.

The case-law of the ECtHR has been attentive to the fundamental relevance of the right of access to justice, as acknowledged in the *Golder versus United Kingdom* case (1975), where it asserted that the right of access to a tribunal, even though not mentioned in Article 6(1) of the ECHR, constituted an 'inherent element' of the right to a fair trial (*procès équitable*) enshrined in Article 6(1). And in the *Airey versus Ireland* case (1979) the Court went further, in affirming that such right of access ought necessarily to be *effective*.[37] The Court also warned, in the *Delcourt versus Belgium* case (1970), that the right to good administration of justice (under Article 6(1) of the Convention) is of crucial importance to the prevalence of the rule of law in a democratic State.[38]

The recognition of the right of access to justice, in concrete terms (such as those expressed by the Court in the *Airey versus Ireland* case, 1979) and not as a theoretical abstraction, constitutes a valuable contribution of the case-law of the ECtHR, leading to the assertion of the States Parties' duty to take positive measures. The effective right of access to justice provides a pertinent illustration of the need of such measures to be taken by the State, which cannot remain passive in face of the essential element of the rule of law.[39] In its decisions in, e.g., the cases *Gaskin versus United Kingdom* (1989) and *Plattform 'Ärzte für das Leben' versus Austria* (1988), the Court again dwelt upon the *positive* obligations on the part of the State.

In the framework of the right to a fair trial, the ECtHR has, moreover, set up criteria for the evaluation of compliance with the principle of the presumption of innocence (Article 6(2)), in the case *Barbera, Messegué and Jabardo versus Spain* (1988).[40] In accordance with the *jurisprudence constante* of the ECtHR, the 'right

---

[36] For a general study, cf., e.g., [Various Authors], *Les nouveaux développements du procès équitable au sens de la Convention Européenne des Droits de l'Homme* (Actes du Colloque de 1996), Bruxelles, Bruylant, 1996, pp. 9–197; J. van Compernolle, 'L'incidence de la Convention Européenne des Droits de l'Homme sur l'administration de la justice: le droit à un procès équitable', in [Various Authors], *La mise en oeuvre de la Convention Européenne des Droits de l'Homme* (Journée d'Études de 1994), Bruxelles, Éd. du Jeune Barreau de Bruxelles, 1994, pp. 63–87; and cf. also J. López Barja de Quiroga, *El Convenio, el Tribunal Europeo y el Derecho a un Juicio Justo*, Madrid, Ed. Akal, 1991, pp. 91–136.

[37] G. Cohen-Jonathan, *La Convention européenne des droits de l'homme*, Aix-en-Provence/Paris, Presses Universitaires d'Aix-Marseille/Economica, 1989, pp. 412–13, 510–11, 394 and 410–11.

[38] D. Gomien, *Short Guide to the European Convention on Human Rights*, Strasbourg, Council of Europe, 1991, p. 37; and cf. J.G. Merrills, *The Development of International Law by the European Court of Human Rights*, 1st. ed., Manchester, University Press, 1988, pp. 27, 92, 201 and 227.

[39] G. Cohen-Jonathan, *op. cit. supra* n. (37), pp. 412–13 and 431. More recently, in the cases *Gaskin versus United Kingdom* (1989) and *Plattform 'Ärzte für das Leben' versus Austria* (1988), for example, the Court once again focused on the positive obligations on the part of the State; D. Gomien, *op. cit. supra* n. (29), pp. 64–5 and 89–90.

[40] For comments, cf. A. Drzemczewski and C. Warbrick, 'The European Convention on Human Rights', 8 *Yearbook of European Law* (1988) pp. 324–6.

to an independent and impartial tribunal', as a component of Article 6 of the ECHR, comprises three elements, namely:

a a tribunal established by law and fulfilling the imperatives of independence and impartiality;

b a tribunal endowed with a sufficiently wide jurisdiction to pronounce on all the aspects of a complaint to which Article 6 of the Convention is applicable; and

c a tribunal to which individuals have free and full access.[41]

In the examination of each case, in all the stages of the procedure, attention ought to be paid to the requisites of the 'superior interests of justice'; hence the centrality of Article 6 in the vast case-law under the ECHR, since, as the ECtHR itself has warned, it occupies a 'prominent place' in 'democratic societies' – this being the reason why a 'restrictive interpretation' of it would not be in conformity with the object and purpose of the ECHR.[42] The right of access to a court (Article 13 of the ECHR) amounts to a right to judicial protection (which has been regarded as corresponding to a general principle of law); in securing that right, courts go further than applying legal norms or provisions, in proceeding to develop the law, and thus to give expression to certain basic values.[43]

In the case-law of the IACtHR, it was not until the case of *Castillo Páez versus Peru* (Merits, 1997) that the Court elaborated for the first time on the contents and extent of the right to an effective remedy before national judges or tribunals. In its Judgment of 03 November 1997 in that case, the Court held that the provision of Article 25 on the right to an effective remedy before the competent national judges or tribunals 'constitutes one of the basic pillars, not only of the American Convention, but of the rule of law [*État de Droit, Estado de Derecho*] itself in a democratic society in the sense of the Convention'. The Court added that 'Article 25 is intimately linked with the general obligation of Article 1(1) of the ACHR, in conferring functions of protection upon the domestic law of States Parties. The remedy of *habeas corpus* has the purpose of not only guaranteeing personal freedom and integrity, but also preventing the disappearance or indetermination of the place of detention and, ultimately, securing the right to life' itself.[44]

This has been the position of the Court ever since. Thus, in its Judgments on the merits in the cases of *Suárez Rosero versus Ecuador* (of 12 November 1997) and of

[41] A. Grotrian, *Article 6 of the European Convention on Human Rights – The Right to a Fair Trial*, Strasbourg, Council of Europe (Human Rights Files n. 13), 1994, p. 27.

[42] Ibid., pp. 53 and 6; not surprisingly, Article 6 is the one which has generated the most voluminous case-law under the European Convention. But even an up-to-date study of the right of access to justice on the basis essentially of Article 6(1) of the ECHR, without taking sufficiently into account its relationship with Article 13 of the ECHR and the growing importance of this latter, does not fail to acknowledge that the right of access to justice amounts ultimately to the right of the realisation of justice; cf. L. Milano, *Le droit à un tribunal au sens de la Convention Européenne des Droits de l'Homme*, Paris, Dalloz, 2006, pp. 51 and 57, and cf. pp. 63, 183 and 479.

[43] F.G. Jacobs, *The Sovereignty of Law – The European Way*, Cambridge, University Press, 2007, pp. 1, 16, 102 and 124.

[44] Paragraphs 82–3 of that Judgment.

Paniagua Morales and Others versus Guatemala (of 08 March 1998),[45] the Court found the respondent States in violation of, *inter alia*, Article 25 in combination with Article 1(1) of the ACHR. In those two cases (pars. 65 and 164, respectively), as well as in that of *Blake versus Guatemala* (Judgment on the merits, of 24 January 1998, par. 102), the Court reiterated its significant *obiter dictum* – now *jurisprudence constante* – to the effect that Article 25 constitutes one of the basic pillars not only of the ACHR but of the rule of law itself in a democratic society, and is intimately linked to the general obligation of Article 1(1) of the ACHR in attributing functions of protection to the domestic law of States Parties.

In addition to these cases, references could be made to other judgments of the IACtHR pertaining to aspects of the due process of law (e.g., cases *Loayza Tamayo versus Peru, Castillo Petruzzi and Others versus Peru, Ivcher Bronstein versus Peru,* cases of the *Constitutional Tribunal* and of *Barrios Altos* concerning Peru, case *Las Palmeras* concerning Colombia, *Trujillo Oroza versus Bolivia, Cantos versus Argentina, Five Pensioners versus Peru*). In this case-law of the IACtHR, several references can be found to the corresponding case-law of the ECtHR. The ACHR requires not only access to justice itself at the level of domestic law (Article 25), but also the realization of material justice. To that end, the ACHR determines the observance of the juridico-procedural guarantees (Article 8), these latter taken *lato sensu*, encompassing the procedural requisites which ought to be observed so that all individuals can adequately defend themselves from any act emanating from the State power which may affect their rights.[46]

In the case *Baena Ricardo and Others versus Panama* (Judgment on the merits, of 02 February 2001), the IACtHR rightly warned that 'in any subject matter, even in labour and administrative matters, the discretionality of the administration has boundaries that may not be surpassed, one such boundary being respect for human rights. (...) The administration (...) may not invoke public order to reduce discretionally the guarantees of its subjects'.[47] The importance of the jurisprudential construction of the IACtHR on the right of access to justice and the right to a fair trial could hardly be minimized; it is far more relevant than assumed until recently, in a continent marked by casuisms which far too often deprive individuals of the protection of the law.[48]

---

[45] In this decision of 08 March 1998, the Court found Guatemala in breach of provisions of *both* the American Convention on Human Rights *as well as* the Inter-American Convention to Prevent and Punish Torture (cf. resolutory points ns. 1 to 5 of the Judgment on the merits in *Paniagua Morales and Others*); this was the first time that the Court found violations of *two* regional human rights treaties (as the judicial supervisory organ of both of them).

[46] Cf., in this sense (wide scope of the due process), the Court's Judgment (on the merits) of 31 January 2001, in the case of the *Constitutional Tribunal,* concerning Peru (par. 69) and the Court's Judgment (on the merits) of 06 February 2001, in the case *Ivcher Bronstein versus Peru* (par. 102).

[47] Paragraphs 125–6 of the Judgment.

[48] A.A. Cançado Trindade, 'Thoughts on Recent Developments in the Case-Law of the Inter-American Court of Human Rights: Selected Aspects', in *Proceedings of the 92nd Annual Meeting of the American Society of International Law – The Challenge of Non-State Actors,* Washington D.C., ASIL, 1998, pp. 192–201, esp. pp. 196–7.

IV

The Interrelation between the Access to Justice (Right to an Effective Remedy) and the Guarantees of the Due Process of Law

I. Introduction   63

II. The Interrelation between the Access to Justice (Right to an
Effective Remedy) and the Guarantees of the Due Process of Law
in the Case-Law of the IACtHR   64

III. The Overcoming of Vicissitudes as to the Right to an Effective
Remedy in the Jurisprudential Construction of the ECtHR   66

IV. The Right of Access to Justice *Lato Sensu*   71

V. Concluding Observations   74

I. Introduction

States Parties to human rights treaties undertake to comply not only with the specific obligations concerning each of the protected rights, but also with the general obligations guaranteeing the exercise of the protected rights, and the harmonization of domestic law so as to remove obstacles to the faithful compliance with those treaties. This includes the prompt removal of obstacles to the access to justice. Such positive measures on the part of States Parties have a bearing not only on the issue of access to international justice in relation to the interaction between international law and domestic law,[1] but also on the relationship of certain conventional provisions of human rights treaties *inter se*, such as those pertaining to the individual's access to justice (right to an effective remedy) and the guarantees of the due process of law.

In the present chapter, I shall review the treatment of the interrelation between those conventional provisions in the evolving case-law of the IACtHR as well as the ECtHR. I shall then focus attention on the issue of the substance, or material content, as well as the extent, of the right of access to justice *lato sensu*. The way will thus be paved for the presentation of my concluding observations on this particular matter.

---

[1] Cf. chapter V, *infra*.

II. The Interrelation between the Access to Justice (Right to an Effective Remedy) and the Guarantees of the Due Process of Law in the Case-Law of the IACtHR

In its Judgment (of 15 September 2005) in the case of the *Massacre of Mapiripán*, concerning Colombia, the IACtHR underlined the ineluctable link between Articles 25 (access to justice, right to an effective remedy) and 8 (guarantees of the due process of law) of the ACHR. According to this latter, 'States Parties are bound to provide effective judicial remedies to the victims of human rights violations (Article 25), remedies which ought to be substantiated in conformity with the rules of the due process of law (Article 8(1))', in the light of the general duty of States Parties, under Article 1(1) of the Convention, to guarantee the free and full exercise of the protected rights (par. 195).

Subsequently, in recalling the origins of this jurisprudential construction of the IACtHR, I pondered, in my Separate Opinion in the case of the *Massacre of Pueblo Bello versus Colombia* (Judgment of 31 January 2006), that:

On the day of the adoption by the Court of the Judgment on the merits (of 03 November 1997) on the case *Castillo Páez [versus Peru]*, – starting point of this lucid *jurisprudence constante* of the Inter-American Court, – I experienced, with satisfaction, a sentiment of accomplishment of a significant advance in the case-law of the Court, which came to situate the right to an effective remedy in the position of importance that corresponds to it, as expression of the right of access to justice itself *lato sensu*, understood as the right to the realization of justice, thus ineluctably encompassing the guarantees of the due process of law, as well as the faithful execution of the sentence. (. . .) Ultimately, what would be the efficacy of the guarantees of the *due process* (Article 8) if the individual were not to count on the right to an effective remedy (Article 25)? And what would be the efficacy of this latter without the guarantees of the due process of law?

It is certain that they complement each other, (. . .) in the juridical framework of the rule of law (*État de droit/Estado de Derecho*) in a democratic society. This is the sane hermeneutics of those two conventional provisions. (. . .) (pars. 28–29).

The IACtHR has so far been faithful to the advanced position it adopted on the matter. Thus, in its well-known Advisory Opinion n. 16, on *The Right to Information on Consular Assistance in the Framework of the Due Process of Law* (of 01 October 1999), the Court once again took into account the right to an effective remedy and the guarantees of the due process of law together. After singling out the need to *interpret* the Convention in the sense of ensuring that 'the regime of protection of human rights has all its proper effects (*effet utile*)' (par. 58), in conformity with the necessarily *evolutive* interpretation of the whole *corpus juris* of international human rights law (pars. 114–115), the Court asserted, in a clear and categorical way, that, in its understanding, 'for the "due process of law" to exist it is necessary that a *justiciable* can vindicate his rights and defend his interests in an effective way and in conditions of procedural equality with the other *justiciables*' (par. 117).

In other words, in the understanding of the Court, there is simply no due process of law without the effective remedy before the competent national judges or tribunals, and the provisions of Articles 25 and 8 of the Convention are ineluctably interrelated, not only at the conceptual, but also – and above all – at the hermeneutic level. The Court added, in its *célèbre* Advisory Opinion n. 16, that one ought to verify and secure that all *justiciables* 'enjoy a true access to justice and benefit from a due process of law (. . .)' (par. 119).

In its *jurisprudence constante*, the IACtHR has to date consistently linked, with the corresponding reasoning to this effect, the consideration of alleged violations of Articles 8 and 25 of the ACHR.[2] On some occasions, the Court has been particularly emphatic as to the necessity to follow a hermeneutics of integration (and never of disaggregation) of Articles 8 and 25, taking them together.[3] Article 8(1) is thus, in the correct understanding of the Court, ineluctably linked to the right to an effective domestic remedy under Article 25 of the Convention.

In this same line of reasoning, in the case *Hilaire, Constantine and Benjamin and Others versus Trinidad and Tobago* (Judgment of 21 June 2002) the Court evoked its *obiter dictum* in the Advisory Opinion n. 16 (*supra*) to the effect that there is no due process of law if a *justiciable* cannot vindicate his rights 'in an effective way' (i.e., if he does not have true access to justice), and added that, 'for true judicial guarantees to exist in a process' the observance is necessary of 'all the requisites' that serve to 'secure the titularity or the exercise of a right' (pars. 146–147).[4] In the case of *Bámaca Velásquez versus Guatemala* (Judgment of 25 November 2000), the Court expressly took 'the guarantees set forth in Article 8 and the judicial protection

---

[2] As duly exemplified by its Judgments on the cases *Durand and Ugarte versus Peru* (of 16 August 2000, par. 130), *Barrios Altos (Chumbipuma Aguirre and Others) versus Peru* (of 14 March 2001, pars. 47–9), *Las Palmeras versus Colombia* (of 06 December 2001, pars. 48–66), *Baena Ricardo and Others versus Panama* (of 02 February 2001, pars. 119–43), *Myrna Mack Chang versus Guatemala* (of 25 November 2003, pars. 162–218), *Maritza Urrutia versus Guatemala* (of 27 November 2003, pars. 107–30), *19 Tradesmen versus Colombia* (of 05 July 2004, pars. 159–206), *Brothers Gómez Paquiyauri versus Peru* (of 08 July 2004, pars. 137–56), *Hermanas Serrano Cruz versus El Salvador* (of 01 March 2005, pars. 52–107), *Caesar versus Trinidad and Tobago* (of 11 March 2005, pars. 103–17), *Community Moiwana versus Suriname* (of 15 June 2005, pars. 139–67), *Indigenous Community Yakye Axa versus Paraguay* (of 17 June 2005, pars. 55–119), *Fermín Ramírez versus Guatemala* (of 20 June 2005, pars. 58–83), *Yatama versus Paraguay* (of 23 June 2005, pars. 145–77), *Massacre of Mapiripán versus Colombia* (of 15 September 2005, pars. 193–241), *Gómez Palomino versus Peru* (of 22 November 2005, pars. 72–86), and *Massacre of Pueblo Bello versus Colombia* (of 31 January 2006, pars. 210 and 216, and cf. par. 192), And cf. also, to the same effect, its Judgments on the cases *Children Yean and Bosico versus Dominican Republic* (of 08 September 2005, par. 201), and *Palamara Iribarne versus Chile* (of 22 November 2005, pars. 120–89).

[3] For example, in the case *Cantos versus Argentina* (Sentencia del 28 November 2002), the Court singled out the importance of the *right of access to justice*, set forth at a time, *lato sensu*, both in Article 25 as in Article 8(1) of the Convention, and promptly added that any norm or measure at domestic law order which imposes costs or renders difficult, in any other manner, the access of individuals to the competent tribunals, is to be understood as being in contravention of the aforementioned Article 8(1) of the Convention' (pars. 50 and 52 of the aforementioned Judgment).

[4] Furthermore, in the case of *Juan Humberto Sánchez versus Honduras* (Judgment of 07 June 2003), the Court warned that local remedies cannot be considered 'effective' if, by the 'general conditions of the country' at issue, or even by the 'particular circumstance' of a given case, they 'result illusory' (par. 121, and cf. par. 135). That is, the access to justice and the effective exercise of the right (with the faithful observance of the judicial guarantees) are ineluctably linked.

established in Article 25 of the Convention' together to analyze the alleged violations of rights in the specific case (par. 187).

In the cases of *Myrna Mack Chang versus Guatemala* (Judgment of 25 November 2003, par. 201), as well as of the '*Street Children*' (*Villagrán Morales and Others versus Guatemala*, Judgment of 19 November 1999, par. 224, and cf. par. 225), the Court significantly affirmed that it:

> ought to undertake an examination of the whole of the domestic legal actions to obtain an integral perception of them and to establish if such actions breach the standards on the judicial guarantees and protection and the right to an effective remedy, which emerge from Articles 8 and 25 of the Convention.

Thus, the provisions of Articles 25 and 8 of the ACHR, taken together, are fundamental for the determination itself of the origin and extent of the responsibility of the State, also for acts or omissions of the Judiciary (or of any other power or agent of the State). In sum and conclusion on this particular point, judicial protection (Article 25) and judicial guarantees (Article 8) form a conceptually organic whole, and conform to the *rule of law* in a democratic society, as indicated by the evolving international case-law on the subject.[5]

III. The Overcoming of Vicissitudes as to the Right to an Effective Remedy in the Jurisprudential Construction of the ECtHR

A distinct posture on the matter at issue has been abandoned by supervisory organs that adopted and followed it earlier on. The early case-law of the ECtHR maintained the 'accessory' character of Article 13 (right to an effective remedy) of the ECHR, understood – as from the eighties – as guaranteeing a subjective substantive individual right. Gradually, in its Judgments in the cases *Klass versus Federal Republic of Germany* (1978), *Silver and Others versus United Kingdom* (1983), and *Abdulaziz, Cabales and Balkandali versus United Kingdom* (1985), the ECtHR began to recognize the autonomous character of Article 13.

At last, after years of hesitation, the ECtHR, in its Judgment (of 18 December 1996) in the case *Aksoy versus Turkey*, established the occurrence of an 'autonomous' violation of Article 13 of the ECHR (pars. 95–100). The Court further warned in the *Aksoy* case that Article 13 imposes the obligation to undertake an 'effective and complete investigation' of incidents of torture.[6] Moreover, in another Judgment, in the case *Akdivar and Others versus Turkey* (16 September 1996), the ECtHR took into account, *inter alia*, the notorious passivity of public authorities as to the condition of victims in a

---

[5] A.A. Cançado Trindade, *Tratado de Direito Internacional dos Direitos Humanos*, vol. II, Porto Alegre/ Brazil, S.A. Fabris Ed., 1999, p. 67, par. 70.

[6] R.A. Lawson and H.G. Schermers, *Leading Cases of the European Court of Human Rights*, Nijmegen, Ars Aequi Libri, 1997, pp. XX and XXIV. And, on the autonomous character of Article 13 of the Convention, cf. A. Drzemczewski and C. Giakoumopoulos, 'Article 13', in *La Convention Européenne des Droits de l'Homme – Commentaire article par article* (eds. L.-E. Pettiti, E. Decaux and P.-H. Imbert), *op. cit. infra* n. (15), pp. 455–74.

situation of armed conflict; to the Court, this situation did not attain the human rights standards of the Council of Europe established in the ECHR.[7]

In an early study of the matter published in 1973, Pierre Mertens criticized the 'poverty' of the initial case-law of the ECtHR, as well as the vague character of the European doctrine on the matter – distinct from the more advanced Latin American doctrine and practice, as from the adoption of the American Declaration on the Rights and Duties of Man of 1948, the first international instrument to set forth the right to an effective remedy.[8] Mertens warned that one ought to pave the way for the right to an effective remedy to generate all its effects in the domestic law of the States Parties. In reality, the 'effectiveness' of that right is measured in the light of the criteria of the guarantees of the due process of law (Article 6 of the ECHR); hence the conclusion of Mertens, that Articles 6 and 13 of the ECHR – which correspond to Articles 8 and 25 of the ACHR – ought to be often 'invoked together' ('invoqués ensemble').[9]

Attention eventually began to turn, with the passing of the years, to the relationship between Articles 13 and 6(1) of the ECHR, the latter (right to a fair trial) becoming the object of considerable case-law of the ECtHR, as well as dense academic debate.[10] In *Mentes and Others versus Turkey* (Judgment of 28 November 1997), for example, the Court examined the alleged violations of Articles 6(1) and 13 together. The applicants were four women, Turkish citizens of Kurdish origin then living in south-east Turkey, who had been forcefully displaced (by security forces) from their village and had their houses destroyed and burnt. Three of the applicants established the facts of their case before the ECtHR.

The latter properly related the access of justice to the 'right to a court' (at domestic level – par. 96). The Court dismissed the preliminary objection of non-exhaustion of local remedies, significantly stating that that condition of admissibility:

must be applied with some degree of flexibility and without excessive formalism. The rule is neither absolute nor capable of being applied automatically. In reviewing whether it has been observed it is essential to have regard to the particular circumstances of each individual case (par. 58).[11]

The ECtHR duly took into account the extent of the problem of the destruction of the village and the situation of 'insecurity and vulnerability' surrounding the alleged victims (par. 59), before dismissing the preliminary objection interposed by the respondent State.

---

[7] Leo Zwaak, 'The European Court of Human Rights Has the Turkish Security Forces Held Responsible for Violations of Human Rights: The Case of Akdivar and Others', 10 *Leiden Journal of International Law* (1997) pp. 99–110.

[8] P. Mertens, *Le droit de recours effectif devant les instances nationales en cas de violation d'un droit de l'homme*, Bruxelles, Éd. de l'Univ. de Bruxelles, 1973, pp. 19–20, 24–5 and 27–9, and cf. pp. 37–9.

[9] Ibid., p. 93.

[10] Cf. L.-E. Pettiti, E. Decaux and P.-H. Imbert, *La Convention Européenne des droits de l'homme*, Paris, Economica, 1995, pp. 455–74.

[11] Cf., in the same sense, 14 years earlier, A.A. Cançado Trindade, *The Application of the Rule of Exhaustion of Local Remedies in International Law*, Cambridge, Cambridge University Press (Series 'Cambridge Studies in International and Comparative Law'), 1983, pp. 1–443.

As to the merits of the case, the Court found a breach of 'the more general obligation' of Article 13 of the ECHR (right to an effective remedy) in respect of three of the applicants (pars. 88 and 92), and found it unnecessary to determine whether there had been a violation of Article 6(1) of the Convention (par. 88). The case of *Mentes and Others versus Turkey* provides yet another example of individuals' access to justice at international level in a situation of great adversity,[12] this time in the European continent.

Subsequently, the ECtHR made an emphatic pronouncement on the matter in *Kudla versus Poland* (Judgment of 18 October 2000), which was a case of unreasonably prolonged criminal proceedings against a person charged with fraud and forgery, and detained on remand, deprived of the rights to a hearing and to trial within a reasonable time or of release pending trial. In its Judgment, the ECtHR affirmed that the moment had come to put an end to the uncertainties of the past and to admit the direct link between Articles 6(1) and 13 of the European Convention (cf. pars. 146–149 and 151). And, in a significant *obiter dictum*, the European Court asserted that:

(...) Article 13, giving direct expression to the State's obligation to protect human rights first and foremost within their own legal system, establishes an additional guarantee for an individual in order to ensure that he or she effectively enjoys those rights. The object of Article 13, as emerges from the *travaux préparatoires* [of the European Convention on Human Rights], is to provide a means whereby individuals can obtain relief at national level for violations of their Convention rights before having to set in motion the international machinery of complaint before the Court. From this perspective, the right of an individual to trial within a reasonable time will be less effective if there exists no opportunity to submit the Convention claim first to a national authority; and the requirements of Article 13 are to be seen as reinforcing those of Article 6(1), rather than being absorbed by the general obligation imposed by that Article not to subject individuals to inordinate delays in legal proceedings (par. 152).

And the ECtHR concluded, in the *Kudla* case, that 'the correct interpretation of Article 13 is that that provision guarantees an effective remedy before a national authority for an alleged breach of the requirement under Article 6(1) to hear a case within a reasonable time' (par. 156). Accordingly, the Court determined that in the concrete case 'there has been a violation of Article 13 in that the applicant had no domestic remedy whereby he could enforce his right to a "hearing within a reasonable time" as guaranteed by Article 6(1) of the Convention' (par. 160).

In fact, since the late 1970s, the ECtHR has often taken into account the requirements of the due process of law (Article 6 of the ECHR) in direct correlation with those of the right to an effective remedy (Article 13).[13] The right to an

---

[12] Cf. chapter VII, *infra*.

[13] For examples, cf. M. de Salvia, *Compendium de la CEDH – Les principes directeurs de la jurisprudence relative à la Convention européenne des droits de l'homme*, Kehl/Strasbourg, Ed. Engel, 1998, p. 280. From the start, the European Court has discarded a restrictive interpretation of Article 6 of the European Convention, given its 'central' and 'prominent' position in the latter, and for being linked to the general principles of law themselves, among which 'the fundamental principle of the rule

effective remedy, in the evolving European case-law, integrates the *État de Droit*, and cannot be dissociated from the rule of law in a democratic society.[14] Its material content, as a subjective and autonomous right, characterizes it as 'un outil fondamental de la mise-en-oeuvre de la protection des droits de l'homme'.[15]

In a thoughtful essay published in 2000, E.A. Alkema argued that, despite the Court's 'quite restrictive' interpretation of Article 13 in the early days, over the years the Convention has developed itself into 'a stronghold for the right to access',[16] and it has become 'the embodiment of the idea of access to justice at three levels'. First, the Convention itself introduced into international law the individual's right to sue a State (including his own) in the vindication of his rights; secondly, 'it entrenched the principle of access' in several of the guaranteed rights, notably in Articles 6 and 13 of the Convention; and thirdly, 'the idea has impregnated', though indirectly, the domestic legal orders of States Parties to the Convention.[17]

In its case-law of the last decade, the ECtHR has devoted growing attention to the autonomous right to an effective remedy (and has increasingly considered its material content and scope). To the ECtHR, Article 13 guarantees 'the availability at the national level of a remedy to enforce the substance of the Convention rights and freedoms in whatever form they might happen to be secured in the domestic legal order'.[18] The remedy required by Article 13 of the ECHR – the Court added – ought to be effective 'in practice as well as in law, in particular in the sense that its exercise must not be unjustifiably hindered by the acts or omissions of the authorities of the respondent State'.[19]

Furthermore, in *Khashiyev and Akayeva versus Russia* (2005), given the fundamental importance of the rights guaranteed under Articles 2 and 3 of the ECHR, the ECtHR stated that 'Article 13 requires, in addition to the payment of compensation where appropriate, a thorough and effective investigation capable of leading to the identification and punishment of those responsible' for deprivation of life (breach

---

of law'; A. Grotrian, *Article 6 of the European Convention on Human Rights – The Right to a Fair Trial*, Strasbourg, C.E., 1994, p. 6.

[14] D.J. Harris, M. O'Boyle and C. Warbrick, *Law of the European Convention on Human Rights*, London, Butterworths, 1995, p. 461.

[15] A. Drzemczewski and C. Giakoumopoulos, 'Article 13', in *La Convention européenne des droits de l'Homme – Commentaire article par article* (eds. L.-E. Pettiti, E. Decaux and P.-H. Imbert), Paris, Economica, 1995, p. 474.

[16] In this sense, cf. E.A. Alkema, 'Access to Justice under the ECHR and Judicial Policy – A Netherlands View', in *Afmaelisrit pór Vilhjálmsson*, Reykjavík, Bókaútgafa Orators, 2000, pp. 29–30.

[17] Ibid., p. 21. And he concluded that 'making access to justice on the domestic level as perfect as possible will reduce the appeal to Strasbourg particularly in a qualitative sense. That is probably the most harmonious answer to the ever and everywhere increasing search for judicial guarantees for legitimacy'; ibid., p. 37.

[18] ECtHR, case of *Tanrikulu versus Turkey*, Judgment of 08 July 1999, par. 117.

[19] Ibid., par. 117; and, likewise, ECtHR, case of *Iatridis versus Greece*, Judgment of 25 March 1999, par. 66; ECtHR, case of *Khashiyev and Akayeva versus Russia*, Judgment of 24 February 2005, par. 182; ECtHR, case of *Isayeva, Yusupova and Bazayeva versus Russia*, Judgment of 24 February 2005, par. 236.

of Article 2) and infliction of ill treatment (contrary to Article 3), 'including effective access for the complainant to the investigation procedure'.[20]

In the same line of thinking, in *Kurt versus Turkey* (1998), the ECtHR characterized the effect of Article 13 as being 'to require the provision of a domestic remedy to deal with the substance of the relevant Convention complaint and to grant appropriate relief'.[21] Where the relatives of a disappeared person have an arguable claim that the disappearance occurred at the hands of the authorities, the Court added, 'the notion of an effective remedy for the purposes of Article 13 entails, in addition to the payment of compensation where appropriate, a thorough and effective investigation capable of leading to the identification and punishment of those responsible and including effective access for the relatives to the investigatory procedure'.[22] In the specific case, given the 'lack of any meaningful investigation', the Court found that 'the applicant was denied an effective remedy in respect of her complaint that her son had disappeared in circumstances engaging the responsibility of the authorities. There has therefore been a violation of Article 13'.[23]

In *Shamayev and Others versus Georgia and Russia* (Judgment of 12 April 2005), the ECtHR recalled its *jurisprudence constante* to the effect that the remedy required by Article 13 must be *effective* 'in practice as well as in law', with no unjustifiable hindrance by the acts or omissions of the State authorities (par. 447). Moreover, the ECtHR has upheld the autonomy of the right to an effective remedy, in clear and emphatic terms; in the Court's view, the 'existence of an actual breach' of another provision of the Convention (a 'substantive' provision) 'is not a prerequisite' for Article 13 to apply (par. 444). The latter, the Court added:

guarantees the availability at the national level of a remedy to enforce (. . .) the substance of the Convention rights and freedoms in whatever form they might happen to be secured (par. 444).

Moreover, in *Markovic and Others versus Italy* (Judgment of 14 December 2006), the ECtHR also recalled its *jurisprudence constante* (since the *Golder* case in 1975) as to the material content of the right of access to a court (pars. 92 and 97), but found that, in the circumstances of the specific case (concerning the complaint brought before the Italian courts in respect of the NATO air strikes against Kosovo in 1999), there had been, in its view, no violation of Article 6 of the ECHR (par. 116). A Joint Dissenting Opinion[24] warned, however, that:

'Reason of State' has little time for law, still less for the 'rule of law', which one can scarcely conceive of without there being a possibility of having access to the courts (par. 3).

---

[20] ECtHR, case of *Khashiyev and Akayeva versus Russia*, Judgment of 24 February 2005, par. 183; and, likewise, ECtHR, case of *Alikhadzhiyeva versus Russia*, Judgment of 05 July 2007, par. 92.
[21] ECtHR, case of *Kurt versus Turkey*, Judgment of 25 May 1998, par. 139.
[22] Ibid., par. 140.
[23] Ibid., p. 142.
[24] Dissenting Opinion of Judge Zagrebelsky, joined by Judges Zupancic, Jungwiert, Tsatsaniko-lovska, Ugrekhelidze, Kovler and D. Thor Bjorgvinsson.

The Dissenting Judges in the *Markovic* case pointed out that 'although the applicants were given access to the Italian courts, it was only to be told that neither the civil courts, nor any other Italian court, had jurisdiction to hear their case' (par. 6). The applicants had argued in the domestic courts that the Italian authorities' actions had 'contravened the rules of national law and international customary law on armed conflict' (as a member of NATO); in so doing, they raised the question of 'the limits that should be placed on the notion of a 'reason of State' free from all judicial scrutiny' (par. 7). The Dissenting Judges regretted that the majority of the Court found that there had been no breach of Article 6 of the ECHR, having thus struck 'a blow at the very foundation of the Convention' (par. 9).

IV. The Right of Access to Justice *Lato Sensu*

It is clear that the right of access to justice comprises not only the right to initiate proceedings before international human rights tribunals, but also the guarantees of due process of law, and the right to protection by means of faithful compliance with judicial decisions. On this particular matter, in my Separate Opinion in the case of the *Massacre of Pueblo Bello* before the IACtHR (Judgment of 31 January 2006), I stated:

In the *Reports* which I presented, as then President of the Inter-American Court, to the competent organs of the Organization of American States (OAS), e.g., on 19 April 2002 and 16 October 2002, I sustained my understanding in the sense of the wide scope of the right of access to justice at international level, of the right of access to justice *lato sensu*.[25] Such right does not reduce itself to the formal access, *stricto sensu*, to the judicial instance (both domestic and international), but comprises, moreover, the right to the realization of justice, and underlies interrelated provisions of the American Convention (such as Articles 25 and 8), besides permeating the domestic law of the States Parties. The right of access to justice, endowed with a juridical content of its own, means, *lato sensu*, the right to obtain justice. In sum, the right to the *realization* itself of justice is thus conformed.

One of the main components of this right is precisely the direct access to a competent tribunal, by means of an effective and expedite remedy, and the right to be promptly heard by such independent and impartial tribunal, at both national and international levels (Articles 25 and 8 of the American Convention). As I allowed myself to point out in a recent work, we can here visualize a true *right to the Law* (*droit au Droit/derecho al Derecho*), that is, the right to a legal order – at both national and international levels – which effectively safeguards the fundamental rights of the human person[26] (pars. 61–62).

---

[25] Cf. A.A. Cançado Trindade, 'El Derecho de Acceso a la Justicia Internacional y las Condiciones para Su Realización en el Sistema Interamericano de Protección de los Derechos Humanos', 37 *Revista del Instituto Interamericano de Derechos Humanos* (2003) pp. 53–83; A.A. Cançado Trindade, 'Hacia la Consolidación de la Capacidad Jurídica Internacional de los Peticionarios en el Sistema Interamericano de Protección de los Derechos Humanos', 37 *Revista del Instituto Interamericano de Derechos Humanos* (2003) pp. 13–52.
[26] A.A. Cançado Trindade, *Tratado de Direito Internacional dos Direitos Humanos*, vol. III, Porto Alegre/Brazil, S.A. Fabris Ed., 2002, ch. XX, p. 524, par. 187.

The wide scope of the right of access to justice has been the object of attention of the ECtHR. Thus, in its Judgment (of 19 March 1997) in *Hornsby versus Greece* case, it warned that the 'right to a court' (Article 6(1) of the ECHR) would be illusory if it applied only to procedural guarantees and the conduct of the parties, without likewise encompassing the proper implementation of judicial decisions – which would hardly be in conformity with the very notion of the rule of law (*prééminence du droit* – par. 40).

Due compliance with the judgments of the international human rights tribunals is a matter of international *ordre public*, in the sense attributed to the latter by human rights treaties.[27] This is a requirement established by the new *corpus juris* of safeguarding the rights of the human person. In the case of non-compliance, recalcitrant States ought to bear the juridical consequences of their breaches of Law. It is no longer the traditional *ordre public* of defence of the legal order of the *forum* (in the face of foreign law), as in classic private international law,[28] but a new international *ordre public* attentive to the imperatives of protection of the human person.

The correct administration of justice is indeed one of the essential elements of the *État de Droit* – a requirement of international *ordre public* in the sense conferred upon it by human rights treaties – necessarily including the faithful execution of judgments, and even more so when these latter seek to secure the intangibility of the guarantees of the due process of law. As the ECtHR aptly added in its Judgment in the *Hornsby* case, the omission or refusal of public authorities to execute a judgment constitutes a *denial of access to justice* (at both national and international levels – pars. 41 and 45), in breach of Article 6(1) of the ECHR.

One decade later, in its recent Judgment (of 31 October 2006) on the case of *Jelicic versus Bosnia and Herzegovina*, the ECtHR further warned that 'it is not open to a State authority to cite lack of funds as an excuse for not honouring a judgment debt', and a delay in the execution of a judgment 'may not be such as to impair the essence of the right protected under Article 6(1)' (par. 39). In the *Jelicic* case the Court reiterated its understanding to the effect that Article 6(1):

embodies the 'right to a court', of which the right of access, that is, the right to institute proceedings before courts in civil matters, constitutes one aspect. However, that right would be illusory if a Contracting State's domestic legal system allowed a final, binding judicial decision to remain inoperative to the detriment of one party. It would be inconceivable that Article 6(1) should describe in detail the procedural guarantees afforded to litigants – proceedings that are fair, public and expeditious – without protecting the implementation of judicial decisions. To construe Article 6 as being concerned exclusively with access to a court and the conduct of proceedings would indeed be likely to lead to situations incompatible with the principle of the rule of law which the Contracting States undertook to respect when they ratified the Convention. Execution of a judgment given by any court

---

[27] Cf., e.g., J.-P. Costa, 'La Cour Européenne des Droits de l'Homme: vers un ordre juridique européen?', in *Mélanges en hommage à L.E. Pettiti*, Bruxelles, Bruylant, 1998, pp. 197–8.

[28] On this distinct, traditional sense of *ordre public*, cf., e.g., J. Foyer, 'Droits internationaux de l'homme et ordre public international', in *Du droit interne au droit international – Mélanges R. Goy*, Rouen, Université de Rouen, 1998, pp. 333–48.

must therefore be regarded as an integral part of the 'trial' for the purposes of Article 6 (par. 38).

In a Colloquium held in 1996 by the University of Strasbourg and the *Cour de Cassation* on '*Les nouveaux développements du procès équitable*' in the sense of the European Convention of Human Rights, J.-F. Flauss rightly underlined the close relationship between access to a tribunal (by means of an effective remedy) and the *procès équitable*, and added that the right to the realization of justice also includes the faithful execution of the Judgment in favour of the victim.[29] In this respect, the Colloquium expressly recognized 'l'intimité profonde' between the access to justice (by means of a simple and effective remedy) and the right to a *procès équitable* (the guarantees of the due process of law), in the framework of the *État de Droit* in a democratic society.[30]

The international human rights case-law on the matter thus converges into the recognition of the right of access to justice *lato sensu*, as indicated in the present chapter. The right of access to justice (right to an effective remedy) is closely interrelated with the guarantees of the due process of law. The effective character of the remedy is linked to the notion of redress, with the guarantees of due process of law assured, bearing always in mind that sometimes non-derogable rights are at stake; in case of non-compliance with, or non-execution of, a judgment, the remedy at issue is not effective,[31] and there is no access to justice *lato sensu*.

It may further be pointed out that, in cases lodged with the African Commission on Human and Peoples' Rights (AfComHPR) concerning human rights protection in situations of armed conflict, the AfComHPR has stressed the fundamental character of non-derogable rights, which ought to be respected in all circumstances (including those of armed conflict). The AfComHPR has, moreover, acknowledged the close relationship between international human rights law and International Humanitarian Law (and the consequences of violations of one upon the other), drawing attention to the same principles underlying both sets of law (such as, e.g., the principle of humanity) and resorting to both of them to seek to secure the effective safeguard of the rights protected under the African Charter on Human and Peoples' Rights (ACHPR) in all situations, including in times of armed conflict.[32]

In fact, the AfComHPR has had the occasion to pronounce on the fundamental importance of the right of access to justice, properly understood *lato sensu*. Thus, in *Bissangou versus Republic of Congo* (2006), the Commission held that the right to be

---

[29] J.-F. Flauss, 'Les nouvelles frontières du procès équitable', in *Les nouveaux développements du procès équitable au sens de la Convention Européenne des Droits de l'Homme* (Actes du Colloque du 22 mars 1996), Bruxelles, Bruylant, 1996, pp. 88–9.

[30] G. Cohen-Jonathan, 'Conclusions générales des nouveaux développements du procès équitable au sens de la Convention Européenne des Droits de l'Homme', in *ibid.*, p. 172.

[31] D. de Bruyn, 'Le droit à un recours effectif', in *Les droits de l'homme au seuil du troisième millénaire – Mélanges en hommage à P. Lambert*, Bruxelles, Bruylant, 2000, pp. 198, 201 and 203.

[32] R. Murray, *The African Commission on Human and Peoples' Rights and International Law*, Oxford/Portland, Hart Publ., 2000, pp. 131, 133 and 142. In these latter, the AfComHPR has imposed duties on governments, insurgents and rebels, so as to secure better protection; moreover, parties to any conflict are bound to respect humanitarian as well as human rights law; *ibid.*, p. 139, and cf. p. 136.

heard by a court, guaranteed by Article 7 of the ACHPR, includes the right to the execution of the judgment. To interpret it in any other way 'would lead to situations which are incompatible with the rule of law'.[33] Thus, the AfComHPR added, the execution of a final judgment issued by a court constitutes 'an integral part of the 'right to be heard' which is protected by Article 7' of the ACHPR; furthermore, the refusal by a minister to honour the Court's judgment in favour of the complainant also amounted to a breach of the ACHPR.[34]

On another occasion, in *Zimbabwe Human Rights NGO Forum versus Zimbabwe* (2006), the AfComHPR, insisting that 'victims must have an effective remedy', further warned that the amnesty (Clemency Order n. 1) of 2000 prohibiting prosecution of, and setting free, perpetrators of 'politically motivated crimes', constituted 'a violation of the victims' right to judicial protection and to have their cause heard under Article 7(1) of the African Charter'.[35] The granting of amnesty 'to absolve perpetrators of human rights violations from accountability' encouraged impunity, rendered the victims 'helpless' and deprived them of justice, in violation of 'the right of victims to an effective remedy".[36] The AfComHPR has, in fact, attempted to safeguard the right of access to justice in the most distinct circumstances.[37]

V. Concluding Observations

The case-law of international human rights tribunals – such as the IACtHR and the ECtHR – provides support for the view that States Parties are bound to secure full access to justice, by means of the provision of effective domestic remedies, in conformity with the guarantees of due process of law. The interrelationship between access to justice and these guarantees soon emerged, and was fully endorsed, by the case-law of the IACtHR, which has consistently linked the consideration –with the corresponding reasoning – of alleged violations of Articles 8 and 25 of the ACHR. In sum, in the understanding of the IACtHR, judicial protection (Article 25) and judicial guarantees (Article 8) go hand in hand, in conformity with the *rule of law* (*État de droit*) in a democratic society, in the sense attributed to this latter by the ACHR.

The corresponding case-law of the ECtHR, in turn, has overcome vicissitudes of the past, and, after years of hesitation, now links the right to an effective remedy (Article 13) with the requirements of the due process of law (of Article 6). Likewise, its case-law has indicated that the two provisions contribute together to conform the *rule of law* (*État de droit*) in a democratic society, in the sense conferred upon

---

[33] Decision reproduced in: *Compendium of Key Human Rights Documents of the African Union* (eds. C. Heyns and M. Killander), Pretoria, Pretoria University Law Press (PULP), 2007, p. 180.

[34] Ibid., p. 180.

[35] Ibid., pp. 266 and 268.

[36] Ibid., p. 268.

[37] On the protection of victims in situations of great adversity (or defencelessness), cf. chapters VIII and IX, *infra*.

this latter by the ECHR. Although the two international human rights tribunals at issue followed initially distinct lines of evolution in their respective case-law on this issue, they have (the ECtHR more lately) come to a similar result, to the effect of enhancing the right of access to justice.

This latter, in the light of the nowadays converging case-law, is to be properly understood in the correct perspective, as comprising not only the right of formal access to justice, enabling individuals to initiate and pursue proceedings before international tribunals, but also the right to protection, to the guarantees of the due process of law, as well as the due and full compliance, by the State concerned, with judicial decisions. This means, ultimately, the right to the realization of justice, in the framework of the *rule of law* (*État de droit*) in a democratic society, in the sense attributed to this latter by the ACHR and the ECHR.

V

Access to International Justice in Relation to the Interaction between International Law and Domestic Law

I. Access to International Justice of Victims of Human Rights
   Violations: General Considerations   76

II. The Interaction between International Law and Domestic Law
   in Human Rights Protection   82

III. The Needed Revision or Control of Reservations to Human
   Rights Treaties   89

IV. The Interaction between International Law and Domestic Law
   and the Rule of Exhaustion of the Local Remedies   98

   1. Human Rights Treaties and the Role of National Courts   98

   2. The State's Duty to Provide Effective Local Remedies and the
      Individual's Duty to Have Recourse to Them: The Emphasis
      on Redress or the Realization of Justice   99

   3. The *Rationale* of the Local Remedies Rule in Human Rights
      Protection   100

V. The Principle of Complementarity in International Criminal Law   107

VI. Beyond Subsidiarity: State Responsibility, Substantive Law, and the
   Interaction between International Law and Domestic Law in the
   Present Domain of Protection   110

I. Access to International Justice of Victims of Human Rights Violations: General Considerations

The protection of human rights has occupied a central position in the international agenda of this first decade of the XXIst century.[1] The multiple international

---

[1] From the adoption of the 1948 Universal Declaration of Human Rights to today, the evolution of the international protection of human rights has undergone two global reassessments. Historically, the First World Conference on Human Rights (Teheran, 1968) represented, in a way, the gradual transition from the legislative phase, of elaboration of the earlier international instruments of human

instruments in the present domain, disclosing a fundamental unity of conception and purpose, started from the assumption that the protected rights are inherent to all human beings, thus pre-existing, and standing above, all forms of political organization. Therefore, those instruments have been made to operate on the understanding that initiatives for the protection of those rights are not – and cannot be – exhausted in the action of the State.

Due to the operation of the organs under these instruments in past decades, numerous victims have been assisted.[2] Due to the endeavours of international supervisory organs at global and regional levels, many lives have been spared, reparations have been granted, legislative measures have been adopted or modified, wrongful administrative practices have been terminated and positive measures and educational programmes have been adopted. International supervisory organs have thus also counted on initiatives at domestic law level. But despite these results, the supervisory organs today confront serious problems, generated mainly by the persistence of human rights violations in different parts of the world, by new and diversified forms of those violations (requiring of them greater agility and capacity of readaptation), and the insufficiency of human and material resources to undertake their work efficiently.

A recurrent challenge has been that of ensuring the individual's access to justice at national and international levels, bearing in mind the interactions between the international and the national legal orders in the present domain of protection. Virtually all existing mechanisms of international protection have been conceived and adopted as *responses* to different kinds of human rights violations.[3] As new needs of protection arise, new responses are needed. Despite all advances achieved in international protection, there occurs today a diversification of the sources of violations of human rights.[4]

---

rights (such as the two U.N. Covenants on Human Rights of 1966), to the phase of implementation of such instruments. The Second World Conference on Human Rights (Vienna, 1993) proceeded to a global reassessment of the application of those instruments and of the perspectives for the new century, paving the way for the examination of the process of consolidation and improvement of the mechanisms of international protection of human rights.

[2] Until to the early nineties, at U.N. level, for example, more than 350 thousand communications denouncing a consistent pattern of human rights violations had been forwarded to the United Nations (under the so-called extraconventional system of ECOSOC resolution 1503). As for the U.N. treaty bodies, under the Covenant on Civil and Political Rights and its first Optional Protocol, for example, the Human Rights Committee had received, up to the mid-nineties, more than 630 communications, and in 73% of the examined cases it concluded that there had occurred violations of human rights. The Committee on the Elimination of All Forms of Racial Discrimination, in its turn, had examined (under the Convention of the same name), in its first two decades of operation, 810 reports (periodical and complementary) of the States Parties. And the United Nations High-Commissioner for Refugees (UNHCR), after almost half a century of operation of the system, was taking care of more than 17 million refugees around the world, apart from internally displaced persons. Cf. data in A.A. Cançado Trindade, *Tratado de Direito Internacional dos Direitos Humanos*, vol. I, 2nd ed., Porto Alegre/Brazil, S.A. Fabris Ed., 2003, pp. 91–100; and cf. further *data*, as to international human rights systems at universal and regional levels, in A.A. Cançado Trindade, *Tratado de Direito Internacional dos Direitos Humanos*, vol. III, Porto Alegre/Brazil, S.A. Fabris Ed., 2003, pp. 27–233.

[3] For a general overview and perspectives, cf. A.A. Cançado Trindade, 'The Future of the International Protection of Human Rights', in *B. Boutros-Ghali Amicorum Discipulorumque Liber – Paix, Développement, Démocratie*, vol. II, Bruxelles, Bruylant, 1998, pp. 961–86.

[4] E.g., those perpetrated by clandestine groups of extermination without apparent signs of the presence of the State, or by financial agencies and the holders of economic power, or by the holders of

There is a significant need to conceive of new forms of protection of the human being in face of new threats. The current paradigm of protection (of the individual vis-à-vis public power) runs the risk of becoming insufficient and anachronistic and not being adequately equipped to confront those threats and violations. In the consideration of new responses, it should be kept in mind that, even in such new circumstances, the State remains responsible for omissions, for not taking positive measures of protection at domestic law level, in pursuance of its international conventional obligations, so as to avoid these violations taking place.

The current concern of international human rights supervisory organs to develop measures both of *prevention* and of *follow-up*, has, therefore, its *raison d'être*. *Prevention* is of the essence, e.g., of the three Conventions against Torture[5] and of the 1948 Convention for the Prevention and Punishment of the Crime of Genocide (Article 8).[6] In the domain of international human rights law, perhaps the most striking illustration of the preventive dimension lies in the jurisprudential construction[7] of the notion of victim (both direct and indirect), comprising the *potential* victim.[8] The 2002 Optional Protocol to the 1984 U.N. Convention against Torture purports to establish a preventive mechanism of regular and independent visits to places of detention,[9] so as to eradicate promptly and definitively the practice of torture.[10]

In the case of non-compliance with decisions of international supervisory organs, the current lack of follow-up procedures generates the problem not only of lack of information but also of lack of means to remedy adequately such situation.[11] In relation to both prevention and follow-up – which may become essential for the realization of justice in some cases – an important role is reserved for the U.N.

---

the power of communications, or else violations resulting from the resurgence of fundamentalist and religious ideologies and various other forms of intolerance, or from corruption and impunity. In the struggle against impunity, a positive initiative has consisted in the establishment of Truth Commissions in recent years in some countries, with distinct mandates and varying results of investigations.

[5] The Inter-American Convention, of 1985, Articles 1 and 6; the European Convention, of 1987, Article 1; and the Convention of the United Nations, of 1984, Articles 2(1) and 16.

[6] Already the *Compilation of International Instruments* of human rights, e.g., prepared by the former Human Rights Centre of the United Nations, for example, listed effectively no less than 13 international instruments devoted to the *prevention* of discrimination of distinct types. Cf. U.N. doc. ST/HR/1/Rev.3, of 1988, pp. 52–142.

[7] Above all under the European Convention on Human Rights.

[8] Cases *Kjeldsen versus Denmark* (1972), *Donnelly and Others versus United Kingdom* (1973), *H. Becker versus Denmark* (1975), *G. Klass and Others versus Germany* (1978), *Marckx versus Belgium* (1979), *Dudgeon versus United Kingdom* (1981), *J. Soering versus United Kingdom* (1989). For a study of this jurisprudential evolution, cf. A.A. Cançado Trindade, 'Co-existence and Co-ordination of Mechanisms of International Protection of Human Rights (At Global and Regional Levels)', 202 *Recueil des Cours de l'Académie de Droit International de La Haye* (1987) pp. 271–83.

[9] Cf. P.V. Kessing, 'New Optional Protocol to the U.N. Torture Convention', 72 *Nordic Journal of International Law* (2003) pp. 571–92.

[10] A mechanism reminiscent of that of the 1987 European Convention for the Prevention of Torture and Inhuman or Degrading Treatment or Punishment.

[11] J. Fodor, 'Future of Monitoring Bodies', *Canadian Human Rights Yearbook* (1991–1992) p. 188. The timely initiative of the Human Rights Committee of appointing a *rapporteur* to follow-up on its views under the U.N. Covenant on Civil and Political Rights and its first Optional Protocol was but one example of the possibilities of action in this regard; as measures of the kind are adopted and develop, a serious gap in the existing machinery of protection (under various human rights treaties) may gradually be filled.

High-Commissioner for Human Rights,[12] a key actor in the current endeavours to establish and consolidate a system of *continuous monitoring* of the observance of human rights in all countries, pursuant to the same criteria. Such monitoring would constitute, ultimately, the response, at procedural level, of the recognition obtained in the Second World Conference on Human Rights in 1993 of the legitimacy of the concern of the whole international community with human rights violations everywhere and at any time.

The Second World Conference on Human Rights drew attention, on the one hand, to the strengthening of the necessary national infrastructure and institutions for the protection of human rights (with the incorporation into the domestic law of States of the international norms of protection), and, on the other hand, to the mobilization of all sectors of the United Nations in favour of the promotion of human rights. From the compartmentalized action of the past, one began seeking to fulfil those objectives jointly and to achieve the incorporation of the dimension of human rights into all programmes and activities of the United Nations.

The observance and prevalance of human rights should be secured in all circumstances, including public emergencies. This draws attention to the necessity of controlling permissible limitations and derogations, as these latter may hinder access to justice. Considerable doctrinal endeavours have in fact been undertaken in recent years in order to give more precision to derogation clauses of human rights treaties, so as to avoid the repetition of human rights violations and abuses resulting, e.g., from the pathological prolongation of so-called states of exception and the chronic suspension of the exercise of rights, as occurred in the recent history of some countries. Such efforts have thus attempted to ensure that, even in situations of *bona fide* declaration of a state of emergency, the State at issue is to refrain from suspending non-derogable rights.[13]

Moreover, they have endeavoured to ensure that emergency measures comply with certain general requisites, namely: the principle of notification (of derogations), the principle of non-discrimination, the principle of proportionality to the exigencies of the situation, the principle of restrictive interpretation of derogations and limitations,[14] the consistency of the measures taken with the other international obligations of the State at issue, and the burden of proof upon the derogating State of the response to a public or social need (legitimate end).[15] Even in emergency cases not covered by human rights instruments or International Humanitarian

---

[12] A post created by the U.N. General Assembly on 20 December 1993, pursuant to a recommendation of II World Conference on Human Rights (of June 1993, held in Vienna).

[13] Such as those referred to by the U.N. Covenant on Civil and Political Rights, Article 4; the European Convention on Human Rights, Article 15; the American Convention on Human Rights, Article 27.

[14] To be foreseen in law and to be compatible with the object and purpose of human rights treaties.

[15] Cf. 'Report of the Committee: Minimum Standards of Human Rights Norms in a State of Exception', in *International Law Association – Report of the LXI Conference Held at Paris in 1984*, I.L.A., 1985, pp. 56–96; cf. also '*The Siracusa Principles on the Limitation and Derogation Provisions in the International Covenant on Civil and Political Rights*', in U.N., document E/CN.4/1985/4, of 28 September 1984, pp. 1–12, and in 7 *Human Rights Quarterly* (1985) pp. 3–14.

Law, all persons and groups remain under the protection of the principles of customary international law and the imperatives of humanity and public conscience.[16]

The protection of human rights is thus extended to states of exception and situations of emergency and subjected likewise to the rule of law. Judicial guarantees (such as, e.g., the remedy of *habeas corpus*) which are essential and indispensable to the protection of non-derogable rights (such as the right to life, the right not to be subjected to torture or slavery, the right not to be incriminated by means of retroactive application of penalties) and for the preservation of legality in a democratic society, can never be suspended.[17] The consideration of this issue is in constant evolution, in the sense of imposing restrictions on the recourse to limitations and derogations to the exercise of protected rights, of establishing with greater precision the conditions for their invocation, and of sustaining the intangibility and prevalence of judicial guarantees – essential to the realization of justice – in any circumstances.

It is not surprising that the 1993 Vienna Conference on Human Rights was particularly attentive to the condition of vulnerable groups and persons.[18] The First World Conference (Teheran, 1968) contributed, years earlier, with the global vision of the indivisibility of all human rights, overcoming resistances characteristic of the cold war period. The Second World Conference (Vienna, 1993), in turn, was bound to contribute to the same end by shifting attention to the means to secure such indivisibility *in practice*, with special regard to discriminated against or disadvantaged persons, to vulnerable groups, to the poor and to all those who are socially marginalized or excluded, in sum, to those in greater need of protection.[19] Nowadays, one and a half decades after the Second World Conference, the situation of victims of human rights violations in situations of great adversity or defencelessness still requires particular attention.[20]

Surely one of the greatest achievements of the international protection of human rights in historical perspective has been the process of its gradual *jurisdictionalization*, along with the access of individuals to international justice. There are clear illustrations

---

[16] Cf. Abo Akademi University, *Declaration of Minimum Humanitarian Standards*, Institute for Human Rights/Abo Akademi Univ., 1991, pp. 2–12.

[17] Cf., to this effect, the 8th and 9th Advisory Opinions (both of 1987) of the Inter-American Court of Human Rights, on the intangibility and prevalence of *habeas corpus* and of other judicial guarantees in states or situations of emergency.

[18] This was an issue which, already by the late eighties, was present in proposals and drafts then under consideration by the former U.N. Sub-Commission of Prevention of Discrimination and Protection of Minorities, the former U.N. Commission on Human Rights, and the U.N. General Assembly (migrant workers and their families, indigenous peoples, minorities, persons subjected to any forms of detention or imprisonment, the mentally ill, the victims of diseases and hunger). Cf. Th. van Boven, 'The Future Codification of Human Rights: Status of Deliberations – A Critical Analysis', 10 *Human Rights Law Journal* (1989) pp. 3–6.

[19] A.A. Cançado Trindade, 'Memória da Conferência Mundial de Direitos Humanos (Viena, 1993)', 87/90 *Boletim da Sociedade Brasileira de Direito Internacional* (1993–1994) pp. 9–57; A.A. Cançado Trindade, 'Balance de los Resultados de la Conferencia Mundial de Derechos Humanos (Viena, 1993)', in *Estudios Básicos de Derechos Humanos*, vol. 3, San José of Costa Rica, IIHR, 1995, pp. 17–45.

[20] Cf. chapters VIII and IX, *infra*.

of this above all in the two regional systems of human rights protection – the European and the Inter-American – endowed with international human rights tribunals in operation for a long time. Their international case-law has indeed secured reparations for the victims of violations of human rights, a domain in which further development is anticipated,[21] hence the overriding importance of securing to individuals direct access to international human rights tribunals.

The universal juridical conscience, as the ultimate material source of all law,[22] has nowadays reached a degree of evolution that acknowledges the permanent need to secure the individuals' right of direct access to international justice. Recent resolutions of the U.N. General Assembly, adopted by the end of 2005, expressly refer to access to justice.[23] In one of such resolutions (60/147, of 16 December 2005), the General Assembly endorsed the *Basic Principles and Guidelines on the Right to a Remedy and Reparation for Victims of Gross Violations of International Human Rights Law and Serious Violations of International Humanitarian Law*, elaborated and adopted by the former U.N. Commission on Human Rights (cf. *infra*), shortly after ECOSOC had done the same (in its resolution 2005/30, of 25 July 2005).

The former U.N. Commission on Human Rights itself had adopted its afore-mentioned document on *Basic Principles and Guidelines on the Right to a Remedy and Reparation for Victims* (by its resolution 2005/35) on 19 April 2005. The document, espousing a victim-oriented systematization of the right to an effective remedy and to adequate forms of reparation, takes into account – expressly, in its preamble – relevant international instruments. In the course of its preparatory work,[24] two decisions may be singled out, duly reflected in the text as adopted by the Commission. Firstly, it was decided, amidst some controversy, to focus

---

[21] Such reparations comprise, in addition to the indemnizations due to the aforementioned victims (in the light of the general principle of *neminem laedere*), the *restitutio in integrum* (reestablishment of the prior situation of the victim, whenever possible), the rehabilitation, the satisfaction, and, signifi-cantly, the guarantee of non-repetition of the acts or omissions in violation of human rights (the duty of prevention). The jurisprudential construction in respect of this issue, in particular that of the Inter-American Court, has developed considerably in recent years, in respect of each of those distinct forms of reparations. Cf., e.g., L. Hennebel, *La Convention Américaine des Droits de l'Homme – Mécanismes de protection et étendue des droits et libertés*, Bruxelles, Bruylant, 2007, pp. 275–312; D. Shelton, *Remedies in International Law*, Oxford, University Press, 2000, pp. 229–31 and 298–302; G. Citroni and K.I. Quintana Osuna, 'Reparations for Indigenous Peoples in the Case Law of the Inter-American Court of Human Rights', in *Reparations for Indigenous Peoples: International and Comparative Perspec-tives* (ed. F. Lenzerini), Oxford, University Press, 2008, pp. 317–44. And cf., on reparations in the European human rights system in general, e.g., L. Wildhaber, 'Reparations for Internationally Wrongful Acts of States – Article 41 of the European Convention on Human Rights: Just Satisfaction under the European Convention on Human Rights', 3 *Baltic Yearbook of International Law* (2003) pp. 1–18.

[22] A.A. Cançado Trindade, 'International Law for Humankind: Towards a New *Jus Gentium* – General Course on Public International Law – Part I', 316 *Recueil des Cours de l'Académie de Droit International de la Haye* (2005) pp. 177–202.

[23] Cf. U.N., General Assembly resolutions 60/159, of 16 December 2005 (on Human Rights in the Administration of Justice), and 60/161, of 16 December 2005 (on the 1998 Declaration on the Right and Responsibility of Individuals, Groups and Organs of Society to Promote and Protect Universally Recognized Human Rights and Fundamental Freedoms).

[24] For a succint account, cf. G. Echeverria, 'Codifying the Rights of Victims in International Law: Remedies and Reparation', in *Redressing Injustices through Mass Claims Processes* (ed. Permanent Court of Arbitration), Oxford, University Press, 2006, pp. 286–97.

specifically on *grave* violations, of international human rights law as well as of International Humanitarian Law. It was further decided that there was need to take account of the fact that persons could be victimized not only individually, but also collectively (preamble and Principle 8).

Reparations should thus be secured to injured persons or groups of persons, and should be proportional to the gravity of the violation and the harm suffered by them (Principle 15). The Commission's document stressed the relevance of securing effective and equal access to justice[25] – including the provision of assistance to victims seeking such access to justice – effective remedies and reparation for the harm suffered (Principles 11–12). The Commission's document added, *inter alia*, that 'obligations arising under international law to secure the right to access justice and fair and impartial proceedings shall be reflected in domestic laws' (Principle 12). Access to justice should also be secured not only to individual victims, but also to groups of victims (Principle 13). In addition, victims should be entitled to learn 'the causes leading to their victimization' and the truth in regard to the grave violations at issue of international human rights law and of International Humanitarian Law (Principle 24).

II. The Interaction between International Law and Domestic Law in Human Rights Protection

We have reached an age when there occurs a reassuring similarity of purpose between international law and domestic public law as to the protection of the human person in any circumstances. In fact, it is the international protection itself which requires national measures of implementation of international instruments of safeguard of human rights, as well as the strengthening of national institutions and procedures aimed at ensuring the full observance of human rights and the rule of law (*État de Droit*).[26] This brings to the fore an issue which seems to be acquiring increasing importance in contemporary debate, namely, that of the relations – or, more precisely, interaction – between international and national jurisdictions in the protection of human rights.[27]

Human rights treaties concluded under the auspices of the United Nations are to be approached through their effects upon the domestic law of States Parties, as it

---

[25] The basic principle of equality and non-discrimination permeates also the right of access to justice, that is, the right to effective remedies, and just and adequate reparation, according to the interpretation pursued in their practice by the international supervisory organs of U.N. human rights treaties; cf. W. Vandenhole, *Non-Discrimination and Equality in the View of the U.N. Human Rights Treaty Bodies*, Antwerpen/Oxford, Intersentia, 2005, pp. 254–5, 277 and 203.

[26] K. Vasak, 'Human Rights as a Legal Reality', *The International Dimensions of Human Rights* (eds. K. Vasak and Ph. Alston), vol. I, Paris, UNESCO/Greenwood, 1982, pp. 3–10; and cf. P.N. Drost, *Human Rights as Legal Rights*, Leyden, Sijthoff, 1965, pp. 61–75.

[27] Cf. A.A. Cançado Trindade, *Reflexiones sobre la Interacción entre el Derecho Internacional y el Derecho Interno en la Protección de los Derechos Humanos*, Guatemala City/Guatemala, Procuraduría de los Derechos Humanos (monograph 3–95), 1995, pp. 7–41; A.Z. Drzemczewski, *European Human Rights Convention in Domestic Law – A Comparative Study*, Oxford, Clarendon Press, 1983, pp. 59–62 and 326–47.

cannot be conceived that a State ratifies one such treaty, depriving it, at the same time, of direct effects in municipal law. Once ratified, there is no space for the invocation of sovereignty in the process of *interpretation* or *application* of such treaties.[28] Furthermore, in the course of the last six decades one has gradually and definitively overcome the objection of exclusive 'domestic jurisdiction', at the same time that the international procedural capacity of individuals and the capacity to act of (conventional and extraconventional) organs of international protection have been recognized and consolidated.

The two Vienna Conventions on the Law of Treaties (of 1969 and 1986, respectively) expressly prohibit (Article 27) a State Party to a treaty to invoke provisions of its domestic law in order to attempt to justify non-compliance with the obligations provided for by the treaty at issue. Beyond the law of treaties, this is a precept of the law of the international responsibility of the State. International (arbitral and judicial) case-law provides numerous examples of the engagement of the international responsibility of the State by any act or omission of any of its organs or agents – of the executive, legislative, or judicial power – in breach of treaty.

In my Separate Opinion in the *Massacre of Pueblo Bello* case, concerning Colombia, before the IACtHR (Judgment of 31 January 2006), I pondered that States Parties:

cannot invoke alleged difficulties or gaps of domestic law, as they are bound to harmonize this latter with the norms of human rights treaties to which they are Parties (American Convention on Human Rights Article 2; U.N. Covenant on Civil and Political Rights, Article 2(2); among others). This being so, if they invoke alleged difficulties or gaps of domestic law, so as not to provide simple and rapid and effective domestic remedies in order to give *effective* application to the international norms of protection of human rights, they are incurring into an *additional* violation of the human rights treaties to which they are Parties (par. 23).

It has, furthermore, been reckoned that the interpretation and application of human rights treaties – which incorporate obligations endowed with an objective character – have been guided by considerations of a superior general interest or *ordre public* which transcend the individual interests of States Parties.[29] Thus,

---

[28]　According to well-established case-law (from that of the PCIJ, in the 1920s and 1930s, to the ICJ case-law), a State Party cannot invoke alleged difficulties of internal or constitutional order in attempting to justify non-compliance with its international obligations. This *jurisprudence constante* holds that international obligations ought to be complied with in good faith, without invoking provisions or alleged difficulties of constitutional or domestic law to evade or circumvent them. Cf. PCIJ, the case of the *Greek-Bulgarian Communities* (1930), Series B, n. 17, p. 32; PCIJ, the case of the *Polish Nationals in Danzig* (1931), Series A/B, n. 44, p. 24; PCIJ, the case of the *Free Zones* (1932), Series A/B, n. 46, p. 167; ICJ, the case of the *Applicability of the Obligation to Arbitrate under the Headquarters Agreement of the United Nations* (case of the *PLO Mission*), *ICJ Reports* (1988) pp. 31–2, par. 47. This applies even more forcefully in the domain of the international protection of human rights, inspired by common superior values, the contents of which constitute a matter of international *ordre public*.

[29]　A.A. Cançado Trindade, 'The Interpretation of the International Law of Human Rights by the Two Regional Human Rights Courts', in *Contemporary International Law Issues: Conflicts and Convergence*

variations as to the *status*, in domestic law, of international norms of protection[30] (a matter delegated by international law to the constitutional law of each country) could not be construed in a way that attempted to revoke conventional obligations, as that would clash with the very notion of *collective guarantee* underlying all human rights treaties.

In the present domain of protection of the human person, it is no longer justified that international law and domestic law are continually approached in a compartmentalized way, as they were in the past. In creating obligations for States Parties vis-à-vis the human beings under their jurisdiction, the norms of human rights treaties apply not only in the joint action (exercise of the collective guarantee) of the States Parties in the realization of the common purpose of protection, but also and above all in the ambit of the domestic legal order of each of them, in the relations between public power and individuals.

Compliance with conventional obligations of protection requires the operation of the internal organs of the States Parties, which are called upon to apply international norms. This is one of the most distinctive features of human rights treaties, endowed with a specificity of their own.[31] In the present domain, international law and domestic law are in a constant interaction, the great beneficiaries being the protected persons. It is thus quite clear that subsequent laws cannot revoke conventional norms which bind the State, above all in the domain of human rights protection.

There is need to strengthen the role of the human rights treaty obligations in the ambit of the domestic legal order. Not only should national laws be interpreted in such a way as not to conflict with the international norms of protection (even if one fails to attribute expressly to treaties primacy over national legislation), but the special character of human rights treaties – requiring the harmonization of domestic law with their norms of protection – is to be clearly recognized.[32] Moreover, as human rights treaties incorporate concepts endowed by jurisprudence with an autonomous meaning and as the object and purpose of human rights treaties are distinct from those of treaties of the classic type (as the former pertain to the relations between the State concerned and the human beings under its jurisdiction), the classic postulates of interpretation of treaties in general are adjusted to this new

(Proceedings of the III Hague Conference, July 1995), The Hague, ASIL/Asser Inst., 1996, pp. 157–62 and 166–7.

[30] For a study, cf., e.g., A.Z. Drzemczewski, *European Human Rights Convention* in *Domestic Law...*, *op. cit. supra* n. (27), pp. 1–347; C. Sciotti-Lam, *L'applicabilité des traités internationaux relatifs aux droits de l'homme en droit interne*, Bruxelles, Bruylant, 2004, pp. 29–626.

[31] For a pioneering study of the specificity of the International Law of Human Rights, cf. K. Vasak, 'Le droit international des droits de l'homme', 140 *Recueil des Cours de l'Académie de Droit International* [RCADI] (1974) pp. 343–413.

[32] A. Cassese, 'Modern Constitutions and International Law', 192 *RCADI* (1985) pp. 398–401. And cf. further, e.g., 'Protection constitutionnelle et protection internationale des droits de l'homme: concurrence ou complémentarité? (9e. Conférence des Cours constitutionnelles européennes – Paris, 1993)', 7 *Revue universelle des droits de l'homme* (1995) pp. 217–94; L. Favoreu (coord.), 'Vers un Droit constitutionnel européen – Quel Droit constitutionnel européen? (Actes du Colloque de Strasbourg, 1993)', 7 *Revue universelle des droits de l'homme* (1995) pp. 357–456.

framework,[33] without in any way detracting from the general rules of interpretation of treaties.[34]

There are human rights treaties which enshrine, parallel to the specific duties of protection of States Parties of the rights set forth thereunder, their general duties to respect and *to ensure respect* for the protected rights, and to harmonize their domestic law with the provisions of those human rights treaties. As to the former, the general and fundamental duty to respect and to ensure respect for the protected rights, stipulated in Article 1(1) of the ACHR, is in parallel with that found in other treaties on the safeguard of the rights of the human person, such as the Covenant on Civil and Political Rights (Article 2(1)), the Convention on the Rights of the Child (Articles 2(1) and 38(1)), the four Geneva Conventions of 1949 on International Humanitarian Law (Article 1) and the Additional Protocol I of 1977 to these latter (Article 1(1)).

The general duty to harmonize domestic law with conventional provisions, set forth in Article 2 of the ACHR, also has equivalents, in its Additional Protocol of 1988 on Economic, Social and Cultural Rights (Article 2), in the Covenant on Civil and Political Rights (Article 2(2)),[35] in the African Charter on Human and Peoples' Rights (Article 1), and in the U.N. Convention against Torture and Other Cruel, Inhuman or Degrading Treatment or Punishment (Article 2(1)). The two afore-mentioned general obligations – as I maintained in my Dissenting Opinion (pars. 9–10) in the case, decided by the IACtHR, of *Caballero Delgado and Santana versus Colombia* (reparations, Judgment of 29 January 1997) – appear to be inextricably intertwined. Hence, the breach of Article 2 always brings about, in my view, a violation of its Article 1(1). As I stated in my aforementioned Dissenting Opinion:

The violation of Article 1(1) takes place whenever there is a breach of Article 2. And in cases of violation of Article 1(1) there is a strong presumption of non-compliance with Article 2, by virtue, e.g., of insufficiencies or lacunae of the domestic legal order as to the regulation of the conditions of the exercise of the protected rights. There is, likewise, no underestimating of the obligation of Article 2, inasmuch as it confers precision on the immediate and fundamental obligation of Article 1(1), of which it appears as almost a corollary. The obligation of Article 2 requires the adoption of the legislation needed to give effect to the conventional norms of protection, filling in eventual lacunae or insufficiencies in the domestic law, or else the modification of national legal provisions so as to harmonize them with the conventional norms of protection (par. 9).

---

[33] A.A. Cançado Trindade, *Tratado*..., vol. II, *op. cit. infra* n. (75), pp. 32–4; and cf. also R. Bernhardt, 'Thoughts on the Interpretation of Human Rights Treaties', in *Protecting Human Rights: The European Dimension – Studies in Honour of G.J. Wiarda* (eds. F. Matscher and H. Petzold), Köln, C. Heymanns, 1988, pp. 66–7 and 70–1; Erik Suy, 'Droit des traités et droits de l'homme', in *Völkerrecht als Rechtsordnung Internationale Gerichtsbarkeit Menschenrechte – Festschrift für H. Mosler* (eds. R. Bernhardt *et alii*), Berlin, Springer-Verlag, 1983, pp. 935–47; J. Velu and R. Ergec, *La Convention européenne des droits de l'homme*, Bruxelles, Bruylant, 1990, p. 51.
[34] Set forth in Articles 31–3 of the two Vienna Conventions on the Law of Treaties (of 1969 and 1986).
[35] Provision which served as source of Article 2 of the American Convention on Human Rights, which was only included in this latter at an already late stage of its preparatory work. Cf. OAS, *International Specialized Conference on Human Rights – Proceedings and Documents* (San José of Costa Rica, 07–22 July 1969), doc. OEA/Ser.K/XVI/1.2, pp. 38, 104, 146, 148, 295, 309, 440 and 481.

Thus, the international obligations of protection, which in their wide scope are incumbent upon all the powers (executive, legislative, and judiciary), organs, and agents of the State, comprise those which pertain to each of the protected rights, as well as the additional general obligations to respect and guarantee these latter, and to harmonize domestic law with the conventional norms of protection (par. 10). Human rights violations and reparations for damages resulting therefrom ought to be determined under the ACHR bearing in mind the specific obligations pertaining to each of the protected rights in conjunction with the general obligations enshrined in Articles 1(1) and 2 of the Convention.[36]

Recognition of the *interrelation* of these two general obligations would constitute a step forward in the evolution of the matter. Furthermore, it discloses the interaction between international law and domestic law in the present domain of protection. Herein, international law and domestic law are indeed in constant interaction: *national* measures of implementation, particularly those of legislative character, assume crucial importance for the future of the *international* protection of human rights itself.[37]

The general obligation to bring domestic law into conformity with human rights treaties requires that the necessary legislation be adopted to give effect to the conventional norms of protection, filling eventual gaps in domestic law, or else that domestic legal provisions be altered in order to harmonize them with the conventional norms of protection.[38] This, in turn, comes to foster the individual's right of access to justice at international level. As all State powers are bound by the conventional obligations of protection, the executive power ought to take all possible measures – administrative and otherwise – to comply faithfully with those obligations. The international responsibility for human rights violations survives governments, precisely for being responsibility of the *State*. The legislative power, in turn, ought to take all measures within its ambit of competence, either to regulate human rights treaties so as to secure their effectiveness at domestic law level, or to alter national laws in order to harmonize them with the provisions of those treaties. And the judicial power ought to apply the treaty norms in the domestic legal order effectively, and to ensure that they are respected.

This means that the national legislature and the judiciary have a duty to provide and apply effective local remedies against violations not only of the rights constitutionally foreseen but also of the rights enshrined in human rights treaties which bind the State at issue. Non-compliance with conventional norms of protection promptly engages the international responsibility of the State, for act or omission, either of the executive

[36] Cf., to this effect, my Dissenting Opinion in the case of *El Amparo versus Venezuela* (reparations, Judgment of 14 September 1996), par. 4.

[37] Cf., in this sense, my Dissenting Opinion in the case of *Caballero Delgado and Santana versus Colombia* (reparations, Judgment of 29 January 1997), par. 20.

[38] Such general obligation, to be duly complied with, naturally implies the co-ordinated operation of all powers, organs and agents of the State. In any case, the classic issue of the relationship between international and domestic law can no longer be approached from a static outlook; cf., generally, C. Santulli, *Le statut international de l'ordre juridique interne – Étude du traitement du droit interne par le droit international*, Paris, Pédone, 2001, pp. 41–469.

power, or the legislative power, or the judiciary. In our days, there continues to exist a pressing need to secure national measures of implementation of international instruments, the adoption and improvement of which is now crucial for the future improvement of the international protection of human rights.

The advances of the *international* protection of human rights also depend nowadays, to a large extent, on *national* measures of implementation. The emphasis on the relevance and urgency of those national measures cannot lose sight of the fact that international standards of protection cannot be lowered; on the contrary, they ought to be preserved and raised. There is a need to understand better the conventional obligations of protection, as the international responsibility of the State Party may indeed be engaged by any act or omission of any of its organs or agents – of the executive, legislative, or judicial power – in breach of the human rights treaties. In the present domain of protection, as already pointed out, international law and domestic law are in a constant interaction.

In addition to measures of implementation of human rights treaties, international protection also requires the strengthening of national institutions linked to the full observance of human rights and the rule of law (*État de Droit*). International instruments of protection were conceived for the realization of the basic purpose of the full observance of human rights. The application of international norms of protection aims at improving, rather than challenging, the domestic norms, to the benefit of all protected human beings. Domestic law is bound to secure better protection to the extent that it incorporates the standards of protection required by human rights treaties. A clear comprehension of this fundamental unity of purpose requires, nevertheless, a change of mentality.

International instruments of protection were conceived and adopted for the realization of the basic purpose of the full observance of human rights, particularly in cases of insufficiencies of the domestic legal order. The application of international norms of protection is meant to improve, rather than to challenge, domestic norms, to the benefit of all protected human beings. Domestic law is bound to secure better protection to the extent that it incorporates the standards of protection required by human rights treaties. A clear comprehension of this fundamental unity of purpose between international law and internal public law in the context of human rights protection still requires, however, a change of mentality. In the present domain, international and domestic jurisdictions complement each other in the constant struggle against all manifestations of arbitrary power.

Several contemporary national Constitutions, expressly referring to human rights treaties, grant special or differential treatment at domestic law level to internationally recognized human rights, and human rights treaties themselves allow for compatibility to be found between conventional provisions and those of domestic law so as to prevent conflicts between international and national jurisdictions in the present domain of protection. Thus, they make it incumbent upon States Parties to provide effective local remedies, and at times to develop the possibilities of judicial remedy; they set forth permissible limitations and derogations, to be restrictively interpreted; they foresee the general duty of adoption by States Parties of legislative, judicial, administrative, and other measures, for the realization of their object and purpose. In sum, they count on the operation of the organs and procedures of domestic public law. There is, thus, an interplay between the international and national jurisdictions in the present ambit of protection to the benefit of the protected persons.[39]

In an integrated system such as that of human rights protection, domestic acts and omissions of States are subject to the supervision of the international organs, when, in the examination of concrete cases, their conformity with international human rights obligations is to be verified. International norms which provide for, and clearly define, an individual right susceptible of vindication before a national court or judge, are directly applicable in domestic law. In the past, relations between international law and domestic law in general were focused *ad nauseam* on the classic and sterile polemic between dualists and monists, erected on false premises. In the vindication of his or her rights, the human person is a subject of domestic law as well as of international law, endowed in both with legal personality and capacity. It is clear that the coincidence of objectives between international law and domestic law, insofar as the protection of the human person is concerned, is to be pursued to its last consequences.

Bearing in mind, on the one hand, the express provisions of human rights treaties and the functions of protection conferred by them upon the organs of the State, and, on the other hand, the opening of contemporary constitutional law – and their *renvoi* – to the rights internationally recognized, there is no longer any sense in insisting – as used to be the case– upon the primacy of the norms of international law or of domestic law, from a purely theoretical standpoint.[40] In fact, human rights treaties themselves significantly and expressly provide for the criterion of the primacy of the *norms most favourable to the alleged victims*,[41] be they norms of international or domestic origin. It is, ultimately, the norm which best protects the human person that always ought to prevail.

---

[39] A.A. Cançado Trindade, *Reflexiones sobre la Interacción...*, *op. cit. supra* n. (27), pp. 7–41, also for references to new trends in contemporary constitutionalism.

[40] On the overcoming of the old and static polemics between dualists and monists, cf., e.g., G. Sperduti, 'Dualism and Monism: A Confrontation to Be Overcome', 3 *Italian Yearbook of International Law* (1977) pp. 31–49; A. Drzemczewski, 'Les faux débats entre monisme et dualisme – Droit international et droit français: L'exemple du contentieux des droits de l'homme', 51 *Boletim da Sociedade Brasileira de Direito Internacional* (1998) n. 113/118, pp. 95–109. And, for an early consideration on 'la pénétration des droits de l'homme dans le droit interne', cf. Ph. Vegleris, 'Préliminaire à la méthodologie des droits de l'homme', in *René Cassin Amicorum Discipulorumque Liber*, vol. IV, Paris, Pédone, 1972, pp. 25–8. And, on the impact of the principle of the '*effet utile*' in the penetration of the norms of international community law into the domestic law of the States concerned, cf. P. Pescatore, 'Monisme, dualisme et "effet utile" dans la jurisprudence de la Cour de Justice de la Communauté Européenne', in *Une communauté de droit – Festschrift für G.C. Rodríguez Iglesias* (eds. N. Colneric *et alii*), Berlin, Berliner Wissenschafts-Verlag, 2003, pp. 330, 332 and 342. And cf. note (85), *infra*.

[41] E.g., U.N. Covenant on Civil and Political Rights, Article 5(2); Convention on the Elimination of All Forms of Discrimination against Women, Article 23; Convention on the Rights of the Child, Article 41; European Convention on Human Rights, Article 60; European Convention for the Prevention of Torture and Inhuman or Degrading Treatment or Punishment, Article 17(1); European Social Charter, Article 32; American Convention on Human Rights, Article 29(b); Additional Protocol to the American Convention on Human Rights in the Matter of Economic, Social and Cultural Rights, Article 4.

III. The Needed Revision or Control of Reservations to Human Rights Treaties

In the same line of reasoning, attention is to be increasingly turned to the need to safeguard the *integrity* of human rights treaties.[42] Some of the latter remain, for example, permeated with reservations, many of which appear manifestly incompatible with their object and purpose. There is, in fact, pressing need to proceed to a wide revision or control of the present system of reservations to multilateral treaties set forth in the two Vienna Conventions on the Law of Treaties (of 1969 and 1986), especially as regards human rights treaties, which find inspiration in common superior values and are applied pursuant to the notion of *collective guarantee*. In my Separate Opinion (pars. 8–29) in the *Blake versus Guatemala* case (Reparations, Judgment of 22 January 1999), as well as in my Separate Opinion (pars. 8–29) in the *Caesar versus Trinidad and Tobago* case (Judgment of 11 March 2005),[43] both decided by the IACtHR, I sought to demonstrate the inadequacy of the current reservations system to human rights treaties, and the need to revise it, so as to secure safer and wider access to international justice. The main points of my arguments may be recalled as follows.

International supervisory organs in the domain of human rights protection have in recent years disclosed their awareness – and, on some occasions, their determination – to the effect of preserving the integrity of human rights treaties. It may be recalled that, inspired in the criterion supported by the ICJ in its Advisory Opinion of 1951 on the *Reservations to the Convention against Genocide*,[44] the present system of reservations set forth in the two Vienna Conventions of the Law of Treaties (of 1969 and 1986, Articles 19–23),[45] in joining the formulation of reservations to the acquiescence or the objections thereto for the determination of their compatibility with the object and purpose of the treaties, is of a markedly voluntarist and contractualist character.

Such a system leads to a fragmentation (in the bilateral relations) of the conventional obligations of the States Parties to multilateral treaties, appearing inadequate

---

[42] Cf. chapter VI, *infra*.

[43] The texts of those two Separate Opinions are reproduced in: A.A. Cançado Trindade, *Derecho Internacional de los Derechos Humanos – Esencia y Trascendencia (Votos en la Corte Interamericana de Derechos Humanos, 1991–2006)*, Mexico, Edit. Porrúa/Univ. Iberoamericana, 2007, pp. 186–204 and 508–38, respectively.

[44] In which, it may be recalled, the Hague Court endorsed the so-called Pan-American practice relating to reservations to treaties, given its flexibility, and in search of a certain balance between the *integrity* of the text of the treaty and the *universality* of participation in it; hence the criterion of the compatibility of the reservations with the object and purpose of the treaties. Cf. *ICJ Reports* (1951) pp. 15–30; and cf., *a contrario sensu*, the Joint Dissenting Opinion of Judges Guerrero, McNair, Read and Hsu Mo (pp. 31–48), as well as the Dissenting Opinion of Judge Álvarez (pp. 49–55), for the difficulties generated by this criterion.

[45] That is, the Vienna Convention on the Law of Treaties of 1969, and the Vienna Convention on the Law of Treaties between States and International Organizations or between International Organizations of 1986, to which one may add, in the same sense, the Vienna Convention on Succession of States in the Matter of Treaties of 1978 (Article 20).

to human rights treaties, which are inspired in superior common values and are applied in conformity with the notion of *collective guarantee*. That system of reservations[46] suffers from notorious insufficiencies when transposed from the law of treaties in general into the domain of international human rights law. To start with, it does not distinguish between human rights treaties and classic treaties, in contrast to the *jurisprudence constante* of the organs of international supervision of human rights, which converge in pointing out such a distinction.

It allows reservations (which have not been objected to) of a wide scope which threaten the very integrity of human rights treaties; it allows reservations (not objected) to provisions of these treaties which incorporate universal minimum standards (undermining, e.g., the basic judicial guarantees of inviolable rights). If certain fundamental rights – starting with the right to life – are non-derogable (in the terms of the human rights treaties themselves), thereby not admitting any derogations which, by definition, are of an essentially temporal or transitory character –it would seem to me, *a fortiori*, they should not admit any reservations, perpetuated in time until and unless withdrawn by the State at issue; such reservations would be, in my understanding, without any *caveat*, incompatible with the object and purpose of those treaties.

Although the two Vienna Conventions on the Law of Treaties prohibit the acceptance of reservations incompatible with the object and purpose of the treaty at issue, they leave, however, various questions without answers. The criterion of compatibility is applied in the relations with the States which effectively objected to the reservations, although such objections are often motivated by factors – including political – other than a sincere and genuine concern on the part of the objecting States with the prevalence of the object and purpose of the treaty at issue. For the same reason, from the silence or acquiescence of the States Parties in relation to certain reservations one cannot necessarily infer a belief on their part that the reservations are compatible with the object and purpose of the treaty at issue.

Such silence or acquiescence, moreover, appears to undermine the application of the criterion of the compatibility of a reservation with the object and purpose of the treaty. And the two Vienna Conventions referred to are not clear, either, as to the legal effects of a non-permissible reservation, or of an objection to a reservation considered incompatible with the object and purpose of the treaty at issue. They do not clarify, either, who ultimately ought to determine the permissibility or otherwise of a reservation, or to pronounce on its compatibility or otherwise with the object and purpose of the treaty at issue.

The present system of reservations ends up permitting even reservations (which have not been objected to) which hinder the possibilities of action of the international supervisory organs, rendering difficult the realization of the object and purpose of the respective human rights treaties. The aforementioned Vienna Conventions not only fail to establish a mechanism to determine the compatibility or otherwise of a

---

[46] Endorsed, e.g., by the American Convention on Human Rights (cross-reference of Article 75).

reservation with the object and purpose of a given treaty,[47] but – even more gravely – do not prevent either that certain reservations or restrictions formulated (in the acceptance of the jurisdiction of the organs of international protection),[48] come to hinder the operation of the mechanisms of international supervision created by the human rights treaties in the exercise of the collective guarantee.

The present system of reservations, reminiscent of the old Pan-American practice, rescued by the ICJ[49] and the two Vienna Conventions on the Law of Treaties, and having crystallized itself in the relations between States, not surprisingly appears entirely inadequate to the treaties whose ultimate beneficiaries are individuals and not the Contracting Parties. Definitively, human rights treaties, focused on the relations between States and human beings under their jurisdiction, do not bear a system of reservations which approaches them from an essentially contractual and voluntarist perspective, undermining their integrity, allowing their fragmentation and leaving at the discretion of the Parties themselves the final determination of the extent of their conventional obligations.

As the two Vienna Conventions of 1969 and 1986 do not provide any indication for an objective application of the criterion of the compatibility or otherwise of a reservation with the object and purpose of a treaty, they leave it, on the contrary, to be applied individually and subjectively by the Contracting Parties themselves, in such a way that, at the end, only the reserving State knows for sure the extent of the implications of its own reservation. Despite the efforts in expert writing to the effect of systematizing the practice of States on the matter,[50] it is difficult to avoid the

---

[47] As neither the aforementioned Vienna Conventions, nor – prior to them – the cited Advisory Opinion of the ICJ on *Reservations to the Convention against Genocide*, define what constitutes the compatibility or otherwise (of a reservation) with the object and purpose of a treaty, the determination is left to the interpretation of this latter, without it having been defined either on whom falls that determination, in what way and when it should be made. At the time of the adoption of that Advisory Opinion (1951), neither the majority of the Hague Court, nor the dissenting Judges on the occasion, foresaw the development of the international supervision of human rights by the conventional organs of protection; hence the insufficiencies of the solution then advanced, and endorsed years later by the two aforementioned Vienna Conventions on the Law of Treaties.

[48] There is a distinction between a reservation *stricto sensu* and a restriction in the instrument of acceptance of the jurisdiction of an international supervisory organ, even though their legal effects are similar.

[49] The Advisory Opinion of the ICJ on the *Reservations to the Convention against Genocide* (1951) marked the gradual passage, in the matter of reservations to treaties, from the rule of unanimity (of its approval by the States Parties), to the test of its compatibility with the object and purpose of the treaty. In a general way, the Vienna Convention incorporated the flexible Pan-American doctrine on reservations, in accordance with a tendency to this effect of the international practice already formed in the epoch; I.M. Sinclair, 'Vienna Conference on the Law of Treaties', 19 *International and Comparative Law Quarterly* (1970) pp. 47–69; and cf. Articles 19–20 of the Vienna Convention.

[50] Cf., e.g., J.M. Ruda, 'Reservations to Treaties', 146 *Recueil des Cours de l'Académie de Droit International de La Haye* (1975) pp. 95–218; D.W. Bowett, 'Reservations to Non-Restricted Multilateral Treaties', 48 *British Year Book of International Law* (1976–1977) pp. 67–92; P.-H. Imbert, *Les réserves aux traités multilatéraux*, Paris, Pédone, 1979, pp. 9–464; K. Holloway, *Les réserves dans les traités internationaux*, Paris, LGDJ, 1958, pp. 1–358; K. Zemanek, 'Some Unresolved Questions Concerning Reservations in the Vienna Convention on the Law of Treaties', *Essays in International Law in Honour of Judge Manfred Lachs* (ed. J. Makarczyk), The Hague, Nijhoff, 1984, pp. 323–36; Ch. Tomuschat, 'Admissibility and Legal Effects of Reservations to Multilateral Treaties', 27 *Zeitschrift für ausländisches öffentliches Recht und Völkerrecht* (1967) pp. 463–82; F. Horn, *Reservations and*

impression that such practice has been surrounded by uncertainties and ambiguities, and has remained inconclusive to date. This lack of definition is not at all reassuring for human rights treaties, endowed as they are with mechanisms of international supervision of their own. This general picture of uncertainty has thus, not surprisingly, led the U.N. International Law Commission (ILC) to engage itself, in 1998, in the preparation of a Draft Practical Guide on Reservations to Treaties.[51]

It draws one's attention, for example, to find an extensive list of reservations, numerous and at times long, and often incongruous, of States Parties to the U.N. Covenant on Civil and Political Rights;[52] and the practical problems generated by many of the reservations (also numerous and not always consistent) of the States Parties to the U.N. Convention on the Elimination of All Forms of Discrimination against Women are well-known, to which one may add the reservations to the U.N. Convention against Torture and the Convention on the Elimination of All Forms of Racial Discrimination.[53]

With persistent inadequacies and insufficiencies of the present system of reservations, it is not at all surprising that, firstly, multiple expressions of dissatisfaction appear in contemporary legal doctrine (both in general studies on the matter[54] and in respect of specific human rights treaties[55]); and secondly, human rights international supervisory organs seem prepared to assert their competence to apply by themselves the criterion of the compatibility (*supra*) and to contribute thereby to secure the integrity of the respective human rights treaties.

At regional level, in its well-known judgment in the *Belilos versus Switzerland* case (1988),[56] *locus classicus* on the issue, the ECtHR considered the declaration

---

Interpretative Declarations to Multilateral Treaties, Uppsala, Swedish Institute of International Law, 1988, pp. 184–222.

[51] Cf. U.N., *Report of the International Law Commission on the Work of Its 50th Session* (1998), *General Assembly Official Records* – Supplement n. 10(A/53/10), pp. 195–214 ('Reservations to Treaties: Guide to Practice').

[52] Compiled by the Secretary-General of the United Nations and collected in the document: U.N., CCPR/C/2/Rev.4, of 24 August 1994, pp. 1–139 (English version), and pp. 1–160 (Spanish version).

[53] For a study of the problems created by the reservations to these four human rights treaties of the United Nations, cf. L. Lijnzaad, *Reservations to U.N. Human Rights Treaties – Ratify and Ruin?*, Dordrecht, Nijhoff, 1995, pp. 131–424.

[54] Cf. D. Shelton, 'State Practice on Reservations to Human Rights Treaties', 1 *Canadian Human Rights Yearbook/Annuaire canadien des droits de la personne* (1983) pp. 205–34; C. Redgwell, 'Universality or Integrity? Some Reflections on Reservations to General Multilateral Treaties', 64 *British Year Book of International Law* (1993) pp. 245–82; L. Lijnzaad, *op. cit. supra* n. (49), pp. 3–424; M. Coccia, 'Reservations to Multilateral Treaties on Human Rights', 15 *California Western International Law Journal* (1985) pp. 1–49; L. Sucharipa-Behrmann, 'The Legal Effects of Reservations to Multilateral Treaties', 1 *Austrian Review of International and European Law* (1996) pp. 67–88.

[55] Cf. B. Clark, 'The Vienna Convention Reservations Regime and the Convention on Discrimination against Women', 85 *American Journal of International Law* (1991) pp. 281–321; W.A. Schabas, 'Reservations to the Convention on the Rights of the Child', 18 *Human Rights Quarterly* (1996) pp. 472–91; A. Sanchez Legido, 'Algunas Consideraciones sobre la Validez de las Reservas al Convenio Europeo de Derechos Humanos', 20 *Revista Jurídica de Castilla – La Mancha* (1994) pp. 207–30; C. Pilloud, 'Reservations to the Geneva Conventions of 1949', *International Review of the Red Cross* (March/April 1976) pp. 3–44.

[56] Followed by the *Weber* case (1990).

amounting to a reservation (of a general character) of Switzerland to the ECHR incompatible with the object and purpose of this latter (in the light of its Article 64). In its turn, the IACtHR, in its 2nd and 3rd Advisory Opinions,[57] pointed out the difficulties of a pure and simple transposition from the system of reservations of the Vienna Convention on the Law of Treaties of 1969 into the domain of the international protection of human rights.

At global level, in the *I. Gueye et alii versus France* case (1989), e.g., the Human Rights Committee (under the U.N. Covenant on Civil and Political Rights), in spite of a reservation *ratione temporis* of the respondent State,[58] understood that the question at issue[59] was justiciable under the Covenant,[60] and concluded that there was a violation of Article 26 of the Covenant.[61] The same Committee, in its *general comment* n. 24(52), of November 1994, warned that the provisions of the two Vienna Conventions and the classic rules on reservations (based upon reciprocity) were not appropriate to the human rights treaties; given the special character of the Covenant as a human rights treaty, the question of the compatibility of a reservation with its object and purpose, instead of being left to the discretion of the States Parties *inter se*, should be objectively determined, on the basis of legal principles, by the Human Rights Committee itself.[62]

Given the specificity of international human rights law, there appears to exist a strong case for leaving the determination of the compatibility or otherwise of reservations with the object and purpose of human rights treaties with the international supervisory organs established by them, rather than with the States Parties themselves; it would be more in keeping with the special character of human rights treaties. To the two international human rights tribunals (the European and Inter-American Courts), the individualistic system of reservations does not seem to be in keeping with the notion of collective control machinery proper to human rights treaties. The *obiter dicta* of the two regional human rights Courts have been rendered despite the fact that the ECHR (Article 64)[63] and the ACHR (Article 75) do not expressly confer this function upon them; the ACHR, in fact, limits itself to referring to the pertinent provisions of the 1969 Vienna Convention on the Law of Treaties.

---

[57] In its 3rd Advisory Opinion on *Restrictions to the Death Penalty* (1983) the Court warned that the question of reciprocity as related to reservations did not fully apply vis-à-vis human rights treaties (pars. 62–3 and 65). Earlier on, in its 2nd Advisory Opinion on the *Effect of Reservations on the Entry into Force of the American Convention* (1982), the Court dismissed the postponement of the entry into force of the American Convention by application of Article 20(4) of the 1969 Vienna Convention (par. 34).

[58] To Article 1 of the [first] Optional Protocol to the Covenant on Civil and Political Rights.

[59] Pertaining to pension benefits of more than 700 retired Senegalese members of the French army.

[60] As the effects of the French legislation on the matter lasted until then.

[61] Communication n. 196/1985, decision of 03 April 1989 (and previous decision of admissibility of 05 November 1987).

[62] Paragraphs 17 and 20; text in: U.N./Human Rights Committee, document CCPR/C/21/Rev.1/Add.6, of 02 November 1994, pp. 6–7.

[63] Prior to Protocol n. 11, in the *Loizidou* case, *supra*.

Given the uncertainties, ambiguities and lacunae in the present system of reservations to treaties of the two Vienna Conventions of 1969 and 1986 (*supra*), proposals have been advanced in contemporary scholarship[64] attempting to alleviate the difficulty of reservations to human rights treaties.[65] The work (as from 1993) of the ILC on the topic of the *Law and Practice Concerning Reservations to Treaties* tends to identify the essence of the question as being the need to determine the powers of the human rights international supervisory organs in the matter, in the light of the general rules of the law of treaties.[66] This posture makes an abstraction of the specificity of international human rights law, attaching itself to the existing postulates of the law of treaties. The debates of 1997 of the ILC, for example, focused effectively on the question of the applicability of the system of reservations of the Vienna Conventions in relation to human rights treaties. Although the point of view prevailed that the pertinent provisions of those Conventions should not be modified,[67] it was acknowledged that that system of reservations should be improved, given its lacunae, above all in relation to non-permissible reservations.[68]

In the debates of the Commission, it was even admitted that the conventional organs of protection of judicial character (the regional ECtHR and the IACtHR) pronounce on the permissibility of reservations when necessary to the exercise of their functions;[69] such considerations were reflected in the 'Preliminary Conclusions on Reservations to Multilateral Normative Treaties Including Human Rights

---

[64] Cf., e.g., references in ns. (54) and (55), *supra*.

[65] Namely: *first*, the inclusion of an express indication in human rights treaties of the provisions which do not admit any reservations (such as those pertaining to the fundamental non-derogable rights), as an irreducible minimum to participate in such treaties; *second*, as soon as the States Parties have proceeded to the harmonization of their domestic legal order with the norms of those treaties (as required by these latter), the withdrawal of their reservations to them (cf., in this line of reasoning, the Vienna Declaration and Programme of Action (1993), the main document adopted by the II World Conference on Human Rights, part II, paragraph 5, and cf. part I, par. 26); *third*, the modification or rectification, by the State Party, of a reservation considered non-permissible or incompatible with the object and purpose of the treaty (cf. n. (53), *supra*), whereby a reservation would thus be seen no longer as a formal and final element of the manifestation of State consent, but rather as an essentially temporal measure, to be modified or removed as soon as possible; *fourth*, the adoption of a possible 'collegial system' for the acceptance of reservations, so as to safeguard the normative character of human rights treaties, bearing in mind, in this respect, the rare example of the Convention on the Elimination of All Forms of Racial Discrimination (system of the two-thirds of the States Parties, set forth in Article 20(2) of that Convention); *fifth*, the elaboration of guidelines (though not binding) on the existing rules (of the two Vienna Conventions of 1969 and 1986) in the matter of reservations, so as to clarify them in practice (such as drawn up in 1998 by the U.N. International Law Commission; cf. n. (51), *supra)*; and *sixth*, the attribution to the depositaries of human rights treaties of the faculty to request periodic information from the reserving States on the reasons why they have not yet withdrawn their reservations to such treaties.

[66] Cf. A. Pellet (special *rapporteur* of the U.N. International Law Commission), *Second Report on the Law and Practice Relating to Reservations to Treaties* (1997), paragraphs 164, 204, 206, 209, 227, 229 and 252.

[67] U.N., *Report of the International Law Commission on the Work of Its 49th Session (1997), General Assembly Official Records* – Supplement n. 10(A/52/10), p. 94, par. 47.

[68] Ibid., p. 112, par. 107. In this respect, it was warned that States often and consciously formulate reservations incompatible with the object and purpose of human rights treaties for knowing that they will not be challenged, and that the lack of sanctions for such reservations thus leads States to become Parties to such treaties without truly committing themselves; ibid., pp. 117–18, pars. 129–30.

[69] Ibid., pp. 106–7, 119 and 121–2, pars. 82, 84, 134, 138 and 143, respectively.

Treaties', adopted by the Commission in 1997 (pars. 4–7).[70] In my understanding, as I stated in my Separate Opinion (par. 36) in the *Caesar versus Trinidad and Tobago* case (2005):

> there are compelling reasons to go further, and the relevant labour of the ILC on the matter could lead to solutions satisfactory to human rights international supervisory organs to the extent that it started from the recognition of the special character of human rights treaties and gave precision to the juridical consequences – for the treatment of the question of reservations – which ensue from that recognition (par. 36).

However, in the subsequent version of its *Draft Guidelines on Reservations to Treaties* (2003), provisionally adopted by the ILC, the latter urged States and international organizations to 'undertake a periodic review' of their reservations to treaties, and to 'consider withdrawing those which no longer serve their purpose',[71] though it did not pursue the aforementioned approach. Such review, added the ILC, 'should devote special attention to the aim of preserving the integrity of multilateral treaties'.[72] Thus, draft guideline 2.5.3 reflects the concerns of monitoring bodies ('particularly but not exclusively in the field of human rights'), to call often upon States to reconsider their reservations and if possible to withdraw them.[73] The ILC has conceded that:

> The reference to the integrity of multilateral treaties is an allusion to the drawbacks of reservations, that may undermine the unity of the treaty regime.[74]

It may be pointed out that human rights treaties have in a way been singled out when one comes to denunciation, and termination and suspension of the operation of treaties; I see, thus, no epistemological or juridical reason why the same could not be done also in relation to reservations. In my view, the conferment of the power of determination of the compatibility or otherwise of reservations with the object and purpose of human rights treaties on the international supervisory organs themselves created by such treaties, would be much more in conformity with the special nature of the latter and with the objective character of the conventional obligations of protection.[75]

There is logic and common sense in attributing such power to those organs, guardians as they are of the integrity of human rights treaties, instead of abandoning such determination to the interested States Parties themselves, as if they were, or could be, the final arbiters of the scope of their conventional obligations.[76] Such

---

[70] Text in ibid., pp. 126–7.

[71] Cf. U.N./ILC, *Report of the International Law Commission* (55th Session, May-June and July-August 2003), *G.A.O.R.* – Suppl. n. 10 (doc. A/58/10), of 2003, p. 184.

[72] Ibid., p. 184.

[73] Ibid., p. 207.

[74] Ibid., p. 208, and cf. pp. 216, 244 and 251 (on the 'limitation' of the scope of previous reservations, conducive to their withdrawal).

[75] A.A. Cançado Trindade, *Tratado de Direito Internacional dos Direitos Humanos*, vol. II, Porto Alegre/Brazil, S.A. Fabris Ed., 1999, pp. 152–70.

[76] Cf. A.A. Cançado Trindade, 'The International Law of Human Rights at the Dawn of the XXIst Century', 3 *Cursos Euromediterráneos Bancaja de Derecho Internacional* – Castellón/Spain (1999) pp. 145–221.

system of objective determination would foster a process of progressive institution-alization of the international protection of human rights,[77] as well as the creation of a true international public order (*ordre public*) based on the full respect for, and observance of, human rights. It is about time for the current process of *humaniza-tion* of International Law[78] to encompass likewise the domain of the law of treaties, traditionally so vulnerable to manifestations of State voluntarism.

It is my understanding that, from the perspective of a minimally institutionalized international community, the regime of reservations to treaties, as it still prevails in our days, is rudimentary and rather primitive. There is pressing need to develop a system of objective determination of the compatibility or otherwise of reservations with the object and purpose of human rights treaties, although to that end an express provision in future human rights treaties may be necessary, or the adoption of protocols to the existing instruments.[79]

Only with such a system of objective determination will we succeed in guarding coherence with the special character of human rights treaties, which set forth obligations of an objective character and are applied by means of the exercise of the collective guarantee. Only thus will we succeed in establishing, in the ambit of the law of treaties, standards of behaviour which contribute to the creation of a true international *ordre public* based on the respect for, and observance of, human rights, with the corresponding obligations *erga omnes* of protection. We stand in need of the renovation and humanization of the law of treaties as a whole, comprising also the forms of manifestation of State consent.

It is necessary to take into account the experience of international supervision accumulated by the conventional organs of protection of human rights in recent decades. Any serious evaluation of the present system of reservations to treaties cannot fail to take into account the practice, on the matter, of such organs of protection. It cannot pass unnoticed that the ICJ, in its already-mentioned Advis-ory Opinion of 1951, effectively recognized, in a pioneering way, the special character of the Convention for the Prevention and Punishment of the Crime of Genocide of 1948, but without having extracted from its acknowledgement all the juridical consequences for the regime of reservations to treaties.

Almost half a century having lapsed, this is the task which is incumbent upon all of us who have the responsibility and the privilege to act in the domain of the international protection of human rights. The words pronounced by the Hague Court in 1951 remain topical nowadays, in pointing out that, in a Convention such as that of 1948, adopted for a 'purely humanitarian' purpose:

---

[77] For the conception of human rights as an 'autonomous juridical imperative', cf. D. Evrigenis, 'Institutionnalisation des droits de l'homme et droit universel', in *Internationales Colloquium über Menschenrechte* (Berlin, Oktober 1966), Berlin, Deutsche Gesellschaft für die Vereinten Nationen, 1966, p. 32.

[78] A.A. Cançado Trindade, 'La Humanización del Derecho Internacional y los Límites de la Razón de Estado', 40 *Revista da Faculdade de Direito da Universidade Federal de Minas Gerais* – Belo Horizonte/Brazil (2001) pp. 11–23.

[79] As suggested in the aforementioned 'Preliminary Conclusions' of 1997 (par. 7) of the ILC; cf. U.N., *Report of the International Law Commission . . .* (1997), *op. cit. supra* n. (67), pp. 126–7.

(...) the Contracting States do not have any interests of their own; they merely have, one and all, a common interest, namely, the accomplishment of those high purposes which are the *raison d'être* of the Convention. Consequently, in a Convention of this type one cannot speak of individual advantages and disadvantages to States, of the maintenance of a perfect contractual balance between rights and duties. The high ideals which inspired the Convention provide, by virtue of the common will of the Parties, the foundation and measure of all its provisions.[80]

I see no sense in attempting to try to escape from the acknowledgement of the specificity of international human rights law as a whole, the recognition of which, in my understanding, in no way threatens the unity of Public International Law; quite on the contrary, it contributes to develop the aptitude of this latter to secure, in the present domain, compliance with the conventional obligations of protection of the States vis-à-vis all human beings under their jurisdiction. With the evolution of international human rights law, it is Public International Law itself which is justified and legitimized, in affirming legal principles, concepts, and categories proper to the present domain of protection, based on premises fundamentally distinct from those which have guided the application of its postulates at the level of purely inter-State relations.[81]

One is not, therefore, proposing here that the development of international human rights law be pursued to the detriment of the law of treaties: my understanding, entirely distinct, is in the sense that the norms of the law of treaties (such as those set forth in the two aforementioned Vienna Conventions, anyway of a residual character) can greatly enrich international human rights law, and develop their aptitude to regulate adequately legal relations at inter-State as well as intra-State levels, under the respective treaties of protection. In sustaining the development of a system of objective determination – which seems to me wholly necessary – of the compatibility or otherwise of reservations with the object and purpose of human rights treaties in particular, in which the organs of international protection created by such treaties exert an important role, I do not see in that any threat to the 'unity' of the law of treaties.

Quite the contrary, there could hardly be something more fragmenting and underdeveloped than the present system of reservations of the two Vienna Conventions, for which reason it would be entirely illusory to assume that, to continue applying it in the same way, one would thereby be fostering the 'unity' of the law of treaties. The true unity of the law of treaties, in the framework of Public International Law, would be better served by the search for improvement in this area, overcoming the ambiguities, uncertainties, and lacunae of the present system of reservations, through the development of a system of objective determination of the compatibility or otherwise of reservations with the object and purpose of human rights treaties (*supra*), in conformity with the special nature of such treaties and the

---

[80] International Court of Justice, Advisory Opinion of 28 May 1951, *ICJ Reports* (1951) p. 23; and, for a study on the matter, cf. A.A. Cançado Trindade, 'La jurisprudence de la Cour Internationale de Justice sur les droits intangibles/The Case-Law of the International Court of Justice on Non-Derogable Rights', *Droits intangibles et états d'exception/Non-Derogable Rights and States of Emergency* (ed. D. Prémont), Brussels, Bruylant, 1996, pp. 53–89.

[81] A.A. Cançado Trindade, 'The International Law of Human Rights at the Dawn of the XXIst Century', *op. cit. supra* n. (76), pp. 145–221.

objective character of the conventional obligations of protection. The unity of Public International Law itself is measured rather by its aptitude to regulate legal relations in distinct contexts with equal adequacy and effectiveness.

IV. The Interaction between International Law and Domestic Law and the Rule of Exhaustion of the Local Remedies

1. Human Rights Treaties and the Role of National Courts

The consideration of the rule of exhaustion of local remedies in international law in relation to the role of national courts touches on the interaction between international law and municipal law with regard to the application of that rule. A useful approach to the matter is possible if attention is directed to, for example, the domestic status of international provisions, the interpretation of domestic provisions by international organs, the relevance of domestic law to international legal procedure, or the implementation of international judicial decisions by domestic courts.

The local remedies rule, it may be recalled, is primarily a prerogative of domestic law (local redress) applied by an international organ; the application of the rule in international law implies the existence of effective remedies under domestic law. In this example, afforded by the application of the aforementioned rule, of interaction between international law and municipal law, the complementary nature of rights and duties can be clearly identified. International supervisory organs pay regard to decisions of domestic courts to verify the conformity of a State's internal acts with its conventional international obligations; this has a bearing on the application of the rule, by, for example, placing the State's international duty to provide effective local remedies in the right perspective.

The general impact of human rights treaties upon the domestic law of member States is thus important for their effect in entailing internal legislative changes to bring domestic laws of member States into harmony with them. International supervisory organs are not courts of appeal from national courts' decisions, or substitutes for national courts, even though they control the compatibility of domestic law with human rights treaties. Whatever the formal domestic status of human rights treaties, the local remedies requirement (where it is provided for) shows that it is primarily before domestic courts that respect must be sought for the internationally guaranteed rights.

This 'positive' outlook of the local remedies requirement appears as an instance of the application of domestic law or remedies in international legal procedure. The subsidiary character of international proceedings (cf. *infra*), while offering an explanation for the *existence* of the local remedies rule, cannot properly be invoked as a justification for an enlargement of the *scope* of application of the rule as generally recognized in international law. The rule at issue appears as one requiring actual local redress and not mere exhaustion *per se* of remedies until the occurrence of a denial of justice.[82] It is

---

[82] Cf. *Collection of Decisions of National Courts Referring to the [European] Convention*, Council of Europe – Directorate of Human Rights, and Supplements 1 to 4, Strasbourg, 1969–74: cf. mainly

a matter of *ordre public* that human rights protection ought to be guaranteed at domestic law level, so as to meet international standards of protection.

The rule at issue is not a principle of immutable approach irrespective of the context of its incidence. The local remedies rule, commonly regarded as a 'precondition' for international proceedings, has thus enjoyed, in classical diplomatic protection and State responsibility for injuries to aliens, a 'negative' or preventive character, with emphasis on the process of exhaustion prior to international interposition on a discretionary State-to-State basis. This approach to the rule is hardly adequate for human rights protection, where the role of local courts and remedies is regarded as a component part of the international system of protection itself, and where the insertion of the rule in international instruments as a mandatory condition makes it possible to accord it detailed treatment. In a system of protection fundamentally victim-oriented, concerned with the rights of individual human beings rather than of States, adopting a more positive outlook of the issue than the one by and large followed so far seems appropriate; and it is likely to lead to more reassuring results than the ones ensuing from an essentially negative or formalistic approach leading to systematic, if not mechanical, rejection of applications for non-exhaustion of local remedies.[83]

2. The State's Duty to Provide Effective Local Remedies and the Individual's Duty to Have Recourse to Them: The Emphasis on Redress or the Realization of Justice

The applicant's duty to exhaust local remedies has as its necessary counterpart the State's duty to provide local remedies. While an analysis of the local remedies rule from the viewpoint of the underlying *interests* at stake may have been adequate in the traditional context of State responsibility for injuries to aliens, in the field of international human rights protection[84] an approach to the rule stressing the complementary *rights and duties*[85] would seem more appropriate. This approach is followed in the application of both the ECHR and ACHR, and the U.N. Covenant on Civil and Political Rights (and its [first] Optional Protocol),[86] when

---

national courts decisions on Articles 26 and 13 of the [original text of the] European Convention (loose-leaf collection, no page references).

[83] A.A. Cançado Trindade, *The Application of the Rule of Exhaustion of Local Remedies in International Law*, Cambridge, Cambridge University Press, 1983, pp. 1–443.

[84] The public hearings in the *Matznetter* case (1969) led the European Court of Human Rights to reject inadequate analogies between diplomatic protection and human rights protection for purposes of application of the rule. Similarly, years earlier, an Opinion of a Committee of Jurists (under the League of Nations) and the oral hearings before the Permanent Court of International Justice in the *Administration of the Prince von Pless* case (1933) provided important elements for a rejection of analogies between State responsibility for injuries to aliens and minorities protection (this latter, e.g., permanent or continuous and not occasional) for purposes of application of the local remedies rule (cf. *supra*).

[85] As already indicated, the correlation between rights and duties is lacking in diplomatic protection (cf. *supra*).

[86] The Covenant goes even further by expressly providing for the duty to develop the possibilities of judicial remedies (cf. *supra*).

they expressly refer to the State's duty to provide local remedies as a necessary and natural counterpart of the local remedies requirement. The applicant's right of individual petition is granted on condition *inter alia* of compliance with that requirement, and the State's right to rely on it is provided to the extent that it has afforded individuals effective local means of redress.

The matter is thus directly related to the measures of implementation of human rights protection. Domestic courts themselves have acknowledged the fact that human rights treaties entrust the protection of those rights to municipal law organs and procedures. It is reassuring to note that they appear to be more often concerned with the State's duty to provide local remedies than with formal technicalities in the operation of the local remedies rule.[87] Recourse to local remedies should terminate in *redress*, thus reserving a more active role to domestic courts in the present domain of protection of the human person.

A clear and current illustration of the growing importance ascribed to the duty of provision of *effective* domestic remedies can be found in recent developments under the ECHR, conferring increasing relevance upon Article 13 of the Convention. Furthermore, in the course of the recent adoption of Protocol n. 14 to the ECHR, opened to the signature of States on 13 May 2004, the Committee of Ministers of the Council of Europe adopted its recommendation Rec.(2004)6, of 12 May 2004, on the improvement of domestic remedies (*amélioration des recours internes*), directly referring to the recent case-law of the ECtHR pertaining to Article 13 (right to an effective remedy).[88]

It is hoped that such improvement may to some extent alleviate the current flood of petitions to the ECtHR. Here one can clearly perceive that access to justice at domestic law level does indeed have a direct bearing upon the operation of the mechanisms of the international protection of human rights. Under human rights treaties, recognition that the duties of providing and of exhausting effective local remedies are complementary has opened a new trend in the application of the local remedies rule in the present domain of protection. One may go yet a step further in considering the guarantee of access to domestic courts and the right to judicial hearing, set forth in some human rights treaties (such as the aforementioned), as allocating a fundamental role to national courts in ensuring respect for and observance of the State's international obligations of protecting human rights.

3. The *Rationale* of the Local Remedies Rule in Human Rights Protection

The issue of the relationship between the rule of exhaustion of local remedies in international law and the role of national courts thus touches on the interaction

---

[87] The duty to provide effective local remedies operates as a safeguard against denial of justice or undue delays throughout the process of exhaustion of local remedies. This close inter-relationship between the individual's duty of exhaustion and the State's duty to provide local remedies illustrates a modern shift of emphasis towards improvement of national systems of judicial protection.

[88] [Various Authors,] *La nouvelle procédure devant la Cour européenne des droits de l'homme après le Protocole n. 14* (ed. F. Salerno), Bruxelles, Bruylant, 2007, pp. 110 and 146.

between international law and domestic law with regard to the application of the rule.[89] The local remedies rule is primarily a prerogative (right of priority) of municipal law (local redress), applied by an international organ; the application of the rule in international law implies the existence of remedies under municipal law. In this example, afforded by the application of the rule, of interaction between international law and municipal law, the complementary nature of rights and duties can be clearly identified.

The *rationale* of the local remedies rule in human rights protection discloses the overriding importance of the element of *local redress*. A matter, raised in the past, on which expert writers seemed at first divided,[90] was whether the rule applied when conventional provisions formed part of the law of the land (i.e. the domestic law of the respondent State) or, in other words, when those provisions had the force of *ordre public* in domestic law, and domestic courts were empowered to supervise *ex officio* their application. In this connection, it appears that the duty to have recourse to local remedies is to be considered solely in respect of the applicant, whether or not domestic courts apply the conventional provisions *ex officio*. The *rationale* behind the rule is to afford the respondent State an opportunity of prior *redress* within the framework of its own domestic legal system; the duty of domestic courts to apply the human rights treaties *ex officio,* where it exists, ensues, for its part, from the fact that it is a matter of *ordre public* that human rights protection ought to be guaranteed (in domestic law).

It ought to be always kept in mind that, in the present domain of protection of the human person – it may here be stressed – the operation of local remedies in international procedures ought to terminate in *redress*. The role of domestic courts in the implementation of international provisions is made important by the 'horizontal' and decentralized structure of international law;[91] when those courts operate pursuant to human rights treaties, a certain uniformity of practice – *inter alia* as to the local remedies rule – can be expected, notwithstanding variations in the domestic legal systems concerned.[92] The role of domestic courts in their horizontal interaction

---

[89] In approaching that interaction one no longer needs to venture into the classical irreconcilable antagonism between dualist and monist positions. Cf., on the former, H. Triepel, *Droit international et droit interne* (trans. R. Brunet), Paris, Pédone, 1920, pp. 11–165; D. Anzilotti, *Corso di Diritto Internazionale*, 3rd. ed, vol. I, Padova, Cedam, 1955, pp. 49–110. And cf., on the monist thesis, H. Kelsen, 'Les rapports de système entre le droit interne et le droit international public', 14 *Recueil des Cours de l'Académie de Droit International de La Haye [RCADI]* (1926) pp. 231–6; H. Kelsen, 'Théorie du Droit international public', 84 *RCADI* (1953) pp. 182–200; G. Scelle, *Précis de Droit des Gens – principes et systématique*, part II, Paris, Rec. Sirey, 1934 [reed. 1984 by CNRS], pp. 5–6 and 10–12. And cf. note (36), *supra*.

[90] Cf., for different views, e g , on the one hand, K. Vasak, *La Convention européenne des droits de l'homme*, Paris, LGDJ, 1964, p. 249; and, on the other hand, J.E.S. Fawcett, *The Application of the European Convention on Human Rights*, Oxford, Clarendon Press, 1969, p. 302, and W.J. Ganshof van der Meersch, 'Does the Convention Have the Force of '*Ordre Public*' in Municipal Law?', in *Human Rights in National and International Law* (ed. A.H. Robertson), Manchester, University Press/Oceana, 1970, pp. 135–43.

[91] Cf. R.A. Falk, *The Role of Domestic Courts in the International Legal Order*, Syracuse, University Press, 1964, pp. 21–59 and 170–77.

[92] Such uniformity ensuing from the co-ordinated activity of domestic courts (under human rights treaties) may be expected particularly in systems of protection largely inspired by the notions of general interest and collective guarantee, with the local remedies rule operating therein as a procedural device for allocating jurisdiction between the municipal and international legal orders.

(as organs for implementation of international provisions) in a way transcends the boundaries of their own respective national legal system; in the application of the local remedies rule in this new perspective, classical abstract definitions of denial of justice (or its component elements) give way to an objective examination of domestic procedures.

This would appear to be a natural course to follow in cases of treaties which require domestic action for their implementation, as do human rights treaties,[93] with the result that States Parties cannot plead municipal law deficiencies as an excuse for non-performance. In the application of the local remedies rule, it is ultimately through domestic court action that the complementary nature of rights and duties is objectively realized. The overriding test of effectiveness of local remedies remains possibly the most adequate test for ascertaining their appropriateness, in constant awareness of the concomitant duties in the application of the local remedies rule; in fact, emphasis on the complementarity of judicially enforceable rights and duties can pave the way for a more balanced application of that rule.

In this connection, a particular group of cases deserves special attention, namely, complaints of allegedly wrongful "legislative measures and administrative practices", or else "general cases", under human rights treaties (such as the European and American Conventions on Human Rights), or cases revealing a "consistent pattern of gross violations of human rights" (in the framework of United Nations organs). If at all applicable in such graver cases, the local remedies rule can here only be properly approached in terms of rights and duties (rather than interests), in particular the State's duty to provide effective local redress and to develop the possibilities of judicial remedies. Not surprisingly, in such cases international supervisory organs have disclosed a clear inclination to approach the local remedies rule with due regard to such underlying duty incumbent upon the State. In such special complaints relating to a whole pattern of domestic measures and practices, the inevitable implication has been a closer scrutiny on the part of international supervisory organs of the real conditions for exhaustion of local remedies in each instance and of the reasons and circumstances for non-exhaustion by the individual petitioners.[94]

Now that a few decades have passed since the crystallization of the right of international individual petition, and a considerable international experience in this area has been accumulated, the original apprehensions which States had with regard to the recognition of procedural status of individuals upon the international level have been gradually fading away, with their recognition that there is no compelling logical or practical reason preventing the application of the local remedies rule from being limited in scope in the cases concerning general practices. These conclusions are meant to take account of the different contexts in which the local remedies rule applies; this latter does not embody a principle of absolute and immutable value irrespective of the domain of its incidence.

The contributions of human rights international supervisory organs on this matter point in the right direction and have been paving the way for develop-

---

[93] E.g., State's duty to provide effective local remedies.

[94] Cf. A.A. Cançado Trindade, *O Esgotamento de Recursos Internos no Direito Internacional*, 2nd. ed., Brasília, Edit. University of Brasília, 1997, pp. 210–22, 228 and 226–38.

ing the application of the local remedies rule with special attention to the needs of protection and the particularities of the present context of international implementation of human rights. The incidence of the local remedies rule in human rights protection is certainly distinct from its application in the practice of diplomatic protection of nationals abroad (in customary international law), and the rule at issue is far from having the dimensions of an immutable or sacrosanct principle of international law. Moreover, the two contexts – human rights protection and diplomatic protection – are also distinct, and there is nothing to impede the application of that rule with greater or lesser rigour in such different situations.

The *jurisprudence constante* of international tribunals of human rights bears witness to the *rationale* of that rule in human rights protection. In fact, over the last three decades, I have been consistently of the view that, in the present domain of protection, the rule of exhaustion of local remedies is to be applied with increasing flexibility, taking local remedies as an element which integrates the system of international human rights protection itself, with emphasis shifted from the process of exhaustion into the overriding element of *redress* itself.[95] There exists a *corpus juris* of *protection* of the human person, endowed with a specificity of its own and based upon premises fundamentally distinct from those that guide a more rigid application of the requisite of exhaustion in other contexts (such as, e.g., that of discretionary diplomatic protection in the inter-State *contentieux*).

This *law of protection* of the rights of the human person, within the framework of which international and domestic law appear in constant interaction, is inspired in common superior values, of *ordre public*. The generally recognized rules of international law – which the formulation of the local remedies requisite in human rights treaties refers to – besides following an evolution of their own in the distinct contexts in which they apply, necessarily undergo, when set forth in human rights treaties, a certain degree of adjustment or adaptation, dictated by the special character of the object and purpose of those treaties, and by the widely reckoned specificity of the International Law of Human Rights.[96] This goes *pari passu* with an increasing emphasis on the State's duty to provide effective local remedies.

This outlook on the matter, which I have been propounding and sustaining throughout the last three decades, is the one which has in effect been adopted and consistently pursued, for several years, by the international tribunals of human rights (the ECtHR and IACtHR), in their *jurisprudence constante* on the matter. This latter has, with the passing of time, supported my understanding and has fully endorsed the thesis I sustained in my original research on the subject.[97] Such has been the position of the IACtHR, quite consistent over the years, redressing the balance in favour of the alleged victims by means of the flexibility in the application of the rule of exhaustion of local remedies – as from its Judgments, on preliminary objections, in the cases of *Gangaram Panday versus Suriname* (of 04 December 1991), of *Castillo Páez*

---

[95] A.A. Cançado Trindade, *The Application of the Rule*..., *op. cit. supra* n. (83), pp. 1–443.

[96] A.A. Cançado Trindade, *O Esgotamento de Recursos Internos*..., *op. cit. supra* n. (94), pp. 265–6.

[97] Cf. A.A. Cançado Trindade, *Developments in the Rule of Exhaustion of Local Remedies in International Law*, 2 vols., Cambridge, University of Cambridge, 1977, pp. 1–1728 (Ph.D. thesis deposited at Cambridge University Library).

versus Peru (of 30 January 1996), and of *Loayza Tamayo versus Peru* (of 31 January 1996), to the present time.[98]

Likewise, in its vast case-law on the subject, the ECtHR has been constantly maintaining for many years that the rule of exhaustion of local remedies ought to be applied, with flexibility and without excessive formalism; and this has indeed been its position, *inter alia*, in its Judgment of 19 March 1991 in the *Cardot versus France* case (par. 34). On several occasions in recent years the ECtHR has referred to its own *jurisprudence constante* in the sense that in the system of protection under the ECHR the local remedies rule ought to be applied with flexibility and without excessive reliance on questions of form. In its Judgment of 16 September 1996, in the case of *Akdivar and Others versus Turkey*, to recall one example, the ECtHR expressly asserted that the application of the rule of exhaustion ought to take into account the specific context of the mechanism of human rights protection in which it operates; it ought, accordingly, to be applied herein with 'a certain degree of flexibility and without excessive formalism' (par. 69).

In the same *Akdivar* case, the ECtHR added that the rule of exhaustion is not absolute and ought not to have automatic application; instead, it ought to take into due account the particular circumstances of the concrete case, including not only the general legal context within which local remedies operate, but also the 'personal circumstances' of the applicants (pars. 68–69). Likewise in the *Aksoy versus Turkey* case (of 18 December 1996), the ECtHR again warned that recourse does not need to be had to remedies which are inadequate or ineffective (pars. 51–52). And in the subsequent Judgment in the *Kurt versus Turkey* case (of 25 May 1998), the ECtHR (Chamber), evoking its own 'settled case-law' (and referring to its reasoning in the *Akdivar* case – *supra*), found that there existed 'special circumstances' dispensing the applicant from the duty of exhausting local remedies, and accordingly dismissed the respondent State's preliminary objection on that account (par. 83).

Subsequently, already under the ECHR as amended by Protocol n. 11, in its Judgment in the case of *Tanrikuly versus Turkey* (of 08 July 1999), the ECtHR properly warned that the rule of exhaustion of local remedies 'must be applied with some degree of flexibility and without excessive formalism', it being essential to have regard to the circumstances of the concrete case and to take due account 'not only of the existence of formal remedies in the legal system of the Contracting State concerned but also of the general context in which they operate, as well as the personal circumstances of the applicant' (par. 82). The Court further observed that the local remedies rule, under Article 35(1) of the ECHR (as amended by Protocol n. 11), requires applicants to use available and effective remedies that 'enable them to obtain redress for the breaches alleged' (par. 76).

---

[98] Cf. A.A. Cançado Trindade, *Tratado de Direito Internacional dos Direitos Humanos*, vol. II, Porto Alegre/Brazil, S.A. Fabris Ed., 1999, pp. 82–123; and cf., on the earlier practice to the same effect, A.A. Cançado Trindade, 'Evolución y Desarrollos Recientes en el Agotamiento de los Recursos Internos en el Sistema Interamericano de Protección de los Derechos Humanos', in *Los Derechos Humanos en América – Una Perspectiva de Cinco Siglos* (International Seminar of Valladolid of 1992), Salamanca, Ed. Cortes de Castilla y León, 1994, pp. 321–52; A.A. Cançado Trindade, *El Agotamiento de los Recursos Internos en el Sistema Interamericano de Protección de los Derechos Humanos*, San José of Costa Rica, IIHR (Series for NGOs), 1991, pp. 35–41.

That is, what ultimately matters is the redress obtained for the wrongs complained of, and not the mechanical exhaustion of local remedies. In the same line of reasoning, in its Judgment in the subsequent case of *Khashiyev and Akayeva versus Russia* (of 24 February 2005), the ECtHR again warned that Article 35(1) 'must be applied with some degree of flexibility and without excessive formalism', as, in the present domain of the international protection of human rights, the rule of exhaustion of local remedies 'is neither absolute nor capable of being applied automatically' (par. 117). Once again, to the same effect, in its Judgment (also of 24 February 2005) in the case of *Isayeva, Yusupova and Bazayeva versus Russia*, concerning the armed hostilities in Chechnya in 1999 (in particular, the bombing of a civilian convoy on 29 October 1999 near Grozny, killing innocent children among those who were trying to escape from the fighting in Grozny), the Court, reiterating its aforementioned *obiter dicta* on the non-application of the local remedies rule in an undue absolute or automatic way (par. 145), took due account of the 'practical difficulties' found by the applicants in the specific case (par. 150).

In particular, in the *Isayeva, Yusupova and Bazayeva* case, the ECtHR noted the fact that 'the law-enforcement bodies were not functioning properly in Chechnya at the time'; consequently, it added that in view of the 'special circumstances' of the case, 'the applicants were not obliged to pursue the civil remedies' suggested by the respondent State, and the Court thereby dismissed the preliminary objection of non-exhaustion of local remedies as 'unfounded' (pars. 150–151 and resolutory point n. 1). More recently, the ECtHR, in its Judgment of 05 April 2007 on the case of *Baysayeva versus Russia*, denied that recourse should be had to inadequate or ineffective remedies, and added that 'the existence of remedies must be sufficiently certain, in practice as well as in theory, failing which they will lack the requisite accessibility and effectiveness' (par. 104). In the *Baysayeva* case, the ECtHR was particularly forceful on the matter; in its words:

The Court emphasizes that the rule of exhaustion of domestic remedies must be applied with some degree of flexibility and without excessive formalism. It has further recognized that the rule of exhaustion is neither absolute nor capable of being applied automatically; for the purposes of reviewing whether it has been observed, it is essential to have regard to the circumstances of the individual case (par. 105).

In the African continent, in a series of cases concerning Zaire, lodged with the African Commission on Human and Peoples' Rights (AComHPR) by the World Organisation against Torture (n. 25/89), the Lawyers' Committee for Human Rights (n. 47/90), *Les Témoins de Jehovah* (n. 56/91), and the *Union Interafricaine des Droits de l'Homme* (n. 100/93), the AComHPR held that the requirement of exhaustion of local remedies did not apply, given the 'seriousness' of the situation, involving 'great numbers of people', added to the fact that recourse to such remedies was 'unavailable' or 'unduly prolonged'.[99]

---

[99] AComHPR, *Decisions of the African Commission on Human and Peoples' Rights* (1986–1997), Series A, vol. I, Banjul, doc. AComHPR/LR/A/1, 1997, p. 22.

The same decision was taken by the AComHPR in three other cases concerning Benin,[100] and other series of cases pertaining to Rwanda,[101] Malawi[102] and Togo.[103] In the *Constitutional Rights Project* case (n. 60/91), concerning Nigeria, the AComHPR further warned that remedies which 'do not operate impartially' are 'neither adequate nor effective', and thereby do not need to be exhausted.[104] Subsequently, in the case of the *Rencontre Africaine pour la Défense des Droits de l'Homme versus Zambia* (n. 71/92), the AComHPR found that:

The mass nature of the arrests, the fact that victims were kept in detention prior to their expulsions, and the speed with which the expulsions were carried out gave the complainants no opportunity to establish the illegality of these actions in the courts. For complainants to contact their families, much less attorneys, was not possible. Thus, the recourse referred to by the government under the Immigration and Deportation Act was as a practical matter not available to the complainants.[105]

Further examples of non-application of the local remedies rule by the AComHPR, given the adverse circumstances surrounding the petitioners, are afforded by the Commission's decisions in the case of *Civil Liberties Organisation in Respect of the Nigerian Bar Association versus Nigeria* (n. 101/93),[106] and in the subsequent case of the *Civil Liberties Organisation versus Nigeria* (n. 129/94), where the Commission concluded that, in the circumstances of the specific case, it was 'reasonable to presume' that local remedies would 'not only be prolonged', but were 'certain to yield no results'.[107]

On yet other occasions, the AComHPR also upheld the non-application of the aforementioned rule, for local remedies being ineffective (*Bissangou versus Republic of Congo* case, 2006), 'impractical or futile' (*Zimbabwe Human Rights NGO Forum versus Zimbabwe* case, 2006), unavailable (case *Purohit and Another versus Gambia*, 2003), or simply non-existent (cases of *Media Rights Agenda and Others versus Nigeria*, 1998; and of *Social and Economic Rights Action Centre (SERAC) and Another versus Nigeria*, 2001).[108] The AComHPR reached the same conclusion in the *Jawara versus Gambia* case (2000), recalling its 'established case-law' to the

---

[100] Lodged by the *Comité Culturel pour la Démocratie au Bénin* (n. 16/88), Badjogoume Hilaire (n. 17/88), and El Hadj Boubacar Diawara (n. 18/88), in ibid., p. 13.

[101] Interposed by the *Organisation Mondiale contre la Torture* (n. 27/89), the *Association Internationale de Juristes Democrates* (n. 46/91), the International Commission of Jurists (n. 49/91), and the *Union Interafricaine des Droits de l'Homme* (n. 99/93), in ibid., p. 31.

[102] Lodged by K. Achuthan (on behalf of A. Banda – n. 64/92), Amnesty International (on behalf of O. and V. Chirwa – n. 68/92), and of O. and V. Chirwa again – n. 78/92), in ibid., p. 66.

[103] Interposed by J.Y. Degli (on behalf of Corporal N. Bikagni – n. 83/93), *Union Interafricaine des Droits de l'Homme* (n. 88/93), International Commission of Jurists (n. 91/93), in ibid., pp. 95–6; cf. also, to the same effect, the case of the *Commission Nationale des Droits de l'homme et des Libertés versus Chad* (n. 74/92), in ibid., p. 87.

[104] Ibid., p. 57. And cf., to the same effect, the case of the *Constitutional Rights Project (in respect of Z. Lekwot and 6 Others) versus Nigeria* (n. 87/93), in ibid., p. 103.

[105] *Cit.* in ibid., p. 79.

[106] Cf. ibid.., p. 113.

[107] *Cit.* in ibid., p. 130.

[108] Cf. AComHPR's decisions reproduced in: *Compendium of Key Human Rights Documents of the African Union* (eds. C. Heyns and M. Killander), Pretoria, Pretoria Univ. Law Press (PULP), 2007, pp. 179, 265, 244, 233 and 254–5.

effect that 'a remedy that has no prospect of success does not constitute an effective remedy', and, in such circumstances, 'it would be reversing the clock of justice to request the complainant to attempt local remedies'.[109] Likewise, in the case of *Lawyers for Human Rights versus Swaziland* (2005), in applying the same test, the AComHPR expressed the view that 'the likelihood of the complainant succeeding in obtaining a remedy that would redress the situation complained of in this matter is so minimal as to render it unavailable and therefore ineffective'.[110]

Last but not least, in the case of the *African Institute for Human Rights and Development (on Behalf of Sierra Leonean Refugees in Guinea) versus Guinea* (2004), the AComHPR held that, given the 'persistent threat' of persecution from State officials, Sierra Leonean refugees found themselves in an 'ongoing situation' of 'constant danger of reprisals and punishment'. This being so, 'any attempt by Sierra Leonean refugees to seek local remedies would be futile'.[111] In its constant practice, the AComHPR has upheld not only the view that there is no need to exhaust ineffective or illusory remedies, but also the understanding that the author of a communication does not need to be a victim of the violation complained of,[112] thus fostering the access to justice and enlarging the scope of protection.

In sum, local remedies form an integral part of the very system of international human rights protection, the emphasis falling on the element of redress rather than on the process of exhaustion. The local remedies rule bears witness to the interaction between international law and domestic law in the present domain of protection, applying only when those remedies are indeed effective and capable to provide redress. We are here before a *droit de protection*, with a specificity of its own, fundamentally *victim-oriented*, concerned with the rights of individual human beings rather than of States. Generally recognized rules of international law (which the formulation of the local remedies rule in human rights treaties refers to), besides following an evolution of their own in the distinct contexts in which they apply, necessarily undergo, when inserted in human rights treaties, a certain degree of adjustment or adaptation, dictated by the special character of the object and purpose of those treaties and by the widely recognized specificity of the international protection of human rights.[113]

V. The Principle of Complementarity in International Criminal Law

Another area wherein international law and domestic law appear in close contact, and which is not to pass unnoticed in the present chapter, is that of contemporary

---

[109] Cf. ibid., p. 211.
[110] Cf. ibid., p. 221.
[111] Ibid., p. 173.
[112] I. Österdahl, *Implementing Human Rights in Africa – The African Commission on Human and Peoples' Rights and Individual Communications*, Uppsala, Iustus Förlag, 2002, pp. 79, 82, 96–9 and 102–5 (also for terminological inconsistencies of the AComHPR).
[113] A.A. Cançado Trindade, *The Application of the Rule...*, *op. cit. supra* n. (83), pp. 1–443.

international criminal law, as illustrated by the *principle of complementarity*. This latter has lately been attracting increasing attention in expert writing, particularly after the principle gradually took shape, along mainly the second half of the XXth century.[114] In recent years the principle has found expression, though in not a uniform way, and pursuant to distinct models[115] which inspired its formulation, though it has a common denominator in the purported aim to ensure that justice is done (either in international or in national criminal justice systems), so as to put an end to impunity.

This is illustrated by the distinct conceptions of the principle found in the Statutes of, on the one hand, the ad hoc International Criminal Tribunal for the Former Yugoslavia (ICTFY) (Article 9) and for Rwanda (ICTR) (Article 8), and, on the other hand, in the Statute of the International Criminal Court (ICC) (preamble and Articles 12–14 and 17). In fact, neither the ICTFY nor the ICTR (both established by resolutions of the U.N. Security Council) have exclusive competence to investigate and judge those responsible for the serious crimes listed in their respective Statutes; the latter attribute to them a principal competence, which has primacy over the concurring competence of national tribunals.[116] In doing so, it intends to have an impact at domestic law so as to strengthen national jurisdictions over those serious crimes and no longer to acquiesce with the impunity of their perpetrators.

Such principle of complementarity is also invoked – in somewhat distinct terms – in the Statute of the permanent ICC (established by a treaty). As invoked in the preamble itself (paragraph 10) of the 1998 Rome Statute, the ICC is, in effect, conceived as complementary to the national criminal jurisdictions; the very conditions of exercise of its competence (Articles 12–14) give primacy to national jurisdictions to investigate and try those responsible for crimes provided for in the Rome Statute, the triggering of the mechanism of the ICC being circumscribed to exceptional circumstances (this approach being distinct, in this particular aspect, from that followed by the Statutes of the ICTFY and the ICTR).[117] In the system of the ICC, the primary responsibility to sanction those responsible for atrocities perpetrated against the human being falls upon domestic jurisdictions,[118] and when these latter fail, the international criminal jurisdiction enters into operation.

The preamble itself of the Rome Statute states that States Parties decided to establish the permanent ICC in order 'to put an end to impunity for the perpetrators' of those serious crimes (par. 5), and thereby to enhance national

---

[114] On the historical development of the principle of complementarity, cf., e.g., J. Stigen, *The Relationship between the International Criminal Court and National Jurisdictions – The Principle of Complementarity*, Leiden, Nijhoff, 2008, pp. 31–86; M.M. El Zeidy, *The Principle of Complementarity in International Criminal Law: Origin, Development and Practice*, Leiden, Nijhoff, 2008, pp. 59–154.

[115] Cf., e.g., M.M. El Zeidy, *op. cit. supra* n. (114), pp. 132–9.

[116] Cf., on the point, e.g., K. Lescure, *Le Tribunal Pénal International pour l'ex-Yougoslavie*, Paris, Montchrestien, 1994, pp. 108–29; O. Dubois, 'Rwanda's National Criminal Courts and the International Tribunal', 37 *International Review of the Red Cross* (1997) n. 321, pp. 717–31.

[117] A.A. Cançado Trindade, *Tratado de Direito Internacional dos Direitos Humanos*, vol. II, Porto Alegre/ Brazil, S.A. Fabris Ed., 1999, pp. 389 and 398–9.

[118] W. Villalpando, *De los Derechos Humanos al Derecho Internacional Penal*, Buenos Aires, Ed. Abeledo-Perrot, 2000, pp. 376–80.

jurisdictions over them. Thus, if there is unwillingness or inability of the State at issue to exercise its jurisdiction, the ICC will exercise its own, so as to ensure that there is no impunity for the perpetrators of the core crimes of genocide, crimes against humanity and war crimes, which shock the conscience of humankind. There is a general and superior concern of the international community as a whole to make sure that justice is done.[119]

The principle of complementarity thus reflects – as the *travaux préparatoires* of the 1998 Rome Statute made clear – the jurisdictional relationship (rather than concurrence) between the ICC and national jurisdictions.[120] In the ICC Statute, complementarity is set forth as a principle accompanied by means of implementation (Article 17);[121] it is not to pass unnoticed that complementarity may thus contribute to improve the application of the related principle of universal jurisdiction.[122]

In this framework of interrelationships, there is another aspect to be pointed out. The presence of the *victims* of international crimes is surely to be taken into account. In recent years, the victims themselves have endeavoured 'to locate forums willing to exercise universal jurisdiction over those at whose hands they had suffered'.[123] The claims of the victims do have a place in the operation of the ICC.[124] In the period 2006–2008, the ICC has been considering the victims' participation in the investigation stage of the proceedings, at the pre-trial and trial phases of a case, and in appeals. Victims mark their presence also at the stage of reparations, as illustrated by the establishment of the Trust Fund for Victims.[125]

Redress for victims of core crimes under international law has lately had its scope enlarged, beyond international human rights law, nowadays being the object of attention of contemporary International Criminal Law, in particular in the operation of the ICC.[126] In our days, the necessity is at last acknowledged of bringing together retributive justice (focused on the sanction of the perpetrators of those

---

[119] Cf. L. Yang, 'On the Principle of Complementarity in the Rome Statute of the International Criminal Court', 4 *Chinese Journal of International Law* (2005) pp. 122–5.

[120] Cf. J. Stigen, *op. cit. supra* n. (114), pp. 69–70.

[121] Cf., e.g., A.L. Zuppi, *Jurisdicción Universal para Crímenes contra el Derecho Internacional*, Buenos Aires, Ed. Ad-Hoc, 2002, pp. 137–8.

[122] X. Philippe, 'The Principles of Universal Jurisdiction and Complementarity: How Do the Two Principles Intermesh?', 88 *International Review of the Red Cross* (2006) n. 862, pp. 375–6, 384 and 398; and, on the relationship between the two principles, cf. also P.-M. Dupuy, 'Principe de complémentarité et Droit international général', in *The International Criminal Court and National Jurisdictions* (eds. M. Politi and F. Gioia), Aldershot, Ashgate, 2008, pp. 23–4; J.K. Kleffner, *Complementarity in the Rome Statute and National Criminal Jurisdictions*, Oxford, University Press, 2008, pp. 237–78 and 288–308.

[123] L. Reydams, *Universal Jurisdiction – International and Municipal Legal Perspectives*, Oxford, University Press, 2004, p. 221.

[124] F. Razesberger, *The International Criminal Court – The Principle of Complementarity*, Frankfurt am Main, P. Lang, 2006, p. 189.

[125] Cf. ICC, *Selected Basic Documents Related to the International Criminal Court*, The Hague, ICC, 2009, pp. 361–74 and 397–403.

[126] Cf., e.g., I. Bottigliero, *Redress for Victims of Crimes under International Law*, Leiden, Nijhoff, 2004, pp. 111, 186 and 250–1.

crimes) and restorative justice (centred on the rehabilitation of the victims). This is another aspect, and a relevant one, of the right to the realization of justice. In the recent cycle of cases pertaining to massacres, brought before the IACtHR,[127] in successive Separate Opinions I have sustained the need to foster an approximation between international human rights law and International Criminal Law, keeping in mind the rights of the victims of grave breaches of human rights.[128]

In this approximation between international human rights law and International Criminal Law, the international subjectivity of individuals appears in both its *active* and *passive* dimensions, respectively. In both domains one is faced with the interaction or interrelationship between the international and domestic legal orders. This suggests that international legal developments which have occurred in the last decades, such as the ones surveyed herein, can no longer be approached from the old outlook of the compartmentalization between international law and domestic law, overcome in our days. The interaction or interrelationship between the international and national legal orders in the present context helps to disclose and consolidate the position of individuals as active as well as passive subjects of international law, endowed with international legal capacity, and thereby to foster the right to the realization of justice, at national as well as international levels.

VI. Beyond Subsidiarity: State Responsibility, Substantive Law, and the Interaction between International Law and Domestic Law in the Present Domain of Protection

Human rights international supervisory organs have often been careful to acknowledge expressly the subsidiary nature of the international enforcement machinery established thereunder. The notion of *subsidiarity* has for a long time been generally invoked in relation to jurisdictional issues or the admissibility of international complaints (in connection, e.g., often with the rule of exhaustion of local remedies). The *rationale* of this subsidiary nature[129] has found support in State practice, case-law, treaties, and doctrine, but it does not follow therefrom that the scope of the local remedies rule is unlimited (cf. *supra*). A misunderstanding of the rationale of the subsidiary role may unduly stress the formal requirement of exhaustion of local

---

[127] Cf. chapter X, *infra*.

[128] Cf., e.g., my Separate Opinions in the cases of the *Massacre of Plan de Sánchez versus Guatemala* (merits, Judgment of 29 April 2004, pars. 34–9 of the Opinion), of the *Massacres of Ituango versus Colombia* (Judgment of 01 July 2006, pars. 25–44 of the Opinion), of *Goiburú and Others versus Paraguay* (Judgment of 22 September 2006, pars. 3–68 of the Opinion), of *Almonacid Arellano versus Chile* (Judgment of 26 September 2006, pars. 26–8 of the Opinion), reproduced in: A.A. Cançado Trindade, *Derecho Internacional de los Derechos Humanos – Esencia y Trascendencia (Votos en la Corte Interamericana de Derechos Humanos, 1991–2006)*, Mexico, Edit. Porrúa/Universidad Iberoamericana, 2007, pp. 413–15, 736–43, 779–804 and 814–16, respectively.

[129] Cf. J.C. Witenberg, 'La recevabilité des réclamations devant les juridictions internationales', 41 *RCADI* (1932) pp. 51–6; G. Dahm, 'Die Subsidiarität des internationalen Rechtsschutzes bei Völkerrechtswidriger Verletzung von Privatpersonen', in *Vom Deutschen zum Europäischen Recht – Festschrift für H. Dölle*, vol. II, Tubingen, Mohr-Siebeck, 1963, pp. 6–27.

remedies. It may be submitted that the subsidiary character of international proceedings, while offering an explanation for the *existence* of the local remedies rule, cannot properly be invoked as a justification for an enlargement of the *scope* of application of the rule as generally recognized in international law. Subsidiarity refers to procedural, and not substantive, law.

In my Separate Opinion in the case of the *Brothers Gómez Paquiyauri versus Peru* (Judgment of 08 July 2004) decided by the IACtHR, I added a precision as to the need to bear in mind the distinction between issues of the material law on State responsibility (starting with its birth or configuration) and the question of the 'subsidiarity' of international jurisdiction in relation to national jurisdiction. In that Opinion I stated that:

In my understanding, any violation of a right protected by the American Convention *immediately* engages the responsibility of the State; the *tempus commissi delicti* is that of the occurrence of the international wrongful act. This entails – as consequences of the original violation – the *conventional* obligations of the State of investigation of the facts, sanction to those responsible for them and reparation to the victims; if the State does not comply with them, it incurs in additional violations of the applicable international law.

(...) The implementation of such responsibility [of the State] (in a moment distinct from that of its birth) takes place necessarily in the light of the norms of the human rights treaty at issue, directly applicable in the domestic law of the State responsible for the breach.

(...) Furthermore, the conditions of admissibility of complaints or petitions under the American Convention pertain to the *implementation* of the responsibility, not to its *origin or birth*. Those conditions are of a procedural nature, whilst the determination of the responsibility of the State falls under the ambit of substantive or material law. Nor do I see how to relate such determination with the so-called 'principle of subsidiarity', which refers directly and specifically to the *mechanisms* of protection, at national and international levels, the international ones being considered as 'subsidiary' to the national ones.

The aforementioned subsidiarity does not encompass material law, that is, cannot be invoked as to the substantive norms pertaining to the protected rights, nor as to the contents and extent of the corresponding obligations. In my view, one cannot attribute to such subsidiarity a dimension which it effectively does not have and has never had. Moreover, the outlook of the relations between the international and national legal orders, from the perspective of the 'principle of subsidiarity', is essentially static. Accordingly, it fails to portray faithfully the dynamics and the current state of the evolution of the *interaction* between international law and the domestic law of the States in the present domain of protection, to the benefit of the protected human beings (pars. 20–21 and 23–24).

As I pointed out, in this respect, earlier on, in my Concurring Opinion in the case of '*The Last Temptation of Christ*' concerning Chile (2001) also before the IACtHR, international law will improve and strengthen the day that human conscience attains a stage of evolution so as no longer to admit the adoption of national laws (or administrative acts or judgments) that obstruct the application of the international norms of protection integrated into the domestic legal order (par. 10). Long before this Concurring Opinion, in an essay published in 1977–1978, I pondered that, as human rights treaties confer functions of protection to the national tribunals themselves in the application of the local remedies rule, such remedies integrate the procedures of international protection; the interaction resulting therefrom, between the international and national legal orders in the present domain of protection, has the purpose and effect of improving the national systems of judicial protection, as required by the international instruments of safeguard of human rights.[130]

---

[130] A.A. Cançado Trindade, 'Exhaustion of Remedies in International Law and the Role of National Courts', 17 *Archiv des Volkerrechts* – Tübingen (1977–1978) pp. 333–70; and cf., to the same effect, two decades later, A.A. Cançado Trindade, *O Esgotamento de Recursos Internos . . .* , *op. cit. supra* n. (94), pp. 176–7 and 244–5.

VI

Access to Justice: The Safeguard and Preservation of the Integrity of International Jurisdiction

I. The Intangibility of International Jurisdiction   113
II. The Position of International Human Rights Tribunals   114
    1. Developments in the European Human Rights System   114
    2. Developments in the Inter-American Human Rights System   115
    3. General Assessment   118
III. Direct Access of Individuals in Provisional Measures of Protection   119
IV. Access to Justice: The Realization of the Right to Justice   120
V. The Prevalence of the Guarantees of the Due Process of Law   122
VI. Concluding Observations   123

I. The Intangibility of International Jurisdiction

Access to justice for the individual at international level requires that the integrity and intangibility of the international jurisdiction be preserved, so as to achieve its mission: the full realization of justice. The importance of this basic requirement has been recognized by the European and American Conventions on Human Rights. In this chapter, attention is focused on the contribution of international human rights tribunals (under the ECHR and the ACHR) to international jurisdiction, and their grant of access to the true complaining party: the individual.

It may here be recalled, *in passim*, that access was not granted to individuals, but only to States, at the time of the drafting of the Statute of the PCIJ (in 1920), a position which has been retained to date, in Article 34(1) of the Statute of the ICJ, despite criticisms of the artificiality of the exclusive inter-State *contentieux*[1] (especially in cases having a direct bearing upon the rights of the human person),

---

[1] Cf. A.A. Cançado Trindade, 'International Law for Humankind: Towards a New Jus Gentium – General Course on Public International Law – Part I', 316 *Recueil des Cours de l'Académie de Droit International de la Haye* (2005) pp. 285–9, and sources referred to therein.

and despite early experiments which granted procedural status to individuals in the first half of the XXth century.[2]

The strict outlook of the PCIJ and ICJ Statute has regrettably led to concessions to inter-State voluntarism.[3] On the other hand, international human rights tribunals have freed themselves from the chains of State voluntarism, and displayed a much greater aptitude for upholding the intangibility of international jurisdiction, as will be shown in the present chapter. In fact, the case-law of the ECtHR and the IACtHR has at times proven decisive as it safeguards and preserves the integrity of the two international jurisdictions of protection of human beings at issue.

II. The Position of International Human Rights Tribunals

1. Developments in the European Human Rights System

In its well-known judgment in the *Belilos versus Switzerland* case (1988), the ECtHR considered the declaration formulated by the respondent State as amounting to a reservation (of a general character) by Switzerland to the ECHR, incompatible with the object and purpose of the latter (in the light of its [then] Article 64). The ECtHR thus contributed to securing the integrity of the mechanism of protection of the ECHR, in particular its petitioning system.

Subsequently, in *Loizidou versus Turkey* (Judgment on Preliminary Objections of 23 March 1995), the Court rejected the possibility of restrictions – by the Turkish declarations (restriction *ratione loci*) – in relation to the key provisions of [then] Article 25 (right of individual petition), and [then] Article 46 (acceptance of its jurisdiction in contentious matters) of the ECHR, prior to Protocol n. 11. To sustain another position, it added:

would not only seriously weaken the role of the Commission and Court in the discharge of their functions but would also diminish the effectiveness of the Convention as a constitutional instrument of the European public order (*ordre public*) (par. 75).

The Court rejected the argument of the respondent State that one could infer the possibility of restrictions to the then optional clauses of Articles 25 and 46 of the Convention by analogy with State practice under Article 36 of the Statute of the ICJ.

The ECtHR not only recalled the contrary State party practice (accepting such clauses without restrictions), but also stressed the fundamentally distinct context in which the two tribunals operate, the ICJ being 'a free-standing international

---

[2] A.A. Cançado Trindade, 'Exhaustion of Local Remedies in International Law Experiments Granting Procedural Status to Individuals in the First Half of the Twentieth Century', 24 *Netherlands International Law Review/Nederlands Tijdschrift voor international Recht* (1977) pp. 373–92.

[3] For a study, cf. A.A. Cançado Trindade, 'The Relevance of International Adjudication Revisited: Reflections on the Need and Quest for International Compulsory Jurisdiction', in *Towards World Constitutionalism – Issues in the Legal Ordering of the World Community* (eds. R.StJ. Macdonald and D.M. Johnston), Leiden, Nijhoff, 2005, pp. 515–42.

tribunal which has no links to a standard-setting treaty such as the Convention' (pars. 82 and 68). The ICJ, reiterated the ECtHR, settles legal questions in the inter-State *contentieux*, distinct from the functions of the supervisory organs of a 'normative treaty' like the ECHR. Accordingly, the 'unconditional acceptance' of the optional clauses of Articles 25 and 46 of the Convention does not leave margin for analogy with the practice of States under Article 36 of the Statute of the International Court of Justice (pars. 84–85).[4]

Subsequently, in its Judgment on Preliminary Objections (of 04 July 2001), in *I. Ilascu, A. Lesco, A. Ivantoc and T. Petrov-Popa versus Moldova and the Russian Federation*, the ECtHR's Grand Chamber confirmed its position on this important issue concerning the very basis of its compulsory jurisdiction in contentious matters. The Grand Chamber of the Court dismissed another attempted restriction of the kind by the respondent States, safeguarded the integrity of its own jurisdiction, and held that 'the concept of 'jurisdiction' within the meaning of Article 1 of the Convention is not limited to the High Contracting Parties' national territory', and further, 'their responsibility can be involved because of acts of their authorities producing effects outside their own territory'.[5]

2. Developments in the Inter-American Human Rights System

Shortly after the IACtHR's Judgment on the merits in *Castillo Petruzzi and Others versus Peru* (of 30 May 1999), the respondent State (under the Presidency of Mr Alberto Fujimori) announced the 'withdrawal' of its instrument of acceptance of the Court's compulsory jurisdiction, with 'immediate effects'. In its two Judgments on competence of 24 September 1999, in the cases of the *Constitutional Tribunal* and *Ivcher Bronstein versus Peru*, the IACtHR, in asserting its competence to adjudicate on those cases, declared the intended 'withdrawal' by the respondent State *inadmissible*. The Court warned that its competence could not be conditional upon acts distinct from its own. It added that, in recognizing its contentious jurisdiction, a State accepts the prerogative of the Court to decide on any question affecting its competence, being unable, later on, to attempt to withdraw suddenly, as that would undermine the whole international mechanism of protection.

The Court noted that there do exist unilateral acts of States which are autonomous (such as the recognition of State or government, diplomatic protest, promise, renunciation), and unilateral acts performed under the ambit of the law of treaties, governed and conditioned by the latter (such as ratification, reservations, acceptance of the clause of contentious jurisdiction of an international tribunal). The ACHR cannot be at the mercy of limitations it does not provide for, imposed

---

[4] For an assessment of the contribution of the Court's Judgments in the *Loizidou* case, and the higher standards of the first Judgment (on Preliminary Objections, 1995) in comparison with the second (on the Merits, 1996), cf., e.g., P. Tavernier, 'Le droit international dans la jurisprudence de la Cour Européenne des Droits de l'Homme: L'apport des arrêts *Loizidou contre Turquie*', in *Du droit interne au droit international – Mélanges R. Goy*, Rouen, Université de Rouen, 1998, pp. 411–27.

[5] ECtHR, the case of *I. Ilascu, A. Lesco, A. Ivantoc and T. Petrov-Popa versus Moldova and the Russian Federation*, Preliminary Objections, Judgment of 04 July 2001, item I.2.a.(ii).(b), p. 17.

suddenly by a State Party for reasons of domestic order. The ACHR does not foresee the unilateral withdrawal of a clause, and even less of a clause of the importance of the one which provides for the acceptance of the contentious jurisdiction of the Court. The sole possibility which it foresees is that of the denunciation of the Convention as a whole, with the observance of a 12-month lapse of time, and without comprising facts prior to the denunciation. This is the same lapse of time set forth in the Vienna Convention on the Law of Treaties of 1969. This is an imperative of juridical security, which ought to be rigorously observed in the interest of all States Parties.

The Court thus proceeded with its examination of the pending contentious cases against the Peruvian State – and it could not have been otherwise: this is a duty incumbent upon it, under the ACHR, as an autonomous judicial organ of international protection of human rights. The respondent State had undertaken an international engagement from which it could not suddenly withdraw on its own terms. The purported unilateral 'withdrawal' with 'immediate effects' of the respondent State had no legal foundation – neither in the ACR, nor in the law of treaties, nor in general international law. The intended 'withdrawal', besides being unfounded, would have brought about the ruin, to the detriment of all States Parties, of the inter-American system of protection as a whole. The Court then decided that the intended 'withdrawal' of the respondent State was 'inadmissible'.

With its important decision in those cases the Court safeguarded the integrity of the ACHR, which, as other human rights treaties, bases its application on the *collective guarantee* in the operation of the international mechanism of protection. The Court's Judgments in *Constitutional Tribunal* and of *Ivcher Bronstein versus Peru*, contributed ultimately to enhancing the foundation of its jurisdiction in contentious matters.[6] With the subsequent change in government in the country, the Peruvian State rendered the earlier purported 'withdrawal' from the Court's competence 'without effects', and 'normalized' its relations with the latter (on 09 February 2001),[7] complying with its Judgments.[8]

---

[6] In that regard, also deserving of special mention are the Judgments of the Court in the *Blake versus Guatemala* case (preliminary objections, 1996; merits, 1998; and reparations, 1999): its decision on the legal issue raised therein, in relation to the alleged limitation *ratione temporis* of the Court's competence, touched the very basis of its jurisdiction in contentious matters.

[7] On that date, the Minister of Justice of Peru visited the headquarters of the Court in San José of Costa Rica, and handed to the Court's President two notes, whereby the Peruvian State expressly recognized its international responsibility for the violation of the rights of the three dismissed Judges of the Constitutional Tribunal, as well as of Mr Baruch Ivcher Bronstein (with regard to the Court's Judgments, on the merits, of 31 January 2001, and 06 February 2001, respectively), and detailed the measures the Peruvian State was taking in order to re-establish the rights of those persons. Inter-American Court of Human Rights, *Press Release CDH-CP2/01*, of 09 February 2001, pp. 1–2.

[8] For an account of the historical significance of the Inter-American Court's decisions in the cases of the *Constitutional Tribunal* and of *Ivcher Bronstein versus Peru*, cf. A.A. Cançado Trindade, 'El Perú y la Corte Interamericana de Derechos Humanos – Una Evaluación Histórica (Part I)', in: 138 *Ideele – Revista del Instituto de Defensa Legal* – Lima/Peru (June 2001) pp. 108–13; A.A. Cançado Trindade, 'El Perú y la Corte Interamericana de Derechos Humanos (Part II)', in: 139 *Ideele – Revista del Instituto de Defensa Legal* – Lima/Peru (July 2001) pp. 85–8.

The basis of the Court's jurisdiction in contentious matters came also to the fore in the cases of *Hilaire, Benjamin, and Constantine versus Trinidad and Tobago* (Preliminary Objections, 2001). The respondent State raised a preliminary objection of a kind not expressly foreseen by Article 62 of the ACHR, which, in the Court's assessment, 'would lead to a situation in which the Court would have as first parameter of reference the Constitution of the State and only subsidiarily the American Convention, situation which would bring about a fragmentation of the international legal order of protection of human rights and would render illusory the object and purpose of the American Convention' (par. 93).

This was clearly unacceptable; as the Court, furthermore, observed, 'the instrument of acceptance on the part of Trinidad and Tobago, of the contentious jurisdiction of the Tribunal, does not fit into the hypotheses foreseen in Article 62(2) of the Convention. It has a general scope, which ends up by subordinating totally the application of the American Convention to the domestic law of Trinidad and Tobago pursuant to what its national tribunals decide. All this implies that this instrument of acceptance is manifestly incompatible with the object and purpose of the Convention' (par. 88). On the basis of this conclusion as to the *rationale* of Article 62(2), the Court retained jurisdiction to adjudicate on the *Hilaire, Benjamin, and Constantine* cases, and safeguarded the integrity of its own jurisdictional basis in particular, and of the mechanism of protection under the ACHR as a whole.[9]

The IACtHR's firm position in tackling these key issues of interpretation and application of the ACHR has played an important role.[10] The Court pointed out that these issues pertained to conventional clauses of fundamental relevance of the international protection of human rights, and warned that any attempt to undermine them would threaten the functioning of the whole mechanism of protection under the ACHR, being thus inadmissible. The Court's decisions, in the cases concerning Peru and Trinidad and Tobago, regarded the provisions on the right of individual petition and on the recognition of its compulsory jurisdiction as constituting the basic pillars of the mechanism whereby the emancipation of the individual vis-à-vis his own State is achieved.[11]

---

[9] Cf. also Separate Opinion of Judge A.A. Cançado Trindade, pars. 1–39.

[10] Such as the right of individual petition (in the case *Castillo Petruzzi and Others versus Peru*, preliminary objections, 1998) and the basis of its own jurisdiction in contentious matters (in the cases of the *Constitutional Tribunal* and of *Ivcher Bronstein versus Peru*, competence, 1999, and in the cases of *Hilaire, Benjamin and Constantine versus Trinidad and Tobago*, preliminary objections, 2001).

[11] For a recent study, cf. A.A. Cançado Trindade, 'Las Cláusulas Pétreas de la Protección Internacional del Ser Humano: El Acceso Directo de los Individuos a la Justicia a Nivel Internacional y la Intangibilidad de la Jurisdicción Obligatoria de los Tribunales Internacionales de Derechos Humanos', in *El Sistema Interamericano de Protección de los Derechos Humanos en el Umbral del Siglo XXI – Memoria del Seminario* (November 1999), vol. I, San José de Costa Rica, Corte Interamericana de Derechos Humanos, 2001, pp. 3–68.

3. General Assessment

The converging case-law of both the European and the Inter-American Courts on international jurisdiction has thus rightly set limits to State voluntarism, has safeguarded the integrity of the European and American Conventions, respectively, as well as the primacy of considerations of *ordre public* over the will of individual States. It has, furthermore, set higher standards of State behaviour, and established some degree of control over the interposition of undue restrictions by States. In has, in addition, reassuringly enhanced the position of individuals as subjects of international human rights law, with full procedural capacity.

In the guest speech I delivered, as President of the IACtHR, at the ceremony of official opening of the judicial year of 2004 of the ECtHR, held at the *Palais des Droits de l'Homme* in Strasbourg, on 22 January 2004, I saw it fit to stress the contribution of the case-law of the two International Human Rights Tribunals in such matters as the right of access to justice – and of obtaining reparation – at international level,[12] and the safeguard and strengthening of the respective mechanisms of international protection.[13] Likewise, both the Inter-American and the European Courts have taken into account basic principles and general International Law.[14]

In the aforementioned speech, I pointed out, *inter alia*, on this particular issue, precisely that:

In the domain of the protection of the fundamental rights of the human person, the growth and consolidation of international human rights jurisdictions in our two continents – Europe and America – bear witness of the notorious advances of the old ideal of international justice in our days. The fruitful dialogue which our two Human Rights Courts have established in recent years, in a spirit of cooperation, mutual respect and coordination in the pursuit of a common cause and ideal, constitutes nowadays an inspiring example to other international tribunals.

---

[12] Cf., on cross-references between their respective case-law and the jurisprudential cross-fertilization, A.A. Cançado Trindade, 'Approximations and Convergences in the Case-Law of the European and Inter-American Courts of Human Rights', in *Le rayonnement international de la jurisprudence de la Cour européenne des droits de l'homme* (eds. G. Cohen-Jonathan and J.-F. Flauss), Bruxelles, Nemesis/Bruylant, 2005, pp. 101–38; and cf. also A.A. Cançado Trindade, 'The Merits of Coordination of International Courts on Human Rights', 2 *Journal of International Criminal Justice* – Oxford (2004) pp. 309–12.

[13] The aforementioned speech is reproduced in: European Court of Human Rights/Cour Européenne des Droits de l'homme, *Annual Report 2004/Rapport annuel 2004*, Strasbourg, ECtHR/Cour-EDH, 2004, pp. 41–50; and cf. A.A. Cançado Trindade, 'The Development of International Human Rights Law by the Operation and the Case-Law of the European and Inter-American Courts of Human Rights', 25 *Human Rights Law Journal* (2004) pp. 157–60; A.A. Cançado Trindade, 'Le développement du Droit international des droits de l'homme à travers l'activité et la jurisprudence des Cours européenne et interaméricaine des droits de l'homme', 16 *Revue universelle des droits de l'homme* (2004) pp. 177–80.

[14] Cf. A.A. Cançado Trindade, 'La Convention Américaine relative aux Droits de l'homme et le droit international général', in *Droit international, droits de l'homme et juridictions internationales* (eds. G. Cohen-Jonathan and J.-F. Flauss), Bruxelles, Bruylant, 2004, pp. 59–71; and L. Caflisch and A.A. Cançado Trindade, 'Les Conventions Américaine et Européenne des Droits de l'homme et le droit international général', 108 *Revue générale de Droit international public* (2004) pp. 5–62.

Both the European and Inter-American Courts have rightly set limits to State voluntarism (. . .). In so far as the basis of their jurisdiction in contentious matters is concerned, eloquent illustrations of their firm stand in support of the integrity of the mechanisms of protection of the two Conventions are afforded, for example, by the decisions of the European Court in the *Belilos versus Switzerland* case (1988), in the *Loizidou versus Turkey* case (Preliminary Objections, 1995), and in the *I. Ilascu, A. Lesco, A. Ivantoc and T. Petrov-Popa versus Moldovia and the Russian Federation* case (2001), as well as by the decisions of the Inter-American Court in the *Constitutional Tribunal* and *Ivtcher Bronstein versus Peru* cases, Jurisdiction (1999), and in the *Hilaire, Constantine and Benjamin and Others versus Trinidad and Tobago* (Preliminary Objection, 2001).

Our two international human rights Tribunals, by correctly resolving basic procedural issues raised in the aforementioned cases, have aptly made use of the techniques of Public International Law in order to strengthen their respective jurisdictions of protection of the human person. They have decisively safeguarded the integrity of the mechanisms of protection of the American and European Conventions on Human Rights, whereby the juridical emancipation of the human person vis-à-vis her own State is achieved (pars. 12–14).[15]

III. Direct Access of Individuals in Provisional Measures of Protection

Under Article 63(2) of the ACHR, the IACtHR can also order any Provisional Measures of Protection that it considers necessary, in cases of extreme gravity and urgency and in order to avoid irreparable damage to persons. It may do so – and it has in fact done so – in relation both to pending cases and to cases which have not yet been submitted to it, upon request of the Commission. The great majority of the petitions of provisional measures have been admitted and ordered by the IACtHR, in relation both to cases pending before it, as well as those not yet submitted, at the request of the Commission.

By means of another development, the position of individuals seeking protection has been lately strengthened in the present domain of provisional measures of protection. In the case of the *Constitutional Tribunal* (2000), concerning Peru, one of the three Judges dismissed from that Tribunal lodged a request for Interim Measures of Protection directly with the IACtHR. As the case was pending before the Court (which was not then in session), its President adopted Urgent Measures, *ex officio* (on 07 April 2000), for the first time in the Court's history, in order to avoid irreparable damage to the petitioner. The same situation occurred in *Loayza Tamayo versus Peru* (2000, then under supervision for execution of the Sentence). In both cases the full Court ratified the Urgent Measures ordered by its President.

Over two years later, in its Resolution of 20 December 2002, in the case of *Bámaca Velásquez versus Guatemala*, the President of the Court once again ordered urgent measures of protection, upon request of the representative of the victims

---

[15] A.A. Cançado Trindade, 'The Development of International Human Rights Law by the Operation and the Case-Law of the European and Inter-American Courts of Human Rights', 25 *Human Rights Law Journal* (2004) pp. 1560.

directly lodged with the Court,[16] so as to safeguard the life and personal integrity of the members of the family Bámaca Velásquez residing permanently in Guatemala (resolutory point n. 1).[17] Such measures were also endorsed by the full Court. Those three significant episodes, which nowadays constitute the practice of the Court on this particular issue, illustrate the importance of the *direct access* of the petitioners to the Court, even more forcefully in situations of extreme gravity and urgency.

IV. Access to Justice: The Realization of the Right to Justice

In the same line of thinking, the Court issued a Judgment on Jurisdiction, on 28 November 2003, in the case of *Baena Ricardo and Others versus Panama*, in which the Court asserted its competence to supervise the execution of its own judgments. In unanimously rejecting the challenge of the respondent State, the Court affirmed that, in its exercise of that competence, it is entitled to request of the responsible States reports on the reparations measures, to evaluate such reports, and to issue instructions and resolutions on compliance (or otherwise) with its judgments. Moreover, the challenge to the Court's competence to supervise compliance with its decisions was not successful, and it decided by unanimity to continue supervising compliance by the respondent State with its earlier Judgment (of 02 February 2001) in the case of *Baena Ricardo and Others versus Panama*.

This landmark Judgment remains the leading case in which the Court upheld, *motu proprio*, its faculty to supervise execution *ex officio*, inherent to its jurisdictional function.[18] From 2003 onwards, the IACtHR has been adopting *motu proprio* resolutions of supervision of compliance with its own Judgments, thus filling a gap in the inter-American human rights system, which, unlike its counterpart the European system, is not endowed with an organ equivalent to the Committee of Ministers. In dismissing the challenge of the respondent State, the IACtHR upheld its faculty to supervise *ex officio* the execution of its Judgments, inherent to its jurisdictional function.[19]

---

[16] Just as he had done, earlier on, in the year 2000, in the *Constitutional Tribunal* and *Loayza Tamayo* cases, concerning Peru; his urgent measures were promptly ratified by the full Court, as soon as this latter restarted sessioning (in August 2000 and February 2001, respectively).

[17] The case had already been decided as to the merits (in 2000) and reparations (in 2002, cf. *supra*), but the Court retained jurisdiction over it so as to supervise the execution of, and compliance with, its earlier judgments on the specific case.

[18] So as to, in due course, in case of manifest non-compliance, inform the General Assembly of the Organization of American States (OAS), for the measures to be taken, in pursuance of the provision of Article 65 of the American Convention. The last occasions in which this sanction was applied, however, were in the OAS General Assemblies of 2000 and 2003, when the then President of the Court informed the main organs of the OAS of the non-compliance of Judgments by Peru, and Trinidad and Tobago, respectively. Ever since, in 2004–2005, the Court kept on supervising the execution of Judgments without applying Article 65, although several Judgments have only been partly complied with by the respective respondent States. This presents a problem which has not found a satisfactory solution so far, in the ambit of the inter-American human rights system.

[19] For the proposal by the [then] President of the Inter-American Court for the creation, within the Commission of Legal and Political Affairs (CAJP) of the Organization of American States (OAS), of a Committee (formed by representatives of States Parties to the American Convention) to be entrusted

The ECtHR, in its turn, irrespective of the fact that the European system of protection counts, for the supervision of the execution of its Judgments, on the Committee of Ministers (in the ambit of the Council of Europe), has insisted that the right to a fair trial by a competent, independent and impartial judge or tribunal (Article 6(1) of the ECHR) would be illusory if it only referred to the formulation of procedural guarantees and the conduct of the contending parties, without also comprising the implementation of judicial decisions, which would hardly be consonant with the very notion of the *rule of law (prééminence du Droit)*.[20]

The correct administration of justice is one of the essential elements of the rule of law, which includes the execution of judgments, and even more forcefully when the latter seek to secure the intangibility of the guarantees of the due process of law (as pointed out by the international case-law on the matter). As the ECtHR warned in its Judgment *Hornsby versus Greece* (of 19 March 1997), the omission or refusal on the part of public authorities to execute a judgment constitutes a *denial of the access to justice* (at both national and international levels).[21]

In fact, the realization of the right to justice is required, and is to be accomplished, at both national and international levels. In its Judgment (of 28 February 2003) in the case of *Five Pensioners versus Peru* (the first case entirely resolved by IACtHR under its new Regulations, in force as from 01 June 2001), the IACtHR declared, by unanimity, that the respondent State had violated the right to property set forth in Article 21 of the ACHR, as a result of modifications introduced in the regime of pensions. The Court further established violations of Article 25 (right to judicial protection), in combination with Articles 1(1) and 2 of the Convention. The Court held that its Judgment constituted per se a form of reparation to the victims, and decided, moreover, that the State should undertake the corresponding investigations and apply the pertinent sanctions to those responsible for non-compliance with the judicial sentences of the Peruvian tribunals (not executed by public administration), in the development of the actions of guarantee interposed by the victims.[22]

In my Concurring Opinion in the *Five Pensioners* case, I expressed my view that the assertion of the legal personality and capacity of the individuals as subjects of both domestic and international law:

specifically with the supervision, on a *permanent* basis, within the OAS, of the execution of the Judgments of the Inter-American Court, cf. A.A. Cançado Trindade, *Bases para un Proyecto de Protocolo a la Convención Americana sobre Derechos Humanos, para Fortalecer Su Mecanismo de Protección*, vol. II, 2nd. ed., San José of Costa Rica, Inter-American Court of Human Rights, 2003, pp. 47–9, 111, 125, 234–5, 664, 793–5 and 918–21, esp. pp. 793–4. The proposal remains still under study at the OAS and taken note of in successive OAS resolutions until the end of 2007 — but no concrete initiative has yet been taken on this particular issue.

[20] Cf., in this sense, ECtHR, *Hornsby versus Greece* case (Judgment of 19 March 1997), Series A, n. 33, pp. 510–11, par. 40.

[21] Cf. ibid., pp. 511–12, pars. 41 and 45 (in violation of Article 6(1) of the European Convention). Subsequently, in its Judgment on reparations (of 01 April 1998) in the same case *Hornsby versus Greece*, the European Court expressed a feeling of 'uncertainty and anxiety' and 'a profound sentiment of injustice' generated by the non-compliance with its Judgment; ECtHR, *Hornsby versus Greece* case (reparations), p. 8, par. 18.

[22] It further ordered the payment of indemnities to the four victims and to the widow of the fifth one, and the payment of the costs of the process.

constitutes the truly revolutionary legacy of the evolution of the international legal doctrine in the second half of the XXth. century. The moment has arrived to overcome the classic limitations of the *legitimatio ad causam* in International Law, which has much refrained its progressive development towards the construction of a new *jus gentium*. (...) (par. 24).[23]

In the circumstances of the case of the *Five Pensioners*, the consolidated international legal personality and capacity of individual petitioners assisted the assertion of that legal personality and capacity in the domain of the Peruvian domestic law.

In summary and conclusion on this particular point, 'a State Party to the American and European Conventions of Human Rights which does not execute a sentence of the Inter-American or European Court of Human Rights fails to put an end to the consequences of the original violation – established by those Courts – of the respective Conventions, thereby incurring into an additional violation of these latter, as well as into a denial of the access to justice thereunder'.[24] There is thus a pressing need to adopt, at national level, mechanisms of domestic law to secure the faithful execution of the sentences of the international human rights tribunals.

At international level there is, likewise, the need to develop the supervision of faithful compliance, by States, with the judgments of these human rights tribunals.[25] In this respect, besides the obligation of all States Parties to those human rights treaties to respect, and to secure respect for, the rights protected thereunder, there is also the obligation of the States Parties *inter se* to secure the integrity and effectiveness of the Conventions at issue: such general duty of protection (the collective guarantee) is of direct interest to each State Party, and to them all jointly.

V. The Prevalence of the Guarantees of the Due Process of Law

Last but not least, the realization of the right to justice necessarily implies the prevalence of the guarantees of the due process of law. Out of the vast international case-law on this particular point, two cases may be singled out, one from the IACtHR and the other from the ECtHR. In *Loayza Tamayo versus Peru* (Judgment of 17 September 1997), the IACtHR declared – for the first time in the so-called cycle of *Peruvian cases* (under the Fujimori regime) – that the Peruvian decrees – laws which typified the delicts of terrorism and '*traición a la patria*' were incompatible with Article 8(4) of the ACHR,[26] in that they were in breach of the

---

[23] More recently, I have recalled this ponderation in my Concurring Opinion (par. 7) in the Provisional Measures of Protection in the case of the *Children and Adolescents Deprived of Freedom in the 'Complexo de Tatuapé' of FEBEM versus Brazil* (Resolution of 30 November 2005).

[24] A.A. Cançado Trindade, 'Las Cláusulas Pétreas de la Protección Internacional del Ser Humano: El Acceso Directo de los Individuos a la Justicia a Nivel Internacional...', *op. cit. supra* n. (11), p. 61 (my own translation).

[25] Cf. E. Lambert, *Les effets des arrêts de la Cour Européenne des Droits de l'homme*, Bruxelles, Bruylant, 1999, pp. 99–527.

[26] For antecedents, in the Court's case-law, in support of the need to determine the incompatibility of domestic laws per se with the ACHR, and urging the Court to proceed to such determination within the context of concrete cases, cf. the Dissenting Opinions of Judge Cançado Trindade in the following cases: *El Amparo*, concerning Venezuela, Judgement (on reparations) of 14 September 1996, and

principle of *non bis in idem* set forth therein. Significantly, some days after the Court's Judgment, the respondent State complied with the Court's order to release the prisoner (Mrs María Elena Loayza Tamayo) and, moreover, announced its decision to put an end to the so-called tribunals of 'faceless judges' (*'jueces sin rostro'*) in Peru.[27] The case thus became a *cause célèbre* in the history of the international protection of human rights in the American continent.

In turn, the ECtHR, in *Kurt versus Turkey* (1998), having (also) established a violation of Article 5, emphasized the 'fundamental importance' of the guarantees enshrined in Article 5 to safeguard the right of the individuals in a democracy to be free from arbitrary detention in the hands of the authorities.[28] As the *rationale* of Article 5 is to protect the individual against arbitrariness, the Court proceeded, the circumstances foreseen in Article 5(1) in which an individual can be legally deprived of his freedom ought to have a 'restrictive interpretation' for constituting exceptions to the most basic guarantee of personal liberty; thus, the detention ought always to be subject to 'judicial scrutiny' in order to secure the responsibility of the authorities for that act.[29] Thus, the secret or clandestine detention of an individual, the Court warned in the aforementioned case *Kurt versus Turkey*, is a 'complete denial' of those guarantees and one of the 'most serious' violations of Article 5; the authorities ought thereby to take effective measures to safeguard the 'risks of disappearance' and ought to conduct a prompt and effective investigation of the whereabouts of a person who was under detention.[30]

VI. Concluding Observations

In their evolving case-law in recent years, both the European and the Inter-American Courts of Human Rights have disclosed their awareness as to the importance of the intangibility of their respective jurisdictions to secure the access to justice of the human person and to achieve the realization of justice. This holds true also in relation to provisional measures of protection. The preservation of the integrity of jurisdiction also extends to the Courts' supervision of the execution of judgments, a faculty which the IACtHR has deemed inherent to its jurisdictional function. After all, the right of access to justice *lato sensu* encompasses guarantees of the due process of law as well as faithful execution of judgments, thus requiring the preservation of the integrity of jurisdiction, altogether essential to the prevalence of the rule of law in a democratic society.

Resolution (on interpretation of judgement) of 16 April 1997; *Caballero Delgado and Santana versus Colombia*, Judgement (on reparations) of 29 January 1997; and *Genie Lacayo versus Nicaragua*, Resolution (on request for revision of judgment) of 13 September 1997.

[27] This decision was announced by the Peruvian government in October 1997, shortly after the release of the prisoner on October 16th, communicated to the Court on October 20th.

[28] ECtHR, *Kurt versus Turkey* case, Judgment of 25 May 1998, in *Recueil des arrêts et décisions/ Reports of Judgments and Decisions*, n. 74, pp. 1184–5, par. 122.

[29] Ibid., p. 1185, pars. 122–3.

[30] Ibid., p. 1185, par. 124, and cf. p. 187, par. 129.

The Inter-American and European Courts of Human Rights have endeavoured to secure compliance with the conventional obligations of protection of States vis-à-vis all human beings under their respective jurisdictions. The current trend towards the strengthening of international compulsory jurisdiction, in the present domain of protection,[31] can only further advance the safeguard and preservation of the integrity of international jurisdiction, as the ineluctable counterpart of the individual right of access to international justice. The ultimate beneficiary of this evolution is the human person.

[31] A.A. Cançado Trindade, 'The Relevance of International Adjudication Revisited: Reflections on the Need and Quest for International Compulsory Jurisdiction', in *Towards World Constitutionalism – Issues in the Legal Ordering of the World Community* (eds. R.St Macdonald and D.M. Johnston), Leiden, Nijhoff, 2005, pp. 515–42.

VII

New Developments in the Notion of 'Potential Victim': The Preventive Dimension of Protection

I. Introduction   125

II. Origins and Development of the Notion of Victim   125

III. The Continuing Evolution of the Notion of 'Potential Victim'   127

IV. New Developments of the Notion of 'Potential Victim'   129

   1. Autonomous Configuration of the Notion of Victim in its
   Preventive Dimension   130

   2. Condition of Victim and *Legitimatio ad Causam*: A Precision   130

V. Concluding Observations   131

I. Introduction

In addressing, in this chapter, the ongoing evolution of the notion of "potential victim", it is particularly fitting to recapitulate, with a new perception, in the light of accumulated experience in time in the protection of victim's rights, the origins and development of the notion of victim. This will be done in addition to the considerations already developed with regard to the titularity (in its distinct formulations) of the right of individual petition under the three regional (European, Inter-American and African) Conventions on Human Rights.[1] Attention will then be focused on new developments of the notion of "potential victim", encompassing its autonomous configuration, and a precision as to the condition of victim and *legitimatio ad causam*. The way will thus be paved for my concluding observations on the matter.

II. Origins and Development of the Notion of Victim

Etymologically, the term *victim* (from the Latin *victima*) was employed originally in relation to a person who was sacrificed (in rituals) or destined to be sacrificed. In the

---

[1] Cf. chapter II, *supra*.

XVIIth century, it acquired the sense of a person who was hurt or harmed, tortured or killed by another. In the XVIIIth century the term began to designate the person injured or oppressed by another, or by some power or situation. The term 'to victimize' came to be used in the XIXth century (1830 onwards).[2] In the XXth century, the new discipline *victimology* focused its attention on the person of the victim,[3] – in counterposition to criminology, which was centred rather on the person of the offender or criminal.

The victim is at times referred to as the 'injured party', under certain present-day human rights treaties; the victim is the human person who has suffered a harm or prejudice, either individually or with other human beings, as a consequence of an internationally wrongful act or omission.[4] Historically, the concept of victim is one of 'the most ancient of humankind', belonging to 'all cultures'.[5] As the State gradually monopolized the means of coercion, the role of victims was somewhat reduced (e.g., to that of a witness) or marginalized in the legal process opposing the State to the accused (in penal procedural law), often to the dissatisfaction of the victim.[6]

In fact, while the conceptual universe of criminology became oriented to the figure of the delinquent, placing the victim in a tangential or marginal position, the emerging discipline of victimology attempted to redress that imbalance, centring attention on the person of the victim, on the need to rehabilitate the latter and to provide her due and adequate reparations.[7] It was, however, the remarkable evolution of international human rights law throughout the second half of the XXth century to the present that propitiated the realization of that aim, by being wholly and duly *victim-oriented*.[8]

The advent and consolidation of the *corpus juris* of international human rights law returned the victim to her *central* position in the normative order. Moreover, the victim has also recovered space, more recently, also in the domain of contemporary criminal law – both domestic and international – as indicated, e.g., by the adoption of the 1985 UN Declaration on Basic Principles of Justice for Victims of Crime and Abuse of Power (pertaining to crimes under domestic law), and the

---

[2] Cf. *The Oxford English Dictionary*, 2nd. ed., vol. XIX, Oxford, Clarendon Press, 1989, p. 607; Asociación H. Capitant, *Vocabulario Jurídico* (dir. G. Cornu), Bogotá, Temis, 1995, p. 904; G. Gómez de Silva, *Breve Diccionario Etimológico de la Lengua Española*, Mexico, El Colegio de Mexico/FCE, 1996 [reimpr.], p. 719.

[3] Cf. E. Neuman, *Victimología – El Rol de la Víctima en los Delitos Convencionales y No Convencionales*, Buenos Aires, Edit. Universidad, 1994, pp. 27–8.

[4] Cf. Union Académique Internationale, *Dictionnaire de la terminologie du Droit international*, Paris, Sirey, 1960, pp. 448–9; J. Salmon (dir.), *Dictionnaire de Droit international public*, Bruxelles, Bruylant, 2001, p. 1131.

[5] A.-J. Arnaud *et alii* (dir.), *Dictionnaire encyclopédique de théorie et de sociologie du Droit*, 2nd. ed., Paris, LGDJ, 1993, p. 641 (entry by E. Viano).

[6] Ibid., pp. 642–3 (entry by E.V.).

[7] Cf., e.g., G. Landrove Díaz, *Victimología*, Valencia, Tirant Lo Blanch, 1990, pp. 22–6, 139–40 and 150; L. Rodríguez Manzanera, *Victimología – Estudio de la Víctima*, 8th. ed., Mexico, Edit. Porrúa, 2003, pp. 25 and 67.

[8] Cf. A.A. Cançado Trindade, *Tratado de Direito Internacional dos Direitos Humanos*, vol. III, Porto Alegre/Brazil, S.A. Fabris Ed., 2003, pp. 447–97.

2006 UN Basic Principles and Guidelines on the Right to a Remedy and Reparation for Victims of Gross Violations of International Human Rights Law and Serious Violations of International Humanitarian Law (concerning international crimes).[9]

This new outlook is an example of what I have termed, in an earlier chapter, the *interaction* between international law and domestic law in the domain of protection of the rights of the human person.[10] The individual's central position in the normative system entitles the victim (or his or her legal representatives), as a subject of international human rights law, to re-vindicate his or her injured rights and to claim for reparation, by means of the free and full exercise of the right of individual petition. It has been in the domain of international human rights law that victims of violations of human rights, who had often lost faith in human justice, have at last recovered that faith and have found redress.

Furthermore, international human rights protection has ineluctably a *preventive* dimension, which brings the notion of 'potential victim' to the fore. This notion has been judicially recognized, and marks presence in the realm of provisional measures of protection, for example, in particular, in the case-law of the IACtHR.[11] The notion of 'potential victim' has been developed over time by the ECtHR in contentious cases. New developments of the notion of potential victim comprise its autonomous configuration, as well as the condition of victim and the *legitimatio ad causam*, in relation to which a word of precision is made in the present chapter.

III. The Continuing Evolution of the Notion of 'Potential Victim'

In requiring individual petitioners to demonstrate they are *victims* of the protected rights (original Article 25, nowadays Article 34), the ECtHR soon developed an interpretation of the *notion of victim* under the Convention itself. In the series of lectures I delivered at The Hague Academy of International Law two decades ago, I devoted a whole chapter of my course of 1987 to the *evolution of the notion of victim* in the international human rights protection.[12] Ever since, new and significant developments have been taking place, but before I turn to them I will briefly recall five cases that I referred to, among a few others, in my aforementioned course at The Hague Academy, as significant precedents of the era prior to Protocols ns. 9 and 11 to the ECHR.

---

[9] Cf., e.g., M.C. Bassiouni, 'International Recognition of Victims' Rights', 6 *Human Rights Law Review* (2006) pp. 221–79; and cf.: I. Melup, 'The United Nations Declaration on [Basic] Principles of Justice for Victims of Crime and Abuse of Power', in *The Universal Declaration of Human Rights: Fifty Years and Beyond* (eds. Y. Danieli, E. Stamatopoulou and C.J. Dias), N.Y., U.N./Baywood Publ. Co., 1999, pp. 53–65; Th. van Boven, 'The Perspective of the Victim', in ibid., pp. 13–26; B.G. Ramcharan, 'A Victims' Perspective on the International Human Rights Treaty Regime', in ibid., pp. 27–35; G. Alfredsson, 'Human Rights and Victims' Rights in Europe', in ibid., 309–17.

[10] Cf. chapter V, *supra*.

[11] Cf. chapter VI, *supra*.

[12] A.A. Cançado Trindade, 'Co-Existence and Co-Ordination of Mechanisms of International Protection of Human Rights (At Global and Regional Levels)', 202 *Recueil des Cours de l'Académie de Droit International de La Haye* (1987), ch. XI, pp. 243–99.

In its Judgment in the case of *G. Klass and Others versus Federal Republic of Germany* (1978), concerning secret surveillance of private life, the European Court found that each of the applicants was entitled to claim to be a victim of a violation of the European Convention, as a result of the 'mere existence of secret measures or of legislation permitting secret measures, without having to allege that such measures were in fact applied to him'. In others words, 'a law may by itself violate the rights of an individual if the individual is directly affected by the law in the absence of any specific measure of implementation'.[13] In the following year, in its Judgment in the case of *P. and A. Marckx versus Belgium* (1979), concerning a challenge to a legal position of the Belgian Civil Code (pertaining to unmarried mothers and children born out of wedlock), the ECtHR reiterated its understanding that 'Article 25 of the Convention entitles individuals to contend that a law violates their rights by itself, in the absence of an individual measure of implementation, if they run the risk of being directly affected by it'.[14]

Subsequently, in *Dudgeon versus United Kingdom* (1981), the ECtHR again found that 'the maintenance in force of the impugned legislation' constituted 'a continuing interference with the applicant's right to respect for his private life (which includes his sexual life)', the threat 'hanging over him' being 'real'; the Court concluded that he had suffered and continued to suffer 'an unjustified interference with his right to respect for his private life' in breach of Article 8 of the Convention.[15] Once again, in its Judgment in the case of *Johnston and Others versus Ireland* (1986), concerning the effects of domestic law on the inability to divorce and re-marry and the issue of respect for family life, the ECtHR found that individual petitioners were entitled 'to contend that a law violates their rights by itself, in the absence of an individual measure of implementation, if they run the risk of being directly affected by it'.[16]

By then, the Court's position had become 'well-established case-law' on the point at issue,[17] as expressly acknowledged by the Court itself. Much earlier on, the notion of 'potential victims' had also been raised by the former European Commission of Human Rights (EComHR) in the case of the *Vietnamese Orphans* (*H. Becker versus Denmark* case, 1975); the applicant had not claimed to have himself been the direct victim of a violation of the Convention, but instead, the Vietnamese orphans (under the risk of being returned to Vietnam in view of the [then] Danish government's policy of repatriation) were, in the words of the EComHR itself, 'the proper applicants and the *potential victims*'. Yet they depended on the applicant (as orphans), and the EComHR accepted that the applicant had been entrusted[18] with 'at least the care of the children' on behalf of their parents. The EComHR accordingly considered the applicant, for the purpose of lodging the application, as

---

[13] *Cit.* in ibid., p. 276.   [14] *Cit.* in ibid., pp. 276–7.
[15] *Cit.* in ibid., p. 277.   [16] *Cit.* in ibid., p. 278.
[17] To the effect that the existence of a violation of the Convention was 'conceivable even in the absence of detriment', as the Court expressly stated in its Judgment in the *De Jong, Baljet and van den Brink versus The Netherlands* case (1984); *cit.* in ibid., p. 278.
[18] By 'the presumably competent Vietnamese authority of the time'; cf. ibid., p. 274.

an 'indirect victim', in that he had a 'valid personal interest in the welfare of the children'.[19]

Thus, over three decades ago, in the aforementioned *Vietnamese Orphans* case, the interrelationship between the notions of *indirect* and *potential* victims had already become apparent. Such concepts emerged in addition to that of direct victim, to fulfill the necessity of protection. In fact, the notion of 'potential victim' soon began to mark its presence in the case-law under the ECHR as a response to the needs and requirements of protection of the human person. It may be recalled, in addition to the five aforementioned cases, that, in the well-known case of *Soering versus United Kingdom* (1989), the ECtHR, in the face of imminent extradition of an individual to a country (the United States) where he could be sentenced to death, held that the situation – the so-called 'death row phenomenon' – exposed him to such psychological suffering that, if the extradition were to be maintained and executed, it would amount to a treatment in breach of his rights under Article 3 of the European Convention.[20] The evolution of the notion of 'potential victim' is still continuing today, as disclosed by the more recent case-law of both the European and the Inter-American Courts of Human Rights.

IV. New Developments of the Notion of 'Potential Victim'

The notion of 'potential victim' has never lost its relevance, as illustrated by the international case-law on the matter, under the European and American Conventions on Human Rights. Under the latter, the notion is present, despite the fact that the Convention does not require that the individual petitioners are victims. In its Judgment in the case of *Suárez Rosero versus Ecuador* (of 12 November 1997), the IACtHR declared that Article 114 *bis* of the Ecuadorean Penal Code, which deprived all persons in detention under the Anti-Drug Law of certain judicial guarantees (as to the length of detention), violated per se Article 2 of the American Convention, *irrespective of whether that norm of the Penal Code had been applied in the present case*. This was the first time that the Court established a violation of Article 2 of the American Convention (the general duty to harmonize national legislation with the norms of the American Convention)[21] by the existence per se of a provision of domestic law.[22] Mr Suárez Rosero was the direct victim in the case, but all other persons that were subject to that provision of the Ecuadorean Penal Code could be considered as potential victims (whether they were aware of that or not). Shortly

---

[19] *Cit.* in ibid., p. 274.

[20] For comments, cf., e.g., F. Sudre, 'Extradition et peine de mort: Arrêt *Soering* de la Cour Européenne des Droits de l'Homme, du 7 juillet 1989', 94 *Revue générale de Droit international public* (1990) pp. 103–21.

[21] The Court's Judgment in the *Suárez Rosero* case significantly devoted a whole section (n. XIV) to the establishment of the violation of Article 2 of the Convention.

[22] As Ecuador, in its view, by the existence of Article 114 *bis* of its Penal Code, had not taken the adequate measures of domestic law in order to render effective the right contemplated in Article 7(5) of the Convention. The Court, moreover, found the respondent State in breach *inter alia* of the judicial guarantees enshrined in Article 8(1) and (2) of the American Convention.

afterwards (on 24 December 1997), the Supreme Court of Ecuador decided to strike down the provision at issue, declaring it unconstitutional.[23] This was the first time that a provision of domestic law was modified as a result of a decision of the IACtHR.

1. Autonomous Configuration of the Notion of Victim in its Preventive Dimension

The relevance of *potential victims* in provisional measures of protection has lately been disclosed by the case-law of the IACtHR, on the basis of Article 63(2). Although the Court refers to 'beneficiaries of provisional measures of protection', they are all in fact *potential* victims, and if these measures of protection are not complied with by the State concerned, in the case of the American Convention there is a breach of the treaty, with the corresponding engagement of the responsibility of the State. In this way, the *notion of victim* clearly appears, in an *autonomous* way, in the domain of provisional measures of protection under the American Convention, irrespective of the decision on the merits of the case at issue.

2. Condition of Victim and *Legitimatio ad Causam*: A Precision

The determination of the condition of victims (including potential victims) thus always marks its presence, in contentious cases and in provisional measures of protection, and is distinct from the *legitimatio ad causam*, as the ACHR does not limit this latter to the petitioner claiming to be a victim himself or herself; Article 44 of the American Convention provides that any person or group of persons, or non-governmental entity legally recognized in one or more States members of the OAS, may lodge a petition or complaint with the Inter-American Commission of Human Rights (IAComHR). In this way, it considerably widens the right of international individual petition, as the mechanism *par excellence* of the direct access of individuals to international justice.

This particular matter was the object of attention of the IACtHR in the case of *Castillo Petruzzi and Others versus Peru*: in its Judgment (on preliminary objections) of 04 September 1998, the Court upheld the integrity of the right of individual petition under the American Convention on Human Rights (Article 44) in the circumstances of the case, by dismissing a preliminary objection on the part of the respondent State which unduly attempted to challenge the *legitimatio ad causam* of the non-governmental entity which lodged the complaint on behalf of the four victims (who were being held under detention).

In this Judgment, the IACtHR drew attention to the importance of the right of individual petition, observing that the broad faculty 'to make a complaint is a characteristic feature of the system for the international protection of human rights'

---

[23] Tribunal Constitucional/Secretaria General, cases ns. 174–92, 106–94 and 61–95 (joined), *Resolución n. 119-1-97*, Quito, December 1997, pp. 1–5 (internal circulation), esp. p. 5, for reference to the Judgment of the Inter-American Court of 12 November 1997 in the *Suárez Rosero* case.

(par. 77). The Court sustained the *legitimatio ad causam*, under Article 44 of the American Convention, not only of 'any person or group of persons' but also of 'any non-governmental entity legally recognised in *one or more* member States' of the OAS (and not necessarily in the respondent State only, as this latter argued).[24]

By thus upholding the *legitimatio ad causam* of the petitioner in the specific case, the IACtHR safeguarded the integrity of the right of individual petition, and, ultimately, of the mechanism of protection as a whole of the American Convention on Human Rights. In my Concurring Opinion in the *Castillo Petruzzi* case (Preliminary Objections, 1998), I pondered that 'without the right of individual petition, and the consequent access to justice at international level, the rights enshrined into the American Convention would be reduced to a little more than dead letter'; thus, the right of individual petition – rendering the protected rights effective – constitutes 'a fundamental clause (*cláusula pétrea*)' upon which was erected 'the juridical mechanism of emancipation of the human being vis-à-vis his own State for the protection of his rights in the ambit of the International Law of Human Rights' (pars. 35–36).

V. Concluding Observations

The notion of victim acquires a central position in the international *contentieux* of human rights. It discloses a temporal – preventive – dimension, as illustrated by the evolution and new developments of the notion of 'potential victim', of much significance for human rights protection, as indicated in the present chapter. The notion of victim marks its presence not only in relation to the *legitimatio ad causam* (as under a human rights treaty such as the European Convention), but *also* for purposes of *reparation* (although legal doctrine, somewhat surprisingly, has not yet dealt sufficiently with this particular point). As to this latter aspect, the notion of *victim*, of relevance to reparations, has experienced a necessary *enlargement*, comprising close relatives (of fatal victims) in their own right, in the settled case-law of the international tribunals (European and Inter-American Courts) of human rights. The case-law of the IACtHR has been particularly rich and revealing in the matter of reparations. In sum, one cannot prescind from the notion of victim, as human rights treaties and instruments have been adopted to protect their rights and to afford them appropriate redress.

---

[24] The non-governmental entity in that case, called FASIC ('Fundación de Ayuda Social de las Iglesias Cristianas'), was legally recognized in Chile, rather than in Peru.

VIII

The Protection of Victims in Situations of Great Adversity or Defencelessness – I

I. Introduction: International Protection of Victims in Distress   132

II. The Drama of Uprootedness and the Growing Need of Protection of Migrants   133

III. The Protection of Migrants in International Case-Law   142

    1. European Human Rights System   142

    2. Inter-American Human Rights System   144

       a. The Advisory Opinion on the *Right to Information on Consular Assistance in the Framework of the Guarantees of the Due Process of Law* (1999)   145

       b. The Advisory Opinion on the *Juridical Condition and Rights of Undocumented Migrants* (2003)   147

IV. Concluding Observations   149

I. Introduction: International Protection of Victims in Distress

The draftsmen of international instruments of human rights could hardly have foreseen that protection would thereby come to be extended to human beings in new situations of great adversity, or defencelessness, that could hardly have been anticipated in their days. This development discloses a reassuring aspect, namely, that due to the evolution of human conscience the international legal personality of the human person has come to be asserted even in situations of complete distress and utmost diversity. In such situations, when the victims had virtually lost all hope in human justice, yet they have had their cases heard and resolved, in recent years, by international human rights tribunals.

The following two chapters are not meant to provide an exhaustive list of such situations, but rather illustrative examples, on the basis of the criterion of selection of those which have succeeded in reaching these tribunals. Bearing this in mind, I purport to cover in the following two chapters the protection of:

a undocumented migrants;

b abandoned or 'street children';

c members of peace communities and other civilians in situations of armed conflict;

d internally displaced persons; and

e persons under sub-human conditions of detention.

Subsequently (in chapter X), I shall also examine the complexties surrounding the safeguard of the rights of victims of massacres or their relatives. The way will thus be paved for presenting my concluding observations on the prevalence of human rights of persons in situations of vulnerability.

II. The Drama of Uprootedness and the Growing Need of Protection of Migrants

The protection of the human rights of migrants has indeed become a key issue in the international human rights agenda in this first decade of the XXIst century. This is hardly surprising, given the growing awareness of the relationships between the intensification of migratory fluxes (from the late 1980s onwards), the speedy internationalization of capitalism, and the growing labour exploitation (generated by the 'requirements of capital', and with the high human costs of unemployment and underemployment, 'informality' in labour relations, search for cheap manpower, impoverishment of living conditions of large segments of the population, and concentration of wealth and income on a world scale).[1]

It was thus to be expected that, in the 1990s, the theme was to become object of increased attention on the part of international organizations at both universal (United Nations) and regional (Organization of American States) levels. At global level, lucid voices from within the Office of the U.N. High Commissioner for Refugees (UNHCR) warned that the UNHCR could no longer only work for the protection of refugees, but should also take into account the denial of human rights of internally displaced persons as well as migrants, and work for their protection, together with that of refugees.[2] In this connection, it should not pass unnoticed that the UNHCR actually intervened in the oral hearings before the IACtHR, in the advisory proceedings that led to the adoption of its Advisory Opinion n. 18 on *The Juridical Condition and Rights of Undocumented Migrants* (of 17 September 2003).[3]

---

[1] Cf., e.g., A.M. Aragonés Castañer, *Migración Internacional de Trabajadores – Una Perspectiva Histórica*, Mexico, Edit. Plaza y Valdés, 2004 [reimpr.], pp. 21, 23, 54, 62, 71–3, 115–20, 125–6, 148 and 154–7.

[2] J. Ruiz de Santiago, 'El Impacto en el Refugio de la Nueva Dinámica Migratoria en la Región – Retos para Asegurar la Protección de Refugiados', in IIHR, *I Curso de Capacitación para Organizaciones de la Sociedad Civil sobre Protección de Poblaciones Migrantes* (June 1999), Mexico/San José of Costa Rica, UNHCR/Universidad Iberoamericana/IIHR, 2002, p. 43; J.C. Murillo, 'La Declaración de Cartagena, el Alto Comisionado de Naciones Unidas para los Refugiados y las Migraciones Mixtas', in *Migraciones y Derechos Humanos* (August 2004), San José of Costa Rica, IIHR/PRODECA, 2004, pp. 174–6.

[3] For the pleadings of the UNHCR before the Inter-American Court, cf. IACtHR, Series B (Pleadings, Oral Arguments and Documents), n. 18 (2003), pp. 211–23 (oral argument of 04 June 2003).

Moreover, international organizations, prompted by the new phenomenon of forced migrations, decided – both in the United Nations and the Organization of American States – to insert it into the scheme of work of their respective *rapporteur* systems. The mandate of the U.N. Special *Rapporteur* on the Human Rights of Migrants was created in 1999, by resolution 1999/44 of the former U.N. Commission on Human Rights (par. 3). The resolution entrusted the Special *Rapporteur* with the tasks of elaboration of reports and undertaking of country visits, and further requested the Special *Rapporteur* to examine 'ways and means to overcome the obstacles existing to the full and effective protection of the human rights of migrants',[4] drawing attention to the 'situation of vulnerability' of these latter.[5]

One decade ago, in a study I prepared for the Inter-American Institute of Human Rights (in Costa Rica, in 1998), published in 2001 in Guatemala, I propounded a human rights approach for the phenomenon of forced migratory fluxes – distinctly from the classic studies on the subject (pursuant to a strictly historical, or else economic, approach) – with attention focused on human beings experiencing great vulnerability.[6] On the occasion, I warned that:

The advances [in this domain] will only be achieved by means of a radical change of mentality. In any scale of values, considerations of a humanitarian order ought to prevail over those of an economic or financial order, over the alleged protectionism of the market of work and over group rivalries. There is, definitively, pressing need to situate the human being in the place that corresponds to him, certainly above capitals, goods and services. This is perhaps the major challenge of the 'globalized' world in which we live, from the perspective of human rights.[7]

Definitively, only the firm determination of reconstruction of the international community[8] on the basis of human solidarity[9] can lead to a mitigation or allevia-

---

[4] U.N., *Special Rapporteur of the [U.N.] Commission on Human Rights on the Human Rights of Migrants*, doc. www.ohchr.org, 2nd. paragraph.

[5] 4th, 6th, and 7th preambular paragraphs. Cf. comments in: C. Villán Durán, 'Los Derechos Humanos y la Inmigración en el Marco de las Naciones Unidas', in *Memorias del Seminario Internacional 'Los Derechos Humanos de los Migrantes'*, (Mexico, June 2005), Mexico, Secretaría de Relaciones Exteriores, 2005, pp. 95–8. In pursuance of that mandate, a series of reports have been prepared and presented by the Special *Rapporteur*, who, in the period 2000–2005, has also undertaken country visits to Canada, Ecuador, Philippines, border Mexico/United States, Mexico, Spain, Morocco, Iran, Italy, Peru and Burkina Faso. In 2005, the then U.N. Commission on Human Rights enlarged the mandate of the Special *Rapporteur*.

[6] A.A. Cançado Trindade, *Elementos para un Enfoque de Derechos Humanos del Fenómeno de los Flujos Migratorios Forzados* (Study of July 1998 prepared for the IIHR), Guatemala City, OIM/IIDH, September 2001, pp. 1–57.

[7] Ibid., p. 26.

[8] Cf., e.g., A.A. Cançado Trindade, 'Human Development and Human Rights in the International Agenda of the XXIst Century', in *Human Development and Human Rights Forum* (August 2000), San José of Costa Rica, UNDP, 2001, pp. 23–38; cf. also, e.g., L. Lippolis, *Dai Diritti dell'Uomo ai Diritti dell'Umanità*, Milano, Giuffrè, 2002, pp. 21–3 and 154–5.

[9] J. Ruiz de Santiago, 'Derechos Humanos, Migraciones y Refugiados: Desafíos en los Inicios del Nuevo Milenio', in *III Encuentro de Movilidad Humana: Migrante y Refugiado – Memoria* (September 2000), San José of Costa Rica, UNHCR/IIHR, 2001, pp. 37–72; and cf. J. Ruiz de Santiago, *Migraciones Forzadas – Derecho Internacional y Doctrina Social de la Iglesia*, Mexico, Instituto Mexicano de Doctrina Social Cristiana, 2004, pp. 9–82. And, on the meaning of solidarity, cf., in general, L. de Sebastián, *La Solidaridad*, Barcelona, Ed. Ariel, 1996, pp. 12–196; J. de Lucas, *El Concepto de Solidaridad*, 2nd. ed., Mexico, Fontamara, 1998, pp. 13–109; among others.

tion of some of the sufferings of the uprooted (whether refugees, internally displaced persons, or migrants).

Paradoxically, the expansion of 'globalization' has been accompanied *pari passu* by the erosion of the capacity of States to protect the economic, social, and cultural rights of persons under their jurisdictions; hence the growing needs of protection of refugees, displaced persons, and migrants, in this first decade of the twenty-first century – what requires solidarity at universal scale.[10] This great paradox appears rather tragic, bearing in mind the considerable advances in science and technology in recent decades, which, nevertheless, have not been able to reduce or eradicate human egoism.[11] Tragically, the material progress of some has been accompanied by the closing of frontiers to human beings and the appearance of new and cruel forms of human servitude (clandestine traffic of persons, forced prostitution, labour exploitation, among others), of which undocumented migrants are often victims.[12] The increasing controls and current hardships imposed upon migrants have led some to behold and characterize a contemporary situation of 'crisis' of the right of asylum.[13]

Migrations and forced displacements, increased and intensified from the 1990s onwards,[14] have been characterized particularly by the disparities in the conditions of life between the country of origin and that of destination of migrants. Their causes are multiple, namely: economic collapse and unemployment, collapse in public services (education, health, among others), natural disasters, armed conflicts generating fluxes of refugees and displaced persons, repression and persecution, systematic violations of human rights, ethnic rivalries and xenophobia, violence of distinct forms.[15] In recent years, the so-called 'flexibility' in labour relations, amidst

---

[10] S. Ogata, *Challenges of Refugee Protection* (Statement at the University of Havana, 11 May 2000), Havana/Cuba, UNHCR, 2000, pp. 7–9 (internal circulation); S. Ogata, *Los Retos de la Protección de los Refugiados* (Statement at the Ministry of External Relations of Mexico, 29 July 1999), Mexico City, UNHCR, 1999, p. 11 (internal circulation). It has recently been pointed out that *early warning* systems (originally devised and used in the domain of International Refugee Law) have disclosed some shortcomings, used at times as they have been, simply to coerce people under stress not to migrate; S. Schmeidl, 'The Early Warning of Forced Migration: State or Human Security?', in *Refugees and Forced Displacement – International Security, Human Vulnerability, and the State* (eds. E. Newman and J. van Selm), Tokyo, United Nations University, 2003, pp. 140, 145 and 149–51. From the perspective of the international civil society as a whole, the argument has been propounded in favour of securing full and effective citizenship to law-abiding migrants; M. Frost, 'Thinking Ethically about Refugees: A Case for the Transformation of Global Governance', in ibid., pp. 128–9.
[11] On the need of 'revaluing' what is human and humanitarian nowadays, cf. J.A. Carrillo Salcedo, 'El Derecho Internacional ante un Nuevo Siglo', 48 *Boletim da Faculdade de Direito da Universidade de Coimbra* (1999–2000) p. 257, and cf. p. 260.
[12] M. Lengellé-Tardy, *L'esclavage moderne*, Paris, PUF, 1999, pp. 26, 77 and 116, and cf. pp. 97–8.
[13] Ph. Ségur, *La crise du droit d'asile*, Paris, PUF, 1998, pp. 110–14, 117, 140 and 155; F. Crépeau, *Droit d'asile – De l'hospitalité aux contrôles migratoires*, Bruxelles, Bruylant/Éd. Université de Bruxelles, 1995, pp. 306–13 and 337–9.
[14] Cf. S. Ogata, *The Turbulent Decade – Confronting the Refugee Crises of the 1990s*, N.Y./London, Norton, 2005, pp. 13–343; UNHCR, *The State of the World's Refugees – Fifty Years of Humanitarian Action*, Oxford, UNHCR/Oxford University Press, 2000, p. 9.
[15] N. Van Hear, *New Diasporas – The Mass Exodus, Dispersal and Regrouping of Migrant Communities*, London, UCL Press, 1998, pp. 19–20, 29, 109–10, 141, 143 and 151; F.M. Deng, *Protecting the Dispossessed – A Challenge for the International Community*, Washington D.C., Brookings Institution, 1993, pp. 3–20. And cf. also, e.g., H. Domenach and M. Picouet, *Les migrations*, Paris, PUF, 1995, pp. 42–126.

the 'globalization' of the economy, has also generated mobility, accompanied by personal insecurity and a growing fear of unemployment.[16]

Migrations and forced displacements, with the consequent uprootedness of so many human beings, bring about traumas. Testimonies of migrants give account of the sufferings of the abandonment of home, at times with family separation or disaggregation, of loss of property and personal belongings, of arbitrarinesses and humiliations on the part of frontier authorities and security agents, generating a permanent feeling of injustice.[17] As Simone Weil warned in the mid-XXth century:

To be rooted is perhaps the most important and least recognized need of the human soul. It is one of the hardest to define.[18]

At the same time and in the same line of thinking, Hannah Arendt warned about the sufferings of the uprooted (the loss of home and of the familiarity of day-to-day life, the loss of profession and of the feeling of usefulness to the others, the loss of the mother tongue as spontaneous expression of feelings), as well as the illusion of trying to forget the past.[19] Also in this line of reasoning, in his book *Le retour du tragique* (1967), J.-M. Domenach observed that one can hardly deny the *roots* of the human spirit itself, since the very form of acquisition of knowledge on the part of each human being – and consequently his way of seeing the world – is to a large extent conditioned by factors such as the place of birth, the mother tongue, the customs, the family and the culture.[20]

In his novel *Le temps des déracinés* (2003), Elie Wiesel[21] remarked that former refugees continue somehow to be refugees for the rest of their lives; they escape from one exile to project themselves into another, everything looking provisional, and without feeling at home anywhere. They continue to remember where they originally come from,[22] cultivating their memories as a means of defence against the adverse conditions of uprooted persons. But the 'celebration of memory' also has its

---

[16] N. Van Hear, *op. cit. supra* n. (15), pp. 251–2. As it has been pointed out, 'the ubiquity of migration is a result of the success of capitalism in fostering the penetration of commoditization into far-flung peripheral societies and undermining the capacity of these societies to sustain themselves. Insofar as this 'success' will continue, so too will migrants continue to wash up on the shores of capitalism's core'; ibid., p. 260. Cf. also R. Bergalli (coord.), *Flujos Migratorios y Su (Des)control*, Barcelona, OSPDH/Anthropos Edit., 2006, pp. 138, 152 and 244–8. For a study of cased, cf., e.g., M. Greenwood Arroyo and R. Ruiz Oporta, *Migrantes Irregulares, Estrategias de Sobrevivencia y Derechos Humanos: Un Estudio de Casos*, San José of Costa Rica, IIHR, 1995, pp. 9–159.

[17] Ibid., p. 152.

[18] Simone Weil, *The Need for Roots*, London/N.Y., Routledge, 1952 (reprint 1995), p. 41. On the contemporary drama of uprootedness, cf. A.A. Cançado Trindade, 'Reflexiones sobre el Desarraigo como Problema de Derechos Humanos Frente a la Conciencia Jurídica Universal', in *La Nueva Dimensión de las Necesidades de Protección del Ser Humano en el Inicio del Siglo XXI* (eds. A.A. Cançado Trindade and J. Ruiz de Santiago), 4th. rev. ed., San José of Costa Rica, UNHCR, 2006, pp. 33–92.

[19] Hannah Arendt, *La tradition cachée*, Paris, Ch. Bourgois Ed., 1987 (orig. ed. 1946), pp. 58–9 and 125–7. And cf. also, on the matter, e.g., C. Bordes-Benayoun and D. Schnapper, *Diasporas et nations*, Paris, O. Jacob Ed., 2006, pp. 7, 11–12, 45–6, 63–5, 68–9, 129 and 216–19.

[20] J.-M. Domenach, *Le retour du tragique*, Paris, Éd. Seuil, 1967, p. 285.

[21] Nobel Peace Prize in 1986, who himself suffered the drama of uprootedness.

[22] E. Wiesel, *O Tempo dos Desenraizados (Le temps des déracinés*, 2003), Rio de Janeiro, Edit. Record, 2004, pp. 18–19.

limitations, as the uprooted are deprived of horizons, and of the sense of belonging to somewhere.[23] They always need help from others. The drama of the victimized seems to be overlooked and forgotten as time passes by, and the uprooted end up having to learn to live with the slow and inevitable diminution even of their own memories.[24]

Whilst in the late 1980s and early 1990s the refugee population surpassed 18 million persons, the displaced population surpassed that total by 7 million more (totalling 25 million persons),[25] and migrants in search of better living and working conditions, in turn, totalled 80 million human beings by the end of the XXth century[26] and – according to IOM recent data – reach nowadays roughly 100 to 120 million migrants all over the world.[27] Yet, the suffering of migrants has been known for many years.[28] The causes of forced migrations are not fundamentally distinct from those of populational forced displacement: natural disasters, chronic poverty,[29] armed conflicts, generalized violence, and systematic violations of human rights.[30]

By the end of last century it became clear that the whole matter was to be approached and examined in the context of the reality of the post-cold war world, as a result of the multiple internal conflicts, of ethnic and religious character, repressed in the past but erupting in recent years with the end of the Cold War.[31] To face this new phenomenon of forced migrations, the U.N. General Assembly approved the International Convention on the Protection of the Rights of All Migrant Workers and Members of their Families on 18 December 1990. This important Convention, which at last entered into force on 01 July 2003, has, however, received very few ratifications – 36 so far (beginning of April 2007) – and has not yet been sufficiently examined in contemporary doctrine, despite its considerable significance.

---

[23] Ibid., pp. 21, 32, 181 and 197.

[24] Ibid., pp. 212, 235, 266 and 278. On his concern with the need of preservation of memory, cf. also Elie Wiesel, *L'oublié*, Paris, Éd. Seuil, 1989, pp. 29, 63, 74–7, 109, 269, 278 and 336.

[25] F.M. Deng, *Protecting the Dispossessed...*, *op. cit. supra* n. (15), pp. 1 and 133.

[26] A.A. Cançado Trindade, 'Preface' to: V.O. Batista, *União Européia: Livre Circulação de Pessoas e Direito de Asilo*, Belo Horizonte/Brazil, Edit. Del Rey, 1998, p. 9.

[27] Jaime Ruiz de Santiago, *El Problema de las Migraciones Forzosas en Nuestro Tiempo*, Mexico, IMDSC, 2003, p. 10; and cf. projections in: S. Hune and J. Niessen, 'Ratifying the U.N. Migrant Workers Convention: Current Difficulties and Prospects', 12 *Netherlands Quarterly of Human Rights* (1994) p. 393.

[28] On the adversities suffered by (foreign) migrant workers (e.g., discrimination on the basis of race, nationality, among others), cf., *inter alia*, S. Castles and G. Kosack, *Los Trabajadores Inmigrantes y la Estructura de Clases en Europa Occidental*, Mexico, FCE, 1984, pp. 11–565.

[29] Which, in accordance with figures of the U.N. Development Programme (UNDP), only in Latin America victimizes today more than 270 million persons (compared to the 250 million of the eighties), who could soon get close to some 300 million people.

[30] *Cit.* in F.M. Deng, *Protecting the Dispossessed...*, *op. cit. supra* n. (15), p. 3.

[31] Ibid., p. 4. It has been warned that, in relation to migrants, the receiving State is always keen to display its power, and the distinct attitudes of Western European countries, of assimilation or else segregation of migrants, have had conflicting implications; E. Todd, *El Destino de los Inmigrantes – Asimilación y Segregación en las Democracias Occidentales* (transl. of *Le destin des immigrés – Assimilation et ségrégation dans les démocraties occidentales*), Barcelona, Tusquet Edit., 1996, pp. 147, 347, 351 and 353. The drama of migrants – their longing for roots and their own cultural identity – has thus persisted.

The 1990 Convention established the Committee on the Protection of the Rights of All Migrant Workers and Members of Their Families as its supervisory organ (Article 72), entrusted with the examination of State reports (Articles 73–74) as well as inter-State and individual communications or complaints (Articles 76–77). In the mid-1990s, the then U.N. Centre for Human Rights itself identified the causes of contemporary fluxes of migrant workers in extreme poverty (below subsistence level), search for work, armed conflicts, personal insecurity, or persecution derived from discrimination (on the ground of race, ethnic origin, colour, religion, language or political opinions).[32] The basic idea underlying the International Convention on the Protection of the Rights of All Migrant Workers and Members of their Families is that *all* migrant workers – thus qualified thereunder – ought to enjoy respect for their human rights irrespective of their legal situation.[33]

Hence the central position occupied, also in this context, by the principle of *non-discrimination* (as set forth in its Article 7). Not surprisingly, the list of protected rights follows a necessarily holistic or integral vision of human rights (comprising civil, political, economic, social, and cultural rights). The Convention took into account both the international labour standards (derived from the experience of the ILO), as well as those of the U.N. Conventions against discrimination.[34] The protected rights are enunciated in three of the nine parts which form the Convention: Part III (Articles 8–35) lists the human rights of *all* migrant workers and the members of their families (including the *undocumented ones*); Part IV (Articles 36–56) covers other rights of migrant workers and members of their families 'who are documented or in a regular situation'; and Part V (Articles 57–63) contains provisions applicable to 'particular categories' of migrant workers and members of their families.[35]

The basic principle of *non-discrimination*, which has a rather long history and to which so much importance was ascribed in the drafting process of the 1948 Universal Declaration of Human Rights,[36] and which subsequently became the main object of two important Conventions of the United Nations (CERD, 1966, and CEDAW, 1979) – which cover only some of its aspects – has, only in recent years, been dwelt upon to a greater degree in its wide potential of application, as in, for example the Advisory Opinions ns. 16 and 18 of the IACtHR, on *The Right to Information on Consular Assistance in the Framework of the Guarantees of the Due Process of Law* (1999), and on *The Juridical Condition and Rights of Undocumented Migrants* (2003), respectively.

As, in the view of States, there is no human right to immigrate, the control of migratory entries is made subject to their own 'sovereign' criteria, and the desire to

---

[32] U.N./Centre for Human Rights, *Los Derechos de los Trabajadores Migratorios* (Foll. Inf. n. 24), Geneva, U.N., 1996, p. 4.

[33] Ibid., pp. 15–16.

[34] Cf. ibid., p. 16.

[35] That is, frontier workers, seasonal workers, itinerant workers, project-tied workers, with concrete employment, on their own, in the terms of the definitions of Article 2(2) of the 1990 Convention. Article 2(1) defines 'migrant worker' as 'a person who is to be engaged, is engaged or has been engaged in a remunerated activity in a State of which he or she is not a national'.

[36] Cf. A. Eide *et alii*, *The Universal Declaration of Human Rights – A Commentary*, Oslo, Scandinavian University Press, 1992, p. 6.

'protect' their internal markets.[37] Furthermore, instead of devising and applying true population policies bearing in mind human rights, most States have been exerting the strictly policing function of 'protecting' their own frontiers and controlling migratory fluxes, and sanctioning so-called 'illegal' migrants. The whole issue has been unduly and unnecessarily 'criminalized'. It is thus not surprising that inconsistencies and arbitrarinesses have ensued therefrom. These latter are manifested in 'democratic regimes', the administration of justice of which has nevertheless failed to free itself from old prejudices against immigrants, particularly when they are undocumented and poor. The programmes of 'modernization' of justice, with international financing, do not dwell upon this aspect, as their main motivation is to ensure the security of investments (capitals and goods).

This provides a revealing picture of the (reduced) dimension which public authorities have conferred upon human beings at the beginning of the XXIst century, placed in a scale of priority inferior to that attributed to capitals and goods, in spite of all the struggles of the past, and all the sufferings of previous generations. The area in which most incongruencies appear manifest nowadays is that pertaining to the guarantees of the due process of law. Yet, the reaction of Law has become prompt and manifest in our days, as demonstrated, for example, by the aforementioned pioneering Advisory Opinions ns. 16 and 18 of the IACtHR. The Advisory Opinion n. 16 has placed the right to consular notification, set forth in Article 36(1)(b) of the 1963 Vienna Convention on Consular Relations in the conceptual universe of international human rights law. It has indeed conferred a human rights dimension to some postulates of classic consular law, as I pointed out in my Concurring Opinion (pars. 1–35)[38] in Advisory Opinion n. 16.

Since it was issued by the Court, Advisory Opinion n. 16, besides inspiring the international case-law *in statu nascendi*, has had a considerable impact on international practice in the American continent (more particularly, in Latin America).[39] However, there is much need of greater and genuine international cooperation to secure assistance to, and protection of, all migrants and members of their families. Legal norms can hardly be effective without the corresponding and underlying values, and, in the present domain, the application of the relevant norms of protection does require a fundamental change of mentality.

In relation to the subject at issue, the norms already exist, but the proper acknowledgment of values seems to be still lacking, as well as a new mentality. It is no mere casuality that the International Convention on the Protection of the Rights of All Migrant Workers and Members of their Families, despite its entry into

---

[37] M. Weiner, 'Ethics, National Sovereignty and the Control of Immigration', 30 *International Migration Review* (1996) pp. 171–95.

[38] Cf. text in: A.A. Cançado Trindade, *Derecho Internacional de los Derechos Humanos – Esencia y Trascendencia* (Votos en la Corte Interamericana de Derechos Humanos, 1991–2006), Mexico, Edit. Porrúa/Universidad Iberoamericana, 2007, pp. 15–27.

[39] Cf. A.A. Cançado Trindade, 'The Humanization of Consular Law: The Impact of Advisory Opinion n. 16 (1999) of the Inter-American of Human Rights on International Case-Law and Practice', 4 *Chinese Journal of International Law* (2007) pp. 1–16.

force, has not been ratified by many States so far.[40] Despite the identity of the basic principles and of the applicable law in distinct situations, the protection of migrants requires, nevertheless, a special emphasis on one and the other aspect in particular. The starting-point seems to lie on the recognition that every migrant has the right to enjoy all the fundamental human rights, as well as the rights derived from employments occupied in the past, irrespective of his legal situation (whether irregular or not).

Here, once again, a necessarily holistic or integral vision of all human rights (civil, political, economic, social, and cultural) applies. Just as the principle of *non-refoulement* constitutes the cornerstone of the protection of refugees (as a principle of customary law and, furthermore, of *jus cogens*), applicable in other situations as well, in the matter of migrants (mainly the undocumented ones) it assumes special importance, beside the due process of law (*supra*); thus, the fundamental human rights and the dignity of irregular or undocumented migrants ought to be preserved also in face of threats of deportation and/or expulsion.[41] Every person in such a situation has the right to be heard by a judge and not to be detained illegally or arbitrarily.[42]

The International Convention on the Protection of the Rights of All Migrant Workers and Members of their Families prohibits measures of collective expulsion and determines that each case of expulsion ought to be 'examined and decided individually' (Article 22(1)), in accordance with the law. Given the great vulnerability which accompanies migrants in a situation of irregularity, the countries of both origin and admission should take positive measures to ensure that all

---

[40] In some cases, the insufficiencies of the instruments of protection result from the very formulation of some of their norms. For example, in so far as the protection of stateless persons is concerned, the 1954 Convention Relating to the Status of Stateless Persons (and, implicitly, also the 1961 Convention of the Reduction of Statelessness) only refers to stateless persons *de jure*, so as to avoid statelessness as of birth, but failing to prohibit – whichwould perhaps be more relevant – the revocation or loss of nationality in given circumstances; C.A. Batchelor, 'Stateless Persons: Some Gaps in International Protection', 7 *International Journal of Refugee Law* (1995) pp. 232–55.

[41] For a compelling argument against arbitrariness in the deportation of migrants, and in support of treating all migrants (including the undocumented ones) with fairness, and a sense of worth and humanity, cf. B.O. Hing, *Deporting Our Souls – Values, Morality and Immigrantion Policy*, Cambridge, University Press, 2006, pp. 1–215. On the provisions of the International Convention on the Protection of the Rights of All Migrant Workers and Members of their Families against unfair and arbitrary expulsion of migrants, pursuant to humanitarian considerations, cf. R. Cholewinski, *Migrant Workers in International Human Rights Law – Their Protection in Countries of Employment*, Oxford, Clarendon Press, 1997, pp. 182–4. And, on the prohibition of massive expulsion of foreigners, cf. A.A. Cançado Trindade, 'El Desarraigo como Problema de Derechos Humanos frente a la Conciencia Jurídica Universal', in *Movimientos de Personas e Ideas y Multicultural idad* (Forum Deusto), vol. I, Bilbao, University of Deusto, 2003, pp. 82–4; H.G. Schermers, 'The Bond between Man and State', in *Recht zwischen Umbruch und Bewahrung – Festschrift für R. Bernhardt* (eds. U. Beyerlin *et alii*), Berlin, Springer-Verlag, 1995, pp. 192–4; H. Lambert, 'Protection against *Refoulement* from Europe: Human Rights Law Comes to the Rescue', 48 *International and Comparative Law Quarterly* (1999) pp. 515–18.

[42] Resettlement, within a reasonable time, in a third country, should also be considered; cf. 'Los Derechos y las Obligaciones de los Migrantes Indocumentados en los Países de Acogida/Protección de los Derechos Fundamentales de los Migrantes Indocumentados', 21 *International Migration/Migraciones Internacionales* (1983) pp. 135–6.

migrations take place in a regular way.[43] This is a challenge to all countries, and even more forceful to those which purport to be 'democratic'. Last but not least, the 1990 Convention ought to be properly appreciated in conjunction with the 1966 U.N. Covenant on Civil and Political Rights, as well the relevant I.L.O. Conventions on the matter.[44]

At regional level, in the American continent, in my Separate Opinion in the case of the *Moiwana Community versus Suriname* before the IACtHR (Judgment of 15 June 2005), I dwelt upon the projection of human suffering in time of the migrants of that Community (some of whom had fled to French Guyana) who survived a massacre (perpetrated on 29 November 1986 in the N'djuka Maroon village of Moiwana, in Suriname). I characterized the harm they suffered as:

a spiritual one. Under their culture, they remain still tormented by the circumstances of the violent deaths of their beloved ones, and the fact that the deceased did not have a proper burial. This privation, generating spiritual suffering, has lasted for almost twenty years, from the moment of the perpetration of the 1986 massacre engaging the responsibility of the State until now. The N'djukas have not forgotten their dead (par. 29).

Only with the aforementioned Judgment of 2005, almost two decades later, they at last found redress, with the judicial recognition of their suffering and the reparations ordered. In the framework of the latter the State is to secure their voluntary and safe return to their native lands.[45] This was not the first time that I addressed the issue of the projection of human suffering in time and the growing tragedy of uprootedness; I also considered it, earlier on, in my Concurring Opinion (pars. 1–25) in the IACtHR's Order of Provisional Measures of Protection (of 18 August 2000) in the case of the *Haitians and Dominicans of Haitian Origin in the Dominican Republic*, as well in my Separate Opinion (pars. 10–14) in the *Bámaca Velásquez versus Guatemala* case (Reparations, Judgment of 22 February 2002),[46] and revisited the point at issue in the more recent *Moiwana Community* case.[47]

---

[43] Cf. ibid., p. 136.

[44] Namely, the 1949 Migration (n. 97) for Employment Convention (Revised), and the 1975 Convention (n. 143) concerning Migrant Workers, as well as Recommendation n. 151 concerning Migrant Workers (of 1975). For a contextual discussion, cf., e.g., B. Boutros-Ghali, 'The U.N. and the I.L.O.: Meeting the Challenge of Social Development', in *Visions of the Future of Social Justice – Essays on the Occasion of the I.L.O.'s 75th Anniversary*, Geneva, I.L.O., 1994, pp. 51–3.

[45] For the full text of my Separate Opinion in the case of the *Moiwana Community versus Suriname*, cf. A.A. Cançado Trindade, *Derecho Internacional de los Derechos Humanos – Esencia y Trascendencia* (Votos en la Corte Interamericana de Derechos Humanos, 1991–2006), Mexico, Edit. Porrúa/ Universidad Iberoamericana, 2007, pp. 539–67.

[46] For the full text of my aforementioned Concurring and Separate Opinions, cf. ibid., pp. 876–83 and 321–30, respectively.

[47] It is significant that, in its Judgment on the case of the *Moiwana Community versus Suriname*, the Inter-American Court, on the basis of the American Convention and in the light of the principle *jura novit curia*, devoted a whole section of the present Judgment to forced displacement – a *malaise* of our times – and established a violation by the respondent State of Article 22 of the American Convention (on freedom of movement and residence) in combination with the general duty of Article 1(1) of the Convention (pars. 101–19).

III. The Protection of Migrants in International Case-Law

1. European Human Rights System

The theme of aliens or migrants has marked its presence in the normative and operational levels of the European system of human rights protection. Thus, Protocol n. 4 (of 1963) to the ECHR effectively prohibits the collective expulsion of foreigners (Article 4). Even in individual cases, if the expulsion of a foreigner generates a separation of the members of the family unit, it brings about a violation of Article 8 of the ECHR; accordingly, the States Parties to the Convention no longer have total discretion to expel from their territory foreigners who already have established a 'genuine link' with them.[48]

The limits of State discretion in the treatment of any persons under the jurisdiction of the States Parties to human rights treaties were stressed, e.g., in the well-known early cases of the *East African Asians*. In those cases, the old European Commission of Human Rights concluded that 25 of the complainants (who had retained their status of British citizens after the independence of Kenya and Uganda to see themselves free from migratory controls) had been victimized by a new British law which put an end to the right of entry of British citizens who did not have ancestral links with the United Kingdom. In the understanding of the old European Commission (Report of 1973), this law constituted an act of racial discrimination which characterized a 'degrading treatment' in the terms of Article 3 of the ECHR.[49]

Years later, the same European Commission confirmed its position on the matter, in the case *Abdulaziz, Cabales and Balkandali versus United Kingdom* (1983), wherein it warned that the State's discretion in the matter of immigration has its limits, as a State cannot, for example, implement policies based upon racial discrimination.[50] The case was referred to the ECtHR by the Commission, as the three applicants (Mrs Abdulaziz, Mrs Cabales and Mrs Balkandali), lawfully and permanently settled in the United Kingdom, had been refused leave to join their husbands in that country. In its turn, the ECtHR (1985) found a violation, not of Article 8 per se, but of Article 8 (respect for private and family life) together with

---

[48] H.G. Schermers, 'The Bond between Man and State', in *Recht zwischen Umbruch und Bewahrung...*, *op. cit. supra* n. (41), pp. 192–4.

[49] Despite the fact that the case was never lodged with the ECtHR, and that the Committee of Ministers did not pronounce on such violation of the ECHR, it awaited until all the complainants were admitted to the United Kingdom to conclude that if was no longer necessary to take any other measure. D.J. Harris, M. O'Boyle and C. Warbrick, *Law of the European Convention on Human Rights*, London, Butterworths, 1995, pp. 81–2 and 695.

[50] *Cit.* in ibid., p. 82. – The old European Commission cared to characterize the 'collective expulsion of foreigners', for the purpose of application of the prohibition contained in Article 4 of Protocol n. 4 to the European Convention, as illustrated, e.g., by its considerations in the case *A. et alii versus The Netherlands* (1988), interposed by 23 applicants of Surinamese nationality; cf. European Commission of Human Rights, application n. 14209/88 (decision of 16 December 1988), in *Decisions and Reports*, vol. 59, Strasbourg, C.E., 1989, pp. 274–80.

Article 14 (prohibition of discrimination), by reason of discrimination on the ground of sex.[51]

In addition, in the case *Abdulaziz, Cabales and Balkandali*, the Court further established a violation of Article 13, for lack of access to justice; the Court pondered that:

the discrimination on the ground of sex of which Mrs Abdulaziz, Mrs Cabales and Mrs Balkandali were victims was the result of norms that were in this respect incompatible with the Convention. In this regard, since the United Kingdom has not incorporated the Convention into its domestic law, there could be no 'effective remedy' as required by Article 13.[52]

In his Concurring Opinion in the *Abdulaziz, Cabales and Balkandali* case, Judge R. Bernhardt aptly argued that:

Article 13 must, in my view, be given a meaning which is independent of the question whether any other provision of the Convention is in fact violated. Whenever a person complains that one of the provisions of the Convention itself or any similar guarantee or principle contained in the national legal system is violated by a national (administrative or executive) authority, Article 13 is in my view applicable and some remedy must be available.[53]

In spite of the fact that the ECHR itself did not contemplate the right not to be expelled from one of the States Parties, very soon it was accepted that there were limits to the faculty of States Parties to control the entry and departure of foreigners, by virtue of the obligations contracted under the Convention itself, as illustrated, e.g., by those pertaining to Article 8 (on the right to respect for private and family life). Thus, although there does not exist a general definition of 'family life', very soon a protective case-law was developed in this respect, in the light of the circumstances of each concrete case. Such case-law, bearing in mind, *inter alia*, the principle of proportionality, has restrictively stipulated the conditions of expulsion.[54]

A study of the protection of migrant workers in the international human rights law has recalled that, on several occasions, the ECtHR found 'an infringement of the right to respect for family life in cases involving second-generation migrants, who had either been expelled, or were under threat of expulsion, because they had been convicted of criminal offences in their country of residence'.[55] Although in each case the expulsions, or threatened expulsions, aimed at preventing disorder or crime, they constituted – the study went on, recalling *inter alia* the Court's

---

[51] Paragraphs 83 and 86, and resolutory point n. 3.
[52] Paragraph 93, and resolutory point n. 6.
[53] ECtHR, the case of *Abdulaziz, Cabales and Balkandali*, Judgment (28 May 1985), Strasbourg, C.E., 1985, Concurring Opinion of Judge R. Bernhardt, p. 41.
[54] Bearing in mind the provision of Article 8 of the European Convention; cf. M.E. Villiger, 'Expulsion and the Right to Respect for Private and Family Life (Article 8 of the Convention) – An Introduction to the Commission's Case-Law', in *Protecting Human Rights: The European Dimension – Studies in Honour of G.J. Wiarda/Protection des droits de l'homme: La dimension européenne – Mélanges en l'honneur de G.J. Wiarda* (eds. F. Matscher and H. Petzold), Köln/Berlin, C. Heymanns Verlag, 1988, pp. 657–8 and 662.
[55] R. Cholewinski, *Migrant Workers in International Human Rights Law – Their Protection in Countries of Employment*, Oxford, Clarendon Press, 1997, p. 341.

Judgments in the cases of *Beldjoudi versus France* (of 26 March 1992) and *Moustaquim versus Belgium* (of 18 February 1991) – 'a disproportionate means of achieving this aim given that the affected individuals had spent most of their lives, together with their immediate families, in the countries concerned and had little or no ties with their country of origin'.[56]

The *Beldjoudi* and the *Moustaquim* cases, together with the *Lamguindaz versus United Kingdom* case (1992), are nowadays regarded as leading cases in this particular respect. As forcefully argued in another study on the matter, given the links (such as family and social ties, schooling, understanding of culture and language) between second-generation migrants and their (new) country of residence, they are *de facto* citizens, and their deportation or expulsion would amount to a violation of their right to private and family life (Article 8 of the ECHR).[57] The protection of the human rights of migrants, under given circumstances, has thus found judicial recognition in the European human rights system. It has done so also in the inter-American human rights system, which has gone even further than the European one in this respect, as it will be examined now.

2. Inter-American Human Rights System

The protection of migrants has likewise marked its presence in the normative and operational levels of the Inter-American system of human rights protection. It has, in fact, been remarkably present in the case-law of the IACtHR in recent years. I have already referred to the Court's Judgment of 15 June 2005 in *Moiwana Community versus Suriname*, as well as the Court's Order of Provisional Measures of Protection (of 18 August 2000) in the case of the *Haitians and Dominicans of Haitian Origin in the Dominican Republic*. In my Concurring Opinion in the latter, I warned as to the pressing need to face the contemporary tragedy of uprootedness, and I further argued that:

the principle of *non-refoulement*, cornerstone of the protection of refugees (as a principle of customary law and also of *jus cogens*), can be invoked even in distinct contexts, such as that of the collective expulsion of (. . .) migrants or of other groups. Such principle has been set forth also in human rights treaties, as illustrated by Article 22(8) of the American Convention on Human Rights.[58]

---

[56] Ibid., pp. 341–2.

[57] R. Cholewinski, 'Strasbourg's "Hidden Agenda"?: The Protection of Second-Generation Migrants from Expulsion under Article 8 of the European Convention of Human Rights', 12 *Netherlands Quarterly of Human Rights* (1994) pp. 287–306. For the *obiter dicta* of the European Court of Human Rights on the question of 'long-term immigrants', despite the fact that it found no violation of Article 8 of the European Convention in the *cas d'espèce*, cf. ECtHR, the case of *Uner versus Netherlands*, Judgment of 18 October 2006, pars. 55–60.

[58] Paragraph 7 n. 5 of my Concurring Opinion (my own translation), text in: A.A. Cançado Trindade, *Derecho Internacional de los Derechos Humanos – Esencia y Trascendencia* (Votos en la Corte Interamericana de Derechos Humanos, 1991–2006), Mexico, Edit. Porrúa/Universidad Iberoamericana, 2007, p. 878.

The relevance of this approach to the point at issue, in relation to the Court's Order of Provisional Measures of Protection in the aforementioned case of the *Haitians and Dominicans of Haitian Origin in the Dominican Republic*, has been promptly acknowledged in expert writing.[59]

As for the already-mentioned Judgment of the IACtHR in the case of the *Moiwana Community versus Suriname* (of 15 June 2005), it was followed by an Interpretation of Sentence (of 08 February 2006), to which I appended a Separate Opinion, wherein I dwelt upon the following points:

a the delimitation, demarcation, and titling and return of land (to the surviving members of the Moiwana Community and their relatives) as a form of reparation;

b the State's duty of guarantee of voluntary and sustainable return; and

c the need of reconstruction and preservation of the cultural identity of the members of the Moiwana Community.[60]

Furthermore, the great contemporary tragedy of *uprootedness*[61] undergone by the growing fluxes of undocumented migrants (in different regions of the world), and the great adversity they face, were eloquently discussed, and duly emphasized, in the course of the whole advisory proceedings before the IACtHR, on two historical occasions, namely, the proceedings conducive to the adoption of the Court's 16th and 18th Advisory Opinions, of 1999 and 2003, respectively. Both Opinions were pioneering in contemporary international case-law (*infra*), and represent the reaction of Law to situations of violations of human rights on a large scale, of persons who at times find themselves in total defencelessness. It is thus proper to review, at this stage, the contribution of those two Advisory Opinions to the safeguard of the human rights of undocumented migrants.

a The Advisory Opinion on the *Right to Information on Consular Assistance in the Framework of the Guarantees of the Due Process of Law* (1999)

The IACtHR delivered, on 01 October 1999, its sixteenth Advisory Opinion on the *Right to Information on Consular Assistance in the Framework of the Due Process of Law*. In this Opinion of transcendental importance, the Court held that Article 36 of the 1963 Vienna Convention on Consular Relations recognizes to the foreigner under detention individual rights – among which the right to information on

---

[59] Cf. Jaime Ruiz de Santiago, *El Problema de las Migraciones Forzosas en Nuestro Tiempo*, Mexico, Instituto Mexicano de Doctrina Social Cristiana, 2003, pp. 27–30.

[60] For the full text of my Separate Opinion in the case of the *Moiwana Community versus Suriname* (Interpretation of Sentence, of 08 February 2006), cf. A.A. Cançado Trindade, *Derecho Internacional de los Derechos Humanos – Esencia y Trascendencia* (Votos en la Corte Interamericana de Derechos Humanos, 1991–2006), Mexico, Edit. Porrúa/Universidad Iberoamericana, 2007, pp. 683–93.

[61] A.A. Cançado Trindade, 'Reflexiones sobre el Desarraigo como Problema de Derechos Humanos Frente a la Conciencia Jurídica Universal', in *La Nueva Dimensión de las Necesidades de Protección del Ser Humano en el Inicio del Siglo XXI* (eds. A.A. Cançado Trindade and J. Ruiz de Santiago), 4th. rev. ed., San José of Costa Rica, UNHCR, 2006, pp. 33–92.

consular assistance – to which correspond duties incumbent upon the receiving State (irrespective of its federal or unitary structure) (pars. 84 and 140).

The IACtHR pointed out that the evolutive interpretation and application of the *corpus juris* of international human rights law have had 'a positive impact on International Law in affirming and developing the aptitude of this latter to regulate the relations between States and human beings under their respective jurisdictions'. The Court thus adopted the 'proper approach' in considering the matter submitted to it in the framework of 'the evolution of the fundamental rights of the human person in contemporary International Law' (pars. 114–115). The Court stated that 'human rights treaties are living instruments, whose interpretation ought to follow the evolution of times and the current conditions of life' (par. 114). It made it clear that, in its interpretation of the norms of the ACHR, it should aim at extending protection into new situations on the basis of pre-existing rights.

The Court expressed the view that, for the due process of law to be preserved, 'a defendant must be able to exercise his rights and defend his interests effectively and in full procedural equality with other defendants' (par. 117). In order to attain its objectives, 'the judicial process ought to recognize and correct the factors of real inequality' of those taken to justice (par. 119); thus, the notification, to persons deprived of their liberty abroad, of their right to communicate with their consul, contributes to safeguard their defence and the respect for their procedural rights (pars. 121–122). The individual right to information under Article 36(1)(b) of the Vienna Convention on Consular Relations thus renders the right to the due process of law effective (par. 124).

The non-observance or obstruction of the exercise of this right affects the judicial guarantees (par. 129). The Court in this way linked the right at issue to the evolving guarantees of due process of law, and added that its non-observance in cases of the imposition and execution of the death penalty amounts to an arbitrary deprivation of the right to life itself (in the terms of Article 4 of the ACHR and Article 6 of the International Covenant on Civil and Political Rights), with all the juridical consequences inherent to a violation of the kind, that is, those pertaining to the international responsibility of the State and to the duty of reparation (par. 137).[62]

This sixteenth Advisory Opinion of the Court, truly pioneering, has served as inspiration for the emerging international case-law, *in statu nascendi*, on the matter,[63] and is having a tangible impact on the practice of the States of the region on the issue. It was the Advisory Opinion which had achieved, until then,

[62] And cf. Concurring Opinions of Judges A.A. Cançado Trindade and S. García Ramírez, and Partially Dissenting Opinion of Judge O. Jackman.
[63] As promptly acknowledged by expert writing; cf., e.g., G. Cohen-Jonathan, 'Cour Européenne des Droits de l'Homme et droit international général (2000)', 46 *Annuaire français de Droit international* (2000) p. 642; M. Mennecke, 'Towards the Humanization of the Vienna Convention of Consular Rights – The *LaGrand* Case before the International Court of Justice', 44 *German Yearbook of International Law/Jahrbuch für internationales Recht* (2001) pp. 430–2, 453–5, 459–60 and 467–8; Ph. Weckel, M.S.E. Helali and M. Sastre, 'Chronique de jurisprudence internationale', 104 *Revue générale de Droit international public* (2000) pp. 794 and 791; Ph. Weckel, 'Chronique de jurisprudence internationale', 105 *Revue générale de Droit international public* (2001) pp. 764–5 and 770.

the greatest mobilization in the advisory proceedings (with eight intervening States, besides several non-governmental organizations and individuals) in the whole history of the Court to date.[64] This historical Advisory Opinion, furthermore, reveals the impact of the International Law of Human Rights in the evolution of Public International Law itself, specifically for having the Inter-American Court been the first international tribunal to warn that, if non-compliance with Article 36(1)(b) of the Vienna Convention on Consular Relations of 1963 takes place, it occurs to the detriment not only of a State Party but also of the human beings at issue.[65]

b The Advisory Opinion on the *Juridical Condition and Rights of Undocumented Migrants (2003)*

In the same line of thinking, Advisory Opinion n. 18 opens new ground for the protection of migrants, in acknowledging the character of *jus cogens* of the basic principle of equality and non-discrimination, and the prevalence of the rights inherent to human beings, irrespective of their migratory status. Its advisory proceedings counted on an even greater mobilization (with 12 accredited States, in addition to the UNHCR, several non-governmental organizations, academic institutions and individuals), the greatest in the whole history of the Court to date. This more recent Opinion n. 18 is likewise having an impact on the theory and practice of International Law in the present domain of protection of the human rights of migrants.[66]

On 10 May 2002 Mexico requested the Inter-American Court of Human Rights to provide its 18th Advisory Opinion, on the juridical condition and rights of undocumented migrants. In the course of the corresponding advisory proceedings, which counted on the greatest public participation in the whole history of the Court, the Court celebrated two public hearings, the first in its headquarters in San José of Costa Rica, in February 2003, and the second outside its headquarters (for the first time in its history), in Santiago of Chile, in June 2003. The advisory

---

[64] In the public hearings (on this 16th Advisory Opinion) before the Court, apart from the eight intervening States, several individuals took the floor, namely: seven individuals representatives of four national and international non-governmental organizations (active in the field of human rights), two individuals of a non-governmental organization working for the abolition of the death penalty, two representatives of a (national) entity of lawyers, four University Professors in their individual capacity, and three individuals in representation of a person condemned to death.

[65] As the ICJ has subsequently also admitted, in the *LaGrand* case.

[66] As also promptly acknowledged by expert writing; cf., e.g., L. Hennebel, 'L'"humanisation' du Droit international des droits de l'homme – Commentaire sur l'Avis Consultatif n. 18 de la Cour Interaméricaine relatif aux droits des travailleurs migrants', 15 *Revue trimestrielle des droits de l'homme* (2004) n. 59, pp. 747–56; S.H. Cleveland, 'Legal Status and Rights of Undocumented Migrants – Advisory Opinion OC-18/03 [of the] Inter-American Court of Human Rights', 99 *American Journal of International Law* (2005) pp. 460–5; C. Laly-Chevalier, F. da Poïan and H. Tigroudja, 'Chronique de la jurisprudence de la Cour Interaméricaine des Droits de l'Homme (2002–2004)', 16 *Revue trimestrielle des droits de l'homme* (2005) n. 62, pp. 459–98. And cf. also, on the impact of the Advisory Opinion n. 18 of the IACtHR in the United States, R. Smith, 'Derechos Laborales y Derechos Humanos de los Migrantes en Estatus Irregular en Estados Unidos', in *Memorias del Seminario Internacional 'Los Derechos Humanos de los Migrantes'* (Mexico, June 2005), Mexico, Secretaría de Relaciones Exteriores, 2005, pp. 299–301.

procedure counted on the participation of twelve accredited States (among which five States intervening in the hearings), the Inter-American Commission on Human Rights, one agency of the United Nations (the U.N. High Commissioner for Refugees – UNHCR), and nine entities of the civil society and academic circles of several countries of the region, besides the Central American Council of Human Rights Ombudsmen [Attorneys-General].

On 17 September 2003 the IACtHR delivered its 18th Advisory Opinion, requested by Mexico, on the *Juridical Condition and Rights of Undocumented Migrants*, wherein it held that States ought to respect and ensure respect of human rights in the light of the general and basic principle of equality and non-discrimination, and that any discriminatory treatment with regard to the protection and exercise of human rights generates the international responsibility of the States. In the view of the Court, the fundamental principle of equality and non-discrimination has entered into the domain of *jus cogens*.

The Court added that States cannot discriminate or tolerate discriminatory situations to the detriment of migrants, and ought to guarantee the due process of law to any person, irrespective of her migratory status. The latter cannot be a justification for depriving a person of the enjoyment and exercise of her human rights, including labour rights. Undocumented migrant workers have the same labour rights as the other workers of the State of employment, and this latter ought to ensure respect for those rights in practice. States cannot subordinate or condition the observance of the principle of equality before the law and non-discrimination to the aims of their migratory or other policies.

In addition, four Individual Opinions were presented. All of them, significantly, were Concurring Opinions. In my extensive Concurring Opinion, as Judge President of the Court, I dwelt upon nine points, namely:

a the *civitas maxima gentium* and the universality of humankind;

b the disparities of the contemporary world and the vulnerability of migrants;

c the reaction of the universal juridical conscience;

d the construction of the individual subjective right of asylum;

e the position and the role of general principles of Law;

f the fundamental principles as *substratum* of the legal order itself;

g the principle of equality and non-discrimination in international human rights law;

h the emergence, the content, and the scope of the *jus cogens*; and

i the emergence and the scope of the obligations *erga omnes* of protection (their horizontal and vertical dimensions).

The 18th Advisory Opinion of the Inter-American Court, on the *Juridical Condition and Rights of Undocumented Migrants*, has already had, for all its implications, a considerable impact in the American continent, and its influence is bound to irradiate elsewhere as well, given the importance of the matter. It propounds the same dynamic or evolutive interpretation of International Human Rights Law heralded by the Inter-American Court, four years earlier, in its pioneering 16th Advisory Opinion, on *The Right to Information on Consular Assistance in the Framework of the Guarantees of the Due Process of Law* (1999),[67] which has ever since been a source of inspiration for the international case-law *in statu nascendi* on the matter. In 2003, the Inter-American Court has reiterated and expanded on its forward-looking outlook, in its 18th Advisory Opinion, on the *Juridical Condition and Rights of Undocumented Migrants*, constructed upon the evolving concepts of *jus cogens* and of obligations *erga omnes* of protection.

IV. Concluding Observations

Advances in the present domain of the international protection of victims in distress – as illustrated by the situation of great adversity of, for example, undocumented migrants – will be achieved in an atmosphere of human solidarity. In this perspective, for example, recent 'constructions' of the type of 'irregular' – or, worse still, 'illegal' – migrants are quite negative,[68] and do not assist at all in seeking lasting solutions to the problems faced by migrants worldwide. Human beings are not deprived of the rights inherent to them as such, as a result of their migratory status or any other circumstance; one can envisage the human rights of the uprooted, and – contrary to what some would appear to try to make one believe nowadays – the principle of *non-refoulement* belongs to the domain of *jus cogens*.[69] The discretion of States has its limits, and their policies on deportation and expulsion ought to abide by the imperative norms of international law.

On the positive side, there is nowadays a greater *consciousness* of the pressing needs of protection of migrants worldwide. The United Nations World Conferences throughout the 1990s and in the passage of the century have contributed decisively to create this new awareness. They have placed due emphasis on the needs of protection of persons and segments of the population in situations of *vulnerability*. Nowadays, seminars and meetings of non-governmental and governmental experts are convened more and more often, in the search for solutions bearing in mind the imperatives of protection of migrants.[70] And yet, greater

---

[67] In that 16th and pioneering Advisory Opinion, of major importance, the IACtHR clarified that, in its interpretation of the norms of the American Convention, it should extend protection in new situations (such as that concerning the observance of the right to information on consular assistance) on the basis of preexisting rights (*supra*).

[68] L. Ortiz Ahlf, 'Derechos Humanos de los Migrantes', 35 *Jurídica – Anuario del Departamento de Derecho de la Universidad Iberoamericana* (2005) pp. 14, 19, 23 and 26–9.

[69] A.A. Cançado Trindade, 'El Desarraigo como Problema de Derechos Humanos frente a la Conciencia Jurídica Universal', in *Movimientos de Personas e Ideas y Multiculturalidad* (Forum Deusto), vol. I, Bilbao, University of Deusto, 2003, pp. 87–103.

[70] Cf., e.g., among many other initiatives: International Institute of Humanitarian Law (IIHL), *Conflict Prevention – The Humanitarian Perspective* (Proceedings, August/September 1994), San Remo, IIHL, 1994, pp. 7–185; Universidad de Sevilla, *La Asistencia Humanitaria en el Derecho Internacional Contemporáneo*, Sevilla, Univ. de Sevilla, 1997, pp. 1–74 (internal circulation); XVI Cumbre Iberoamericana, *Compromiso de Montevideo sobre Migraciones y Desarrollo*, of 05 November 2006, pp. 1–10 (internal circulation).

concertation at universal level is much needed, as the protection of migrants, in increasing numbers from distinct parts of the world, has become a *legitimate concern of the international community as a whole*.

It is reassuring that the 2000 United Nations Millennium Declaration was attentive enough to include (par. 25) a call:

to take measures to ensure respect for and protection of the human rights of migrants, migrant workers and their families, to eliminate the increasing acts of racism and xenophobia in many societies and to promote greater harmony and tolerance in all societies.

Half a decade later, in September 2005, the U.N. document 2005 World Summit Outcome, reassuringly also enlarged the express reference to the issue of migrations (pars. 61–63), relating migration to development (par. 61), and reaffirming 'our resolve to take measures to ensure respect for and protection of the human rights of migrants, migrant workers and members of their families' (par. 62).

Advances in this domain, however, will only be achieved amidst a radical change of mentality, and a greater consciousness of the pressing needs to protect the basic rights of migrants, and other persons in situation of great vulnerability. On any scale of values, considerations of a humanitarian order ought to prevail over those of an economic or financial order, over the alleged 'protectionism' of the 'work market', over group rivalries. There is a pressing need to situate the human beings in the place that corresponds to them, certainly above capitals, goods and services. This is one of the major challenges of the 'globalized' world in which we live, from the perspective of human rights.

IX

The Protection of Victims in Situations of Great Adversity or Defencelessness – II

I. Introduction: The Centrality of the Suffering of the Victims   151

II. The Protection of Abandoned or 'Street Children'   152

III. The Protection of Members of Peace Communities and Other
Civilians in Situations of Armed Conflict   157

IV. The Protection of Internally Displaced Persons   163

V. The Protection of Persons under Sub-human Conditions
of Detention   171

VI. Concluding Observations: The Prevalence of Human Rights
of Persons in Situations of Vulnerability   174

I. Introduction: The Centrality of the Suffering of the Victims

The international protection of victims in situations of considerable distress and adversity – such as the ones surveyed in the previous and the present chapters – shifts our attention to the undisputed centrality of the suffering of the victims, in the conceptual universe of international human rights law. This latter is essentially *victim-oriented*. The wide scope of its *corpus juris* is to be approached from this outlook; after all, it is in the protection extended to the victims, in any circumstances, that human rights law reaches its plenitude. The circle of protected persons in the most adverse circumstances is nowadays much wider than one would *prima facie* be inclined to assume.

The centrality of the suffering of the victims becomes notorious with their access to justice, when international mechanisms of protection are seized by them, in search of prevention (of further damage), but also of safeguard and reparation, and when their complaints are examined in international instances. The International Law of Human Rights has thus contributed, in a decisive way, to the process of *humanization* of International Law itself, as I have been stressing, in my Separate Opinions in the IACtHR, throughout the last decade (e.g., in the cases of *Blake versus Guatemala*, Merits, 1998, and Reparations, 1999; of *Bámaca Velásquez versus Guatemala*, Merits, 2000, and Reparations, 2002; besides my Concurring Opinion in the already referred to Advisory Opinion of 1999, on the *Right to Information on Consular Assistance in the Framework of the Guarantees of the Due Process of Law*).

We have already considered, in the preceding chapter, the access to justice, e.g., of undocumented migrants, and of persons affected by uprootedness in general, usually in circumstances of great adversity. In the present chapter, we shall examine, as further examples, the access to justice of abandoned or so-called 'street children', of members of peace communities and other civilians in situations of armed conflict, of internally displaced persons, of individuals under sub-human conditions of detention. This list is meant to be illustrative, but by no means exhaustive; yet it paves the way for my remaining and concluding observations, on the prevalence of human rights of persons in situations of vulnerability.

II. The Protection of Abandoned or 'Street Children'

In the exercise of its jurisdiction on contentious matters, the IACtHR delivered its Judgment in the paradigmatic case of the so-called *'Street Children' (Villagrán Morales and Others versus Guatemala* (Merits, Judgment of 19 November 1999)), establishing a violation of the right to life of the five murdered adolescents under Article 4 of the ACHR; the Court significantly stated that, 'owing to the fundamental nature of the right to life, restrictive approaches to it are inadmissible. In essence, the fundamental right to life includes, not only the right of every human being not to be deprived of his life arbitrarily, but also the right that he will not be prevented from having access to the conditions that guarantee a dignified existence' (par. 144).

In a Joint Concurring Opinion on the merits of the case, it was pointed out that 'the duty of the State to take positive measures is stressed precisely in relation to the protection of life of vulnerable and defenceless persons, in situation of risk, such as the children in the streets' (par. 4); 'the needs of protection of the weaker, – such as the children in the streets, – require definitively an interpretation of the right to life so as to comprise the minimum conditions of life with dignity' (par. 7).[1] This case, a microcosm of the reality of human rights in many parts of the American continent, as well as other regions of the world, has attracted considerable attention in the region, because the IACtHR correctly addressed one of the most serious current problems of human rights, that pertaining to children abandoned in the streets.

As to reparations, in my Separate Opinion in the same case of the *'Street Children'* (Judgment on Reparations, of 26 May 2001), I stressed the need to determine the reparations of human rights violations in cases of the kind 'as from the gravity of the facts and their impact upon the integrality of the personality of the victims, – both the direct (the murdered persons) and the indirect ones (their surviving close relatives)' (par. 2). I developed my reasoning centred on the triad formed by *victimization, human suffering,* and *rehabilitation of the victims,* – to be

---

[1] Joint Concurring Opinion of Judges A.A. Cançado Trindade and A. Abreu Burelli.

considered as from the integrality of the personality of the victims, so as to approach reparations not only on the basis of the distinction of its diverse forms, but also – and above all – to identify their true meaning on the basis of 'a prior comprehension of the real sense of human suffering' (par. 3). The intensity of human suffering, so amply and eloquently demonstrated in the case of the '*Street Children*', constituted, I proceeded, the element of utmost importance for the determination of the reparations (par. 10). And I pondered:

Nowadays, there is simply no news at all of numerous other cases, similar to the *cas d'espèce*, of the '*Street Children*', daily victimizing likewise poor and humble persons, who do not achieve to reach the international jurisdiction, nor the national one, and who are not even conscious of their rights. But even if those responsible for the established order do not perceive it, the suffering of the excluded ones is ineluctably projected into the whole social *corpus*. The supreme injustice of the state of poverty inflicted upon the unfortunate ones contaminates the whole social *milieu*, which, in valuing violence and aggressiveness, relegates to a secondary position the victims, forgetting that the human being represents the creative force of the whole community. Human suffering has a dimension which is both personal and social. Thus, the damage caused to each human being, however humble he might be, affects the community itself as a whole. As the present case discloses, the victims are multiplied in the persons of the surviving close relatives, who, furthermore, are forced to live with the great pain inflicted by the silence, the indifference and the oblivion of the others.

(...) One cannot deny nowadays the importance and pressing need to devote greater attention to victimization, human suffering, and rehabilitation of the victims, – keeping in mind the current diversification of the sources of violations of human rights.[2] The systematic violations of human rights and the growth of violence (in its multiple forms) in our days and everywhere disclose that, regrettably, the much praised material progress (enjoyed, in reality, by very few) has simply not been accompanied *pari passu* of concomitant advances at spiritual level (pars. 22–23).

The conclusion of my aforementioned Separate Opinion was to the effect that:

in circumstances such as those of the present case of the *Street Children*, there is *stricto sensu* no true or full reparation possible, in the literal sense of the term (from the Latin *reparatio*, derived from *reparare*, 'to prepare or dispose again') (...). The impossibility of a full reparation – the *restitutio in integrum* – takes place, in my understanding, not only as to the direct victims and the fundamental right to life, as commonly assumed, but also as to the indirect (surviving) victims and other rights (such as that of not being subjected to torture, nor to cruel, inhuman or degrading treatment).[3] Juridically, above all in circumstances such as those of the present case of the *Street Children*, the reparations – of the *consequences* of the measure or situation in violation of the protected human rights (in the terms of Article 63(1)

---

[2] Of which bear witness the violations perpetrated by unidentified agents or death squads, by the persistence of impunity, by the manipulation of the power of communications, by the exclusions generated by the economic power (in particular by the concentration of income in a world scale, which many insist on continuing to call 'globalization' of the economy).

[3] On the jurisprudential development of this latter, cf. ECtHR, the case of *Selmouni versus France* (Judgment on the merits of 28 July 1999), pars. 95 and 101; IACtHR, the case of *Cantoral Benavides versus Peru* (Judgment on the merits of 18 August 2000), pars. 99–100 (on the torture perpetrated by acts producing in the victim 'an acute physical, psychic or moral suffering').

of the American Convention), – instead of truly *repairing*, rather *alleviate* the human suffering of the surviving relatives, seeking to rehabilitate them for life, – and *thereby* they become absolutely necessary.

This is, in my understanding, the true meaning, with the inevitable limitations of its real extent, of the juridical concept of *reparations*, in the framework of the International Law of Human Rights. The evil committed, as I have already pointed out, does not disappear: it is only fought against, and mitigated. The reparations granted render the life of the surviving relatives perhaps bearable, by the fact that, in the *cas d'espèce*, the silence and the indifference and the oblivion have not succeeded to cover the atrocities, and that the evil perpetrated has not prevailed over the perennial search for justice (proper of the spirit). In other words, the reparations granted mean that, in the concrete case, the *human conscience* has prevailed over the impulse of destruction. In *this sense*, the reparations, although not full, are endowed with an unquestionable importance in the work of safeguard of the rights inherent to the human being (pars. 41–43).

The contentious proceedings before the Court in the '*Street Children*' case (1999–2001), by the turn of the century, counted on the effective access to justice, and the participation of the mothers of the five murdered children (and the grandmother of one of them), as poor and as abandoned as their sons (and grandson); they appeared before the Court (public hearings of 28/29 January 1999 and 12 March 2001), and, due to the judgments of IACtHR (as to the merits, of 19 November 1999, and as to reparations, of 26 May 2001), which brought some consolation to them, they could at least recover their faith in human justice.

The Court ordered a series of reparations. Besides indemnities to the close relatives of the five murdered children, the Court ordered the harmonization of the domestic legislation, the legislative, administrative, and any other measures with the relevant provisions of the ACHR (such as Article 19, on the rights of the child); it further ordered the investigation of the facts of the case, and the identification and sanction of those responsible for them, so as to guarantee their non-repetition. The Court also ordered the respondent State to 'designate an educational centre with a name allusive to the young victims in this case and place, in this centre, a plaque' with their names,[4] so as to honour their memory. This pioneering and *leading case*, which already forms part of the history of the international protection of human rights, has been drawing special attention from expert writing.[5]

Four years later, the case of the '*Institute of Rehabilitation of Minors*' versus *Paraguay* (Judgment of 02 September 2004) came once again to demonstrate, as I pointed out in my Separate Opinion (pars. 3–4), that the human person, even in the most adverse conditions, emerges as a subject of international human rights law endowed with full international juridicio-procedural capacity. In this case concerning

[4] Resolutory point n. 7.
[5] Cf., on the present case of the '*Street Children*' (*Villagrán Morales and Others versus Guatemala*), *inter alia*, the books: CEJIL, *Crianças e Adolescentes – Jurisprudência da Corte Interamericana de Direitos Humanos*, Rio de Janeiro, CEJIL/Brazil, 2003, pp. 7–237; Casa Alianza, *Los Pequeños Mártires*..., San José of Costa Rica, Casa Alianza/A.L., 2004, pp. 13–196; and cf. also, e.g., K. Quintana Osuna and G. Citroni, 'I minori d'età di fronte alla Corte Interamericana dei Diritti dell'Uomo', 2 *Pace Diritti Umani* – Università di Padova (2005) pp. 55–101, esp. pp. 69–72.

children and adolescents virtually abandoned to their own fate in sub-human conditions in a centre of detention, the IACtHR established violations of the rights to life
and to humane treatment, and of the rights of the child.[6]

The Judgment of the Court in this case duly recognized the high relevance of the
historical reforms introduced by the Court in its fourth Regulations,[7] in force as
from 01 June 2001,[8] in favour of the *titularity* of the individuals of the protected
rights, granting *locus standi in judicio* in *all* the stages of the contentious procedure
before the Court. The aforementioned cases of the '*Street Children*' and of the
'*Institute of Rehabilitation of Minors*' bear eloquent testimony of such titularity,
asserted and exercised before the Court, even in situations of utmost adversity.[9]

Subsequently, in its Judgment on the case of the *Children Yean and Bosico versus
Dominican Republic* (08 September 2005), concerning two children deprived of
nationality for four years, the Court, for the first time, pronounced on the issue of
statelessness, and, bearing in mind the wide scope of the general duties of protection under Articles 1(1) and 2 of the ACHR, it further warned as to the prohibition
imposed upon States Parties to the Convention to adopt administrative practices or
legislative measures which are discriminatory in the matter of nationality (starting
with its attribution and acquisition).[10]

The drama of the kidnapped and disappeared children in the armed conflict in El
Salvador in the 1980s was brought to the fore by the Court's Judgment (on merits
and reparations, of 01 March 2005) in the case of the *Sisters Serrano Cruz versus El
Salvador*; in this case, however, the Court did not dwell further on the issue as it
limited itself on a jurisdictional ground.[11] In my Dissenting Opinion, I drew
attention to the need to bear in mind the situation as a whole of the utmost
vulnerability of children kidnapped in a prolonged situation of armed conflict, with
all its consequences (also for the right to life with dignity and the right to cultural
identity – pars. 1–75).[12]

---

[6] Articles 4 and 5, and 19, in combination with Article 1(1) of the American Convention.

[7] Paragraphs 107, 120–1 and 126.

[8] Cf., in this respect, A.A. Cançado Trindade, 'Le nouveau Règlement de la Cour Interaméricaine
des Droits de l'Homme: quelques réflexions sur la condition de l'individu comme sujet du Droit
international', *in Libertés, justice, tolérance – Mélanges en hommage au Doyen G. Cohen-Jonathan*, vol. I,
Bruxelles, Bruylant, 2004, pp. 351–65.

[9] Such as that suffered by the children and adolescents who were inmates in the '*Institute of
Rehabilitation of Minors*' (amidst three fires in 2000–2001, and some of them killed or injured by
the burns), and even in face of the limitations of their juridical capacity as a result of their existential
condition of children or adolescents (minors of age); notwithstanding, their *titularity* of rights
emanated directly from International Law has subsisted intact, and their cause reached an international
tribunal of human rights.

[10] Paragraphs 141–2 of the Court's Judgment.

[11] For a criticism of this self-limitation, on the basis of a restriction interposed by the respondent
State, cf. the Dissenting Opinion of Judge A.A. Cançado Trindade, paragraphs 1–75.

[12] In my Dissenting Opinion in the earlier Judgment of the Court (on preliminary objections, of 23
November 2004) in the same case of the *Sisters Serrano Cruz versus El Salvador*, I strongly criticized the
Court for the undue self-limitation of its own jurisdiction, bearing also in mind the gravity of the
situation of the specific case (pars. 1–49). My two aforementioned Dissenting Opinions in the case of
the *Sisters Serrano Cruz* are reproduced in: A.A. Cançado Trindade, *Derecho Internacional de los
Derechos Humanos – Esencia y Trascendencia (Votos en la Corte Interamericana de Derechos Humanos,*

Half a decade after the 'Street Children' case, the drama of the 'street children' was brought again to the attention of the Court in the case of *Servellón and Others versus Honduras* (Merits and Reparations, Judgment of 21 September 2006). Of the four victims killed in the streets in Tegucigalpa, two were children and one was adolescent. In my Separate Opinion in that case, I observed that the facts which originated the *cas d'espèce* 'represented a microcosm of the violence perpetrated, without frontiers, against children in the streets of the world', victimized by marginalization and exclusion (par. 18). But, however brief and ephemeral their lives had been, as abandoned children, I added, they:

occupy, notwithstanding, as victims, a *central position* in the International Law of Human Rights. The centrality of the victims in the conceptual universe of the International Law of Human Rights is nowadays solidly established (. . .).

Before this international jurisdiction, those forgotten by the world are treated as full subjects of law, endowed with international juridico-procedural capacity. Their sufferings do not pass in vain. (. . .) (pars. 19 and 33).

Cases such as the aforementioned ones, concerning 'street children' or abandoned children, disclose a high intensity of human suffering, and further reveal that the links of affection survive and that the violent death of the beloved ones can have devastating effects on the close relatives and disrupting effects on the respective family units already surviving in social marginalization and exclusion and chronic poverty. On the other hand, the outcome of such cases brought to the attention of the IACtHR indicates not only their resolution as to reparations, but has further contributed to raise the standards of human behaviour with regard to the dispossessed.

It further discloses that human conscience has attained a degree of evolution that has rendered it possible to impart justice by means of the protection of the rights of the marginalized or excluded, in granting to them and/or their relatives, and their legal representatives – as to every human being – direct access to an international judicial instance in order to vindicate their rights, as the true complaining party. The human being, even in the most adverse conditions, thus emerges as subject of international human rights law, endowed with full international juridico-procedural capacity.

It may be added that, in the exercise of its advisory jurisdiction, the IACtHR delivered, on 28 August 2002, the 17th. Advisory Opinion of its history, of particular importance, on the *Juridical Condition and Human Rights of the Child*, wherein the Court dwelt upon the duties which both the family and the State have vis-à-vis the child.[13] The Court warned that the child is the subject (*titulaire*) of rights rather than simply an object of protection. In this connection, the Court furthermore held that the juridicial personality is ineluctably recognized by Law to every human being

---

1991–2006), México, Edit. Porrúa/Universidad Iberoamericana, 2007, pp. 466–82 and 483–507, respectively.

[13] In the light of the rights of this latter provided for in the American Convention on Human Rights and the U.N. Convention on the Rights of the Child.

(whether a child or an adolescent), irrespective of his existential condition or the extent of his legal capacity to exercise his rights for himself (capacity of exercise). In fact, the recognition and the consolidation of the position of the human being as a full subject of international human rights law constitutes, nowadays, an unequivocal and eloquent manifestation of the advances of the current process of *humanization* of International Law itself (the new *jus gentium* of our times).[14]

III. The Protection of Members of Peace Communities and Other Civilians in Situations of Armed Conflict

In recent years, the IACtHR has extended protection to members of peace communities in situations of armed conflict, particularly in view of the persistence and aggravation of situations of the kind of the one in present-day Colombia. It has done so by means of orders of Provisional Measures of Protection. One such community, whose members are nowadays thus protected, is that of San José of Apartadó, since the first Provisional Measures ordered, in the case of the *Community of Peace of San José of Apartadó versus Colombia*, to their benefit, in the year 2000. Two years later, the IACtHR expanded those Measures of Protection, so as to cover, besides the members of that Community, also persons who render services to it.

The Court, furthermore, pointed out the duty of the State to protect the life and personal integrity of all persons under the protection of those measures, also vis-à-vis *third parties* (notably clandestine groups and paramilitary). The expansion of those measures of protection coincided with the aggravation of the human rights situation in Colombia. By means of the adoption of those reiterated measures, the IACtHR has acknowledged the pressing need of developing the obligations *erga omnes* of protection in the framework of the ACHR.[15]

In the following year (2003), the IACtHR kept on ordering in an increasing way Provisional Measures of Protection,[16] this time to the benefit also of the members of the *Communities of Jiguamiandó and Curbaradó* (2003), also in Colombia, with an additional total of 2125 protected persons. In my Concurring Opinion in that case, I drew attention to the special interest of Provisional Measures of Protection of the kind for the study and development of the obligations *erga omnes* of protection, as well as of the emerging right of *humanitarian assistance* (under the American Convention) in a situation of generalized internal armed conflict such as that plaguing Colombia nowadays. In my aforementioned

---

[14] Cf., on this point, A.A. Cançado Trindade, *Tratado de Direito Internacional dos Direitos Humanos*, vol. III, Porto Alegre/Brazil, S.A. Fabris Ed., 2003, pp. 447–97.

[15] A.A. Cançado Trindade, 'The Developing Case-Law of the Inter-American Court of Human Rights', 3 *Human Rights Law Review* (2003) pp. 22–3.

[16] As an illustration of the constant pattern of the increasing use of such measures, comprising an increasingly greater number of protected persons, it may be pointed out that, the total of about 1500 protected persons verified in mid-2001 had risen by mid-2003, to a total of about 4500 protected persons.

Separate Opinion, I further stressed the convergences between international human rights law and International Humanitarian Law, particularly in situations of the kind. In the year 2005, the IACtHR issued new Resolutions on Provisional Measures of Protection, which have continued to enlarge the circles of protected persons, continuously benefiting members of entire peace communities, as in the cases of the *Peace Community of San José of Apartadó versus Colombia*[17] and of the *Communities of Jiguamiandó and Curbaradó*.[18]

In its resolutions on Provisional Measures of Protection, the IACtHR, besides the adoption of such measures, has also required the State concerned to inform periodically on the measures, and the Inter-American Commission to present to the Court its observations on State reports. This has enabled the Court itself to exert, besides the protection of a preventive character, a *continuous monitoring* of the compliance, on the part of the States at issue, with the aforementioned Provisional Measures ordered by it. In my Concurring Opinion in the case of the *Peace Community of San José of Apartadó* (Resolution of 18 June 2002), I stressed the importance of the recognition of the effects of the ACHR vis-à-vis third parties, particularly in a situation such as that of the armed conflict in Colombia, and in my Concurring Opinion in the case of the *Communities of the Jiguamiandó and of the Curbaradó* (Resolution of 06 March 2003) I insisted that the recognition of the *Drittwirkung* was relevant so as to comprise the protection of human rights in the relations of the human person not only vis-à-vis the State power but also in the framework of inter-individual relations (encompassing clandestine groups, the paramilitary and other groups of individuals – pars. 2–4).

In sum, the preventive dimension of such Measures is to be properly stressed, as well as their being of the utmost importance to persons in situations of great adversity and vulnerability, such as members of peace communities in situations of armed conflict. Under the ACHR, these Provisional Measures of Protection have certainly contributed to the strengthening of the protection of the fundamental rights of the human person in any circumstances.[19] Other pertinent references are found in the exercise of the Court's contentious as well as advisory functions.

In the course of the contentious proceedings before the IACtHR in the case of the *Massacre of Pueblo Bello*, also concerning Colombia, it was pointed out that a chronic situation of armed conflict of high risk had been established by the creation of the so-called 'paramilitarism' (to which the State itself had originally contributed) involved with drug-trafficking and assisted by 'forces of intelligence';[20] the specific case fitted into this situation of chronic violence, the generalization and

---

[17] IACtHR, Resolutions of 17 November 2004 and 15 March 2005.

[18] IACtHR, Resolution of 15 March 2005. Such measures of protection have also comprised large numbers of members of whole indigenous communities (as in the case of the *Sarayaku Indigenous People* concerning Ecuador, Resolutions of 06 July 2004 and 17 June 2005).

[19] Cf. A.A. Cançado Trindade, 'The Evolution of Provisional Measures of Protection under the Case-Law of the Inter-American Court of Human Rights (1987–2002)', 24 *Human Rights Law Journal* – Strasbourg/Kehl (2003) n. 5–8, pp. 162–8; A.A. Cançado Trindade, 'Les Mesures provisoires de protection dans la jurisprudence de la Cour Interaméricaine des Droits de l'Homme', 4 *Revista do Instituto Brasileiro de Direitos Humanos* (2003) pp. 13–25.

[20] As indicated by the Court's Judgment (of 31 January 2006) itself, par. 65(k).

intensification of which[21] had generated the internal displacement of people in large scale.[22] The facts of the case of the *Massacre of Pueblo Bello* thereby brought to the fore the relevance of the general duty of guarantee set forth in Article 1(1) of the ACHR; the whole Judgment (of 31 January 2006) of the Court in that case underlined the State's *duty of due diligence* to avoid the occurrence of more human rights violations.

As to the Court's advisory function, it may here be recalled that, in its memorable Advisory Opinion n. 18, on the *Juridical Condition and Rights of Undocumented Migrants* (of 17 September 2003), the Court sustained precisely that the rights protected by the ACHR ought to be respected both in the relations between the individuals and State power and in inter-individual relations, in the light of the general duty of guarantee by the States Parties (par. 140) under Article 1(1) of the Convention. This general obligation *erga omnes* of protection, as I pointed out in my Concurring Opinion (par. 80), was endowed with a necessarily objective character, and encompassed all the addressees of the juridical norms (*omnes*), both those who integrate the organs of the State public power as well as private persons themselves (*particuliers*, par. 76). And I added:

In my view, we can consider such obligations *erga omnes* from *two dimensions, one horizontal and the other vertical*, which complement each other. Thus, the obligations *erga omnes* of protection, in a horizontal dimension, are obligations pertaining to the protection of the human beings due to the international community as a whole.[23] In the framework of conventional international law, they bind all the States Parties to human rights treaties (obligations *erga omnes partes*), and, in the ambit of general international law, they bind all the States which compose the organized international community, whether or not they are Parties to those treaties (obligations *erga omnes lato sensu*). In a vertical dimension, the obligations *erga omnes* of protection bind both the organs and agents of (State) public power, and the individuals themselves (in the inter-individual relations).

For the conformation of this vertical dimension have decisively contributed the advent and the evolution of the International Law of Human Rights. But it is surprising that, until now, these horizontal and vertical dimensions of the obligations *erga omnes* of protection have passed entirely unnoticed from contemporary legal doctrine. Nevertheless, I see them clearly shaped in the legal regime itself of the American Convention on Human Rights. Thus, for example, as to the vertical dimension, the general obligation, set forth in Article 1(1) of the American Convention, to respect and to ensure respect for the free exercise of the rights protected by it, generates effects *erga omnes*, encompassing the relations of the individual both with the public (State) power as well as with other individuals (*particuliers*)[24] (pars. 77–78).

In the European human rights system, the case *Issa and Others versus Turkey* (Judgment of 16 November 2004), e.g., concerned a large-scale trans-frontier raid

---

[21] Above all between 1988 and 1990, when 'there occurred more than 20 massacres of peasants and trade union members perpetrated by the paramilitary'; ibid., par. 95(27).

[22] Cf. ibid., pars. 65(1) and 66(c).

[23] IACtHR, case *Blake versus Guatemala* (Merits), Judgment of 24 January 1998, Separate Opinion of Judge A.A. Cançado Trindade, par. 26, and cf. pars. 27–30.

[24] Cf., in this respect, in general, the resolution adopted by the *Institut de Droit International* (I.D.I.) at the session of Santiago de Compostela of 1989 (Article 1), in: I.D.I., 63 *Annuaire de l'Institut de Droit International* (1989)-II, pp. 286 and 288–9.

undertaken by Turkish military forces into northern Iraq. Although the Chamber of the ECtHR concluded that the applicants had not succeeded in establishing the facts contained in their complaint to the required standard of proof (pars. 81–82), it stated, in the light of Article 1 of the ECHR, that in the case of military action carried out in an area outside its national territory over which the State at issue exercises effective control, its international responsibility may be engaged for breach of the obligation to secure the rights protected by the ECHR (pars. 66–69). The ECtHR added that 'accountability in such situations stems from the fact that Article 1 of the Convention cannot be interpreted so as to allow a State Party to perpetrate violations of the Convention on the territory of another State, which it could not perpetrate on its own territory' (par. 71).

In fact, earlier on, with the eruption and aggravation (as from the emergency situation of 1987 onwards) of the internal armed conflict in the South-East region of Turkey, successive cases[25] lodged with the ECtHR disclosed a pattern of operations of Turkish security forces amidst arbitrary detentions, torture, and killings of civilians by 'unknown perpetrators' and disappearances of persons.[26] Some of the petitions have met with evidential hurdles; yet the Court has stressed the State's duty to take precautions to protect civilians whenever deliberate force is used by the State, as well as the State's duty to conduct an effective investigation of the human rights breaches,[27] starting with the violations of the fundamental right to life.

In the cycle of the so-called *Turkish cases*, the ECtHR noted that it had 'to bear in mind the insecurity and vulnerability of the applicants' position', deprived of their basic needs and with their homes destroyed, as in, *inter alia*, the case of *Akdivar and Others* (Judgment of 16 September 1996).[28] In this case, the Court further stressed the need to secure the free and effective operation of the petitioning system; in the same line of thinking, a finding of the existence of an administrative practice incompatible with the ECHR relieved the petitioners from the duty of prior exhaustion of local remedies, and the respondent State could not rely on the exhaustion of these latter.[29]

The Court realized that, with the successive petitions from individuals in *South East Turkey*, it had entered into a new stage of evolution in the history of the application of the ECHR, not only in the scale of the human rights violations at issue, but also in the obstacles to overcome as to the procedural and jurisprudential issues raised, calling for a judicial investigation of State policies in the context of a prolonged emergency situation: it was at least clarified that in South East Turkey local

---

[25] Cf., e.g., cases *Akdivar and Others* (1996), *Aksoy* (1996), *Yasa* (1998), *Ergi* (1998), *Kurt* (1998–1999), *Tanrikulu* (1999), *Akdeniz and Others* (1999), *Cakici* (1999), *Kilic* (2000), *Kaya* (2000), *Akkoc* (2000), *Gul* (2000), *Timurtas* (2000), *Ertak* (2000), *Tas* (2000).

[26] C. Buckley, 'The European Convention on Human Rights and the Right to Life in Turkey', 1 *Human Rights Law Review* (2001) p. 35.

[27] Ibid., pp. 44–7 and 65.

[28] L. Zwaak, 'The European Court of Human Rights Has the Turkish Security Forces Held Responsible for Violations of Human Rights: The Case of *Akdivar and Others*', 10 *Leiden Journal of International Law* (1997) p. 104.

[29] Ibid., pp. 107 and 109.

remedies were then manifestly inadequate and ineffective, and did not need to be exhausted by the applicants, in face of 'the existence of administrative practices which permit or authorise gross violations of human rights'.[30]

Like the IACtHR from the very start of the exercise of its contentious function, the ECtHR also began to face massive or structural violations of human rights, with the flow of petitions against the Turkish security forces in large scale. The systematic violations of human rights in this new cycle of cases led the Court to adopt a more proactive role in pursuance of a *pro victima* interpretation of the relevant norms of the Convention and its mechanism of control (and in particular the local remedies rule).[31] Thus, particularly from the mid-1990s onwards, the ECtHR began to put greater stress on the State's 'positive obligations of protection', on its duty to conduct an effective investigation of the circumstances surrounding murders linked to the uncontrolled use of force (and to identify, try, and sanction the perpetrators), as well as on the growing importance of the right to an effective remedy – in its wide scope – set forth in Article 13 of the ECHR (including the petitioners' access to the procedure of investigation).[32] In sum, faced with such grave and systematic violations of human rights, the Court has become more and more concerned with the much-needed improvement of the existential condition of the victims.

In September 2003, a study was submitted to the Steering Committee for Human Rights of the Council of Europe, of the case-law under the ECHR dealing with the principles governing its application during armed conflicts and internal disturbances and tensions. The author of the study (J. McBride), in upholding the view that International Humanitarian Law standards can inform the specific application of the ECHR in such circumstances (pars. 13 and 17), focused on the needed availability and accessibility of judicial supervision even in times of emergency measures and derogations of certain rights, so as to determine whether such derogations were strictly required by the exigencies of the situation and did not encroach upon non-derogable rights (par. 14). In any case, recourse to the ECtHR should be secured in any circumstances (par. 14).

A central place was thus reserved, in the aforementioned study, to the imperative of preserving access to justice, at both national and international levels. The study

---

[30] A. Reidy, F. Hampson and K. Boyle, 'Gross Violations of Human Rights: Invoking the European Convention on Human Rights in the Case of Turkey', 15 *Netherlands Quarterly of Human Rights* (1997) pp. 172 and 162.

[31] J.-F. Flauss, 'La Cour de Strasbourg face aux violations systématiques des droits de l'homme', in *Les droits de l'homme au seuil du troisième millénaire – Mélanges en hommage à P. Lambert*, Bruxelles, Bruylant, 2000, pp. 343–4, 347 and 354; the author points out that 'le devoir d'épuiser les recours internes peut se trouver réduit à l'obligation de solliciter une enquête sur les faits dénoncés comme constitutifs d'une atteinte aux droits indérogeables' (p. 355).

[32] Ibid., pp. 349–51 and 353. On the 'objective character' of the conventional obligations of protection of States Parties to human rights treaties, cf. A.A. Cançado Trindade, *Tratado de Direito Internacional dos Direitos Humanos*, vol. II, Porto Alegre/Brazil, S.A. Fabris Ed., 1999, pp. 28–31. On the European Court's early acknowledgement of 'positive obligations' of protection and the 'considerable enlargement of State responsibility by the incidence of Article 1 of the European Convention on Human Rights', cf. D. Spielmann, *L'effet potentiel de la Convention Européenne des Droits de l'Homme entre personnes privées*, Bruxelles, Bruylant, 1995, pp. 75–84.

further warned that the independence and impartiality of national courts should always be secured, as well as independent legal advice, even amidst security measures (pars. 41–42); there was 'no scope for compromise in the need to provide a fair procedure', and the right of access to courts should always be preserved (pars. 40 and 46). So, even in times of armed conflicts, there persisted the duties to provide appropriate remedies and judicial supervision of any actions, so as to ensure the protection of those vulnerable against abuse (par. 88).[33]

In November 2003, the Steering Committee for Human Rights of the Council of Europe adopted its *Final Activity Report* on the protection of human rights during armed conflicts and internal disturbances and tensions. It drew attention to prevention and investigation of human rights in such circumstances (par. 4). It regarded the Council of Europe's Commissioner for Human Rights as 'the most suitable body to undertake broad fact-finding in crisis situations' (pars. 12–13). At last, the Committee of Ministers of the Council of Europe adopted, on 21 January 2004, the 'Declaration on the Protection of Human Rights during Armed Conflict, Internal Disturbances and Tensions', which, drawing attention to such circumstances (par. 10), firmly condemned 'all situations of serious and massive violations of human rights' (par. 5), and recalled that, 'in any event, States cannot derogate from the peremptory norms of international law or from those of International Humanitarian Law where applicable' (par. 4).[34]

Although legal issues concerning the access to justice of victims of massacres and crimes of State are studied in detail in the following chapter, at this stage reference is to be made also to a relevant case in the framework of the African human rights system. In the inter-State case of the *Democratic Republic of Congo versus Burundi, Rwanda and Uganda* (2003),[35] the complainant State alleged 'grave and massive violations' of human and peoples' rights, committed in its Eastern provinces by the armed forces of the respondent States, in the form of a 'series of massacres, rapes, mutilations, mass transfers of populations and looting of the peoples' possessions'.[36]

The African Commission on Human and Peoples' Rights (AfComHPR) found that 'the killings, massacres, rapes, mutilations and other grave human rights abuses committed while the respondent States' armed forces were still in effective occupation of the Eastern provinces of the complainant State' (as from the beginning of August 1998) were 'reprehensible', as well as 'inconsistent with their

---

[33] J. McBride, *Study on the Principles Governing the Application of the European Convention on Human Rights during Armed Conflict and Internal Disturbances and Tensions*, Strasbourg, C.E./Steering Committee for Human Rights, doc. DH-DEV(2003)001, of 19 September 2003, pp. 1–11.

[34] Council of Europe/Steering Committee for Human Rights, *Final Activity Report on the Protection of Human Rights during Armed Conflict as well as during Internal Disturbances and Tensions*, Strasbourg, C.E. doc. CDDH(2003)026/Add. II, of 26 November 2003, pp. 1–6.

[35] Communication 227/99, Decision of May 2003, at the 33rd. Session of the African Commission on Human and Peoples' Rights, *Report of the African Commission on Human and Peoples' Rights* (June 2006), doc. EX.CL/279(IX), pp. 111–31.

[36] Case reproduced also in: C. Heyns and M. Killander (eds.), *Compendium of Key Human Rights Documents of the African Union*, 3rd. ed., Pretoria, University Law Press (PULP), 2007, p. 192, par. 69; this was the first inter-State communication decided by the AfComHPR.

obligations' under the 1949 Geneva Convention Relative to the Protection of Civilian Persons in Time of War (Part III) and Protocol I to the Convention.[37] Furthermore, the AfComHPR held that they also constituted 'flagrant violations' of the rights to life and the integrity of the person, in breach of Articles 2 and 4 of the African Charter on Human and Peoples' Rights.[38]

In this case of massacres, it is significant that the African Commission based its decision on relevant and pertinent provisions of both international human rights law and International Humanitarian Law. It found further violations of the African Charter, such as of Articles 18(1) and 12(1) and (2), resulting from the 'mass transfer of persons from the Eastern provinces of the complainant State to camps in Rwanda' (as alleged by the complainant and not refuted by the respondent).[39] It further condemned the plunder and lootings of the natural resources of the Eastern provinces of the Congo, in contravention of Articles 21–22 of the African Charter,[40] and found that there had been a serious lack of respect for the mortal remains of the victims of massacres and for their gravesites, adding that the 'barbaric' and 'reckless' dumping and mass burial of those mortal remains (following the massacres), besides being forbidden under Article 34 of Additional Protocol I of 1977 to the Geneva Conventions of 1949, were a violation of the Congolese people's right to cultural development, in breach of Articles 60 and 61 of the African Charter.[41]

IV. The Protection of Internally Displaced Persons

In the last three decades, the problem of internal displacement has challenged the very bases of the international norms of protection, demanding an *aggiornamento* of these latter and new responses to a situation not originally foreseen at the time of the drafting or elaboration of the relevant international instruments. These latter have revealed flagrant insufficiencies, such as, for example, the original lack of norms expressly directed to overcome the alleged non-applicability of the norms of protection to non-State actors, the non-typification of internal displacement under the original norms of protection, and the possibility of restrictions or derogations undermining protection in critical moments. Such insufficiencies have generated initiatives of protection at both global (United Nations) and regional (Latin American) levels – initiatives which have sought a conceptual framework which allows the development responses, at operative level, to the new needs of protection.

---

[37] Which, as added by the AfComHPR, laid down – the four Geneva Conventions of 1949 and the two Additional Protocols of 1977 – rules recognized by member States of the African Union (formerly OAU) and that form part of 'the general principles recognized by African States'; ibid., p. 193, pars. 78–9.

[38] Cf. ibid., p. 193, par. 80.
[39] Ibid., p. 194, par. 81.
[40] Ibid., pp. 195–6, pars. 90–1 and 94–5.
[41] Ibid., pp. 194–5, par. 87.

At global (U.N.) level, one decade ago, early in 1998, the former U.N. Commission on Human Rights, bearing in mind the reports by the U.N. Secretary-General's Representative on Internally Displaced Persons (F.M. Deng),[42] at last adopted the *Guiding Principles on Internal Displacement*,[43] despite the persistence of the problem of internal displacement for mainly the last two decades. The basic purpose of the *Guiding Principles* is that of reinforcing and strengthening the already existing means of protection; to this effect, the proposed new principles apply both to governments and insurgent groups, at all stages of the displacement. The basic principle of *non-discrimination* occupies a central position in the 1998 document on *Principles*,[44] which lists the same rights of internally displaced persons, which other persons in their country enjoy.[45]

The *Guiding Principles* determine that the displacement cannot take place in a way that violates the rights to life, to dignity, to freedom and security of the affected persons;[46] they also assert other rights, such as the right to respect for family life, the right to an adequate standard of living, the right to equality before the law, and the right to education.[47] The basic idea underlying the whole document[48] is that internally displaced persons do not lose their inherent rights as a result of displacement, and can invoke the pertinent international norms of protection (of both international human rights law and International Humanitarian Law) to safeguard their rights.

In a significant resolution adopted in 1994, the then U.N. Commission on Human Rights, bearing in mind in particular the problem of internally displaced persons, recalled the relevant norms of international human rights law and International Humanitarian Law, as well as International Refugee Law, of pertinence to the problem at issue.[49] Resolution 1994/68, adopted by the Commission on 09 March 1994, further recalled the 1993 Vienna Declaration and Programme of Action (adopted by the II World Conference on Human Rights), which called for 'a comprehensive approach by the international community with regard to refugees and displaced persons'.[50]

It stressed the 'humanitarian dimension' of 'the problem of internally displaced persons and the responsibilities this poses for States and the international

---

[42] Those reports stressed the importance of prevention (e.g., reinforcing the protection of the rights to life and personal integrity, as well as the rights to property of lands and goods); cf. F.M. Deng, *Internally Displaced Persons* (Interim Report), N.Y., RPG/DHA, 1994, p. 21; and cf. U.N., doc. E/CN.4/1995/50/Add.1, of 03 October 1994, p. 34.

[43] For comments, cf. W. Kälin, *Guiding Principles on Internal Displacement – Annotations*, Washington D.C., ASIL/Brookings Institution, 2000, pp. 1–276.

[44] Principles 1(1), 4(1), 22, 24(1).

[45] It affirms, moreover, the prohibition of the 'arbitrary displacement' (Principle 6).

[46] Principles 8 and following.

[47] Principles 17, 18, 20, and 23, respectively.

[48] On a 'comprehensive approach' to displacement so as to address as well the problem of forced migration as a whole, bearing in mind the U.N. Guiding Principles on Internal Displacement, cf. C. Phuong, *The International Protection of Internally Displaced Persons*, Cambridge, University Press, 2004, pp. 54–5 and 237.

[49] 2nd. preambular paragraph.

[50] 7th preambular paragraph.

community'.[51] It further drew attention to 'the need to address the root causes of internal displacement',[52] as well as 'to continue raising the level of *consciousness* about the plight of the internally displaced'.[53] More than a decade later, its considerations are likewise valid and relevant to migrants, who add an even greater dimension to the sufferings of the uprooted in our so-called and improperly called 'globalized' world.

Still at global (U.N.) level, resolution 2005/47 of the former U.N. Commission on Human Rights, adopted on 19 April 2005, expressed concern, in its preamble, at 'the increasing number of migrants worldwide', a worrisome phenomenon with a 'global character' (par. 6), and called upon States to revise their immigration policies with a view to eliminating all discriminatory practices against migrants and their families (par. 4). It urged States to put an end to arbitrary arrests and deprivation of liberty of migrants (par. 15), to prevent the violation of the human rights of migrants while in transit (par. 18), and to combat and prosecute international trafficking and smuggling of migrants (endangering their lives and entailing 'different forms of servitude or exploitation' – par. 19).[54] Resolution 2005/47 recalled, in its preamble, the contributions of the pioneering Advisory Opinions ns. 16 and 18 of the IACtHR, on *The Right to Information on Consular Assistance in the Framework of the Guarantees of the Due Process of Law* (1999), and on *The Juridical Condition and Rights of Undocumented Migrants* (2003), as well as the Judgments of the International Court of Justice in the *LaGrand* (2001) and the *Avena and Other Mexican Nationals* (2004) cases.[55]

At regional level, in the American continent, the 1984 Declaration of Cartagena on Refugees, the 1994 San José Declaration on Refugees and Displaced Persons, and the 2004 Mexico Declaration and Plan of Action to Strengthen the International Protection of Refugees in Latin America, are each a product of a given historical moment. The first one, the Declaration of Cartagena, was motivated by the urgent need generated by a concrete crisis of great proportions; to the extent that this crisis was being overcome, due in part to that Declaration, its legacy began to project itself to other regions and subregions of the American continent.

The second Declaration was adopted amidst a distinct crisis, a more diffuse one, marked by the deterioration of the socio-economic conditions of wide segments of the population in distinct regions. In sum, Cartagena and San José were both products of their time. The *aggiornamento* of the Colloquium of San José likewise gave special emphasis on the identification of the *needs of protection* of the human

---

[51] 5th. preambular paragraph.
[52] 12th. preambular paragraph.
[53] Paragraph 3 (emphasis added).
[54] The resolution further encouraged States Parties to implement fully the U.N. Convention against Transnational Organized Crime and the two Additional Protocols thereto, namely, the Protocol against the Smuggling of Migrants by Land, Sea and Air, and the Protocol to Prevent, Suppress and Punish Trafficking in Persons, Especially Women and Children, and urged States that had not done so to ratify them (par. 33).
[55] 6th. preambular paragraph.

being in any circumstances.[56] There remained no place for the *vacatio legis*.[57] The 1994 Declaration of San José gave a special emphasis not only on the whole problem of internal displacement, but also, more widely, on the challenges presented by the new situations of human uprootedness in Latin America and the Caribbean, including the forced migratory movements originated by causes different from those foreseen in the Declaration of Cartagena.

The 1994 Declaration recognized that the violation of human rights is one of the causes of forced displacements and that therefore the protection of those rights and the strengthening of the democratic system constitute the best measures for the search for lasting solutions, as well as for the prevention of conflicts, the exoduses of refugees and the grave humanitarian crises.[58] Recently, at the end of consultations with wide public participation, undertaken at the initiative of the UNHCR, the 2004 Mexico Declaration and Plan of Action to Strengthen the International Protection of Refugees in Latin America was adopted,[59] on the occasion of the twentieth anniversary of the Cartagena Declaration. For the first time in the present process, a document of this kind was accompanied by a Plan of Action. This can be explained by the aggravation of the humanitarian crisis in the region, particularly in the Andean subregion.

As the *rapporteur* of the Committee of Legal Experts of the UNHCR observed in his presentation of the final report to the Mexico Colloquium, at its first plenary session, on 15 November 2004, although the 1984 Cartagena Declaration and the 1994 San José Declaration applied to specific situations is distinct moments, their achievements 'cumulate, and constitute today a juridical patrimony' of all the peoples of the region, disclosing the new trends of the development of the international safeguard of the rights of the human person in the light of the needs of protection, and projecting themselves into the future.[60] Thus:

the Declaration of Cartagena faced the great human drama of the armed conflicts in Central America, but furthermore *foresaw* the aggravation of the problem of internally displaced persons. The Declaration of San José, in turn, dwelt deeper upon the issue of protection of, besides refugees, also of internally displaced persons, but moreover *foresaw* the aggravation of the problem of forced migratory fluxes.

Ever since anachronical compartmentalizations were overcome, proper of a way of thinking of a past which no longer exists, and one came to recognize the *convergences* between the three regimes of protection of the rights of the human person, namely, the

---

[56] Instead of subjective categorizations of persons (in accordance with the reasons which led them to abandon their homes), proper of the past, nowadays the objective criterion of the needs of protection came to be adopted, encompassing thereby a considerably greater number of persons (including the internally displaced persons) so vulnerable as the refugees, or even more than the latter.

[57] Ibid., pp. 14–15.

[58] Ibid., pp. 431–2.

[59] Cf. text reproduced in: UNHCR, *Memoria del Vigésimo Aniversario de la Declaración de Cartagena sobre los Refugiados (1984–2004)*, Mexico City/San José of Costa Rica, UNHCR, 2005, pp. 385–98.

[60] Cf. 'Presentación por el Dr. A.A. Cançado Trindade del Comité de Consultores Jurídicos del ACNUR' (Mexico City, 15 November 2004), in *UNHCR, Memoria del Vigésimo Aniversario de la Declaración de Cartagena . . .* , *op. cit. supra* n. (59), pp. 368–9.

International Law of Refugees, International Humanitarian Law and the International Law of Human Rights. Such convergences – at normative, hermeneutic and operative levels – were reaffirmed in all preparatory meetings of the present Commemorative Colloquy of Mexico City, and have repercussions nowadays in other parts of the world, conforming the most lucid international legal doctrine on the matter.[61]

Those convergences[62] were, not surprisingly, further reflected in the 2004 Mexico Declaration and Plan of Action to Strengthen the International Protection of Refugees in Latin America itself. Thus, as the *rapporteur* of the Committee of Legal Experts of the UNHCR at last warned at the Mexico Colloquium of November 2004:

there is no place for the *vacatio legis*, there is no legal vacuum, and *all* (. . .) persons are under the protection of the Law, in all and any circumstances (also in face of security measures).[63]

Still at regional level, the Inter-American Commission on Human Rights (IAComHR), pursuant to a request of the General Assembly of the Organization of American States (OAS),[64] established the mandate of its Special *Rapporteur* on Migrant Workers and their Families in 1997, with due emphasis on their situation of 'special vulnerabilities'. Since 1997the Special *Rapporteur* has been engaged in the work of monitoring of the situation of migrants and their families in the region, so as to increase 'general awareness' of the States' duty to protect them and 'to act promptly' on petitions or communications on their part. The Special *Rapporteur* has issued recommendations to States, has prepared reports and special studies, and has carried out visits to countries of the region, including the United States, Mexico, Guatemala and Costa Rica. The research topics examined so far, in order 'to enhance the awareness' of the adversities faced by migrant workers and their families, include discrimination in general, racism and xenophobia, lack of access to the due process of law, detention conditions, smuggling of migrants and trafficking in persons, and migratory practices and their economic consequences.[65]

These developments are significant for addressing the issue of forced internal displacement, and the guarantee of voluntary and safe return. Yet, the problem of forced migrations has a wider dimension, and presents, nowadays, a considerable challenge to the international community as a whole. Only during the 1990s was

[61] Ibid., p. 369.
[62] Cf. A.A. Cançado Trindade, 'Derecho Internacional de los Derechos Humanos, Derecho Internacional de los Refugiados y Derecho Internacional Humanitario: Aproximaciones y Convergencias', in *10 Años de la Declaración de Cartagena sobre Refugiados – Memoria del Coloquio Internacional* (San José of Costa Rica, December 1994), San José of Costa Rica, IIDH/UNHCR, 1995, pp. 77–168; A.A. Cançado Trindade, 'Aproximaciones y Convergencias Revisitadas: Diez Años de Interacción entre el Derecho Internacional de los Derechos Humanos, el Derecho Internacional de los Refugiados, y el Derecho Internacional Humanitario (De Cartagena/1984 a San José/1994 y México/2004)', in *Memoria del Vigésimo Aniversario de la Declaración de Cartagena sobre Refugiados (1984–2004)*, San José of Costa Rica, UNHCR, 2005, pp. 139–91.
[63] Ibid., p. 369.
[64] OAS, G.A. resolutions AG/RES.1404/XXVI-O/96 (of 1996) and AG/RES.1480/XXVII-0/97 (of 1997).
[65] OAS, *Special Rapporteurship on Migrant Workers and Their Families*, Washington D.C., IAComHR, document www.cidh.oas.org/migrants, 2007, pp. 1–10.

the larger problem of the fluxes of forced migrations identified and began to be dealt with as such, in a systematized way. In fact, the drama of the internally displaced persons manifests nowadays, in an alarming way, in distinct parts of the world,[66] as one of the major human rights problems. It is not surprising that it has reached international human rights tribunals such as the IACtHR and the ECtHR.

That drama, of the internally displaced persons, has been a central problem for the IACtHR in the cases of the *Indigenous Community Yakye Axa versus Paraguay* (Judgment of 17 June 2005) and of the *Indigenous Community Sawhoyamaxa versus Paraguay* (Judgment of 29 March 2006), as well as in the case of the *Moiwana Community versus Suriname* (Judgment of 15 June 2005); in this latter, the grave human rights violations generated internally displaced persons as well as refugees. This trilogy of recent cases discloses, once again, the convergences between international human rights law, the International Law of Refugees and International Humanitarian Law.[67] I purport herein to concentrate on the vulnerability of internally displaced persons, in particular.

In this trilogy of cases, the IACtHR stressed the need of positive measures on the part of the respondent States to protect the fundamental right to life, including the right to cultural identity, as well as to secure the voluntary and safe *return* of the members of the respective communities to their ancestral lands, from which they had been forcefully displaced. The Court deemed the *devolution* of their lands[68] to them as essential to the preservation of their cultural identity and, ultimately, of their fundamental right to life *lato sensu*.

In fact, during the proceedings before the Court in the cases of the *Yakye Axa* and *Sawhoyamaxa Indigenous Communities*, it was pointed out that the forcibly displaced members of those communities were surviving at the border of a road, in a situation of total destitution; some had already died. Besides suffering the humiliation of the extreme poverty forced upon them, they could not, in all probability, even develop a project of life. Moreover, they were being deprived – by their forced displacement – of their cultural identity, which was closely linked to their ancestral lands, and, ultimately, of their right to life *lato sensu*, their right to live with dignity.[69]

---

[66] Cf., generally, *inter alia*, e.g., J.E. Serrano, *La Acción Humanitaria en Colombia desde la Perspectiva del Restablecimiento*, Bilbao, University of Deusto, 2004, pp. 17–102; A.B. Çelik, 'Transnationalization of Human Righs Norms and Its Impact on Internally Displaced Kurds', 27 *Human Rights Quarterly* (2005) pp. 969–97.

[67] For a recent treatment of this particular issue, cf. A.A. Cançado Trindade, 'International Law for Humankind: Towards a New *Jus Gentium*' – Part II, 317 *Recueil des Cours de l'Académie de Droit International de La Haye* (2005), ch. XXIII, pp. 150–71. And cf., earlier on, A.A. Cançado Trindade, *Derecho Internacional de los Derechos Humanos, Derecho Internacional de los Refugiados y Derecho Internacional Humanitario – Aproximaciones y Convergencias*, Geneva, ICRC, [2000], pp. 1–66.

[68] On the particular issue of the devolution of their lands to members of indigenous communities, cf., *inter alia*, e.g., F. Gómez Isa (ed.), *El Caso Awas Tingni contra Nicarágua: Nuevos Horizontes para los Derechos de los Pueblos Indígenas*, Bilbao, University of Deusto, 2003, pp. 9–279; C. Binder, 'The Case of the Atlantic Coast of Nicaragua: The *Awas Tingni* Case', in *International Law and Indigenous Peoples* (eds. J. Castellino and N. Walsh), Leiden, Nijhoff/R. Wallenberg Institute, 2005, pp. 249–67.

[69] Cf., on this point, e.g., [Various Authors,] *Actes du Symposium sur le droit à la vie – Quarante ans après l'adoption de la Déclaration Universelle des Droits de l'Homme: évolution conceptuelle, normative et jurisprudentielle* (eds. D. Prémont and F. Montant), Geneva, CID, 1992, pp. 1–91; J.G.C. van Aggelen, *Le rôle des organisations internationales dans la protection du droit à la vie*, Bruxelles,

The State's duty of due diligence thus came to the fore, even more clearly in view of the social oblivion into which the members of the indigenous communities were relegated. These cases, as well as that of the *Moiwana Community*, portray forced internal displacement as effectively a problem of human rights. As I stated in my Separate Opinion in the case of the *Sawhoyamaxa Indigenous Community* (Judgment of 29 March 2006):

(. . .) The vulnerability of the situation of the displaced persons results precisely from the fact that they find themselves under the jurisdiction of the State[70] (their own State) which did not take sufficient measures to avoid or impede the situation of virtual abandonment which they came to suffer. The situation de the internally displaced persons can perfectly – and ought to – be solved in the light of the norms of human rights treaties like the American Convention. As I allowed myself to point out in my Separate Opinion (par. 17) in the case of the *Moiwana Community versus Suriname* (Merits, Judgment of 15 June 2005), the *Guiding Principles on Internal Displacement* of 1998 of the United Nations determine that the displacement cannot take place in violation of the right to life – including herein the right to an adequate standard of life, the right to live; – of the right to personal dignity, to the freedom and security of the affected persons; of the *right to respect* for family life; of the right to education; of the right to equality before the law.[71] (. . .)

The present case of the *Sawhoyamaxa Community* reveals the centrality (. . .) of the victims, in a situation of high vulnerability, and who, though surviving in conditions of total indigence, and virtual abandonment, (. . .) have nevertheless succeeded in having had their cause examined by an international tribunal of human rights for the determination of the international responsibility of the State at issue. The centrality of the victims, in the most adverse circumstances, as subjets of the International Law of Human Rights, brings to the fore their *right to the Law* (*droit au Droit*/*derecho al Derecho*), their right to justice under the American Convention, which encompasses the judicial protection (Article 25) together with the judicial guarantees (Article 8). Such right comprises the whole jurisdictional protection, until the faithful execution of the international Judgment (the right of access to international justice *lato sensu*), duly motivated, and founded on the applicable law in the *cas d'espèce*. Article 25 of the American Convention constitutes effectively a pillar of the rule of law in a democratic society, in close relationship with the guarantees of the due process of law (Article 8), giving due expression to the general principles of law universally recognized, which belong to the domain of the international *jus cogens*. (. . .)

Seven years after the Judgment on the merits of this Court in the paradigmatic case of the 'Street Children' (*Villagrán Morales and Others versus Guatemala*, Judgment of 19 November 1999),[72] the abandoned and forgotten of the world again happen to reach an international tribunal of human rights in search of justice, in the cases of the members of the *Communities Yakye Axa* (Judgment of 17 June 2005) and *Sawhoyamaxa* (the present Judgment). In the *cas d'espèce*, those forcefully displaced from their homes and ancestral lands, and socially

E. Story-Scientia, 1986, pp. 1–89; [Various Authors,] *The Right to Life in International Law* (ed. B.G. Ramcharan), Dordrecht, Nijhoff, 1985, pp. 1–314.

[70] M. Stavropoulou, 'Searching for Human Security and Dignity: Human Rights, Refugees, and the Internally Displaced', in *The Universal Declaration of Human Rights: Fifty Years and Beyond* (eds. Y. Danieli, E. Stamatopoulou and C.J. Dias), Amityville/N.Y., Baywood Publ. Co., 1999, pp. 181–2.

[71] Principles 8 and following, 17–18, 20 and 23, respectively; cf. U.N., document E/CN.4/1998/53/Add.2, of 11 February 1998, pp. 6–10.

[72] And cf. also the Judgment on reparations on the same case, of 26 May 2001.

marginalized and excluded, have *effectively* reached an international jurisdiction, before which they have at last found justice. (. . .)

The present case of the *Sawhoyamaxa Indigenous Community*, preceded by the case of the *Yakye Axa Indigenous Community*, insert themselves in the line of emancipation of the human being vis-à-vis his own State for the vindication of the rights which are inherent to him, and which are prior and superior to such State. The members of the indigenous communities referred to, abandoned at the border of roads, had their cause examined and resolved (. . .) by an international tribunal like the Inter-American Court of Human Rights. Perhaps this development of the universal human conscience could not have been anticipated by the so-called 'realists' some years ago. Something has effectively changed in the world, and, in this particular, for better.

With the impact of the International Law of Human Rights, human conscience seems to have awakened to the suffering of those abandoned in the streets and at the border of the roads of the world. The human being begins to understand that he cannot live in peace with himself in face of the silent suffering of the others, including those who surround him. (. . .)[73]

Other cases of forced displacement resolved by the IACtHR in recent years included those of the massacres of *Mapiripán* (2005) and *Ituango* (2006), concerning Colombia, and of the *Moiwana Community* (2005), pertaining to Suriname; in all of them the IACtHR was attentive to the need to secure the safe and voluntary return, of those forcefully displaced, to their homes and land. In the Court's decision of 08 February 2006 on Interpretation of Judgment in the case of the *Moiwana Community versus Suriname*, this was in fact the central issue addressed by the IACtHR; in my Separate Opinion, I related that return to their homes and land to the actual demarcation, devolution, and title of their land as a form of reparation, and to their right to cultural identity (pars. 1–32).

The great adversity undergone by forcefully displaced persons has been brought to the fore not only under the ACHR, but also under the ECHR. Thus, in the *Cyprus versus Turkey* case (Judgment of 10 May 2001), the ECtHR was faced with a situation of forced internal displacement and the complaint that the rights of the displaced persons to 'respect for their private life and home' were being violated (pars. 165 and 167). The ECtHR found that not only were the displaced persons unable to apply to public authorities to reoccupy the homes which they had left behind, but they were moreover physically prevented from even visiting them (par. 172). The Court established a 'complete denial' of the right of the displaced persons to respect for their homes, in breach of Article 8(2) of the Convention; that was – it added – a continuing violation 'as a matter of policy' since 1974, comprising 'the refusal to allow the return of any Greek-Cypriot displaced persons to their homes in northern Cyprus' (pars. 174–175).

Such refusal of voluntary return provides an illustration of the convergences between international human rights law and International Refugee Law in the *cas d'espèce*.[74] The ECtHR concluded, furthermore, that there had been in the *Cyprus*

---

[73] Paragraphs 14, 35, 37 and 52–3 of the aforementioned Separate Opinion.

[74] On such convergences, cf. A.A. Cançado Trindade, 'Derecho Internacional de los Derechos Humanos, Derecho Internacional de los Refugiados y Derecho Internacional Humanitario: Aproximaciones y Convergencias', in *10 Años de la Declaración de Cartagena sobre Refugiados – Declaración de*

versus Turkey case, a continuing violation also of Article 1 of Protocol n. 1 to the ECHR, by virtue of the fact that Greek-Cypriot owners of property in northern Cyprus were being 'denied access to and control, use and enjoyment of their property as well as any compensation for the interference with their property rights' (par. 189). And the Court also found that the displaced persons had no remedies to contest interferences with their rights, what accordingly amounted also to a breach of Article 13 (right to an effective remedy) under the Convention. The ECtHR concluded that such violation of Article 13 occurred as a result of 'the respondent State's failure to provide the Greek Cypriots not residing in northern Cyprus any remedies to contest interferences with their rights under Article 8 of the Convention and Article 1 of Protocol n. 1' (pars. 192 and 194).

V. The Protection of Persons under Sub-human Conditions of Detention

Among the groups of persons who stand in a particularly vulnerable situation are those deprived of liberty; although prisoners are under the custody of the State, they often find themselves in sub-human conditions of detention. This being a recurrent problem, it is not surprising to find continuing attention devoted to such issues as protection against arbitrary detention and deprivation of liberty, prevention of ill-treatment in prisons and control of the conditions of detention, assurance of a criminal process with the guarantees of due process of law, and provision of medical treatment and assistance to detainees.[75]

The matter has been the object of an extensive case-law of the ECtHR (particularly under Article 5 of the ECHR), in providing international remedies against torture and other ill-treatment. This suggests, on the one hand, that abuses against prisoners remain a recurrent human rights problem,[76] and, on the other hand, that, notwithstanding, persons under the most adverse conditions of detention had attained access to international justice. But this access to justice by persons in detention, clearly inferred from the vast case-law under the ECHR, has been often surrounded by difficulties, including in the very exercise of the right of individual petition under the ECHR.

Thus, in the leading case of *Petra versus Romania* (Judgment of 23 September 1998), the ECtHR took note of the applicant's statement that 'he had twice been

---

San José sobre Refugiados y Personas Desplazadas 1994 (Memoria del Coloquio Internacional de San José de Costa Rica de 1994), San José of Costa Rica, UNHCR/IIHR, 1995, pp. 79–116 and 166–8.

[75] Cf., e.g., J. Murdoch, *The Treatment of Prisoners – European Standards*, Strasbourg, Council of Europe, 2006, pp. 71–364; Various Authors, *Le contrôle des conditions de détention dans les prisons d'Europe* (Actes du Colloque de Marly-le-Roi, France, de 1996), Paris, CCE, 1997, pp. 33–67.

[76] The experience at domestic law level (in different latitudes) shows unfortunately the recurrence of the problem of persons detained without trial (the excesses and abuses of preventive detention), and the need for further judicial control and determination of the rights of such detainees; cf., e.g., J.J. Paust, 'Judicial Power to Determine the Status and Rights of Persons Detained without Trial', 44 *Harvard International Law Journal* (2003) n. 2, pp. 503–32.

threatened by the Aiud prison authorities' when he had asked to write to the former EComHR, and his statements were not contradicted by the respondent State. The Court, having due regard to the 'vulnerability of the complainant' and the undue pressures exerted upon him by the prison authorities, found that such pressures were 'illegitimate and unacceptable', and concluded that they had 'hindered the right of individual petition' under the then Article 25 (1) of the ECHR (pars. 43–44). The Court warned, in the *Petra* case, that:

> it is of the utmost importance for the effective operation of the system of individual petition instituted by Article 25 that applicants or potential applicants should be able to communicate freely with the Commission without being subjected to any form of pressure from the authorities to withdraw or modify their complaints (par. 43).

Difficulties experienced by individual petitioners under detention have led the ECtHR itself to warn, in its Judgment in the case *Campbell and Fell versus United Kingdom* (of 28 June 1984), that 'la justice ne saurait s'arrêter à la porte des prisons'.[77] In any case, it ought to be reckoned that the vast case-law on the matter under the ECHR has disclosed a notable evolution, in raising standards of protection of detainees, e.g., from the old days of the classic decisions of both the former EComHR and ECtHR in the *Northern Ireland* case (1976), to the more recent times of the Judgments of the ECtHR in the *Tomasi versus France* case (of 27 August 1992) and in the *Selmouni versus France* (28 July 1999) case.[78]

In historical perspective, some of the ECtHR's rulings, drawing attention to the marginalization and vulnerability of prisoners, have entailed changes in practices at domestic law level in respect of imprisonment.[79] Yet, there remain to date problems of ill-treatment in prison,[80] prolonged detention on remand, detention in high security cells, in isolation[81] or *incommunicado*. This latter has indeed become a world-wide problem nowadays.[82]

In the inter-American human rights system, the IACtHR has exercised its competence, regarding contentious cases as well as Provisional Measures of Protection, disclosing ill-treatment in prisons, overcrowded prisons, cells containing convicted persons as well as persons still awaiting judgment, inter-individual

---

[77] As recalled by one of its former Judges; A. Spielmann, *Au diapason des droits de l'homme – Écrits choisis (1975–2003)*, Bruxelles, Bruylant, 2006, p. 333, and cf. pp. 330–2; A. Spielmann, 'Les détenus et leurs droits (de l'homme)', in *Les droits de l'homme au seuil du troisième millénaire – Mélanges en hommage à P. Lambert*, Bruxelles, Bruylant, 2000, p. 787, and cf. pp. 777–88.

[78] Cf. N.S. Rodley, *The Treatment of Prisoners under International Law*, 2nd. ed., Oxford, Univ. Press, 2000 [reprint], pp. 75–106.

[79] Cf., *inter alia*, C. Harvey and S. Livingstone, 'Protecting the Marginalised: The Role of the European Convention on Human Rights', 51 *Northern Ireland Legal Quarterly* (2000) 448–56.

[80] A. Cassese, *Inhuman States – Imprisonment, Detention and Torture in Europe Today*, Cambridge, Polity Press, 1996, pp. 48, 66–7 and 124–6.

[81] Cf., e.g., Various Authors, *La détention en isolement dans les prisons européennes* (eds. M. Zingoni-Fernández and N. Giovannini), Bruxelles, Bruylant, 2004, pp. 1–179.

[82] For a contemporary case-study, cf., e.g., H. Hillgenberg, '*Incommunicado* in Guantanamo', in *Internationale Gemeinschaft und Menschenrechte – Festschrift für G. Ress* (eds. J. Bröhmer *et alii*), Köln/Berlin/München, 2005, pp. 133–40; M. Cohn, 'Torture of Prisoners in U.S. Custody', 16 *I Diritti dell'Uomo – Cronache e Battaglie* (2005) pp. 59–62.

violence within prisons, among other situations of much gravity. The IACtHR has, in recent years, extended its Provisional Measures of Protection also to persons in large numbers and in great need of them, held under sub-human conditions of detention.

In 2002, in the case of the *Prison 'Urso Branco'* concerning Brazil,[83] the IACtHR ordered Provisional Measures of Protection of the life and personal integrity of all persons detained in the Prison 'Urso Branco', and further ordered the State to undertake investigation of the facts which led to the adoption of those measures and to provide further information thereon to the Court. Two years later, the IACtHR ordered new Measures of Protection in that same case.[84] The IACtHR continued to enlarge considerably the circles of protected persons held under detention, in further adopting new Provisional Measures of Protection to the benefit of entire human collectivities, such as the detainees in the case of the *Prisons of Mendoza*, concerning Argentina,[85] as well as the adolescents deprived of their freedom and confined in centres of 'rehabilitation or reeducation' (as in the case of the *'Unit of Tatuapé of FEBEM'*, concerning Brazil).[86]

In the exercise of its function of resolving contentious cases, the IACtHR acknowledged the suffering of the young victims detained in sub-human conditions, in its aforementioned Judgment (of 02 September 2004) in the case of the *'Institute of Rehabilitation of Minors' versus Paraguay* (*supra*). The young people detained were victims of violations of the rights to life and to humane treatment (as well as of the rights of the child), established by the Court; they endured even fires within the detention centre; yet, their case was brought to an international tribunal (the IACtHR), disclosing the assertion of human rights of defenceless persons in situations of overwhelming adversity.

The human rights violations also established by the IACtHR in the case of the *Prison Castro Castro*, concerning Peru (Judgment of 25 November 2006) – which amounted to a massacre – with no less than 42 detainees being killed, while 175 others suffered injuries, and 322 (mainly female detainees) were subjected to cruel, inhuman, and degrading treatment. Such violations resulted from an armed operation conducted by the respondent State against the defenceless detainees (on 06 and 09 May 1992 and the following days). Their case was likewise brought before an international tribunal (the IACtHR). Another episode of the kind was the case of *Montero Aranguren and Others (Detention Centre of Catia)*, concerning Venezuela (Judgment of 05 July 2006), which amounted likewise to a massacre of persons under detention.

Despite the extreme vulnerability of persons under sub-human conditions of detention, their cases have reached international human rights tribunals such as the ECtHR and the IACtHR. Their deprivation of freedom for wrongs committed does not deprive them of other human rights. They have also had access to

---

[83] IACtHR, Resolutions of 18 June and 29 August 2002.
[84] IACtHR, Resolutions of 22 April 2004 and of 07 July 2004.
[85] IACtHR, Resolutions of 22 November 2004 and of 18 June 2005.
[86] IACtHR, Resolutions of 17 and 29 November 2005.

international justice for the abuses they suffered in the hands of public authorities. In such circumstances, the effectiveness of their right of individual petition to the ECtHR and the IACtHR bears special witness to the *prééminence du Droit*, of the rule of law in a democratic society, in the sense of the ECHR and the ACHR.

VI. Concluding Observations: The Prevalence of Human Rights of Persons in Situations of Vulnerability

In recent years, individuals surrounded by circumstances of much vulnerability, on the verge of losing any hope in human justice, have nevertheless reached international instances of protection. This bears witness to the advances of international human rights law in recent years; yet this particular aspect has not been significantly dwelt upon, or singled out, by expert writing to date. The fact remains that access to international justice has often been achieved in situations of extreme vulnerability, if not defencelessness, of the human person. Examples of this development can be found in virtually all petitioning systems, either in the practice of the so-called treaty bodies, or supervisory organs, operating under human rights treaties,[87] or in the practice of specialized agencies of the United Nations system at global level, or else in the case-law of international human rights tribunals at regional level. In so far as U.N. specialized agencies are concerned, the long-standing experience of the International Labour Organization (ILO), for example, should not pass unnoticed here.

Already for some decades, the ILO has 'tackled conditions of near-servitude in industry and agriculture, and generally worked to raise standards of employment and to strengthen trade union freedom'.[88] In fact, protection of vulnerable individuals or groups of individuals has become 'an essential part' of the regular work of the ILO, often when 'the effects of discrimination or of exploitation are expressed through the means of access to or denial of economic activity'.[89] Shortly after the 50th anniversary of the ILO, C.W. Jenks remarked that the ILO had consistently

---

[87] Cf., e.g., M. Nowak, *U.N. Covenant on Civil and Political Rights – CCPR Commentary*, Kehl/Strasbourg, N.P. Engel, 1993, pp. 126–57 and 480–505; T. Zwart, *The Admissibility of Human Rights Petitions*, Dordrecht, Nijhoff, 1994, pp. 7–22 and 41–4 (also on the U.N. Human Rights Committee); [Various Authors,] *Convención CEDAW y Protocolo Facultativo*, 2nd ed., San José de Costa Rica, IIHR, 2004, pp. 37–93 and 115–30; J. Dhommeaux, 'Le rôle du Comité des Droits de l'Enfant dans le contrôle, l'interprétation et l'évolution de la Convention relative aux Droits de l'Enfant', in *Les droits de l'homme à l'aube du XXIe. siècle – K. Vasak Amicorum Liber*, Bruxelles, Bruylant, 1999, pp. 553–80; P. Thornberry, 'Confronting Racial Discrimination: A CERD Perspective', 5 *Human Rights Law Review* (2005) pp. 239–69; C. Ingelse, 'The Committee against Torture: One Step Forward, One Step Back', 18 *Netherlands Quarterly of Human Rights* (2000) pp. 307–27.

[88] As recalled by J.E.S. Fawcett almost four decades ago. Cf. J.E.S. Fawcett, *The Law of Nations*, 2nd. ed., Penguin Books, London, Middlesex/England, 1971, p. 161.

[89] L. Swepston, 'Protection of Vulnerable Groups by the International Labour Organisation', in *The Living Law of Nations – Essays in Memory of A. Grahl-Madsen* (eds. G. Alfredsson and P. Macalister-Smith), Kehl/Strasbourg, N.P. Engel, 1996, p. 409, and cf. pp. 410–19.

established a tradition of 'the strongest condemnation of discrimination'.[90] The ILO Constitution provides for two procedures for petitions or complaints, which have been often resorted to, namely, *representations* (under Article 24) and *complaints* (under Article 26).[91]

Particularly vulnerable individuals and groups of individuals who have sought, and achieved, access to justice under such ILO procedures, include migrant workers, members of workers' organizations in adverse conditions of labour, children and young workers, women at work, and persons subject to discrimination on distinct grounds.[92] A recent study on the protection of vulnerable persons and groups by the ILO has indicated that this latter has been sensitive to 'the terrible conditions under which migrant workers must often survive, and their need for protection'.[93] The ILO has, furthermore, set up as one of its priorities the equality of women at work, and has from the beginning endeavoured to prevent child labour, 'the most tragic exploitation of all'.[94]

A collection of essays published on the occasion of the ILO's 75th anniversary, in 1994, besides denouncing the recurrent tragedy of child labour in 'abominably inhuman' conditions, disclosing that 'the market system and the profit motive are used to justify this most hideous child abuse',[95] went on to ponder that 'labour is not a commodity' and that the 'dehumanizing process' of breaches of social justice offend the 'universal conscience'.[96] In its turn, UNESCO instituted its communications or complaints procedure (in 1978), so as to examine, within its sphere of competence, not only individualized cases, but also questions of 'massive, systematic or flagrant violations of human rights', resulting 'either from a policy contrary to human rights applied *de jure* or *de facto* by a State or from an accumulation of individual cases forming a consistent pattern'.[97]

---

[90] C. Wilfred Jenks, *Social Justice in the Law of Nations – The ILO Impact After Fifty Years*, Oxford, University Press, 1970, p. 63.

[91] Cf., e.g., N. Valticos, 'The International Labour Organisation (ILO)', in *The International Dimensions of Human Rights* (eds. K. Vasak and Ph. Alston), vol. I, Paris/Westport, UNESCO/ Greenwood Press, 1982, pp. 377–82. Access to justice has also been object of attention in the domain of regional community law; cf., as to the European Union, e.g., M. Ortega, *El Acceso de los Particulares a la Justicia Comunitaria*, Barcelona, Ed. Ariel, 1999, pp. 11–230.

[92] E.g., race, colour, ethnic, social or national origin, or religion, as well as members of indigenous and tribal peoples.

[93] L. Swepston, 'Protection of Vulnerable Groups . . .', *op. cit. supra* n. (89), p. 416.

[94] Ibid., p. 415.

[95] A. Adedeji, 'Can There Be a Human-Centred Holistic Global Work and Employment Policy?', in *Visions of the Future of Social Justice – Essays on the Occasion of the ILO's 75th Anniversary*, Geneva, International Labour Office, 1994, p. 13.

[96] M.E. Ackerman, 'Return to the Source, Reaffirm the Principles', in *Visions of the Future of Social Justice . . .*, *op. cit. supra* n. (95), pp. 3 and 6; B.F. Ople, 'Notes on the 75th Anniversary of the ILO', in ibid., p. 230.

[97] J. Symonides, 'UNESCO's Contribution to the Progressive Development of Human Rights', 5 *Max Planck Yearboook of United Nations Law* (2001) p. 331, and cf. pp. 317 and 340; and cf. also, on the UNESCO complaints procedure, H. Saba, 'UNESCO and Human Rights', in *The International Dimensions of Human Rights* (eds. K. Vasak and Ph. Alston), vol. II, UNESCO/Greenwood Press, Paris/Westport Conn., 1982, pp. 418–22; B. Say, 'Procédure d'examen des communications relatives aux violations alléguées des droits de l'homme dans les domaines de compétence de l'UNESCO: problème du double emploi et réflexion sur la réforme envisagée', in *Les droits de l'homme à l'aube du*

Underlying most of the human rights problems at issue are the recurrent root causes of chronic poverty and exploitation, and the pressing need to attain poverty alleviation and eradication, and to secure access to social justice. Despite this overwhelming obstacle to the enjoyment of basic human rights, it appears nonetheless significant that, notwithstanding situations of acute or extreme vulnerability, and great adversity, individuals have often succeeded in bringing their cases to international instances, and have duly exercised their right to access to international justice, as subjects of international law endowed with international procedural capacity.

If, on the one hand, the drama of victims in distress discloses recurring violations of human rights of persons who find themselves in situations of utmost adversity, on the other hand it should not pass unnoticed that such victims have, not seldom, in our times, reached international jurisdiction, whether they are undocumented migrants, abandoned or 'street children', those affected by social marginalization or exclusion and chronic poverty, those detained in sub-human conditions of detention, or those victimized in situations of armed conflict. That some of their cases have been heard and resolved by international tribunals such as the IACtHR and the ECtHR suggests that there have been advances in international justice in our times.

In its Judgment of 10 May 2001 on the *Cyprus versus Turkey* case[98] – to recall but one example – the ECtHR asserted the positive obligation of the respondent State to conduct effective investigation of the 'arrests and killings on a large scale' resulting from the use of force by agents of the State as well as non-State agents (pars. 131 and 133); the Court determined that there had been 'a continuing violation' of Article 2 of the Convention 'on account of the failure of the authorities of the respondent State to conduct an effective investigation aimed at clarifying the whereabouts and fate of Greek-Cypriot missing persons who disappeared in life-threatening circumstances' (par. 136). The Court aptly warned that:

the acquiescence or connivance of the authorities of a Contracting State in the acts of private individuals which violate the Convention rights of other individuals within its jurisdiction may engage that State's responsibility under the Convention. Any different conclusion would be at variance with the obligation contained in Article 1 of the Convention (par. 81).

The ECtHR also established a violation of Article 3 of the Convention, given the 'discrimination amounting to degrading treatment' suffered by the victims (pars. 309–311). In this case, the Court proceeded to determine the condition of 'victims' on the basis of their actual suffering. It is notable, in this respect, that the Court did not consider, in the circumstances of the case, that the fact that certain relatives of the

---

XXIe. siècle – K. Vasak Amicorum Liber, Bruxelles, Bruylant, 1999, pp. 819–61; M. Paszkowski, 'Evocation of an "Unknown" Procedure Concerning Human Rights Protection by UNESCO', in ibid., pp. 707–21.

[98] Originated in application n. 25.781/94, the first (opposing Cyprus to Turkey) to have been referred to the Court, preceded by three inter-State (*Cyprus versus Turkey*) applications decided by the European Commission, in 1976 (the first two) and in 1983 (the third one).

(direct) victims might not have actually witnessed the detention of family members, or complained about such detention to the authorities of the respondent State, deprived them of 'victim' status under Article 3 of the Convention. Not at all. The Court recalled, in this connection, that:

> the military operation resulted in a considerable loss of life, large-scale arrests and detentions and enforced separation of families. The overall context must still be vivid in the minds of the relatives of persons whose fate has never been accounted for by the authorities. They endure the agony of not knowing whether family members were killed in the conflict or are still in detention or, if detained, have since died. The fact that a very substantial number of Greek-Cypriots had to seek refuge in the south coupled with the continuing division of Cyprus must be considered to constitute very serious obstacles to their quest for information. The provision of such information is the responsibility of the authorities of the respondent State. This responsibility has not been discharged. For the Court, the silence of the authorities of the respondent State in the face of the real concerns of the relatives of the missing persons attains a level of severity which can only be categorised as inhuman treatment within the meaning of Article 3. (. . .) The Court concludes that, during the period under consideration, there has been a continuing violation of Article 3 of the Convention in respect of the relatives of the Greek-Cypriot missing persons (pars. 157–8).

The determination of the condition of 'victim', in such instances by the ECtHR, and even in cases of massacres by the IACtHR,[99] has been undertaken on the basis of the recognition of human suffering and the fulfilment of the pressing need of reparation to the victims. This has evidenced that the mechanisms of international protection of human rights are, as already pointed out, essentially and ineluctably *victim-oriented*.[100] In this understanding, protection and redress have been extended to victims in situations of great adversity or defencelessness.

Even in situations of armed conflict, as already seen, individuals, despite their utmost vulnerability, have found relief and protection in the approximations and convergences of international human rights law, International Humanitarian Law, and International Refugee Law. The centrality of the suffering of the victims comes clearly to the fore also in the determination of the reparations due to them. These latter, as I noted in another study, are to be approached from the triad formed by *victimization, human suffering,* and *rehabilitation of the victims*, which is to be:

> considered as from the integrality of the personality of the victims. These latter cease to appear, as in the classic doctrine, as 'neutral object' of the juridical relation caused by the delictual fact, and emerge as subjects (*titulaires*) of the violated rights, as subjects of law victimized by a human conflict.[101]

Any assessment of the long saga of human beings for attaining access to international justice – sometimes in the most adverse circumstances – is to guard itself against approaches to the matter which may be misleading. One of them consists in

---

[99] Cf. chapter X, *infra*.

[100] A.A. Cançado Trindade, *The Application of the Rule of Exhaustion of Local Remedies in International Law*, Cambridge, Cambridge University Press, 1983, pp. 1–443.

[101] A.A. Cançado Trindade, *Tratado de Direito Internacional dos Direitos Humanos*, vol. III, Porto Alegre/Brazil, S.A. Fabris Ed., 2003, p. 442.

bringing into the picture the so-called 'realist' thinking. This latter has always paid lip service to power, and, worse still, power as it stands at a given moment in history.[102] It has proven incapable of understanding or explaining the advances in the international protection of human rights.

As a pertinent example in this respect, there is an inescapable incongruity in conceding that the human rights movement emerged as an understandable reaction against the trust in the State's 'unlimited authority' (as propounded by J. Bodin and Thomas Hobbes, among others) and, at the same time, in insisting on the 'centrality' of the State as the 'key actor' in 'human rights discourse'.[103] In the present domain of protection, *the centrality is of the victims, not of the State*, and all the advances achieved in the long journey of individuals towards access to international justice can only be explained by the fact that international human rights law is, and has always been, as from its beginnings, essentially victim-oriented. This is what so-called 'realists' appear unable to understand, or to accept.

---

[102] For a strong criticism of the myopia of so-called 'realist' thinking, cf., e.g., A.A. Cançado Trindade, 'International Law for Humankind: Towards a New *Jus Gentium* – General Course on Public International Law' – Part I, 316 *Recueil des Cours de l'Académie de Droit International de la Haye* (2005) pp. 79–82.

[103] Cf. C. Tomuschat, *Human Rights – Between Idealism and Realism*, Oxford, University Press, 2003, pp. 57 and 320.

X

Access to Justice of Victims of Massacres and Crimes of State

I. Massacres and Crimes of State: Introductory Observations   179

II. Victims of Massacres   182

III. The Determination of the Aggravated Responsibility of the State   183

IV. The Determination of the Condition of Victim   186

     1. Identified and Identifiable Victims: Identification of Victims at Distinct Stages of the Procedure   186

     2. Classification or Categorization of Victims   187

     3. Centrality and Expansion of the Notion of Direct Victim   188

V. The Victims' Right to Redress   189

VI. Concluding Observations   190

I. Massacres and Crimes of State: Introductory Observations

The cases of massacres that have lately reached the international human rights tribunals (IACtHR and ECtHR) have generated great difficulties not only for the Law (e.g., the determination of the victims for the effects of reparations) but also for the social sciences in general. To start with, the phenomenon of massacres challenges any attempt of comprehension: it does not seem to have any meaning or purpose, it is profoundly disturbing, it appears as product of human madness and cruelty. Furthermore, it does not lend itself to attempts at 'general theory': each massacre – extermination of non-combatants, among women and men, children and elderly people, in general entirely defenceless – is perpetrated in a given distinct historical, political, and cultural context.[1]

On the other hand, the intellectual and material authors of massacres try to characterize the victims, even though innocent and defenceless, as 'enemies' who

---

[1] J. Sémelin, 'Analysing Massacres and Genocide: Contribution of the Social Sciences', in: [Various Authors,] *Violence and Its Causes: A Stocktaking*, Paris, UNESCO, 2005, pp. 63–5, and cf. p. 62 and 67. Although such massacres begin to attract attention in human rights legal writing, the matter remains insufficiently explored to date, and the legal problems faced by international human rights tribunals in settling such cases remain to a large extent unknown to the public at large so far.

ought to be eliminated or exterminated – they seek, in sum, to dehumanize them (even by undue uses of the language and misleading uses of neologisms and euphemisms) before killing them.[2] They seek thereby to 'protect themselves' from their own feeling of guilt for their acts of extreme cruelty. The element of *intentionality* seems to be always present, in my view as an *aggravating* circumstance, also for the effects of reparations. At last, in any endeavour to achieve restorative justice, one ought necessarily to take into account the profound traumatic effects of massacres, not only and obviously on the victims and their relatives, but also on the social *milieu* itself, on the population itself affected by the massacres as a whole.

Over the last half decade, the IACtHR has in fact had the occasion to pronounce itself on a new cycle of cases, configuring, in my understanding, true *crimes of State*, planned at the highest levels of public power and executed amidst genuine State policies of systematic extermination of human beings. Reference can be made, in this connection, to the Judgments of the Court in the cases of the *Massacres of Barrios Altos* (of 14 March 2001), of *Caracazo* concerning Venezuela (reparations, of 29 August 2002), of *Plan de Sánchez* (of 29 April 2004), of the *19 Tradesmen* (of 05 July 2004), of *Mapiripán* (of 17 September 2005), of the *Moiwana Community* (of 15 June 2005), of *Pueblo Bello* (of 31 January 2006), of *Ituango* (of 01 July 2006), of *Montero Aranguren and Others* (of 05 July 2006), and of the *Prison of Castro Castro* (of 25 November 2006), as well as in the cases of assassinations planned at the highest level of the State power and executed by order of this latter (such as that of *Myrna Mack Chang*, Judgment of 25 November 2003).

In the respective contentious proceedings before the IACtHR, almost all those cases of massacres counted, significantly, on the recognition of international responsibility on the part of the respondent States themselves for the occurrence of the crimes, to the effect of determining the wrongful acts of the past so as to avoid their repetition. This phenomenon, of major historical relevance, does not find parallels in other contemporary international tribunals. As I pointed out in some of my Separate Opinions in the aforementioned cases, it should certainly suffice to lead to a reconsideration, by the U.N. International Law Commission [ILC], of the evasive and unconvincing position that it assumed in 2001, rendered nowadays unsustainable, in shelving the notion of *crimes of State* so as to obtain the approval of its Articles on the International Responsibility of the State. Whether the ILC

---

[2] For dramatic personal accounts, cf. Primo Levi, *The Drowned and the Saved*, N.Y., Vintage, 1989 [reprint], pp. 11–203; J. Améry, *At the Mind's Limits*, Bloomington, Indiana Univ. Press, 1980, pp. 1–101. And cf. also B.A. Valentino, *Final Solutions: Mass Killing and Genocide in the Twentieth Century*, Ithaca/London, Cornell Univ. Press, 2004, pp. 17, 49, 55, 57, 71 and 235; Y. Ternon, *Guerres et génocides au XXe. siècle*, Paris, O. Jacob, 2007, pp. 14–15, 81–3, 138, 191, 279 and 376; G. Bensoussan, *Europe – Une passion génocidaire*, Paris, Éd. Mille et Une Nuits, 2006, pp. 53, 134, 220 and 228–9; J.A. Berry and C.P. Berry (eds.), *Genocide in Rwanda – A Collective Memory*, Washington D.C., Harvard University Press, 1999, pp. 3–4, 28–9 and 87; B. Bruneteau, *Le siècle des génocides*, Paris, A. Colin, 2004, pp. 41, 43, 222 and 229; E. Staub, *The Roots of Evil – The Origins of Genocide and Other Group Violence*, Cambridge, University Press, 2005 [16th printing], pp. 29, 103, 121, 142 and 227; R.J. Bernstein, *El Mal Radical – Una Indagación Filosófica*, Buenos Aires, Lilmod, 2005, pp. 110–11, 145 and 290–1.

recognizes it or not, crimes of State do indeed exist, as have some of the respondent States themselves expressly confessed before the IACtHR.

In addition to these cases, the IACtHR has recently delivered two new Judgments of historical transcendence, in which it reiterates its assertion of the *aggravated* international responsibility of the State, namely, the Judgments pertaining to the regime of Pinochet in Chile (of 27 September 2006, on the case *Almonacid Arellano*) and to the regime of Stroessner in Paraguay (of 22 September 2006, on the case *Goiburú and Others*). The respective contentious proceedings once again counted on the reassuring procedural cooperation of the respondent States, willing to clarify past facts for the realization of justice; in the second case (*Goiburú and Others*), the respondent State also proceeded to a recognition of its international responsibility, in a sign of maturity, as further exemplified by what occurred in earlier aforementioned cases. In both Judgments, in my lengthy Separate Opinions, I developed my personal reflections on the *crimes of State*, bearing in mind above all the horrors of the sinister *Operation Condor*.[3]

The lessons which one can extract from these two historic cases[4] are clear. At conceptual level, there continue to coexist the *objective* international responsibility of the State, and its international responsibility *aggravated* by *intentionality* (*mens rea*). At operational level, it becomes evident that one cannot struggle against terror with the same means of terror, but, instead of that, necessarily within the Law (for which purpose several international Conventions exist). One cannot consent in a contemporary reedition of the *Operation Condor*, materialized, in our days, in Guantánamo, Abu Ghraib, and in the network of clandestine prisons and concentration camps today in operation in distinct continents (recently denounced and condemned by the European Union and by the Parliamentary Assembly of the Council of Europe).[5]

---

[3] Cf. A.A. Cançado Trindade, *Évolution du Droit international au droit des gens – L'accès des particuliers à la justice internationale: le regard d'un juge*, Paris, Pédone, 2008, pp. 121–84.

[4] Which victimized more than 30 thousand Latin Americans, in their great majority, young innocent people who were kidnapped, tortured and 'disappeared', many having been thrown alive from airplanes into the sea, for 'there no longer being place' for their mortal remains in clandestine cemeteries.

[5] Cf. D. Marty (*rapporteur*), 'Alleged Secret Detentions in Council of Europe Member States', Strasbourg, Council of Europe Parliamentary Assembly/Committee on Legal Affairs and Human Rights, doc. AS/Jur(2006)03.rev., del 22 January 2006, pp. 1–25; D. Marty (*rapporteur*), 'Alleged Secret Detentions and Unlawful Inter-State Transfers Involving Council of Europe Member States', Strasbourg, Council of Europe Parliamentary Assembly/Committee on Legal Affairs and Human Rights, doc. AS/Jur(2006)16-II, del 07 June 2006, pp. 1–71 (restricted circulation). On its turn, on 06 July 2006, the European Parliament adopted a resolution on 'the alleged use of European countries by the CIA for the transportation and illegal detention of prisoners'; European Parliament, doc. A6-0213/2006, pp. 1–6. In its long resolution the European Parliament began by warning that 'the fight against terrorism cannot be won by sacrificing the very principles that terrorism seeks to destroy, notably that the protection of fundamental rights must never be compromised; terrorism must be fought by legal means and it must be defeated while respecting international and national law' (preamble, *considerandum* C). It then asserted that the practices of 'secret detention' and kidnapping of suspected persons in the territory of the member States engaged the international responsibility of the State (pars. 2 and 8). It expressed its deep concern with the use of European air space and airports for transferring suspected persons 'illegally to the custody of the CIA or the US military or to other countries' (par. 13). The aforementioned resolution condemned 'the practice of extraordinary renditions, which is aimed at ensuring that suspects are not brought before a court but are transferred

Violations of the absolute prohibition of torture, and undue restrictions to remedies which protect fundamental rights, cannot be admitted. The fact that victims (and their relatives) of the *Operation Condor*, three decades after the perpetration of its horrors, have seized an international tribunal of human rights (such as the IACtHR) of their case (cases *Goiburú* and *Almonacid*), which reaffirmed and expanded the international *jus cogens*, is due to the awakening of the *universal juridical conscience* (as the ultimate material source of all Law),[6] so that crimes of State will no longer be repeated in the future.

II. Victims of Massacres

Circumstances of massacres of course vary from case to case, and it is virtually impossible to determine with precision the point at which a case of grave violations of human rights is to be regarded as a massacre. However, the element of intentionality, of premeditation, is always present, among other aggravating circumstances. There have been two recent cases, resolved by the IACtHR, of massacres conducted by security forces of the respondent States, even of persons under detention, i.e., under the custody of the State itself, namely, the cases of the *Prison Castro Castro*, concerning Peru (Judgment of 25 November 2006), and of *Montero Aranguren and Others (Detention Centre of Catia)*, concerning Venezuela (Judgment of 05 July 2006) (cf. *supra*).

Circumstances vary, but the aggravating element of intentionality, of planning, is always there. In some cases there has been a plurality of victims (all identified), in others there has been a considerable number of them, to the extent of disclosing a situation wherein the exact total of victims is not even known. Such cases of massacres

to third countries to be interrogated, where they could be tortured, and detained in facilities controlled by the USA or local authorities'; the same resolution stressed that 'the prohibition of torture or cruel, inhuman and degrading treatment as defined in Article 1 of the U.N. Convention against Torture, is absolute and allows no exceptions whether in times of war or threat of war, domestic political instability or any other emergency; recalls that cases of *incommunicado* detention, abduction or extraordinary rendition constitute violations of fundamental rights in International Law, in particular Articles 3 and 5 of the European Convention on Human Rights, especially since these acts are synonymous with torture or inhuman and degrading treatment' (par. 29). Besides that resolution of the European Parliament, the Secretary General of the Council of Europe presented recommendations – in the light of Article 52 of the European Convention of Human Rights – in its recent *Reports* to the Governments of European States, on news suggesting that 'individuals, notably persons suspected of involvement in acts of terrorism, may have been arrested and detained, or transported while deprived of their liberty, by or at the instigation of foreign agencies, with the active or passive co-operation of States Parties to the Convention or by States Parties themselves at their own initiative, without such deprivation of liberty having been acknowledged'; cf. Council of Europe, doc. SG/Inf(2006)5, of 28 February 2006, pp. 1–15; Council of Europe, doc. SG/Inf (2006)13, of 14 June 2006, pp. 1–8. And cf. the recent publications of the Council of Europe itself: C.E., *CIA Above the Law? Secret Detentions and Unlawful Inter-State Transfers of Detainees in Europe*, Strasbourg, C.E. Publ., 2008, pp. 5–301; C.E., *Guantánamo: Violation of Human Rights under International Law?*, Strasbourg, C.E. Publ., 2007, pp. 5–110.

[6] A.A. Cançado Trindade, 'International Law for Humankind: Towards a New *Jus Gentium* – General Course on Public International Law – Part I', 316 *Recueil des Cours de l'Académie de Droit International de la Haye* (2005), ch. VI, pp. 177–202.

reveal a most regrettable distortion of the ends of the State: this latter is expected to extend protection to all persons under its jurisdiction (and indeed is under the duty to do so), but instead it utilizes the monopoly of force that it exercises to victimize groups of persons under its jurisdiction, who often happen to be the most vulnerable ones, in situations of defencelessness.

The State has here incurred into grave violations of human rights, and has, in some instances, in my understanding, committed true *crimes of State*.[7] Two particular legal issues may be singled out in those cases of massacres: first, the determination of the aggravated responsibility of the State (aggravating circumstances of the wrongs perpetrated); and secondly, the determination of the condition of victim in such cases. This latter has disclosed the complexities of those cases, as well as the continuing presence and evolution of the notion of victim in the international *contentieux* of human rights.

III. The Determination of the Aggravated Responsibility of the State

The new cycle of cases of massacres lodged with the IACtHR in the last half decade, disclosing a pattern of grave and systematic violations of human rights – starting with the fundamental right to life – has led the Court to establish the *aggravating circumstances* of such violations.[8] In the same line of reasoning, under the ECHR, the ECtHR has likewise established *aggravating circumstances* in cases disclosing an 'administrative practice' to the detriment of victims of torture and inhuman or degrading treatment (under Article 3 of the ECHR).[9]

The recent cases before the IACtHR[10] raise the issue of the *aggravated* international responsibility of the respondent States. This cycle of cases featured aggravating circumstances, as the grave violations of human rights were planned and perpetrated in pursuance of State policies of a *systematic* practice of extermination

---

[7] Cf., on this point, A.A. Cançado Trindade, 'Complementarity between State Responsibility and Individual Responsibility for Grave Violations of Human Rights: The Crime of State Revisited', in *International Responsibility Today – Essays in Memory of O. Schachter* (ed. M. Ragazzi), Leiden, M. Nijhoff, 2005, pp. 253–69.

[8] Cf., e.g., the cases of the *Massacres of Barrios Altos* (of 14 March 2001), of *Plan de Sánchez* (of 29 April 2004), of the *19 Tradesmen* (of 05 July 2004), of *Mapiripán* (of 17 September 2005), of the *Moiwana Community* (of 15 June 2005), of *Ituango* (of 01 July 2006), of *Montero Aranguren and Others* (of 05 July 2006), and of the *Prison of Castro Castro* (of 25 November 2006), among others.

[9] H. Fourteau, *L'application de l'article 3 de la Convention Européenne des Droits de l'Homme dans le droit interne des États membres*, Paris, LGDJ, 1996, pp. 73–4 and 76–7.

[10] Such as, *inter alia*, the cases of the *Massacre of Plan de Sánchez versus Guatemala* (Judgments on Merits and Reparations, of 29 April 2004 and 19 November 2004, respectively), of the massacre of the *Moiwana Community versus Suriname* (Judgment of 15 June 2005), of the *Massacre of Mapiripán*, concerning Colombia (Judgment of 15 September 2005), of the *19 Tradesmen* against Colombia (Judgment of 05 July 2004), of the *Massacres of Ituango versus Colombia* (Judgment of 01 July 2006), of the *Massacres of Barrios Altos* and of *La Cantuta*, concerning Peru (Judgments of 14 March 2001 and of 29 November 2006, respectively), of the massacre of the *Prison Castro Castro versus Peru* (Judgment of 25 November 2006), among others.

of human beings.[11] In the respective contentious proceedings before the IACtHR, almost all those cases of massacres have counted, significantly, on the recognition of international responsibility on the part of the respondent States for the occurrence of the grave violations of human rights, to the effect of determining the wrongful acts of the past so as to avoid their repetition. Such successive recognition of international responsibility under the ACHR by the respondent States before the IACtHR[12] is a phenomenon of historic importance, which finds no parallel in other contemporary international tribunals.

Its Judgment on the merits in the case of the *Massacre of Plan de Sánchez* (of 29 April 2004), concerning Guatemala, for example, the Court established violations of the rights to humane treatment, to a fair trial and to judicial protection, to privacy, to freedom of conscience and religion, to freedom of thought and expression, to freedom of association, to property, and to equal protection,[13] and further held that the respondent State had failed to comply with the general duty, set forth in Article 1(1) of the ACHR, to respect, and ensure respect for, the rights protected thereunder. In the course of the proceedings in that case, the respondent State recognized its international responsibility under the American Convention for the grave human rights violations resulting from the massacre of Plan de Sánchez.

As demonstrated in this case, the crimes committed in the course of the execution, by military operations, of a State policy of '*tierra arrasada*', including the massacre itself of Plan de Sánchez (perpetrated on 18 July 1982), were intended to destroy wholly or in part the members of indigenous Maya communities. In its aforementioned Judgment of 29 April 2004, the IACtHR determined that those violations 'gravely affected the members of the *maya-achí* people in their identity and values', and, in so far as they occurred within a 'pattern of massacres', they had 'an aggravated impact' in the establishment of the international responsibility of the State.[14]

Earlier on, the Guatemalan Commission for the Historical Clarification, in its report *Guatemala – Memoria del Silencio*, had established the occurrence of 626 massacres committed by the forces of the State during the armed conflict, mainly

---

[11] Reference could also be added to cases of murders planned at the highest level of State power and perpetrated by order of this latter (such as the case of *Myrna Mack Chang versus Guatemala*, Judgment of 25 November 2003). Cf. A.A. Cançado Trindade, 'The Inter-American System of Protection of Human Rights (1948–2006): Evolution, Present State and Perspectives', in *Dossier Documentaire/ Documentary File – XXXVI Session d'Enseignement* (2006), vol. II, Strasbourg, Institut International des Droits de l'Homme, 2006, pp. 80–1.

[12] There have been over 20 cases of such acceptance by respondent States of their international responsibility under the American Convention, of which 15 cases have been of full recognition of responsibility, and the remaining ones of partial acceptance of responsibility. For a study of this aspect of the case-law of the Inter-American Court to date, cf. A.A. Cançado Trindade, 'Responsabilidad, Perdón y Justicia como Manifestaciones de la Conciencia Jurídica Universal', 8 *Revista de Estudios Socio-Jurídicos* – Universidad del Rosario/Bogotá (2006) n. 1, pp. 23–4, and cf. pp. 15–36. And cf. further the Separate Opinion of Judge Cançado Trindade (pars. 1–31) in the case *Gutiérrez Soler versus Colombia*, Court's Judgment of 12 September 2005.

[13] Articles 5, 8(1) and 25, 11, 12, 13, 16, 21, and 24, respectively, of the American Convention on Human Rights.

[14] Par. 51 of the Judgment. The Court ordered reparations in its subsequent Judgment on the case, of 19 November 2004.

the Army, supported by paramilitary structures; 95% of them had been perpetrated between 1978 and 1984 (with violence intensified in 1981–1983), and in this period 90% had been executed in areas inhabited predominantly by the Maya people. The acts of extreme violence, in the assessment of that Commission, disclosed the characteristics of 'acts of genocide'.[15] In my Separate Opinion in the IACtHR's Judgment in the case of the *Massacre of Plan de Sánchez* (pars. 1–43), I dwelt upon the evolution of the material content of international *jus cogens*, and argued that, in circumstances such as those of the present case, the occurrence of a true *crime of State* cannot be denied, nor can the co-existence of the (aggravated) international responsibility of the State and of the international penal responsibility of individuals (perpetrators of the atrocities).[16]

In such cases of massacres, conducted by State agents as part of a State policy, brought to the attention of the IACtHR, in my Separate Opinions I have insisted on my view that the facts disclosed therein made it impossible to deny the existence of true *crimes of State*, entailing all their juridical consequences: in this context, I upheld the *complementarity* of the international responsibility of the State and the international penal responsibility of the individuals concerned – as, for example, in the case of the *Massacre of Mapiripán versus Colombia* (Judgment of 15 September 2005).[17]

In the case of *La Cantuta*, concerning Peru (Judgment of 29 November 2006), the victims (one professor and a group of students) were kidnapped from the premises of the University of La Cantuta, Lima, by security forces of the respondent State, after midnight, in the early hours of 18 July 1992, were 'disappeared', and some of them promptly and summarily executed; following that, the facts were not duly investigated. In the earlier case of *Barrios Altos* (Judgment of 14 March 2001), the victims had been members of trade unions.

In submitting the case of *Goiburú and Others versus Paraguay* (2006) to the Court, the IAComHR described it as a case occurred in a context of unlawful and prolonged detentions (in the mid-1970s) of the victims by agents of the State; the victims remained *incommunicado*, were tortured and murdered, and their mortal remains were hidden, all as a result of their opposition to the dictatorial regime of President A. Stroessner. The IACtHR established the grave violations of human rights that took place, in the context of the so-called 'Operation Condor', in which security agents of the States of the Southern Cone of South America 'cooperated' to exterminate political opponents of the repressive regimes of those days.

---

[15] Specifically against members of the peoples *maya-ixil, maya-achi, maya-k'iche', maya-chuj* and *maya-q'anjob'al*, in four regions of the country; Comisión para el Esclarecimiento Histórico, *Guatemala – Memoria del Silencio*, vol. III, Guatemala, CEH, 1999, pp. 316–18, 358, 375–6, 393, 416 and 417–23. In the view of the Guatemalan Truth Commission, the grave and massive human rights violations engaged both the individual responsibility of the 'intellectual or material authors' of the 'acts of genocide' as well as the 'responsibility of the State', as most of those acts were the product of a State 'policy preestablished by a superior command to its material authors'; ibid., p. 422.

[16] For a study, cf. A.A. Cançado Trindade, 'Complementarity between State Responsibility and Individual Responsibility for Grave Violations of Human Rights . . . ', *op. cit. supra* n. (7), pp. 253–69.

[17] And, earlier on, in the case of the *Massacre of Plan de Sánchez versus Guatemala* (Judgments on Merits and Reparations, of 29 April 2004 and 19 November 2004, respectively).

In the case of the *Massacre of Mapiripán*, concerning Colombia, occurred between 15 and 20 July 1997, one hundred members of the paramilitary forces (*Autodefensas Unidas de Colombia*), counting on 'the collaboration and acquiescence' of State agents, unlawfully detained and tortured and murdered at least 49 civilians in the town of Mapiripán, and then destroyed their bodies and sent their mortal remains into the river Guaviare. The case of the *Massacres of Ituango* (Judgment of 01 July 2006) fits into the same pattern of chronic violence in Colombia,[18] directly involving State agents (together with the paramilitary, against the guerrilla) in the murders of the victims. And in the case of the *Moiwana Community*, concerning Suriname, on 29 November 1986 the armed forces attacked the members of the Community, murdered many of them and the survivors were forcefully displaced from their traditional lands (of the Ndjuka Maroon Community, in the small town of Moiwana), unable to rebuild their communal *modus vivendi*.

In its Judgments (of, respectively, 15 September 2005 and 15 June 2005) in both cases of the *Massacre of Mapiripán* and of the massacre of the *Moiwana Community*, the IACtHR ordered a series of measures of reparations (comprising indemnities as well as distinct kinds of non-pecuniary reparations), including measures to foster the voluntary return of the displaced persons to their original lands and communities, in Colombia and Suriname, respectively. The Judgments of the Court, in that respect, disclosed the contemporary drama of the flows of forcefully displaced persons and their uprootedness, as well as the pressing need to secure their safe and voluntary return.

IV. The Determination of the Condition of Victim

Recently, the IACtHR has had to face, as already pointed out, the difficulty of the determination of the condition of victim in the aforementioned cases of massacres. The criteria it has adopted for such determination in those cases have disclosed the awareness that the American Convention, like all other human rights treaties, is essentially *victim-oriented*. The fact is that the recent cycle of cases of which the Court has been seized has led to a new jurisprudential development as to the determination of the condition of victim. Such development has been fostered by the endeavours of the Court to face and overcome difficulties in the identification of the alleged victims in such cases of massacres.

1. Identified and Identifiable Victims: Identification of Victims at Distinct Stages of the Procedure

Thus, to start with, the IACtHR has considered, in such cases, as alleged victims, besides the persons *identified* by the Inter-American Commission on Human Rights in the petition it lodged with the Court, *those who can be identified*

---

[18] In the case of the *Massacres of Ituango*, the facts occurred in June 1996 and as from October 1997: the raids in the town of Ituango (Department of Antioquia) were undertaken by paramilitary groups of '*Autodefensas Unidas de Colombia*', which, counting on the 'omission, acquiescence and collaboration' on the part of the security forces of the State, murdered defenceless persons, deprived them of their goods, and generated terror and forced displacement.

subsequently, given that the difficulties found in their individualization lead to presume that there are still victims pending of determination (Court's Judgments in the cases of the *Massacres of Plan de Sánchez, Mapiripán* and *Ituango*).[19] To overcome such difficulties, the Court has considered as alleged victims some whose names derived from documents[20] other than the petition presented by the Inter-American Commission.[21] The Court has, on more than one occasion, requested the Commission to correct such defects by providing lists of alleged victims *identified subsequently* to the presentation of the petition.[22]

The Court has, furthermore, ordered the respondent State *to individualize and to identify* the victims and their relatives for the purpose of reparations.[23] The IACtHR has taken these measures, in the light of the applicable law (the ACHR and its Regulations), bearing in mind the complexities of each case, making sure that the right of defence of the parties has been respected (at the corresponding procedural moment), and that the alleged victims subsequently identified keep relation with the facts described in the petition and the evidence produced before the Court (Court's Judgments in the cases of *Goiburú and Others*, and of the *Massacres of Ituango*).[24]

In this way the Court has taken the initiative of correcting, by means of its own analysis and assessment of the evidence produced by the parties, eventual gaps or defects in the identification of the alleged victims in the petition presented by the Commission, even when the parties themselves have admitted that some persons 'by mistake were not included in the lists of alleged victims'[25] originally presented before the Court. In the exercise of its duty of protection, the Court has deemed it fit to proceed in this way, in cases disclosing a plurality of alleged victims, above all in the recent cycle of cases of massacres.

2. Classification or Categorization of Victims

The case of the *Caracazo*, concerning Venezuela, pertained to the street riots that occurred in the city of Caracas, in February–March 1989, which, as a result of the indiscriminate and disproportional use of force by the State, caused the deaths of no less than 276 persons. However, the problem of identification of the victims arose from the very start of the submission of the case – a true massacre – to the IACtHR by the Inter-American Commission. In the complaint it lodged with the Court, it

---

[19] IACtHR, Judgments in the cases of the *Massacre of Plan de Sánchez* (2004), par. 48; of the *Massacre of Mapiripán* (2005), pars. 183 and 305; of the *Massacres of Ituango* (2006), par. 92.

[20] Incorporated into the *dossiers* of the cases.

[21] IACtHR, Judgment on the case of the *Massacres of Ituango* (2006), par. 94.

[22] IACtHR, Judgments on cases of *Aloeboetoe and Others* (Reparations, 1991), pars. 39, 64, 66 and 69; of *El Amparo* (Reparations, 1996), pars. 39 and 42; of *Caballero Delgado and Santana* (Reparations, 1997), pars. 13 and 38; of the '*Institute of Rehabilitation of Minors*' (2004), pars. 107 and 111.

[23] IACtHR, Judgment on the case of the *Massacre of Mapiripán* (2005), pars. 305–6; and cf. Judgment on the case of the '*Street Children*' (*Villagrán Morales and Others*, Reparations, 2001), par. 17.

[24] IACtHR, Judgments on the cases of *Goiburú and Others* ('Operation Condor', 2006), par. 33; and of the *Massacres of Ituango* (2006), par. 95.

[25] IACtHR, Judgment on the case of *Acevedo Jaramillo and Others* (2006), par. 227; and cf. case of *Aloeboetoe and Others* (Reparations, 1991), par. 66.

referred to the hiding of evidence (clandestine graves); the IAComHR was able to identify no more than 44 victims of the *Caracazo* disturbances. The Court, in its turn, in its Judgment of 29 August 2002 on reparations, in determining the beneficiaries of these latter, saw it fit to single out distinct 'categories of victims'.

The 44 victims in the *Caracazo* case were thus classified by the IACtHR's Judgment: 35 victims of extra-judicial executions, engaging the direct responsibility of the State; 2 forcefully disappeared persons by State agents; 3 victims of violations of the right to personal integrity; and 4 victims of breach of judicial protection and guarantees, in the context of the facts of the case (par. 67). The Court added that the relatives of the 44 victims were also beneficiaries of reparations for violation of Articles 8 and 25 of the ACHR (judicial protection and guarantees) (pars. 67–73); they were regarded also as 'direct victims' (of violation of Articles 8 and 25) in their own right (par. 74). The complexity of the *Caracazo* case illustrates the difficulties faced by the IACtHR in a case of a massacre with a great number of victims, and a prolonged lapse of time between the occurrence of the facts and the decision of the Court (par. 72).

In another case of massacre (that of *Montero Aranguren and Others (Detention Centre of Catia) versus Venezuela*, Judgment of 05 July 2006),[26] the IACtHR faced yet another difficulty, namely, that of the co-existence of two versions of the facts (par. 60.16–17). Be that as it may, the Court proceeded to the determination of the victims and of their relatives. To consider the victims' complaints of the kind, particularly in cases of massacres involving a great number of victims, adjudicated after a long lapse of time, the IACtHR has, in the solutions it has adopted, displayed its concern not to leave out of its Judgments (for the purpose of reparations) any of the victims of the brutalities perpetrated.

3. Centrality and Expansion of the Notion of Direct Victim

To this effect it has, in some instances, been considered preferable to leave the list of victims 'open' (for subsequent additions, due to the factual complexities of the cases at issue), rather than establishing a 'categorization of victims'. However, this has been done by providing that eventual additional victims bear of course a direct link with the facts described in the original complaints lodged with the Court. This balancing of distinct criteria adopted by the Court reveals, in its turn, its concomitant concerns to ensure juridical security and to impart justice in the circumstances of the cases.

The Court has thus – in a particularly forceful way in cases of massacres – given testimony of the ineluctable *centrality of the victims* in the present domain of protection of the human person. As from the paradigmatic case of the '*Street Children*' (Reparations, 2001), the Court has come *to enlarge the notion of victim*, in considering as the *injured party* also the immediate relatives of the direct victims (tortured and

---

[26] The case pertained to the killing of approximately 63 detainees by the guards of the Detention Centre of Catia, which took place between 27 and 29 November 1992, in addition to 28 disappeared persons and 52 injured persons (par. 60.18).

executed), in their own character of victims,[27] on their own. In the same line of reasoning (expansion of the notion of victim), in the recent cycle of cases of massacres, the Court has declared as a '*victim*' or '*injured party*', persons who keep relation with the facts described in the petition and in the evidence produced before it.[28]

The aforementioned cases of massacres resolved by the IACtHR have, in a sense, transcended the distinction between direct and indirect victims, in favour of the *expansion of the notion of direct victim*. Thus, the relatives of the *direct victims* as a consequence of the *violation of the right to life* (that is, the relatives of the murdered victims), become, in their turn, as a direct consequence of the violent death of their beloved ones, also *direct victims* as a result of the *violation of the right to personal integrity* (psychic and moral integrity, of the relatives), followed by the *violation of the right of access to justice and to the due process of law*.[29] This jurisprudential evolution is comprehensible and reassuring: ultimately, the reaction of Law to its breaches is proportional to the gravity of the facts, of the violations of the protected rights.

V. The Victims' Right to Redress

The increasing participation of victims themselves, or of their legal representatives, in international proceedings before international human rights tribunals (such as the IACtHR and the ECtHR), has, over the years, enhanced their right to redress (envisaged in a variety of forms) for grave violations of their rights. Such redress encompasses the rights to truth and justice: the former, materialised by means of a thorough investigation of the facts, conducive to the identification and sanction of those responsible for the violations, and the latter, consubstantiated by means of the reparations in their diverse forms (including the rehabilitation of the victims); it is nowadays generally acknowledged that the IACtHR has much contributed to this effect.[30]

At universal (U.N.) level, on 29 November 1985 the U.N. General Assembly adopted the Declaration of Basic Principles of Justice for Victims of Crime and Abuse of Power, which came to be known as the 'Victims' Declaration'. The *Handbook on Justice for Victims*, published by the U.N. (Centre for International Crime Prevention) in 1999, focused on the use and application of the 1985 Victims' Declaration. It started by disclosing the social impact of victimization, bearing not only on victims and their close relatives themselves, but also on their

---

[27] IACtHR, Judgment on the case of the '*Street Children*' (*Villagrán Morales and Others*, Reparations, Judgment of 26 May 2001), par. 68.

[28] IACtHR, Judgments on the cases of *Goiburú and Others* (22 July 2006), par. 29; of the *Massacres of Ituango* (01 July 2006), par. 91; of the *Massacre of Mapiripán* (15 September 2005), par. 183; of *Acevedo Jaramillo and Others* (07 February 2006), par. 227.

[29] IACtHR, Judgments on the cases of *Vargas Areco* (26 September 2006), pars. 95–6; of *Goiburú and Others* (22 July 2006), par. 96; and cf. Judgments on the cases of *Ximenes Lopes* (04 July 2006), par. 156; of *Montero Aranguren and Others* (*Retén de Catia*, 05 July 2006), par. 104; and of *Baldeón García* (06 April 2006), par. 128.

[30] Cf. I. Bottigliero, *Redress for Victims of Crimes under International Law*, Leiden, Nijhoff, 2004, pp. 111, 144, 177, 181, 183 and 250–1.

social *milieu*, and affecting particularly the most vulnerable persons.[31] The document then stressed the importance of the direct access of all victims to the justice system, overcoming obstacles thereto; it warned that:

There is an urgent need to provide more effective remedies and protective mechanisms for victims to enable them to gain access to, and participate effectively in, the justice system. This includes sensitization of practitioners to the specific needs and concerns of victims.[32]

Providing justice to victims is a way of contributing to their rehabilitation and, furthermore, of condemning victimization in general.[33] Compensation to victims has become a 'key feature' of restorative justice, and, on this latter, the *Handbook* stated:

Restorative justice is a new term for an old concept. Throughout the history of humankind restorative justice approaches have been used in order to solve conflicts between parties and to restore peace in communities. Retributive or rehabilitative approaches to crime are, by comparison, relatively new approaches. In recent years, however, dissatisfaction with the retributive and rehabilitative approaches has given rise to a renewed interest in restorative justice.[34]

At last, the document drew attention to the temporal dimension of victimization, warning that 'the intergenerational aspect should also be considered: what happened in one generation will affect what happens in the next'.[35] Hence the reestablishment of the value and dignity of victims, e.g., by socially recognizing their suffering, honouring their memory, relieving their stigmatization, providing an apology and full reparations to victims, rehabilitating the survivors and securing education to their descendants. The 1985 Victims' Declaration addressed victims of crime as well as of certain abuses of power;[36] it is thus not surprising that the Declaration has been recalled in the framework not only of inter-individual relations, but also in connection with State-perpetrated crimes.[37]

VI. Concluding Observations

The massacre cases recently brought before the IACtHR clearly indicate that, in particularly aggravating circumstances, crimes of State do indeed exist – whether doctrine wishes to admit it or not. There have been instances in which the respondent States themselves have recognized their international responsibility

---

[31] U.N./Centre for International Crime Prevention, *Handbook on Justice for Victims*, Vienna/N.Y., U.N., 1999, pp. 4–5.
[32] Ibid., p. 34.
[33] Ibid., p. 35.
[34] Ibid., p. 42.
[35] Ibid., p. 80.
[36] Namely, non-enforcement abuse of power, and unethical abuse of power.
[37] Cf., e.g., R. Aldana-Pindell, 'An Emerging Universality of Justiciable Victims' Rights in the Criminal Process to Curtail Impunity for State-Sponsored Crimes', 26 *Human Rights Quarterly* (2004) pp. 652–3.

for the atrocities and criminal policies pursued and criminal acts perpetrated. Contemporary legal doctrine still tries to circumvent the issue, but, with the awakening of human conscience, and the disclosure nowadays of atrocities which in the past did not reach international justice, it becomes increasingly difficult for those attached to the notion of State sovereignty to deny the existence and repeated occurrence of crimes of State.

Sometimes contemporary legal doctrine seems to attempt to minimize the gravity of State crimes, by resorting to euphemistic expressions such as 'State-sponsored' crime. This responds to a reductionist outlook. Crimes of State have occurred in a sustained pattern of extermination of human beings, prolonged in time. No one can deny that this is precisely what happened in cases like, for example, those of the *Massacre of Plan de Sánchez* (one among 626 massacres, which occurred mainly between 1978 and 1984, as established by the Guatemalan Truth Commission) and of *Goiburú and Others versus Paraguay* (one among numerous other atrocities committed by the so-called 'Operation Condor' in the Southern Cone of South America three decades ago).

Crimes of State have been not only 'State-sponsored': they have been State-conceived, State-planned (at the highest level), State-financed, pursuant to State policies, and executed by the State, and often covered up by the State concerned. They have victimized numerous defenceless persons, and prevented an investigation of the facts and the access to justice of numerous other human beings. In my view, it does great harm to the legal profession to try continually to deny the existence of State crimes; contemporary international legal doctrine will gain much credibility when it no longer circumvents the issue, and proceeds to determine the juridical consequences of the perpetration of State crimes. To that end, it can now count, for example, on the recent case-law of an international human rights tribunal such as the IACtHR, which has been seized of cases disclosing such crimes: it is reassuring that, in our lifetimes, even victims of massacres and crimes of State and their relatives have had their cause to reach international justice.

XI

The Overcoming of Obstacles to Direct Access to Justice

I. Introduction 192

II. The Proper Role of International Human Rights Tribunals 193

III. Towards the End of Self-Amnesties 194

IV. The Right to the Law (*droit au Droit/Derecho al Derecho*) as an Imperative of *Jus Cogens* 196

V. The Expansion of the Material Content of *Jus Cogens* 198

VI. The Evolving Presence of Victims in International Criminal Jurisdictions 201

VII. Concluding Observations: The Protection of the Human Person in the Light of Considerations of International *Ordre Public* 205

I. Introduction

We have already seen that there have been situations of great adversity wherein the direct victims or their relatives (also victims themselves) have, notwithstanding, succeeded in bringing their cause to an international human rights tribunal.[1] Consideration of the problem is now to be completed by turning attention to those extreme situations where the victims or their relatives are in a state of complete defencelessness, and where, furthermore, the apparatus of the public power of the State is put at the service of systematic breaches of fundamental human rights (in a most regrettable distortion and denial of the ends of the State), in criminal practices at times followed by self-amnesties. Even in such cases of grave violations *de facto* and *de jure* of human rights, significantly the direct victims or their relatives (also victims in their own right) have succeeded in bringing their cases before the international jurisdiction.

In the present chapter I shall focus attention, successively, on the proper role of international human rights tribunals, on the endeavours of an international human rights tribunal such as the IACtHR to put an end to the so-called 'self-amnesties', on what I term the right to the Law (*droit au Droit/derecho al Derecho*), on the

---

[1] Cf. chapters VIII and IX, *supra*.

recent endeavours of the IACtHR towards the expansion of the material content of *jus cogens*, and on the evolving presence of victims in contemporary international criminal jurisdictions. The way will thus be paved for the presentation of my concluding observations on the protection of the human person in the light of considerations of international *ordre public*.

II. The Proper Role of International Human Rights Tribunals

Judgments of an international human rights tribunal serve the wide purpose not only of resolving the legal questions raised in a given case, but also of clarifying and developing the meaning of the norms of the human rights treaty at issue, and of thereby contributing to its observance by the States Parties.[2] Thus, an international human rights tribunal not only settles the cases brought to its attention, but, furthermore, says what the Law is. It goes further than simply the settlement of human rights cases. This is evidenced when international human rights tribunals come to determine, in the framework of a contentious case, the compatibility of a domestic law with the human rights treaty at issue.

In this connection, in its Judgment (of 05 February 2001) in the case of the '*Last Temptation of Christ*' (*Olmedo Bustos and Others versus Chile*), concerning freedom of expression (movie censorship on the basis of a constitutional provision), the IACtHR emphasized the general duty that Article 2 of the ACHR imposes upon the States Parties to harmonize their domestic legal orders with the norms of protection of the ACHR (par. 87).[3] In this case, the Court established a violation of Article 13 of the ACHR, as a result of Article 19(12) of the 1980 Chilean Constitution, and ordered the respondent State to modify that norm so as to put an end to previous film censorship, so as to allow the public exhibition of the movie the '*Last Temptation of Christ*'.[4]

On 19 March 2003 the respondent State reported to the Court that the domestic law had been so modified, and on 19 March 2003 further informed the Court that the movie at issue was already being exhibited in Chile (as from 11 March 2003). The individual petitioners and the IAComHR, in their turn, informed the Court[5] that they were satisfied with Chile's compliance with the IACtHR's Judgment. In a resolution of 28 November 2003, the Court declared that its Judgment of 05 February 2001 had been fully complied with by the respondent State, and the case was thus terminated. This is an example of the Court properly exercising its function of settling a contentious case and, moreover, of saying what the Law is.

---

[2] In this sense, ECtHR, *Ireland versus United Kingdom* case (Merits), Judgment of 18 January 1978, Series A, n. 25, p. 62, par. 154.

[3] The foundations of this position can be found in my lenghty Concurring Opinion in the aforementioned Judgment (pars. 2–40), as well as, earlier on, in my Dissenting Opinions in the Jugments on the case of *El Amparo versus Venezuela* (Reparations, 14 September 1996, pars. 2–3 and 6 of my Opinion, and Interpretation of Judgment, 16 April 1997, pars. 22–3 of my Opinion).

[4] Resolutory point n. 4 of the Court's Judgment.

[5] In their reports of 21 October 2003 and 27 October 2003, respectively.

The aforementioned Judgment of the IACtHR in the case of the '*Last Temptation of Christ*' is more than a remarkable precedent (given the exemplary compliance with it by the respondent State, and its repercussions in the region): it is endowed with a truly historic significance, as the Chilean State modified a provision of its own Constitution so as to comply fully with a Judgment of an international human rights tribunal. This historic episode reveals that, in the present domain of protection, the primacy of international law over domestic law at normative level comes to constitute, more than an academic construction, a real feature of Law in our days, which has evolved and been moved ultimately by human conscience.

International tribunals, in general, in facing the most diverse situations, and in their quest for justice, are bound to contribute to the development of International Law,[6] thus upholding values and contributing to the prevalence of the rule of law[7] in a changing world, with emphasis on considerations of humanity.[8] This is very significant, given the expansion of international jurisdiction in our days,[9] with the reassuring co-existence of multiple contemporary international tribunals, giving their share to the prevalence of the rule of law in democratic societies. It is in this general framework that international human rights tribunals, such as the IACtHR and the ECtHR – lately joined by the African Court on Human and Peoples' Rights – have been developing the International Law of Human Rights itself by means of their evolving case-law of protection of the human person in any circumstances,[10] even those of the utmost adversity.

III. Towards the End of Self-Amnesties

These considerations acquire an even greater relevance in cases when the manifest incompatibility of domestic law with the provisions of human rights treaties lead to grave violations of human rights, denial of access to justice and perpetuation of impunity. This leads the victims or their relatives to a situation of virtually defencelessness. It is the case of the so-called self-amnesties, which purport to subtract from justice those who, in the name of the State, perpetrated atrocities or grave violations of human rights. Among the so-called laws of amnesty, there is a particularly perverse type, the so-called *self-amnesties* – which purport to subtract from justice those responsible for grave violations of human rights and International Humanitarian Law, and of crimes against humanity – which has lately been duly buried by the *jurisprudence constante* of the IACtHR.

Shortly afterwards, in its historic judgment in the case of the massacre of *Barrios Altos* (Merits, 14 March 2001) pertaining to Peru, the IACtHR, under

---

[6] H. Lauterpacht, *The Development of International Law by the International Court*, London, Stevens, 1958, pp. 5–6 and 397.

[7] J.G. Merrills, *The Development of International Law by the European Court of Human Rights*, 2nd. ed., Manchester, University Press, 1993, pp. 129, 132, 234, 249 and 252.

[8] L.J. van den Herik, *The Contribution of the Rwanda Tribunal to the Development of International Law*, Leiden, Nijhoff, 2005, pp. 270–1 and 276.

[9] Cf., e.g., [Various Authors,] *La juridictionnalisation du Droit international* (SFDI, Colloque de Lille de 2002), Paris, Pedone, 2003, pp. 3–545; T. Koopmans, 'Judicialization', in *Une communauté de droit – Festschrift für G.C. Rodríguez Iglesias* (eds. N. Colneric *et alii*), Berlin, Berliner Wissenschafts-Verlag (BMV), 2003, pp. 51–7.

[10] Cf., e.g., A.A. Cançado Trindade, *El Desarrollo del Derecho Internacional de los Derechos Humanos Mediante el Funcionamiento y la Jurisprudencia de la Corte Europea y la Corte Interamericana de Derechos Humanos*, CtIADH, San José de Costa Rica, 2007, pp. 1–75.

my Presidency, determined that the 'laws' of self-amnesty are incompatible with human rights treaties such as the ACHR, and are *devoid of juridical effects*.[11] This was the first time in contemporary International Law that an international tribunal quashed a 'law' of self-amnesty.[12] In the Judgment of *Barrios Altos*, the IACtHR sustained that self-amnesties (such as those of the Peruvian laws ns. 26479 and 26492), attempting to exclude responsibility for grave violations of human rights (such as torture, summary and extralegal executions, forced disappearances of persons), are inadmissible, and, in hindering or impeding the access of victims and their relatives to truth and justice, are in breach of Articles 1(1), 2, 8 and 25 of the Convention (pars. 41 and 43). In my Concurring Opinion in this Judgment, I pondered that the alleged 'legality' at domestic law level of those self-amnesties, in leading to impunity and injustice, was in flagrant incompatibility with the norms of protection of international human rights law, bringing about violations *de jure* of the rights of the human person, in 'an inadmissible affront to the juridical conscience of humanity' (pars. 5–6 and 26). In other words, the 'laws' of self-amnesty were vitiated of nullity *ex tunc*, of nullity *ab initio*, and are thus devoid of every and any juridical effect.

The aforementioned Judgment of *Barrios Altos* is nowadays acknowledged in expert legal writing in distinct continents,[13] as a landmark in the history of the International Law of Human Rights. In its Interpretation of Judgment (of 03.09.2001) of *Barrios Altos*, the IACtHR clarified, in relation to the State's duty to suppress from its legal order the norms in force which imply or amount to a violation of the American Convention (par. 17), that the promulgation of a law manifestly in breach of the obligations undertaken by a State Party to the Convention 'constitutes *per se* a violation' of this latter; the Court added that what it had decided in the Judgment as to the merits (*supra*) had, thus, 'general effects'.[14] This being so, such 'laws' of self-amnesty are not applicable, they are not truly laws.

Recently, in the same line as *Barrios Altos* (pertaining to the Fujimori regime), the Court took another step in the same direction, in its Judgment (of 26 September 2006) in the case *Almonacid Arellano versus Chile*, concerning the self-amnesty of the Pinochet regime. The IACtHR declared that the attempt to extend amnesty to those responsible for crimes against humanity by the Chilean decree-law n. 2191 was 'incompatible with the American Convention', and thus devoid of juridical effects.[15] The IACtHR determined that the aforementioned self-amnesty cannot continue to represent an obstacle to the investigation, trial and sanction of those responsible for grave violations of human rights.[16] In my

---

[11] Resolutory point n. 4 of the aforementioned Sentence.

[12] A. Cassese and M. Delmas-Marty (eds.), *Crimes internationaux et juridictions internationales*, Paris, PUF, 2002, pp. 16 and 246–7.

[13] A. Salado Osuna, *Los Casos Peruanos ante la Corte Interamericana de Derechos Humanos*, Trujillo/Peru, Edit. Normas Legales, 2004, pp. 228–36, 353–4, 412–13 and 457–9; A. Cassese and M. Delmas-Marty (eds.), *op. cit. supra* n. (12), pp. 16 and 246–7; A. Cassese, *International Criminal Law*, Oxford, Univ. Press, 2003, pp. 313–14 and 318; M. Scalabrino, *Per Non Dimenticare – Violazioni dei Diritti Umani e Leggi di Amnistia in America Latina*, Milano, Vita e Pensiero (V&P), 2007, pp. 93–145 and 169–213; V.F.D. Cançado Trindade, 'Uma Análise das Leis de Auto-Anistia na Evolução Jurisprudencial da Corte Interamericana de Direitos Humanos', 8 *Revista do Instituto Brasileiro de Direitos Humanos* (2008) pp. 281–91.

[14] Paragraph 18 and resolutory point n. 2.

[15] Resolutory point n. 3.

[16] Resolutory points ns. 5–6.

lengthy Separate Opinion in the *Almonacid case*, I reiterated the lack of juridical validity of the self-amnesties, which obstruct justice and violate the prohibitions (in expansion) of *jus cogens* (thus being the denial itself of Law), and I situated the crimes against humanity in the confluence between international human rights law and International Criminal Law (pars. 7, 10 and 28).

Moreover, this jurisprudential construction was confirmed by the IACtHR in its recent Judgment (of 29 November 2006) on the case of the massacre in the University of *La Cantuta*, concerning Peru, in which the Court asserted that 'the incompatibility *ab initio* of the laws of amnesty with the Convention was materialized in general in Peru' since it was impugned by the Court in its Judgment on the case *Barrios Altos*; that is, 'the State suppressed the effects which at some moment those laws may have generated' (pars. 186–187). The same impact of the case-law of the IACtHR has occurred recently in the domestic law of other South American countries. In its Judgment on the case of *La Cantuta*, the Court clearly determined that the aforementioned 'laws' of self-amnesty 'have not been able to generate effects, do not have them at present, nor can they generate them in the future'.[17]

In sum, the Judgments of the IACtHR on the cases of *Barrios Altos* (2001), of *Almonacid* (2006), and of *La Cantuta* (2006), constitute a decisive contribution of the Court to the end of self-amnesties and to the definitive primacy of Law. Such 'laws' of self-amnesty are not true laws, they are nothing but a juridical aberration, an affront to the *recta ratio*. It should not pass unnoticed that this jurisprudential construction, of emancipation of the human person *vis-à-vis* her own State,[18] was rendered possible due to the exercise of the right of international individual petition, whereby the victims and their relatives affirm themselves as true subjects of contemporary International Law, endowed with full juridico-procedural capacity.[19]

IV. The Right to the Law (*droit au Droit/Derecho al Derecho*) as an Imperative of *Jus Cogens*

In its Advisory Opinion n. 18, on the *Juridical Condition and Rights of Undocumented Migrants* (of 17 September 2003), the IACtHR rightly warned that 'the State must guarantee that access to justice is genuine and not merely formal' (par. 126); such access encompasses, in my view, by means of an effective remedy, all the guarantees of the due process of law, up to faithful and final compliance with the sentence. The same Advisory Opinion n. 18 lucidly sustained that the principle of equality and non-discrimination integrates nowadays the domain of *jus cogens* (pars. 111–127).

---

[17] Paragraph 189, and resolutory point n. 7.
[18] Cf., for a study of this point, A.A. Cançado Trindade, 'The Emancipation of the Individual from His Own State – The Historical Recovery of the Human Person as Subject of the Law of Nations', *in Human Rights, Democracy and the Rule of Law – Liber Amicorum Luzius Wildhaber* (eds. S. Breitenmoser *et alii*), Zürich/Baden-Baden, Dike/Nomos, 2007, pp. 151–71.
[19] Cf. A.A. Cançado Trindade, 'International Law for Humankind: Towards a New *Jus Gentium* – General Course on Public International Law – Part I', 316 *Recueil des Cours de l'Académie de Droit International de la Haye* (2005), ch. IX-X, pp. 252–317.

Attention has already been focused on the interrelation between the access to justice (right to an effective remedy) and the guarantees of the due process of law.[20] In my Separate Opinion in the case of the *Massacre of Pueblo Puello* (Judgment of 31 January 2006), concerning Colombia, I sustained that such interrelation (between Articles 25 and 8 of the American Convention):

leads one to characterize as being of the domain of *jus cogens* the access to justice understood as the *full realization* of this latter, that is, as being of the domain of *jus cogens* the intangibility of all the judicial guarantees and protection in the sense of Articles 25 and 8 taken *jointly*. There can be no doubt that the fundamental guarantees, common to the International Law of Human Rights and International Humanitarian Law,[21] have a universal vocation in applying in all and any circumstances, conform an imperative norm (belonging to the *jus cogens*), and bring about obligations *erga omnes* of protection[22] (par. 64).

Accordingly, I expressly called for (par. 65) the continuing expansion of the material content of *jus cogens* by the Court, so as to comprise the access to justice thus understood, just as it had done earlier on, in Advisory Opinion n. 18 of 2003, in relation to the basic principle of equality and non-discrimination.

In the domain of international human rights law, moved by considerations of international *ordre public*, we stand before common and superior values, truly fundamental and irreducible.[23] Such values, in their turn, are consubstantiated, ultimately, in the central concept of 'democratic society' based upon respect for the rights of the human person.[24] We can here visualize a true *right to the Law*, that is, the right to a legal order which effectively safeguards the fundamental rights of the human person.[25] The new *corpus juris* of international human rights law, applicable by means of the instrumentality of the law, is endowed with a specificity and a system of values of its own, which find expression in the counterposition of the human person vis-à-vis the public power, aiming at protecting the human being in any circumstances and against all manifestations of the arbitrary power. The two international human rights tribunals – the European and Inter-American

---

[20] Cf. chapter III, *supra*.

[21] E.g., Article 75 of Protocol I (of 1977) to the Geneva Conventions (of 1949) on International Humanitarian Law.

[22] Cf., also in this sense, e.g., M. El Kouhene, *Les garanties fondamentales de la personne en Droit humanitaire et droits de l'homme*, Dordrecht, Nijhoff, 1986, pp. 97, 145, 148, 161 and 241.

[23] Cf., in this sense, F. Sudre, 'Existe t-il un ordre public européen?', in *Quelle Europe pour les droits de l'homme?* (ed. P. Tavernier), Bruxelles, Bruylant, 1996, pp. 41, 50 and 54–67. And, for a classic study of the legal order, which purported to transcend pure normativism, cf. Santi Romano, *L'ordre juridique*, Paris, Dalloz, 2002 [reimpr.], pp. 3–163.

[24] A. Kiss, 'La Convention Européenne des Droits de l'Homme a-t-elle créé un ordre juridique autonome?', in *Mélanges en hommage à L.E. Pettiti*, Bruxelles, Bruylant, 1998, pp. 496, 501 and 504–5.

[25] A.A. Cançado Trindade, *Tratado de Direito Internacional dos Direitos Humanos*, vol. III, Porto Alegre/Brazil, S.A. Fabris Ed., 2003, pp. 524–5. And, for a case-study in this respect, cf. A.A. Cançado Trindade, E. Ferrero Costa and A. Gómez-Robledo, 'Gobernabilidad Democrática y Consolidación Institucional: El Control Internacional y Constitucional de los *Interna Corporis* – Informe de la Comisión de Juristas de la OEA para Nicarágua (Febrero de 1994)', 67 *Boletín de la Academia de Ciencias Políticas y Sociales* – Caracas (2000–2001) n. 137, pp. 593–669.

Courts, in operation for years, have effectively contributed to the crystallization of the notion of international *ordre public* in the present domain of protection of the human person.

V. The Expansion of the Material Content of *Jus Cogens*

Turning to a related point, in my *General Course on Public International Law*, delivered at the Hague Academy of International Law in 2005, I characterized the doctrinal and jurisprudential construction of international *jus cogens* as proper of what I perceive as a new *jus gentium*, the International Law for Humankind. I sustained, moreover, that, in this understanding, international *jus cogens* by definition goes well beyond the law of treaties, extending itself to the domain of State responsibility and, ultimately, to any juridical act. It encompasses the whole *corpus juris* of contemporary International Law, and projects itself into domestic law as well, invalidating any measure or act incompatible with it. *Jus cogens* has a direct bearing on the foundations of a universal International Law, and is a basic pillar of the new *jus gentium*.[26]

It is not my intention here to reiterate the considerations that I developed in my aforementioned *General Course* at the Hague Academy, but rather to complement them with an additional aspect, of great relevance, which cannot pass unnoticed here: that of the expansion of the material content of *jus cogens*, the construction of which I have been much engaged in, via the case-law of the IACtHR in recent years. Thus, in the Judgments of the IACtHR in the cases of the *Brothers Gómez Paquiyauri versus Peru* (of 08 July 2004, pars. 111–112), and of *Tibi versus Ecuador* (of 07 September 2004, par. 145), concerning arbitrary detention and torture, the Inter-American Court, *inter alia*, in establishing violations of the rights to personal liberty and to humane treatment under Articles 7 and 5 of the American Convention,[27] asserted that there exists nowadays 'an international legal regime of absolute prohibition of all forms of torture, physical as well as psychological, a regime which belongs nowadays to the domain of *jus cogens*'. The Court added that:

the prohibition of torture is complete and non-derogable, even in the most difficult circumstances, such as war, threat of war, 'fight against terrorism' and any other delicts, state of siege or of emergency, commotion or internal conflict, suspension of constitutional guarantees, internal political instability or other public emergencies or calamities.[28]

Shortly afterwards, the IACtHR's Judgment (of 11 March 2005) in the case of *Caesar versus Trinidad and Tobago*, tackled some issues pertaining to the law of

---

[26] A.A. Cançado Trindade, 'International Law for Humankind: Towards a New *Jus Gentium* – General Course on Public International Law – Part I', 316 *Recueil des Cours de l'Académie de Droit International de la Haye* (2005), ch. XII, pp. 336–46.

[27] In addition, in the *Gómez Paquiyauri* case, of the violation of the right to life (Article 4) itself.

[28] Paragraphs 111–12 of the Judgment on the *Brothers Gómez Paquiyauri versus Peru* case, and paragraph 145 of the Judgment on the *Tibi versus Ecuador* case. And, on the matter at issue – the absolute prohibition of torture as belonging to the domain of *jus cogens* – cf. the Separate Opinions of Judge A.A. Cançado Trindade in both cases.

treaties.[29] The Judgment at issue, fitting squarely into its *jurisprudence constante* on the evolutive interpretation of *jus cogens*, rightly took a step forward, in upholding the absolute prohibition, proper to the domain of *jus cogens*, of torture *as well as any other cruel, inhuman, and degrading treatment.*

Earlier on, in its pioneering Advisory Opinion n. 18 (of 17 September 2003), on the *Juridical Condition and the Rights of Undocumented Migrants,* the IACtHR rightly enlarged the material content of *jus cogens* so as to comprise also the fundamental principle of equality and non-discrimination (including equality before the law) (par. 101). In my Concurring Opinion, I endorsed the Court's position, acknowledging that that basic principle permeates the whole legal order, and drawing attention to its importance, and of all general principles of law, from which norms and rules emanate, and without which there is ultimately no 'legal order' at all (pars. 44–46 and 65). In sum, such principles form, in my view, the *substratum* of the legal order itself (pars. 52–58).

Ever since the IACtHR upheld this view, in successive contentious cases I insisted on the need of widening further that material content of *jus cogens,* so as to encompass likewise the right of access to justice.[30] I did so, *inter alia,* in my Separate Opinion (devoted to the right of access to justice *lato sensu*) in the Court's Judgment (of 31 January 2006) in the case of the *Massacre of Pueblo Bello versus Colombia,* drawing attention to the fundamental importance precisely of that right of access to justice, and stating that:

The interrelatedness that I sustain between Articles 25 and 8 of the American Convention (...) leads to characterize as belonging to the domain of *jus cogens* the access to justice understood as the *full realization* of it, that is, as belonging to the domain of *jus cogens* the intangibility of all the judicial guarantees in the sense of Articles 25 and 8 taken *altogether.* There can be no doubt that the fundamental guarantees, common to the International Law of Human Rights and to International Humanitarian Law, have a universal vocation in applying in all and any circumstances, conforming an imperative law (belonging to *jus cogens*), and entailing obligations *erga omnes* of protection (par. 64).

But it was in the case of *Goiburú and Others versus Paraguay* (Judgment of 22 September 2006), concerning the sinister 'Operation Condor' of the so-called 'intelligence services' of the countries of the Southern Cone of South America (at the time of the dictatorships of three decades ago), that the IACtHR at last espoused the thesis that I had been sustaining within it for already more than two

---

[29] Such as interpretation, reservations, denunciation, termination and suspension of the operation of treaties.

[30] Cf., to this effect, my Separate Opinions in the Court's Judgments in the cases of the *Massacre of Plan de Sánchez versus Guatemala* (merits, of 29 April 2004), pars. 22, 29–33 and 35 of the Opinion; and (reparations, of 19 November 2004), pars. 4–7 and 20–7 of the Opinion; of the *Brothers Gómez Paquiyauri versus Peru* (of 08 July 2004), pars. 37–44 of the Opinion; of *Tibi versus Ecuador* (of 07 September 2004), pars. 30–2 of the Opinion; of *Caesar versus Trinidad and Tobago* (of 11 March 2005), pars. 85–92 of the Opinion; of *Yatama versus Nicaragua* (of 23 June 2005), pars. 6–9 of the Opinion; of *Acosta Calderón versus Ecuador* (of 14 June 2005), pars. 4 and 7 of the Opinion; of the *Massacres of Ituango versus Colombia* (of 01 July 2006), par. 47 of the Opinion; of *Baldeón García versus Peru* (of 06 April 2006), pars. 9–10 of the Opinion; of *López Álvarez versus Honduras* (of 01 February 2006), pars. 53–5 of the Opinion; of *Ximenes Lopes versus Brazil* (of 04 July 2006), pars. 19–26 and 38–47 of the Opinion.

years,[31] in effectively further expanding the material content of *jus cogens,* so as to comprise the right of access to justice at national and international levels. In my Separate Opinions in the case *Goiburú and Others,*[32] as well as in the subsequent cases of *Almonacid Arellano versus Chile* (Judgment of 26 September 2006, pars. 58–60 of the Opinion), and of *La Cantuta versus Peru* (Judgment of 29 November 2006, pars. 49–62 of the Opinion), I stressed the considerable importance of such expansion of the material content of *jus cogens.*

On this further expansion of the material content of *jus cogens,* I sustained, in my Separate Opinion in the case of *La Cantuta versus Peru* (Judgment of 29 November 2006), that:

In cases such as the present one, in which the apparatus of the State power was unduly utilized to commit crimes of State (in a shocking distortion of the ends of the State), constituting inadmissible violations of the *jus cogens,* and afterwards to cover-up such crimes and to maintain its agents, perpetrators of them, in impunity, and the relatives of the victims (also victimized) in the most complete desolation and despair, – in cases such as those of *La Cantuta* and of *Barrios Altos* [concerning Peru], in which the crimes against human rights were perpetrated in the framework of a proven criminal practice of the State, – the patient reconstitution and determination of the facts by this Court constitute, themselves, one of the forms of providing satisfaction – as a form of reparation – due to the surviving relatives of the victims (who are also victims), and to honour the memory of the victims who died.

Jus cogens resists to the crimes of State, and imposes sanctions to them, by virtue of the prompt engagement of the *aggravated* international responsibility of the State. As a result of those crimes, the due reparations assume the form of distinct obligations of doing, including the investigation, trial and sanction of those responsible for the crimes of State that they perpetrated (by action or omission). The Law does not cease to exist by the violation of its norms, as the 'realists' attempt to hint, degenerated by their ineluctable and pathetic idolatry of the established power. Quite on the contrary, the imperative law (*jus cogens*) immediately reacts to such violations, and imposes sanctions.

During the years, within this Court, I have insisted on the necessity of the recognition and on the identification of the *jus cogens,* and I have elaborated, in numerous [Individual] Opinions (in the exercise of both the contentious and the advisory functions of the Tribunal), the doctrinal construction of the expansion of the material content of the *jus cogens* and of the corresponding obligations *erga omnes* of protection, in both their horizontal dimension (vis-à-vis the international community as a whole) and their vertical dimension (encompassing the relations of the individual with the public power as well as with non-State entities and other individuals). Accordingly, the very notion of 'victim' under the American Convention has evolved and expanded, the parameters of the protection due to the *justiciables* as well as the circle of protected persons have enlarged' (pars. 58–60).

The gradual expansion of the material content of *jus cogens* has taken place *pari passu* with the recent judicial condemnation of grave violations of human rights and

---

[31] Cf. the text of my Separate Opinion therein, reproduced in: A.A. Cançado Trindade, *Derecho Internacional de los Derechos Humanos – Esencia y Trascendencia (Votos en la Corte Interamericana de Derechos Humanos, 1991–2006),* Mexico, Édit. Porrúa/Universidad Iberoamericana, 2007, pp. 779–804.
[32] Pars. 62–8 of the Opinion, text in ibid., pp. 801–4.

massacres which amount, in my understanding, to crimes of State.[33] In my Separate Opinion in the case of *Almonacid and Others*[34] I sought to demonstrate the lack of juridical validity of the so-called self-amnesties (as exemplified by the much-criticized Decree-Law n. 2191, of 18 April 1978, of the Pinochet regime), incompatible with the ACHR, in generating the obstruction and denial of justice, and the consequent impunity of those responsible for the atrocities. I insisted on the necessity of the enlargement of the material content of the prohibitions of *jus cogens* (so as to secure the access to justice at both national and international levels), and I situated, at last, the conceptualization of the crimes against humanity in the confluence between international human rights law and International Criminal Law.

The significance of the further expansion of the material content of *jus cogens*,[35] by the IACtHR in its Judgment of 22 September 2006, in the case of *Goiburú and Others*, so as to encompass the right of access to justice, and the importance and the implications of this remarkable jurisprudential advance, are stressed in my Separate Opinion (pas. 62–68) in that case, in which, furthermore, I dwelt upon the criminalization of grave violations of human rights; the crime of State in the context of State terrorism (of the aforementioned 'Operation Condor', and the cover-up by the State of the atrocities perpetrated); the international responsibility of the State aggravated by the crime of State;[36] and new elements of the necessary complementarity between international human rights law and contemporary International Criminal Law.

VI. The Evolving Presence of Victims in International Criminal Jurisdictions

Recent advances in the domains of international human rights law and of International Criminal Law have drawn increasing attention to the individual's active as well as passive international subjectivity, respectively. Within this framework the issue of the evolving presence of victims in international legal procedures can be appropriately addressed. In fact, before the ad hoc International Criminal Tribunals for the Former Yugoslavia (ICTFY) and for Rwanda (ICTR), the role of the victims is limited to presenting their testimony as witnesses,[37] what has led to criticisms

---

[33] Cf. chapter VIII, *supra*.

[34] The public hearings of which took place in the external session of the IACtHR held in Brasilia, on 29 March 2006.

[35] Cf., recently, A.A. Cançado Trindade, 'Some Reflections on the Reassuring Expansion of the Material Content of *Jus Cogens*', in *Diritti Individuali e Giustizia Internazionale – Liber F. Pocar*, Milano, Giuffrè Ed., 2009, pp. 65–79.

[36] Cf., on this point, A.A. Cançado Trindade, 'Complementarity between State Responsibility and Individual Responsibility for Grave Violations of Human Rights: The Crime of State Revisited', in *International Responsibility Today – Essays in Memory of O. Schachter* (ed. M. Ragazzi), Leiden, M. Nijhoff, 2005, pp. 253–69.

[37] They cannot access evidence, nor be provided with information concerning proceedings, nor instigate criminal investigation or prosecution, nor claim reparations.

that it does not satisfy the conception of the victims themselves of what (international) justice is or ought to be.[38]

But the International Criminal Court (ICC) breaks new grounds in this respect, innovating in the role conferred upon the victims before an international criminal jurisdiction: they can present their views and concerns at all stages of the proceedings before the ICC,[39] participating in these latter in their own right; they can transmit information to the Prosecutor (requesting the initiation of an investigation), can obtain information from the ICC throughout the proceedings, and can obtain legal representation when necessary.[40]

Furthermore, in September 2002 the Assembly of States Parties of the ICC decided to create a *Trust Fund for Victims*,[41] which was in fact established by decision of the Assembly on 03 December 2005,[42] in an acknowledgement of the fact that true justice can only be achieved if due account is taken of the suffering of the victims. The ICC thus counts on a mechanism that provides for access to justice and redress for victims.[43] Before the ICC, victims are 'natural persons who suffered harm', either in a 'situation' falling within the jurisdiction of the ICC, or else in a specific case where an individual is formally charged and prosecuted.[44]

The Trust Fund is meant to provide assistance to a broad class of victims;[45] after all, participation by the victims themselves secures access to justice, and a mechanism for judicial review and redress.[46] There appears to be here an approximation between contemporary International Criminal Law and international human rights law, in so far as the recognition of the relevance of the presence of victims (and their relatives) is concerned. It now remains to be seen how the Trust Fund for Victims will operate in practice in the years to come. Parallel to the establishment of the Trust Fund for Victims (*supra*), there is also the Victims Participation and Reparations Section, within the ICC Registry (Statute, Article 43(6), and Rules 16–19).[47]

The case *Goiburú and Others versus Paraguay* (Judgment of 22 September 2006) brought to the fore, before the IACtHR, the defencelessness of the victims in a systematic practice of arbitrary detentions followed by forced 'disappearances' of

---

[38] G. Bitti and G. González Rivas, 'The Reparations Provisions for Victims under the Rome Statute of the International Criminal Court', in *Redressing Injustices Through Mass Claims Processes* (ed. Permanent Court of Arbitration), Oxford, University Press, 2006, pp. 303–4.

[39] Where their personal interests are affected.

[40] With financial assistance when appropriate; cf. ibid., pp. 299–300 and 306.

[41] Established (independently of the ICC) pursuant to Article 79 of the 1998 Rome Statute of the ICC (and cf. also Court's Rule 98).

[42] The decision was adopted by consensus; cf. ICC, *4th Assembly of the States Parties of the International Criminal Court* (The Hague, 28.11–03 December 2005), p. 2. For the text of the Trust Fund for Victims, cf. ICC, *Trust Fund for Victims*, resolution ICC-ASP/4/Res.3, pp. 320–33.

[43] G. Bitti and G. González Rivas, 'The Reparations Provisions for Victims . . .', *op. cit. supra* n. (38), pp. 300–1.

[44] 1998 Rome Statute of the ICC, Articles 13–14; and Rule 85 of the ICC Rules.

[45] Its role in the distribution of (collective) awards for reparations is set forth in Rule 98 of the ICC Rules; cf. G. Bitti and G. González Rivas, *op. cit. supra* n. (38), pp. 315 and 317.

[46] It further provides relevant information, generates greater awareness of what occurred, and enhances 'a general climate of respect for the rule of law'; ibid., p. 320, and cf. pp. 321–2.

[47] Ibid., pp. 32 and 122–4.

persons, during the years of operation, three decades ago, of the sinister 'Operation Condor', perpetrated by the so-called 'intelligence services' of dictatorships in the Southern Cone of South America three decades ago. In my Separate Opinion in that case, I *inter alia* identified, as elements demonstrating the complementarity between international human rights law and contemporary International Criminal Law, the following ones:

a the international legal personality (active as well as passive) of the individual;

b the complementarity of the international responsibility of the State and of the individual;

c the conceptualization of crimes against humanity;

d the prevention and the guarantee of non-repetition (of the grave human rights violations); and

e the reparatory justice in the confluence of international human rights law and International Criminal Law (par. 34).

In that complementarity (first element), the individual emerges in his juridical condition of both *active* subject (international human rights law) and *passive* subject (International Criminal Law) of International Law, that is, as *titulaire* of rights and bearer of duties which emanate directly from International Law. Such condition of the individual represents, as I have repeatedly been stressing, the most precious legacy of the juridical thinking as from the mid-XXth century[48] (par. 35). In fact, in relation to the ad hoc ICTFY and the ICTR, the ICC represents an advance, in particular, as to the presence and participation of the victims in the course of its proceedings.[49]

As I pondered in my aforementioned Separate Opinion in the *Goiburú and Others* case:

The presence of the victims in the procedure before the ICC represents, in my understanding, a significant point of confluence between contemporary International Criminal Law and the International Law of Human Rights. It is no longer only a punitive or sanctioning justice, but, moreover, also a reparatory one (Rome Statute, Article 75), and foreseeing distinct forms and modalities of reparation (Rules of the ICC, Rule 98),[50] both individual and collective. It is not surprising that, in its first pronouncements, – in the case

---

[48] Cf., *inter alia*, A.A. Cançado Trindade, 'International Law for Humankind: Towards a New *Jus Gentium* – General Course on Public International Law', 316 *Recueil des Cours de l'Académie de Droit International de la Haye* (2005) chs. IX-X, pp. 252–17; A.A. Cançado Trindade, *El Derecho Internacional de los Derechos Humanos en el Siglo XXI*, 2nd. ed., Santiago, Editorial Jurídica de Chile, 2006, pp. 319–76; A.A. Cançado Trindade, *El Acceso Directo del Individuo a los Tribunales Internacionales de Derechos Humanos*, Bilbao, University of Deusto, 2001, pp. 9–104; A.A. Cançado Trindade, *Tratado de Direito Internacional dos Direitos Humanos*, vol. III, Porto Alegre/Brazil, S.A. Fabris Ed., 2003, pp. 447–97.

[49] Rome Statute, Articles 68 and 75, and Rules 16, 89 and 90–3; ICC, *Selected Basic Documents Related to the International Criminal Court*, The Hague, ICC Secretariat, 2005, pp. 47, 52, 122 and 151–3.

[50] ICC, *Selected Basic Documents Related to the International Criminal Court*, The Hague, ICC Secretariat, 2005, pp. 52 y 155.

Th. Lubanga Dyilo and the investigation of the *situation in the Democratic Republic of Congo*,[51] – the ICC has made express reference to the rich case-law of the Inter-American Court.[52] The International Law of Human Rights and contemporary International Criminal Law can here mutually reinforce each other, to the ultimate benefit of the human beings.

The consolidation of the international criminal [penal] personality of the individuals, as active as well as passive subjects of international law, strengthens the *accountability* in International Law for abuses perpetrated against human beings. In this way, individuals are also bearers of duties under International Law, what reflects the consolidation of their international juridical personality.[53] Developments in the international juridical personality and international responsibility take place *pari passu*, and all this evolution bears witness of the formation of the *opinio juris communis* in the sense that the gravity of certain violations of the fundamental rights of the human person directly affects basic values shared by the international community as a whole[54] (pars. 37–38).

The presence of the victims, which is central in the domain of international human rights law (wholly victim-oriented), begins to become noticeable also in the domain of contemporary International Criminal Law, as disclosed by the Rome Statute of the International Criminal Court.[55] This may prove to be the beginning of a new development, bringing international human rights law and International Criminal Law closer together, to the benefit and redress of the victims.

There still seems to be a long way to go – though the first steps are already being taken – in properly developing the reparations due to victims of grave and massive violations of human rights,[56] which are of direct concern to both international human rights law and International Criminal Law. After all, there is a strong case for asserting the responsibility and accountability of all subjects of law[57] – among them States as well as individuals. As I have sustained in my *General Course on Public International Law* (2005) at The Hague Academy of International Law, the expansion of international legal personality in contemporary

[51] Cf. International Criminal Court (ICC)/Pre-Trial Chamber I, doc. ICC-01/04, of 17 January 2006, pp. 14–15, 29 and 34; ICC-01/04, of 31 March 2006, p. 12; and ICC-01/04, of 31 July 2006, pp. 8–9.

[52] E.g., references to cases, e.g., *Blake versus Guatemala*, 1998; *'Street Children' versus Guatemala*, 1999; *El Amparo versus Venezuela*, 1996; *Neira Alegría versus Peru*, 1996; *Paniagua Morales versus Guatemala*, 2001; *Baena Ricardo and Others versus Panama*, 2001, among others.

[53] H.-H. Jescheck, 'The General Principles of International Criminal Law Set Out in Nuremberg, as Mirrored in the ICC Statute', 2 *Journal of International Criminal Justice* (2004) p. 43.

[54] Cf., e.g., A. Cassese, 'Y a-t-il un conflit insurmontable entre souveraineté des États et justice pénale internationale?', in *Crimes internationaux et juridictions internationales* (eds. A. Cassese and M. Delmas-Marty), Paris, PUF, 2002, pp. 15–29; and cf., generally, [Various Authors], *La Criminalización de la Barbarie: La Corte Penal Internacional* (ed. J.A. Carrillo Salcedo), Madrid, Consejo General del Poder Judicial, 2000, pp. 17–504.

[55] Articles 15(3), 19(3), 68, 75 and 79.

[56] Cf. F. Rigaux, 'La condition des victimes de crimes de Droit international', in *Man's Inhumanity to Man – Essays on International Law in Honour of A. Cassese* (eds. L.C. Vohrah, F. Pocar *et alii*), The Hague, Kluwer, 2003, p. 788, and cf. pp. 771–89.

[57] Cf., e.g., B. Simma, 'Does the U.N. Charter Provide an Adequate Legal Basis for Individual or Collective Responses to Violations of Obligations *Erga Omnes*?', in *The Future of International Law Enforcement: New Scenarios – New Law?* (Proceedings of the 1992 Symposium of the Kiel Institute of International Law, eds. J. Delbrück and U.E. Heinz), Berlin, Duncker and Humblot, 1993, pp. 129 and 134.

International Law has taken place *pari passu* with the evolution of international responsibility itself, no longer only of States, but also of individuals, and other subjects of International Law.[58]

VII. Concluding Observations: The Protection of the Human Person in the Light of Considerations of International *Ordre Public*

When reference is made to 'international *ordre public*' in the present domain of the international protection of human rights, the expression becomes endowed, in my view, with a meaning of its own. It is certainly not equated with the classic sense in which it was invoked in other branches of law (such as civil law or administrative law); nor is it herein utilized in the sense of the well-known 'exception of *ordre public*' (of non-application by the judge of given norms of 'foreign law'), proper to private international law (where it is a recurrent theme). It is my understanding that, in the domain of international human rights law, the notion of international *ordre public* is endowed with an entirely distinct meaning, and of difficult definition, as it enshrines values which pre-exist and are superior to the norms of positive law.[59] We are before a humanized public order, or even a truly humanist one, in which the public interest or the general interest fully coincides with the prevalence of human rights.[60]

This implies the recognition that human rights constitute the basic foundation, themselves, of the legal order, and the values, always underlying human rights themselves, care to ascribe to them concrete expression. These values are perfectly identifiable,

---

[58] A.A. Cançado Trindade, 'International Law for Humankind: Towards a New *Jus Gentium* – General Course on Public International Law – Part I', 316 *Recueil des Cours de l'Académie de Droit International de la Haye* (2005) pp. 203–333; A.A. Cançado Trindade, 'International Law for Humankind: Towards a New *Jus Gentium* –General Course on Public International Law – Part II', 317 *Recueil des Cours de l'Académie de Droit International de la Haye* (2005) pp. 274–6.

[59] J. Foyer, 'Droits internationaux de l'homme et ordre public international', *Du droit interne au droit international – Mélanges Raymond Goy*, Rouen, Publ. Université de Rouen, 1998, pp. 333–48; G. Karydis, 'L'ordre public dans l'ordre juridique communautaire: un concept à contenu variable', 1 *Revue trimestrielle de droit européen* (2002) pp. 1 and 25. And, on the evolution of the so-called 'communitarian juridical order', cf. also L.S. Rossi, '"Constitutionnalisation" de l'Union Européenne et des droits fondamentaux', 1 *Revue trimestrielle de droit européen* (2002) pp. 29–33. In the ambit of Public International Law, the international community itself needs the concept of *ordre public* ('*international public order*'), so as to preserve its basic juridical principles; H. Mosler, 'The International Society as a Legal Community', 140 *Recueil des Cours de l'Académie de Droit International de La Haye* (1974) pp. 33–4; and cf. also, in this respect, G. Jaenicke, 'International Public Order', *Encyclopedia of Public International Law* (ed. R. Bernhardt/Max Planck Institute), vol. 7, Amsterdam, North-Holland, 1984, pp. 314–18.

[60] In this sense, one has suggested the emergence of a true *jus commune* of human rights at international level; cf. M. de Salvia, 'L'élaboration d'un *'jus commune'* des droits de l'homme et des libertés fondamentales dans la perspective de l'unité européenne: l'oeuvre accomplie par la Commission et la Cour Européennes des Droits de l'Homme', in *Protection des droits de l'homme: la dimension européenne – Mélanges en l'honneur de G.J. Wiarda* (eds. F. Matscher and H. Petzold), 2nd. ed., Köln/Berlin, C. Heymanns Verlag, 1990, pp. 555–63; G. Cohen-Jonathan, 'Le rôle des principes généraux dans l'interprétation et l'application de la Convention Européenne des Droits de l'Homme', in *Mélanges en hommage à L.E. Pettiti*, Bruxelles, Bruylant, 1998, pp. 168–9.

along the operative part of international treaties and instruments of human rights, but made explicit above all in their preambles. These latter tend to invoke the ideals which inspired the respective treaties and instruments (of importance to the identification of their 'spirit'), or to enunciate their foundations or general principles.[61]

It is notable, for example, that the preamble of the Universal Declaration of Human Rights of 1948 already invoked the 'conscience of mankind'.[62] In the present context of protection, there is no longer space for the 'autonomy of the will', for the bargains of reciprocity, for mutual concessions, to which yield several branches of law (mainly of private law); in the domain of international human rights law, moved ahead by considerations of international *ordre public*, we are, as already pointed out, before common and superior values, which are truly fundamental and irreducible.[63]

In their turn, these values are consubstantiated, ultimately, in the central concept of 'democratic society' based on respect for the rights of the human person.[64] One can here visualize a true *right to the Law*, that is, the right to a legal order which effectively safeguards the fundamental rights of the human person.[65] The ECtHR and the IACtHR have, in this respect, effectively contributed to the crystallization of the notion of international *ordre public* in the present domain of protection.

It may here be recalled, to invoke but a couple of examples from their recent case-law, that the ECtHR, in the case *Loizidou versus Turkey* (preliminary objections, 1995), expressly qualified the ECHR as a 'constitutional instrument of the European public order' (par. 75). The IACtHR, in its turn, pondered, in the case *Castillo Páez versus Peru* (merits, 1997), that the right to an effective remedy before competent national tribunals or judges, set forth in Article 25 of the ACHR, constitutes one of the 'basic pillars', not only of the ACHR, but of the rule of law

[61] N. Bobbio, 'Il Preambolo della Convenzione Europea dei Diritti dell'Uomo', 57 *Rivista di Diritto Internazionale* (1974) pp. 437–8. The author added that the appeal to values, often formulated in the preambles of the human rights treaties, 'può assumere (...) l'aspetto di un'indicazione: a) dei fini o degli obiettivi; b) delle motivazioni; c) del fundamento della decisione' taken in the process of elaboration of the treaty at issue; ibid., pp. 439–40.

[62] 2nd. preambular paragraph. It may be observed, moreover, that, along the last decades, the notion of 'elementary considerations of humanity' have at times marked presence in the case-law of the International Court of Justice itself, but it has been the two international tribunals – the Inter-American and the European Courts – of human rights operating today that have most elaborated on the matter, in relation particularly to the minimum and irreducible nucleus of non-derogable human rights, which count on a truly universal recognition. Cf., in this respect, e.g., A.A. Cançado Trindade, 'La jurisprudence de la Cour Internationale de Justice sur les droits intangibles', in *Droits intangibles et états d'exception* (eds. D. Prémont, C. Stenersen and I. Oseredczuk), Bruxelles, Bruylant, 1996, pp. 53–71 and 73–89; P.-M. Dupuy, 'Les 'considérations élémentaires d'humanité' dans la jurisprudence de la Cour Internationale de Justice', in *Mélanges en l'honneur de N. Valticos – Droit et justice* (eds. R.-J. Dupuy and L.A. Sicilianos), Paris, Pédone, 1999, pp. 117–30.

[63] Cf., in this sense, F. Sudre, 'Existe t-il un ordre public européen?', in *Quelle Europe pour les droits de l'homme?* (ed. P. Tavernier), Bruxelles, Bruylant, 1996, pp. 41, 50 and 54–67. And cf., in general, Santi Romano, *L'ordre juridique*, Paris, Dalloz, 2002 [reimpr.], pp. 3–163.

[64] A. Kiss, 'La Convention Européenne des Droits de l'Homme a-t-elle créé un ordre juridique autonome?', in *Mélanges en hommage à L.E. Pettiti*, Bruxelles, Bruylant, 1998, pp. 496, 501 and 504–5.

[65] For a case-study in this respect, cf. A.A. Cançado Trindade, E. Ferrero Costa and A. Gómez-Robledo, 'Gobernabilidad Democrática y Consolidación Institucional...', *op. cit. supra* n. (25), pp. 593–669.

itself in a democratic society in the sense of the Convention (par. 82). Ever since the IACtHR has reiterated this important *obiter dictum*, which is now integrated into its *jurisprudence constante*.[66] The significance of this jurisprudential development of the IACtHR has been stressed in an earlier chapter,[67] together with its positive impact on the improvement of administration of justice at national level.

Attention has recently and reassuringly been drawn to the rule of law at both national and international levels. Thus, at the U.N. 2005 World Summit, and subsequently, attention has been focused on the need to strengthen the rule of law at national and international levels.[68] Shortly after the adoption of the document *World Summit Outcome* (2005), it was pointed out to the U.N. Secretary General that the international and national dimensions of the rule of law were 'strongly interlinked', and that 'the strengthening of the rule of law at the international level thus had a direct impact on the rule of law at national level'.[69] As a follow-up to the commitment to that end given at the U.N. World Summit, the subject was taken up for further consideration, in 2006, by the VI Committee of the U.N. General Assembly.

This latter recommended, in its turn, on 17 November 2006, a 'solemn commitment to an international legal order based on the rule of law and international law', bearing in mind the 'indivisible core values and principles of the United Nations'.[70] The U.N. General Assembly, on its part, endorsed the recommendation of its VI Committee, in its resolution on 'The Rule of Law at the National and International Levels', adopted on 18 December 2006.[71] The fact that the subject has been taken up at the highest level by the United Nations seems to disclose a new consciousness of the pressing need to secure the preservation and strengthening of the rule of law at national and international levels. In this domain, the right of direct access to justice at national and international levels has a key role to play.

Pursuant to the U.N. General Assembly resolution 61/39, of 2006, the U.N. Secretary General presented an interim report, circulated on 15 August 2007, on '*The Rule of Law at the National and International Levels*', containing a survey of current activities of the organs, bodies, offices, departments, funds and programmes within the U.N. system devoted to the promotion of the rule of law at the national and international levels, for consideration of the U.N. General Assembly. The survey covered, *inter alia*, assistance in the domestic implementation of international law, and administration of justice and law enforcement.[72]

Furthermore, the U.N. Secretary General presented another report, on 11 July 2007, also on '*The Rule of Law at the National and International Levels*', on the

---

[66] Cf. A.A. Cançado Trindade, 'Thoughts on Recent Developments in the Case-Law of the Inter-American Court of Human Rights: Selected Aspects', in *Proceedings of the 92nd Annual Meeting of the American Society of International Law – The Challenge of Non-State Actors*, Washington D.C., American Society of International Law, 1998, pp. 192–201.

[67] Cf. chapter II, section II, *supra*.

[68] U.N., G.A. resolution 60(1), of 2005.

[69] Annex to the letter from Liechtenstein and Mexico to the U.N. Secretary General, of 11 May 2006, U.N. doc. A/61/142, par. 2, and cf. par. 4.

[70] U.N., *Report of the VI Committee*, U.N. doc. A/61/456, of 17 November 2006, p. 3, par. 9.

[71] U.N., G.A. resolution 61/39, of 18 December 2006, pars. 1–5.

[72] Cf. U.N. document A/62/261, of 15 August 2007, pp. 1–12.

comments and information received from governments on the subject at issue.[73] Attention was drawn, *inter alia*, to the broad concept of rule of law, encompassing also the subjects of rights,[74] the *justiciables*. It is significant that the subject has indeed gathered growing attention at the U.N., in a clear sign of the awakening of conscience as to its importance in our times. This can clearly be seen in converging comments made by Delegations of countries from different continents and distinct cultural backgrounds on the matter under consideration.[75]

Humankind has undergone indescribable sufferings until attaining the degree of human consciousness that nowadays warns that the *raison d'État* has its limits.[76] The State was originally conceived for the realization of the common good, and exists for the human being, and not *vice-versa*. In the struggle against grave and systematic violations of universal human rights, the recognition, for example, of the principle of universal jurisdiction, as well as the exercise of the collective guarantee exercised by the States Parties to human rights treaties, assert themselves in our days. This evolution ought to be appreciated in its wide dimension.

In reaction to the successive atrocities which, throughout the XXth century, victimized millions and millions of human beings, on a scale hereto unknown in the history of mankind, the *universal juridical conscience* has emerged, with vigour, as the ultimate *material source* of all Law – restoring to the human being his condition of subject of both domestic as well as international law, and final addressee of all juridical norms, of both national and international origin. Hence the emergence of higher considerations of *ordre public*, reflected, at normative level, in the conceptions of the imperative norms of general international law (*jus cogens*), and of the non-derogable fundamental rights, and, at procedural level, in the conception of the obligations *erga omnes* of protection (due to the international community as a whole).

By means of this evolution, human beings are benefitted, and International Law is enriched and justified, freeing itself from the chains of Statism, and meeting its original vocation, that of a true *jus gentium* (*droit des gens*), which, in its early beginnings, inspired its formation and historical development. This new trend of International Law has been guided, to a large extent, by the impact, in the last decades, of what has been conceived as the International Law of Human Rights. The consolidation and expansion of this latter – essentially victim-oriented – disclose the new *ethos* of our times: that of the emerging primacy – hopefully a definitive one – of the *raison d'humanité* over the old *raison d'État*.[77]

---

[73] Cf. U.N. document A/62/121, of 11 July 2007, pp. 1–35.

[74] Statement by Mexico, in ibid., pp. 24–7.

[75] Some of them expressly recalled and endorsed the commitment of the 2005 World Summit Outcome document to the rule of law at national and international levels.

[76] A.A. Cançado Trindade, 'La Humanización del Derecho Internacional y los Límites de la Razón de Estado', 40 *Revista da Faculdade de Direito da Universidade Federal de Minas Gerais* – Belo Horizonte/Brazil (2001) pp. 11–23.

[77] Cf. A.A. Cançado Trindade, 'International Law for Humankind: Towards a New *Jus Gentium* – General Course on Public International Law – Part I', 316 *Recueil des Cours de l'Académie de Droit International de la Haye* (2005) pp. pp. 31–439; A.A. Cançado Trindade, 'International Law for Humankind: Towards a New *Jus Gentium* – General Course on Public International Law – Part II', 317 *Recueil des Cours de l'Académie de Droit International de la Haye* (2005) pp. 19–312.

Conclusions

Contemporary international law has, over more than half a century, rescued the international juridical subjectivity of the human being. It has restored to the human person the place that is hers in the international legal order, as foreseen by the so-called founding fathers of the law of nations (the *droit des gens*)[1]. International law has freed itself from the chains of statism, and the human person has emancipated herself from her own State, with the acknowledgement of her rights, which are prior and superior to this latter. In this framework of the historical process of *humanization* of international law, the *raison d'humanité* has come to prevail over the old *raison d'État*. The individual's international legal personality emerges as a definitive and irreversible achievement of international legal thinking in the last decades.

Parallel to the impressive doctrinal developments to this effect, stands the equally significant historical evolution, in practice, of the right of individual petition at international level. This right secures nowadays the direct access of individuals to contemporary international human rights tribunals.[2] The right of individual petition, which has given rise to a remarkable jurisprudential development in the last few decades, is a cornerstone of the international protection of human rights. The current passage from the individuals' *locus standi in judicio* to their *jus standi* before international human rights tribunals bears witness to the individuals' full juridico-procedural capacity at the international level, in the vindication of their rights.

The international case-law (of the European and Inter-American Courts of Human Rights) of emancipation of individuals from their own State comes to approach the conditions of admissibility of petitions without losing sight of the pressing need to secure their access to international justice. That case-law converges into the acknowledgment of the right to an effective domestic remedy as a basic pillar of the rule of law in a democratic society, and stresses the intangibility of judicial guarantees in all circumstances. We are here before a *law of protection (droit de protection)* of the human person, the International Law of Human Rights being essentially *victim-oriented*.

That gradually evolving case-law of protection has duly underlined the interrelation between the access to justice (right to an effective remedy) and the guarantees

---

[1] On this historical development, cf. A.A. Cançado Trindade, *Évolution du Droit international au droit des gens*, Paris, Pédone, 2008, pp. 1–188.

[2] The European and Inter-American Courts of Human Rights, and the African Court of Human and Peoples' Rights.

of the due process of law, which is borne out in the *jurisprudence constante* of the Inter-American Court of Human Rights. The European Court of Human Rights, which has a vast case-law on the latter, has in recent years been devoting growing attention to the former. From this emerges the correct understanding of the right of access to justice *lato sensu*, comprising not only the right to initiate proceedings before international human rights tribunals, but also the aforementioned guarantees of the due process of law, and the right to due protection by means of the faithful compliance with, or execution of, the judicial decisions at issue.

This brings to the fore the interaction between international law and domestic law in the present domain of protection. Human rights treaties confer upon national tribunals a relevant role in safeguarding internationally-recognized rights. Conventional obligations of protection are incumbent upon all powers (executive, legislative and judiciary), organs and agents of the States Parties. These latter are under the duty to provide effective domestic remedies. The *rationale* of the local remedies rule, as a prerequisite of the admissibility of international petitions, is to lay emphasis on *redress*, rather than on the process of exhaustion of those remedies.[3]

The interaction between international law and domestic law in the present context can be ascertained also from other angles. Contemporary doctrine and international case-law have lately drawn attention to the needed revision or control of reservations to human rights treaties endowed with judicial supervisory organs[4] of their own. In the domain of contemporary international criminal law, another illustration is provided by the principle of complementarity. The international subjectivity of individuals thus comes to the fore in both its active as well as its passive dimensions.

The plea of the subsidiary nature of the international enforcement machinery set up by human rights treaties is to be properly understood as pertaining to procedural, and not substantive, law. In so far as this latter is concerned, it is to be kept in mind that the *corpus juris* of international human rights law is meant to improve, by means of its interaction with domestic law, the national systems of judicial protection. Domestic remedies integrate the procedures of international protection, and international law and domestic public law operate together, sharing the same common purpose of providing effective protection to all human beings subject to the jurisdiction of the States concerned.

The ineluctable counterpart of the right of international individual petition is the integrity of international jurisdiction. Its preservation has been the concern of international tribunals such as the Inter-American and the European Courts of Human Rights, which, faced at times with challenges from one State Party or another, have upheld the intangibility of their international jurisdiction, and have thus set limits to manifestations of State voluntarism. In this way, the Inter-American and the European Courts have safeguarded ultimately the access to

---

[3] To this effect, A.A. Cançado Trindade, *The Application of the Rule of Exhaustion of Local Remedies in International Law*, Cambridge, Cambridge University Press, 1983, pp. 1–445.

[4] Namely, the European Court of Human Rights, the Inter-American Court of Human Rights, and the African Court of Human and Peoples' Rights.

justice of the human person at international level, on the basis of the primacy of considerations of *ordre public*, thus creating higher standards of State behaviour.

The European Court's decision in the *Loizidou versus Turkey* case (Preliminary Objection, 1995) is often recalled in that connection, and the Inter-American Court's decisions on jurisdiction in the *Constitutional Tribunal* and *Ivcher Bronstein versus Peru* cases (1999) – followed by its decision in the *Hilaire, Benjamin, Constantine and Others versus Trinidad and Tobago* case (Preliminary Objections, 2001) – are indeed of historical relevance, as turning-points in the evolution of the international protection of human rights. The current trend towards the enhancement of international compulsory jurisdiction is reassuring. The acknowledgement of the right of individual petition and the integrity of international jurisdiction as ineluctable counterparts have, as ultimate beneficiary, the human person, as a subject of international law.

The notion of *victim* itself, particularly under the petitioning systems that require that condition as *legitimatio ad causam* for the exercise of the right of petition, has undergone a significant evolution in recent years, of relevance also for reparations. International human rights law has restored the *victim* to his or her central position in the normative order. The notion of 'potential victim' discloses the preventive dimension of human rights protection. The notion of victim acquires a central position also in the operation of mechanisms of protection, which were devised and adopted in order to protect his or her rights, and to afford the victim appropriate redress.

We have reached a stage in the evolution of international human rights law wherein human beings, in situations of the utmost adversity, or even defencelessness, have notwithstanding had access to international justice. The right of individual petition has also been effectively made use of in such situations – something that could hardly have been anticipated, in their days, by the draftsmen of international human rights treaties and instruments endowed with petitioning systems.

Contemporary international case-law contains eloquent illustrations of such access to international justice amidst great adversity and vulnerability, in cases concerning, for example, undocumented migrants, children abandoned in streets, members of peace communities and other civilians in situations of armed conflict, internally displaced persons, individuals (including minors of age) under subhuman conditions of detention, members of dispossessed indigenous communities, among others. In such cases, the centrality of the suffering of the victims became notorious with their access to justice at international level.

In the light of the experience on the matter accumulated thus far, *the centrality is precisely that of the victim, not of the State*. This can hardly be surprising, considering that international human rights law is surely *victim-oriented*. The extension of protection to persons living, or rather surviving, in situations of extreme vulnerability or adversity, is ultimately linked to the awakening of human conscience as to the imperatives of their protection. It is in such extreme circumstances that the international protection of human rights appears to attain its plenitude.

Thus, massacres and crimes of State, which a few decades ago tended to fall into oblivion, have lately been brought to the cognizance of international human rights tribunals (such as the Inter-American and the European Courts), in order to determine State responsibility (under the respective regional Conventions) for grave breaches of human rights protected thereunder. New developments have here lately taken place, in the international legal procedures, such as those relating to the determination of the aggravated responsibility of the States concerned, and to the identification of the victims at distinct stages of the procedure.

In such cases of massacres, perpetrated by State agents as part of a State policy, the facts disclosed have proven the occurrence of true crimes of State. Once again, one can here verify the centrality and expansion of the notion of direct victim, and the relevance of the victims' right to redress. It is highly significant that, nowadays, surviving victims of massacres, and relatives of fatal victims, have had access to international justice.

In fact, international human rights tribunals – such as the Inter-American and the European Courts of Human Rights – have overcome obstacles to the individual petitioners' direct access to justice. The Inter-American Court was the first contemporary international tribunal to quash a self-amnesty law, in its historical Judgment of 14 March 2001 in the case of the massacre of *Barrios Altos*, concerning Peru, thus paving the way for its jurisprudential construction on the matter. This latter has stressed the imperative of access to justice, conforming a true *right to the Law* (*droit au Droit/derecho al Derecho*).

The Inter-American Court has, furthermore, expressly acknowledged the gradual expansion of the material content of *jus cogens*, encompassing the absolute prohibition of all forms of torture (and any other cruel, inhuman or degrading treatment), the basic principle of equality and non-discrimination, and, indeed, the right of access to justice. Without this latter, there is no legal system at all. We are before a humanized public order, or even a truly humanist one, enshrining common superior values. This reassuring evolution is ultimately due to the awakening of the universal juridical conscience (as the ultimate material source of all Law), freeing international law from the chains of statism, and heralding the advent of a new *jus gentium*, in this first decade of the XXIst century.

Select Bibliography

I. BOOKS

Accioly, H., *Tratado de Direito Internacional Público*, vol. I, 1st. ed., Rio de Janeiro, Imprensa Nacional, 1933.

Aggelen, J.G.C. van, *Le rôle des organisations internationales dans la protection du droit à la vie*, Bruxelles, E. Story-Scientia, 1986.

Álvarez, A., *La Reconstrucción del Derecho de Gentes – El Nuevo Orden y la Renovación Social*, Santiago de Chile, Ed. Nascimento, 1944.

Améry, J., *At the Mind's Limits*, Bloomington, Indiana Univ. Press, 1980.

Anzilotti, D., *Corso di Diritto Internazionale*, 3rd. ed., vol. I, Padova, Cedam, 1955.

Aragonés Castañer, A.M., *Migración Internacional de Trabajadores – Una Perspectiva Histórica*, Mexico, Edit. Plaza y Valdés, 2004 [reimpr.].

Arangio-Ruiz, G., *Diritto Internazionale e Personalità Giuridica*, Bologna, Coop. Libr. Univ., 1972.

Arendt, H., *La tradition cachée*, Paris, Ch. Bourgois Ed., 1987 (orig. ed. 1946).

Arnaud, A.-J., *et alii* (dir.), *Dictionnaire encyclopédique de théorie et de sociologie du Droit*, 2nd. ed., Paris, LGDJ, 1993.

Azcárate, P. de, *League of Nations and National Minorities: An Experiment*, Washington, Carnegie Endowment for International Peace, 1945.

Bassiouni, M.Ch., *Crimes against Humanity in International Criminal Law*, 2nd. rev. ed., The Hague, Kluwer, 1999.

Beauté, J., *Le droit de pétition dans les territoires sous tutelle*, Paris, LGDJ, 1962.

Bensoussan, G., *Europe – Une passion génocidaire*, Paris, Éd. Mille et Une Nuits, 2006.

Bentwich, N., *The Mandates System*, London, Longmans, 1930.

Bergalli, R. (coord.), *Flujos Migratorios y Su (Des)control*, Barcelona, OSPDH/Anthropos Edit., 2006.

Bernstein, R.J., *El Mal Radical – Una Indagación Filosófica*, Buenos Aires, Lilmod, 2005.

Berry, J.A., and Berry, C.P. (eds.), *Genocide in Rwanda – A Collective Memory*, Washington D.C., Harvard University Press, 1999.

Bettati, M., and Dupuy, P.-M., *Les O.N.G. et le Droit international*, Paris, Economica, 1986.

Bordes-Benayoun, C., and Schnapper, D., *Diasporas et nations*, Paris, O. Jacob Ed., 2006.

Bottigliero, I., *Redress for Victims of Crimes under International Law*, Leiden, Nijhoff, 2004.

Bruneteau, B., *Le siècle des génocides*, Paris, A. Colin, 2004.

Cançado Trindade, A.A., *Tratado de Direito Internacional dos Direitos Humanos*, vol. I, 2nd. ed., Porto Alegre/Brazil, S.A. Fabris Ed., 2003; and vol. II, 1999; and vol. III, 2003.

Cançado Trindade, A.A., *The Application of the Rule of Exhaustion of Local Remedies in International Law*, Cambridge, Cambridge University Press, 1983.

Cançado Trindade, A.A., *Developments in the Rule of Exhaustion of Local Remedies in International Law*, 2 vols., Cambridge, University of Cambridge, 1977, pp. 1–1728 (Ph.D. thesis deposited at Cambridge University Library).

Cançado Trindade, A.A., *O Esgotamento de Recursos Internos no Direito Internacional*, 2nd. ed., Brasília, Edit. University of Brasília, 1997.

Cançado Trindade, A.A., *El Acceso Directo del Individuo a los Tribunales Internacionales de Derechos Humanos*, Bilbao, University of Deusto, 2001.

Cançado Trindade, A.A., *El Derecho Internacional de los Derechos Humanos en el Siglo XXI*, 2nd. ed., Santiago, Editorial Jurídica de Chile, 2006.

Cançado Trindade, A.A., *Derecho Internacional de los Derechos Humanos – Esencia y Trascendencia (Votos en la Corte Interamericana de Derechos Humanos, 1991–2006)*, México, Edit. Porrúa/Universidad Iberoamericana, 2007.

Cançado Trindade, A.A., *Évolution du Droit international au droit des gens*, Paris, Pédone, 2008.

Cançado Trindade, A.A., *Bases para un Proyecto de Protocolo a la Convención Americana sobre Derechos Humanos, para Fortalecer Su Mecanismo de Protección*, vol. II, 2nd. ed., San José of Costa Rica, Inter-American Court of Human Rights, 2003.

Cançado Trindade, A.A., *A Humanização do Direito Internacional*, Belo Horizonte/Brazil, Edit. Del Rey, 2006.

Cançado Trindade, A.A., *O Direito Internacional em um Mundo em Transformação*, Rio de Janeiro, Ed. Renovar, 2002.

Cançado Trindade, A.A, *Direito das Organizações Internacionais*, 3rd. ed., Belo Horizonte/ Brazil, Edit. Del Rey, 2003.

Carrillo Salcedo, J.A., *Dignidad frente a Barbarie – La Declaración Universal de Derechos Humanos, Cincuenta Años Después, Madrid*, Ed. Trotta, 1999.

Casa Alianza, *Los Pequeños Mártires...*, San José of Costa Rica, Casa Alianza/A.L., 2004.

Cassese, A., *International Law*, Oxford, University Press, 2001.

Cassese, A., *International Criminal Law*, Oxford, University Press, 2003.

Cassese, A., *Inhuman States – Imprisonment, Detention and Torture in Europe Today*, Cambridge, Polity Press, 1996.

Cassese, A., and Delmas-Marty, M. (eds.), *Crimes internationaux et juridictions internationales*, Paris, PUF, 2002.

Castles S., and Kosack, G., *Los Trabajadores Inmigrantes y la Estructura de Clases en Europa Occidental*, Mexico, FCE, 1984.

CEJIL, *Crianças e Adolescentes – Jurisprudência da Corte Interamericana de Direitos Humanos*, Rio de Janeiro, CEJIL/Brazil, 2003.

Cholewinski, R., *Migrant Workers in International Human Rights Law – Their Protection in Countries of Employment*, Oxford, Clarendon Press, 1997.

Cohen-Jonathan, G., *La Convention européenne des droits de l'homme*, Aix-en-Provence/ Paris, Presses Universitaires d'Aix-Marseille/Economica, 1989.

Crépeau, F., *Droit d'asile – De l'hospitalité aux contrôles migratoires*, Bruxelles, Bruylant/Éd. Université de Bruxelles, 1995.

Dekeuwer-Défossez, F., *Les droits de l'enfant*, 5th. ed., Paris, PUF, 2001.

Deng, F.M., *Protecting the Dispossessed – A Challenge for the International Community*, Washington D.C., Brookings Institution, 1993.

Drost, P.N., *Human Rights as Legal Rights*, Leyden, Sijthoff, 1965.

Drzemczewski, A.Z., *European Human Rights Convention in Domestic Law*, Oxford, Clarendon Press, 1983.

Eide, E., *et alii*, *The Universal Declaration of Human Rights – A Commentary*, Oslo, Scandinavian University Press, 1992.

El Kouhene, M., *Les garanties fondamentales de la personne en Droit humanitaire et droits de l'homme*, Dordrecht, Nijhoff, 1986.

El Zeidy, M.M., *The Principle of Complementarity in International Criminal Law: Origin, Development and Practice*, Leiden, Nijhoff, 2008, pp. 59–154.

Falk, R.A., *The Role of Domestic Courts in the International Legal Order*, Syracuse, University Press, 1964.

Fawcett, J.E.S., *The Application of the European Convention on Human Rights*, Oxford, Clarendon Press, 1969.

Fawcett, J.E.S., *The Law of Nations*, 2nd. ed., Penguin Books, London, Middlesex/England, 1971.

Fourteau, H., *L'application de l'article 3 de la Convention Européenne des Droits de l'Homme dans le droit interne des États membres*, Paris, LGDJ, 1996.

Gómez Isa, F. (ed.), *El Caso Awas Tingni contra Nicarágua: Nuevos Horizontes para los Derechos de los Pueblos Indígenas*, Bilbao, University of Deusto, 2003.

Harris, D.J., O'Boyle, M., and Warbrick, C., *Law of the European Convention on Human Rights*, London, Butterworths, 1995.

Herik, L.J. van den, *The Contribution of the Rwanda Tribunal to the Development of International Law*, Leiden, Nijhoff, 2005.

Heyns, C., and Killander, M. (eds.), *Compendium of Key Human Rights Documents of the African Union*, 3rd. ed., Pretoria, University Law Press (PULP), 2007.

Hing, B.O., *Deporting Our Souls – Values, Morality and Immigration Policy*, Cambridge, University Press, 2006.

Kälin, W., *Guiding Principles on Internal Displacement – Annotations*, Washington D.C., ASIL/Brookings Institution, 2000.

Kleffner, J.K., *Complementarity in the Rome Statute and National Criminal Jurisdictions*, Oxford, University Press, 2008.

Lescure, K., *Le Tribunal Pénal International pour l'ex-Yougoslavie*, Paris, Montchrestien, 1994.

Jacobs, F.G., *The Sovereignty of Law – The European Way, Cambridge*, University Press, 2007.

Jessup, Ph.C., *A Modern Law of Nations – An Introduction*, New York, MacMillan Co., 1948.

Jiménez de Aréchaga, E., *El Derecho Internacional Contemporáneo*, Madrid, Tecnos, 1980.

Lador-Lederer, J.J., *International Group Protection*, Leyden, Sijthoff, 1968.

Lambert, E., *Les effets des arrêts de la Cour Européenne des Droits de l'Homme*, Bruxelles, Bruylant, 1999.

Landrove Díaz, G., *Victimología*, Valencia, Tirant Lo Blanch, 1990.

Lauterpacht, H., *International Law and Human Rights*, London, Stevens, 1950.

Lauterpacht, H., *The Development of International Law by the International Court*, London, Stevens, 1958.

Lengellé-Tardy, M., *L'esclavage moderne*, Paris, PUF, 1999.

Levi, Primo, *The Drowned and the Saved*, N.Y., Vintage, 1989 [reprint].

Lippolis, L., *Dai Diritti dell'Uomo ai Diritti dell'Umanità*, Milano, Giuffrè, 2002.

Mandelstam, A.N., *Les droits internationaux de l'homme*, Paris, Éds. Internationales, 1931.

McNair, Lord, *Selected Papers and Bibliography*, Leiden/N.Y., Sijthoff/Oceana, 1974.

Meijknecht, A., *Towards International Personality: The Position of Minorities and Indigenous Peoples in International Law*, Antwerpen/Groningen, Intersentia, 2001.

Merrills, J.G., *The Development of International Law by the European Court of Human Rights*, 2nd. ed., Manchester, University Press, 1993.

Mertens, P., *Le droit de recours effectif devant les instances nationales en cas de violation d'un droit de l'homme*, Bruxelles, Éd. de l'Univ. de Bruxelles, 1973.

Milano, L., *Le droit à un tribunal au sens de la Convention Européenne des Droits de l'Homme*, Paris, Dalloz, 2006.

Murdoch, J., *The Treatment of Prisoners – European Standards*, Strasbourg, Council of Europe, 2006.

Murray, R., *The African Commission on Human and Peoples' Rights and International Law*, Oxford/Portland, Hart Publ., 2000.

Neuman, E., *Victimología – El Rol de la Víctima en los Delitos Convencionales y No Convencionales*, Buenos Aires, Edit. Universidad, 1994.

Norgaard, C.A., *The Position of the Individual in International Law*, Copenhagen, Munksgaard, 1962.

Nowak, M., *U.N. Covenant on Civil and Political Rights – CCPR Commentary*, Kehl/Strasbourg, N.P. Engel, 1993.

Nowak, M. (ed.), *World Conference on Human Rights (Vienna, June 1993) – The Contribution of NGOs, Reports and Documents*, Wien, Manzsche Verlags- und Universitätsbuchhandlung, 1994.

Ogata, S., *The Turbulent Decade – Confronting the Refugee Crises of the 1990s*, N.Y./London, Norton, 2005.

Ortega, M., *El Acceso de los Particulares a la Justicia Comunitaria*, Barcelona, Ed. Ariel, 1999.

Österdahl, I., *Implementing Human Rights in Africa – The African Commission on Human and Peoples' Rights and Individual Communications*, Uppsala, Iustus Förlag, 2002.

Ouguergouz, F., *The African Charter on Human and Peoples' Rights*, The Hague, Nijhoff, 2003.

Petit de Gabriel, E.W., *Las Exigencias de Humanidad en el Derecho Internacional Tradicional (1789–1939)*, Madrid, Tecnos, 2003.

Phuong, C., *The International Protection of Internally Displaced Persons*, Cambridge, University Press, 2004.

Razesberger, F., *The International Criminal Court – The Principle of Complementarity*, Frankfurt am Main, P. Lang, 2006.

Reuter, P., *Droit international public*, 7th. ed., Paris, PUF, 1993.

Reydams, L., *Universal Jurisdiction – International and Municipal Legal Perspectives*, Oxford, University Press, 2004.

Rodley, N.S., *The Treatment of Prisoners under International Law*, 2nd. ed., Oxford, Univ. Press, 2000 [reprint].

Rodríguez Manzanera, L., *Victimología – Estudio de la Víctima*, 8th. ed., Mexico, Edit. Porrúa, 2003.

Röling, B.V.A., *International Law in an Expanded World*, Amsterdam, Djambatan, 1960.

Salado Osuna, A., *Los Casos Peruanos ante la Corte Interamericana de Derechos Humanos*, Trujillo/Perú, Edit. Normas Legales, 2004.

Salvia, M. de, *Compendium de la CEDH – Les principes directeurs de la jurisprudence relative à la Convention européenne des droits de l'homme*, Kehl/Strasbourg, Ed. Engel, 1998.

Santi Romano, *L'ordre juridique*, Paris, Dalloz, 2002 [reimpr.].

Santulli, C., *Le statut international de l'ordre juridique interne – Étude du traitement du droit interne par le droit international*, Paris, Pédone, 2001.

Scalabrino, M., *Per Non Dimenticare – Violazioni dei Diritti Umani e Leggi di Amnistia in America Latina*, Milano, Vita e Pensiero (V&P), 2007.

Scelle, G., *Précis de Droit des Gens – Principes et systématique*, part I, Paris, Libr. Rec. Sirey, 1932 (CNRS reprint, 1984).

Scelle, G., *Précis de Droit des Gens – principes et systématique*, part II, Paris, Rec. Sirey, 1934 [reed. 1984 by CNRS].

Ségur, Ph., *La crise du droit d'asile*, Paris, PUF, 1998.

Serrano, J.E., *La Acción Humanitaria en Colombia desde la Perspectiva del Restablecimiento*, Bilbao, University of Deusto, 2004.

Sperduti, G., *L'Individuo nel Diritto Internazionale*, Milano, Giuffrè Ed., 1950.

Spielmann, A., *Au diapason des droits de l'homme – Écrits choisis (1975–2003)*, Bruxelles, Bruylant, 2006.

Spielmann, D., *L'effet potentiel de la Convention Européenne des Droits de l'Homme entre personnes privées*, Bruxelles, Bruylant, 1995.

Staub, E., *The Roots of Evil – The Origins of Genocide and Other Group Violence*, Cambridge, University Press, 2005 [reprint].

Stigen, J., *The Relationship between the International Criminal Court and National Jurisdictions – The Principle of Complementarity*, Leiden, Nijhoff, 2008.

Stone, J., *International Guarantees of Minorities Rights*, Oxford, University Press, 1932.

Ternon, Y., *Guerres et génocides au XXe. siècle*, Paris, O. Jacob, 2007.

Thornberry, P., *International Law and the Rights of Minorities*, Oxford, Clarendon Press, 1992 [reprint].

Todd, E., *El Destino de los Inmigrantes – Asimilación y Segregación en las Democracias Occidentales* (transl. of *Le destin des immigrés – Assimilation et ségrégation dans les démocraties occidentales*), Barcelona, Tusquet Edit., 1996.

Tomuschat, C., *Human Rights – Between Idealism and Realism*, Oxford, University Press, 2003.

Toussaint, C.E., *The Trusteeship System of the United Nations*, London, Stevens, 1956.

UNESCO, *Los Derechos del Hombre – Estudios y Comentarios en torno a la Nueva Declaración Universal*, Mexico/ Buenos Aires, Fondo de Cultura Económica, 1949.

Valentino, B.A., *Final Solutions: Mass Killing and Genocide in the Twentieth Century*, Ithaca/ London, Cornell Univ. Press, 2004.

Vandenhole, W., *Non-Discrimination and Equality in the View of the U.N. Human Rights Treaty Bodies*, Antwerpen/Oxford, Intersentia, 2005.

Van Hear, N., *New Diasporas – The Mass Exodus, Dispersal and Regrouping of Migrant Communities*, London, UCL Press, 1998.

Various Authors, *Le contrôle des conditions de détention dans les prisons d'Europe* (Actes du Colloque de Marly-le-Roi, France, de 1996), Paris, CCE, 1997.

[Various Authors,] *La détention en isolement dans les prisons européennes* (eds. M. Zingoni-Fernández and N. Giovannini), Bruxelles, Bruylant, 2004.

[Various Authors,] *La juridictionnalisation du Droit international* (SFDI, Colloque de Lille de 2002), Paris, Pedone, 2003.

[Various Authors,] *La Criminalización de la Barbarie: La Corte Penal Internacional* (ed. J.A. Carrillo Salcedo), Madrid, Consejo General del Poder Judicial, 2000.

[Various Authors,] *Visions of the Future of Social Justice – Essays on the Occasion of the ILO's 75th Anniversary*, Geneva, International Labour Office, 1994.

[Various Authors,] *La nouvelle procédure devant la Cour européenne des droits de l'homme après le Protocole n. 14* (ed. F. Salerno), Bruxelles, Bruylant, 2007.

[Various Authors,] *La Criminalización de la Barbarie: La Corte Penal Internacional* (ed. J.A. Carrillo Salcedo), Madrid, Consejo General del Poder Judicial, 2000.

[Various Authors,] *The Universal Declaration of Human Rights: Fifty Years and Beyond* (eds. Y. Danieli, E. Stamatopoulou and C.J. Dias), N.Y., U.N./Baywood Publ. Co., 1999.

[Various Authors,] *Les nouveaux développements du procès équitable au sens de la Convention Européenne des Droits de l'Homme* (Actes du Colloque de 1996), Bruxelles, Bruylant, 1996.

[Various Authors,] *The Right to Life in International Law* (ed. B.G. Ramcharan), Dordrecht, Nijhoff, 1985.

[Various Authors,] *Actes du Symposium sur le droit à la vie – Quarante ans après l'adoption de la Déclaration Universelle des Droits de l'Homme: évolution conceptuelle, normative et jurisprudentielle* (eds. D. Prémont and F. Montant), Geneva, CID, 1992.

Vasak, K., *La Convention européenne des droits de l'homme*, Paris, LGDJ, 1964.

Vasak, K., and Alston, Ph. (eds.), *The International Dimensions of Human Rights*, vol. I, Paris, UNESCO/Greenwood Press, 1982; and vol. II, 1982.

Verdoodt, A., *Naissance et signification de la Déclaration Universelle des Droits de l'Homme*, Louvain/Paris, Éd. Nauwelaerts, [1963].

Viljoen, F., *International Human Rights Law in Africa*, Oxford, Univ. Press, 2007.

Villalpando, W., *De los Derechos Humanos al Derecho Internacional Penal*, Buenos Aires, Ed. Abeledo-Perrot, 2000.

Weil, S., *The Need for Roots*, London/N.Y., Routledge, 1952 [reprint].

Wiesel, E., *O Tempo dos Desenraizados* (*Le temps des déracinés*, 2003), Rio de Janeiro, Edit. Record, 2004.

Wilfred Jenks, C., *Social Justice in the Law of Nations – The ILO Impact After Fifty Years*, Oxford, University Press, 1970.

Wright, Quincy, *Mandates under the League of Nations*, Chicago, University Press, 1930.

Youf, D., *Penser les droits de l'enfant*, Paris, PUF, 2002.

Zuppi, A.L., *Jurisdicción Universal para Crímenes contra el Derecho Internacional*, Buenos Aires, Ed. Ad-Hoc, 2002.

Zwart, T., *The Admissibility of Human Rights Petitions*, Dordrecht, Nijhoff, 1994.

II. COURSES, COLLECTIONS, CONTRIBUTIONS TO BOOKS

Alkema, E.A., 'Access to Justice under the ECHR and Judicial Policy – A Netherlands View', in *Afmaelisrit pór Vilhjálmsson*, Reykjavík, Bókaútgafa Orators, 2000, pp. 21–37.

Barberis, J.A., 'Nouvelles questions concernant la personnalité juridique internationale', 179 *Recueil des Cours de l'Académie de Droit International de La Haye* (1983) pp. 157–238.

Binder, C., 'The Case of the Atlantic Coast of Nicaragua: The *Awas Tingni* Case', in *International Law and Indigenous Peoples* (eds. J. Castellino and N. Walsh), Leiden, Nijhoff/R. Wallenberg Institute, 2005, pp. 249–67.

Bitti, G., and González Rivas, G., 'The Reparations Provisions for Victims under the Rome Statute of the International Criminal Court', in *Redressing Injustices Through Mass Claims Processes* (ed. Permanent Court of Arbitration), Oxford, University Press, 2006, pp. 303–4.

Bruyn, D. de, 'Le droit à un recours effectif', in *Les droits de l'homme au seuil du troisième millénaire – Mélanges en hommage à P. Lambert*, Bruxelles, Bruylant, 2000, pp. 198–203.

Caflisch, L., and Cançado Trindade, A.A., 'Les Conventions Américaine et Européenne des Droits de l'Homme et le droit international général', 108 *Revue générale de Droit international public* (2004), pp. 5–62.

Cançado Trindade, A.A., 'International Law for Humankind: Towards a New *Jus Gentium* – General Course on Public International Law – Part I', 316 *Recueil des Cours de l'Académie de Droit International de la Haye* (2005), pp. 31–439.

Cançado Trindade, A.A., 'International Law for Humankind: Towards a New *Jus Gentium* – General Course on Public International Law – Part II', 317 *Recueil des Cours de l'Académie de Droit International de la Haye* (2005), pp. 19–312.

Cançado Trindade, A.A., 'Co-existence and Co-ordination of Mechanisms of International Protection of Human Rights (At Global and Regional Levels)', 202 *Recueil des Cours de l'Académie de Droit International de La Haye* (1987), pp. 32–412.

Cançado Trindade, A.A., 'Derecho Internacional de los Derechos Humanos, Derecho Internacional de los Refugiados y Derecho Internacional Humanitario: Aproximaciones y Convergencias', in *10 Años de la Declaración de Cartagena sobre Refugiados – Declaración de San José sobre Refugiados y Personas Desplazadas 1994* (Memoria del Coloquio Internacional de San José de Costa Rica de 1994), San José of Costa Rica, UNHCR/ IIHR, 1995, pp. 77–168.

Cançado Trindade, A.A., 'Aproximaciones y Convergencias Revisitadas: Diez Años de Interacción entre el Derecho Internacional de los Derechos Humanos, el Derecho Internacional de los Refugiados, y el Derecho Internacional Humanitario (De Cartagena/1984 a San José/1994 y México/2004)', in *Memoria del Vigésimo Aniversario de la Declaración de Cartagena sobre Refugiados (1984–2004)*, San José of Costa Rica, UNHCR, 2005, pp. 139–91.

Cançado Trindade, A.A., 'Complementarity between State Responsibility and Individual Responsibility for Grave Violations of Human Rights: The Crime of State Revisited', in *International Responsibility Today – Essays in Memory of O. Schachter* (ed. M. Ragazzi), Leiden, M. Nijhoff, 2005, pp. 253–69.

Cançado Trindade, A.A., 'Responsabilidad, Perdón y Justicia como Manifestaciones de la Conciencia Jurídica Universal', 8 *Revista de Estudios Socio-Jurídicos* – Universidad del Rosario/Bogotá (2006), n. 1, pp. 15–36.

Cançado Trindade, A.A., 'The International Law of Human Rights at the Dawn of the XXIst Century', 3 *Cursos Euromediterráneos Bancaja de Derecho Internacional* – Castellón/ Spain (1999), pp. 186–207.

Cançado Trindade, A.A., 'The Procedural Capacity of the Individual as Subject of International Human Rights Law: Recent Developments', in *Les droits de l'homme à l'aube du XXIe. siècle – K. Vasak Amicorum Liber*, Bruxelles, Bruylant, 1999, pp. 521–44.

Cançado Trindade, A.A., 'Las Cláusulas Pétreas de la Protección Internacional del Ser Humano: El Acceso Directo de los Individuos a la Justicia a Nivel Internacional y la Intangibilidad de la Jurisdicción Obligatoria de los Tribunales Internacionales de Derechos Humanos', *El Sistema Interamericano de Protección de los Derechos Humanos en el Umbral del Siglo XXI – Memoria del Seminario* (Nov. 1999), San José de Costa Rica, CtIADH, 2001, pp. 3–68.

Cançado Trindade, A.A., 'The Future of the International Protection of Human Rights', in *B. Boutros-Ghali Amicorum Discipulorumque Liber – Paix, Développement, Démocratie*, vol. II, Bruxelles, Bruylant, 1998, pp. 961–86.

Cançado Trindade, A.A., 'Some Reflections on the Reassuring Expansion of the Material Content of *Jus Cogens*', in *Diritti Individuali e Giustizia Internazionale – Liber F. Pocar*, Milano, Giuffrè Ed., 2009, pp. 65–79.

Cançado Trindade, A.A., 'The Emancipation of the Individual from His Own State – The Historical Recovery of the Human Person as Subject of the Law of Nations', in *Human Rights, Democracy and the Rule of Law – Liber Amicorum L. Wildhaber* (eds. S. Breitenmoser et alii), Zürich/Baden-Baden, Dike/Nomos, 2007, pp. 151–71.

Cançado Trindade, A.A., 'La jurisprudence de la Cour Internationale de Justice sur les droits intangibles', in *Droits intangibles et états d'exception* (eds. D. Prémont, C. Stenersen and I. Oseredczuk), Bruxelles, Bruylant, 1996, pp. 53–89.

Cançado Trindade, A.A., 'Complementarity between State Responsibility and Individual Responsibility for Grave Violations of Human Rights: The Crime of State Revisited', in

International Responsibility Today – Essays in Memory of O. Schachter (ed. M. Ragazzi), Leiden, M. Nijhoff, 2005, pp. 253–69.

Cançado Trindade, A.A., 'Reflexiones sobre el Desarraigo como Problema de Derechos Humanos Frente a la Conciencia Jurídica Universal', in *La Nueva Dimensión de las Necesidades de Protección del Ser Humano en el Inicio del Siglo XXI* (eds. A.A. Cançado Trindade and J. Ruiz de Santiago), 4th. rev. ed., San José of Costa Rica, UNHCR, 2006, pp. 33–92.

Cançado Trindade, A.A., 'The Right to a Fair Trial under the American Convention on Human Rights', in *The Right to Fair Trial in International and Comparative Perspective* (ed. A. Byrnes), Hong Kong, University of Hong Kong, 1997, pp. 4–11.

Cançado Trindade, A.A., 'Judicial Protection and Guarantees in the Recent Case-Law of the Inter-American Court of Human Rights', in *Liber Amicorum in Memoriam of Judge J.M. Ruda*, The Hague, Kluwer, 2000, pp. 527–35.

Cançado Trindade, A.A., 'The Emancipation of the Individual from His Own State: The Historical Recovery of the Human Person as Subject of the Law of Nations', in *Human Rights, Democracy and the Rule of Law – Liber Amicorum L. Wildhaber* (eds. S. Breitenmoser et alii), Zürich/Baden-Baden, Dike/Nomos, 2007, pp. 151–71.

Cançado Trindade, A.A., 'Le nouveau Règlement de la Cour Interaméricaine des Droits de l'Homme: quelques réflexions sur la condition de l'individu comme sujet du Droit international', in *Libertés, justice, tolérance – Mélanges en hommage au Doyen G. Cohen-Jonathan*, vol. I, Bruxelles, Bruylant, 2004, pp. 351–65.

Cançado Trindade, A.A., 'Approximations and Convergences in the Case-Law of the European and Inter-American Courts of Human Rights', in *Le rayonnement international de la jurisprudence de la Cour européenne des droits de l'homme* (eds. G. Cohen-Jonathan and J.-F. Flauss), Bruxelles, Nemesis/Bruylant, 2005, pp. 101–38.

Cançado Trindade, A.A., 'Evolución y Desarrollos Recientes en el Agotamiento de los Recursos Internos en el Sistema Interamericano de Protección de los Derechos Humanos', in *Los Derechos Humanos en América – Una Perspectiva de Cinco Siglos* (International Seminar of Valladolid of 1992), Salamanca, Ed. Cortes de Castilla y León, 1994, pp. 321–52.

Cançado Trindade, A.A., 'Balance de los Resultados de la Conferencia Mundial de Derechos Humanos (Viena, 1993)', in *Estudios Básicos de Derechos Humanos*, vol. 3, San José de Costa Rica, IIDH, 1995, pp. 17–45.

Cançado Trindade, A.A., 'Las Cláusulas Pétreas de la Protección Internacional del Ser Humano: El Acceso Directo de los Individuos a la Justicia a Nivel Internacional y la Intangibilidad de la Jurisdicción Obligatoria de los Tribunales Internacionales de Derechos Humanos', in *El Sistema Interamericano de Protección de los Derechos Humanos en el Umbral del Siglo XXI – Memoria del Seminario* (November 1999), vol. I, San José of Costa Rica, Inter-American Court of Human Rights, 2001, p. 3–68.

Cançado Trindade, A.A., 'The Development of International Human Rights Law by the Operation and the Case-Law of the European and Inter-American Courts of Human Rights', 25 *Human Rights Law Journal* (2004), pp. 157–60.

Cançado Trindade, A.A., 'La Convention Américaine relative aux Droits de l'Homme et le droit international général', in *Droit international, droits de l'homme et juridictions internationales* (eds. G. Cohen-Jonathan and J.-F. Flauss), Bruxelles, Bruylant, 2004, pp. 59–71.

Cançado Trindade, A.A., 'The Relevance of International Adjudication Revisited: Reflections on the Need and Quest for International Compulsory Jurisdiction', in *Towards World Constitutionalism – Issues in the Legal Ordering of the World Community* (eds. R.St. Macdonald and D.M. Johnston), Leiden, Nijhoff, 2005, pp. 515–42.

Cançado Trindade, A.A., 'The Interpretation of the International Law of Human Rights by the Two Regional Human Rights Courts', in *Contemporary International Law Issues: Conflicts and Convergence* (Proceedings of the III Hague Conference, July 1995), The Hague, ASIL/Asser Inst., 1996, pp. 157–67.

Cançado Trindade, A.A., 'Human Development and Human Rights in the International Agenda of the XXIst Century', in *Human Development and Human Rights Forum* (August 2000), San José of Costa Rica, UNDP, 2001, pp. 23–38.

Cassese, A., 'Y a-t-il un conflit insurmontable entre souveraineté des États et justice pénale internationale?', in *Crimes internationaux et juridictions internationales* (eds. A. Cassese and M. Delmas-Marty), Paris, PUF, 2002, pp. 15–29.

Cassin, R., 'L'homme, sujet de droit international et la protection des droits de l'homme dans la société universelle', in *La technique et les principes du Droit public – Études en l'honneur de G. Scelle*, vol. I, Paris, LGDJ, 1950, pp. 81–2.

Cassin, R., 'La Déclaration Universelle et la mise en oeuvre des droits de l'homme', 79 *Recueil des Cours de l'Académie de Droit International de La Haye* (1951), pp. 328–9.

Cohen-Jonathan, G., 'Le rôle des principes généraux dans l'interprétation et l'application de la Convention Européenne des Droits de l'Homme', in *Mélanges en hommage à L.E. Pettiti*, Bruxelles, Bruylant, 1998, pp. 168–9.

Costa, J.-P., 'La Cour Européenne des Droits de l'Homme: vers un ordre juridique européen?', in *Mélanges en hommage à L.E. Pettiti*, Bruxelles, Bruylant, 1998, pp. 197–8.

Dahm, G., 'Die Subsidiarität des internationalen Rechtsschutzes bei Völkerrechtswidriger Verletzung von Privatpersonen', in *Vom Deutschen zum Europäischen Recht – Festschrift für H. Dölle*, vol. II, Tubingen, Mohr-Siebeck, 1963, pp. 6–27.

Delvaux, H., 'The Notion of Victim under Article 25 of the European Convention on Human Rights', in *Protection of Human Rights in Europe – Limits and Effects* (ed. I. Maier), Heidelberg, C.F. Müller Juristischer Verlag, 1982, pp. 41–64.

Dhommeaux, J., 'Le rôle du Comité des Droits de l'Enfant dans le contrôle, l'interprétation et l'évolution de la Convention relative aux Droits de l'Enfant', in *Les droits de l'homme à l'aube du XXIe. siècle – K. Vasak Amicorum Liber*, Bruxelles, Bruylant, 1999, pp. 553–80.

Diena, G., 'Les mandats internationaux', 5 *Recueil des Cours de l'Académie de Droit International de La Haye* (1924), pp. 246–61.

Drzemczewski, A., 'A Major Overhaul of the European Human Rights Convention Control Mechanism: Protocol n. 11', 6 *Collected Courses of the Academy of European Law* (1997)-II, pp. 121–244.

Drzemczewski, A., and Giakoumopoulos, C., 'Article 13', in *La Convention européenne des droits de l'Homme – Commentaire article par article* (eds. L.-E. Pettiti, E. Decaux and P.-H. Imbert), Paris, Economica, 1995, p. 473–4.

Dupuy, P.-M., 'Les 'considérations élémentaires d'humanité' dans la jurisprudence de la Cour Internationale de Justice', in *Mélanges en l'honneur de N. Valticos – Droit et justice* (eds. R.-J. Dupuy and L.A. Sicilianos), Paris, Pédone, 1999, pp. 117–30.

Dupuy, P.-M., 'Principe de complémentarité et Droit international général', in *The International Criminal Court and National Jurisdictions* (eds. M. Politi and F. Gioia), Aldershot, Ashgate, 2008, pp. 23–4.

Echeverria, G., 'Codifying the Rights of Victims in International Law: Remedies and Reparation', in *Redressing Injustices through Mass Claims Processes* (ed. Permanent Court of Arbitration), Oxford, University Press, 2006, pp. 286–97.

Ermacora, F., 'The Protection of Minorities before the United Nations', 182 *RCADI* (1983), pp. 257–347.

Eustathiades, C.Th., 'Une nouvelle expérience en Droit international – Les recours individuels à la Commission des droits de l'homme', in *Grundprobleme des internationalen Rechts – Festschrift für J. Spiropoulos*, Bonn, Schimmlebusch, 1957, pp. 77–137.

Eustathiades, C.Th., 'Les sujets du Droit international et la responsabilité internationale – Nouvelles tendances', 84 *Recueil des Cours de l'Académie de Droit International de La Haye* (1953), pp. 402–612.

Feinberg, N., 'La pétition en droit international', 40 *Recueil des Cours de l'Académie de Droit International de La Haye* (1932), pp. 576–639.

Flauss, J.-F., 'Les nouvelles frontières du procès équitable', in *Les nouveaux développements du procès équitable au sens de la Convention Européenne des Droits de l'Homme* (Actes du Colloque du 22 March 1996), Bruxelles, Bruylant, 1996, pp. 88–9.

Flauss, J.-F., 'La Cour de Strasbourg face aux violations systématiques des droits de l'homme', in *Les droits de l'homme au seuil du troisième millénaire – Mélanges en hommage à P. Lambert*, Bruxelles, Bruylant, 2000, pp. 343–55.

Foyer, J., 'Droits internationaux de l'homme et ordre public international', in *Du droit interne au droit international – Mélanges R. Goy*, Rouen, Université de Rouen, 1998, pp. 333–48.

Ganshof van der Meersch, W.J., 'Does the Convention Have the Force of *'Ordre Public'* in Municipal Law?', in *Human Rights in National and International Law* (ed. A.H. Robertson), Manchester, University Press/Oceana, 1970, pp. 135–43.

Glaser, S., 'Les droits de l'homme à la lumière du droit international positif', *Mélanges offerts à H. Rolin – Problèmes de droit des gens*, Paris, Pédone, 1964, pp. 105–18.

Gowlland-Debbas, V., 'Judicial Insights into Fundamental Values and Interests of the International Community', in *The International Court of Justice: Its Future Role after Fifty Years* (eds. A.S. Muller *et alii*), The Hague, Kluwer, 1997, pp. 344–6.

Guggenheim, P., 'Les principes de Droit international public', 80 *Recueil des Cours de l'Académie de Droit International de La Haye* (1952), pp. 116–18.

Heydte, F.A. von der, 'L'individu et les tribunaux internationaux', 107 *Recueil des Cours de l'Académie de Droit International de La Haye* (1962), pp. 301–15.

Hillgenberg, H., 'Incommunicado in Guantanamo', in *Internationale Gemeinschaft und Menschenrechte – Festschrift für G. Ress* (eds. J. Bröhmer *et alii*), Köln/Berlin/München, C. Heymanns Verlag, 2005, pp. 133–40.

Kelsen, H., 'Les rapports de système entre le droit interne et le droit international public', 14 *Recueil des Cours de l'Académie de Droit International de La Haye* (1926), pp. 231–6.

Kelsen, H., 'Théorie du Droit international public', 84 *Recueil des Cours de l'Académie de Droit International de La Haye* (1953), pp. 182–200.

Kiss, A., 'La Convention Européenne des Droits de l'Homme a-t-elle créé un ordre juridique autonome?', in *Mélanges en hommage à L.E. Pettiti*, Bruxelles, Bruylant, 1998, pp. 496–505.

Koopmans, T., 'Judicialization', in *Une communauté de droit – Festschrift für G.C. Rodríguez Iglesias* (eds. N. Colneric *et alii*), Berlin, Berliner Wissenschafts-Verlag (BMV), 2003, pp. 51–7.

Mandelstam, A.N., 'La protection des minorités', 1 *Recueil des Cours de l'Académie de Droit International de La Haye* (1923), pp. 363–519.

Matscher, F., 'La Posizione Processuale dell'Individuo come Ricorrente dinanzi agli Organi della Convenzione Europea dei Diritti dell'Uomo', in *Studi in Onore di Giuseppe Sperduti*, Milano, Giuffrè, 1984, pp. 601–20.

Mosler, H., 'The International Society as a Legal Community', 140 *Recueil des Cours de l'Académie de Droit International de La Haye* (1974), pp. 33–4.

Mosler, H., 'Réflexions sur la personnalité juridique en Droit international public', in *Mélanges offerts à H. Rolin – Problèmes de droit des gens*, Paris, Pédone, 1964, pp. 228–51.

Mubiala, M., 'L'accès de l'individu à la Cour africaine des droits de l'homme et des peuples', in *La promotion de la justice, des droits de l'homme et du règlement des conflits par le Droit international – Liber amicorum L. Caflisch* (ed. M.G. Kohen), Leiden, Nijhoff, 2007, pp. 369–78.

Murillo, J.C., 'La Declaración de Cartagena, el Alto Comisionado de Naciones Unidas para los Refugiados y las Migraciones Mixtas', in *Migraciones y Derechos Humanos* (August 2004), San José of Costa Rica, IIHR/PRODECA, 2004, pp. 174–6.

Parry, C., 'Some Considerations upon the Protection of Individuals in International Law', 90 *Recueil des Cours de l'Académie de Droit International* (1956), pp. 686–722.

Pescatore, P., 'Monisme, dualisme et 'effet utile' dans la jurisprudence de la Cour de Justice de la Communauté Européenne', in *Une communauté de droit – Festschrift für G.C. Rodríguez Iglesias* (eds. N. Colneric *et alii*), Berlin, Berliner Wissenschafts-Verlag, 2003, pp. 330–42.

Rigaux, F., 'La condition des victimes de crimes de Droit international', in *Man's Inhumanity to Man – Essays on International Law in Honour of A. Cassese* (eds. L.C. Vohrah, F. Pocar *et alii*), The Hague, Kluwer, 2003, p. 771–89.

Rogge, K., 'The "Victim" Requirement in Article 25 of the European Convention on Human Rights', in *Protecting Human Rights: The European Dimension – Studies in Honour of G.J. Wiarda* (eds. F. Matscher and H. Petzold), Köln/Berlin, C. Heymanns Verlag, 1988, pp. 539–45.

Ruiz de Santiago, J., 'Derechos Humanos, Migraciones y Refugiados: Desafíos en los Inicios del Nuevo Milenio', in *III Encuentro de Movilidad Humana: Migrante y Refugiado – Memoria* (September 2000), San José of Costa Rica, UNHCR/IIHR, 2001, pp. 37–72.

Ruiz de Santiago, J., 'El Impacto en el Refugio de la Nueva Dinámica Migratoria en la Región – Retos para Asegurar la Protección de Refugiados', in IIHR, *I Curso de Capacitación para Organizaciones de la Sociedad Civil sobre Protección de Poblaciones Migrantes* (June 1999), Mexico/San José of Costa Rica, UNHCR/Universidad Iberoamericana/IIHR, 2002, p. 40–43.

Saito, Y., 'Judge Tanaka, Natural Law and the Principle of Equality', in *The Living Law of Nations – Essays in Memory of A. Grahl-Madsen* (eds. G. Alfredsson and P. Macalister-Smith), Kehl/Strasbourg, N.P. Engel Publ., 1996, pp. 401–8.

Salvia, M. de, 'L'élaboration d'un *"jus commune"* des droits de l'homme et des libertés fondamentales dans la perspective de l'unité européenne: l'oeuvre accompli par la Commission et la Cour Européennes des Droits de l'Homme', in *Protection des droits de l'homme: la dimension européenne – Mélanges en l'honneur de G.J. Wiarda* (eds. F. Matscher and H. Petzold), 2nd. ed., Köln/Berlin, C. Heymanns Verlag, 1990, pp. 555–63.

Say, B., 'Procédure d'examen des communications relatives aux violations alléguées des droits de l'homme dans les domaines de compétence de l'UNESCO: problème du double emploi et réflexion sur la réforme envisagée', in *Les droits de l'homme à l'aube du XXIe. siècle – K. Vasak Amicorum Liber*, Bruxelles, Bruylant, 1999, pp. 819–61.

Scelle, G., 'Some Reflections on Juridical Personality in International Law', in *Law and Politics in the World Community* (ed. G.A. Lipsky), Berkeley/L.A., University of California Press, 1953, pp. 49–58.

Schermers, H.G., 'The Bond between Man and State', in *Recht zwischen Umbruch und Bewahrung – Festschrift für R. Bernhardt* (eds. U. Beyerlin *et alii*), Berlin, Springer-Verlag, 1995, pp. 1924.

Schmeidl, S., 'The Early Warning of Forced Migration: State or Human Security?', in *Refugees and Forced Displacement – International Security, Human Vulnerability, and the State* (eds. E. Newman and J. van Selm), Tokyo, United Nations University, 2003, pp. 140–51.

Smith, R., 'Derechos Laborales y Derechos Humanos de los Migrantes en Estatus Irregular en Estados Unidos', in *Memorias del Seminario Internacional 'Los Derechos Humanos de los Migrantes'* (Mexico, June 2005), Mexico, Secretaría de Relaciones Exteriores, 2005, pp. 299–301.

Sperduti, G., 'L'individu et le droit international', 90 *Recueil des Cours de l'Académie de Droit International* (1956), pp. 764–822.

Spielmann, A., 'Les détenus et leurs droits (de l'homme)', in *Les droits de l'homme au seuil du troisième millénaire – Mélanges en hommage à P. Lambert*, Bruxelles, Bruylant, 2000, pp. 777–88.

Stavropoulou, M., 'Searching for Human Security and Dignity: Human Rights, Refugees, and the Internally Displaced', in *The Universal Declaration of Human Rights: Fifty Years and Beyond* (eds. Y. Danieli, E. Stamatopoulou and C.J. Dias), Amityville/N.Y., Baywood Publ. Co., 1999, pp. 181–2.

Sudre, F., 'Existe t-il un ordre public européen?', in *Quelle Europe pour les droits de l'homme?* (ed. P. Tavernier), Bruxelles, Bruylant, 1996, pp. 41–67.

Swepston, L., 'Protection of Vulnerable Groups by the International Labour Organisation', in *The Living Law of Nations – Essays in Memory of A. Grahl-Madsen* (eds. G. Alfredsson and P. Macalister-Smith), Kehl/Strasbourg, N.P. Engel, 1996, pp. 409–19.

Vasak, K., 'Le droit international des droits de l'homme', 140 *Recueil des Cours de l'Académie de Droit International* (1974), pp. 343–413.

Vedovato, G., 'Les accords de tutelle', 76 *Recueil des Cours de l'Académie de Droit International* (1950), pp. 613–94.

Villán Durán, C., 'Los Derechos Humanos y la Inmigración en el Marco de las Naciones Unidas', in *Memorias del Seminario Internacional 'Los Derechos Humanos de los Migrantes'*, (Mexico, June 2005), Mexico, Secretaría de Relaciones Exteriores, 2005, pp. 95–8.

Villiger, M.E., 'Expulsion and the Right to Respect for Private and Family Life (Article 8 of the Convention) – An Introduction to the Commission's Case-Law', in *Protecting Human Rights: The European Dimension – Studies in Honour of G.J. Wiarda/Protection des droits de l'homme: La dimension européenne – Mélanges en l'honneur de G.J. Wiarda* (eds. F. Matscher and H. Petzold), Köln/Berlin, C. Heymanns Verlag, 1988, pp. 657–62.

Witenberg, J.-C., 'La recevabilité des réclamations devant les juridictions internationales', 41 *Recueil des Cours de l'Académie de Droit International de La Haye* (1932), pp. 5–135.

III. MONOGRAPHS AND REPORTS

AComHPR, *Decisions of the African Commission on Human and Peoples' Rights* (1986–1997), Series A, vol. I, Banjul, IHRDA, doc. AComHPR/LR/A/1, 1997.

Association for the Prevention of Torture (APT), *The African Court on Human and Peoples' Rights – Presentation, Analysis and Commentary: The Protocol to the African Charter on Human and Peoples' Rights, Establishing the Court* (Occasional Paper), Geneva, APT, 2000.

Cançado Trindade, A.A., *El Desarrollo del Derecho Internacional de los Derechos Humanos Mediante el Funcionamiento y la Jurisprudencia de la Corte Europea y la Corte Interamericana de Derechos Humanos*, CtIADH, San José of Costa Rica, 2007, pp. 1–75.

Cançado Trindade, A.A., *El Agotamiento de los Recursos Internos en el Sistema Interamericano de Protección de los Derechos Humanos*, San José of Costa Rica, IIHR (Series for NGOs), 1991.

Cançado Trindade, A.A., *Reflexiones sobre la Interacción entre el Derecho Internacional y el Derecho Interno en la Protección de los Derechos Humanos*, Guatemala City/Guatemala, Procuraduría de los Derechos Humanos (monograph 3-95), 1995, pp. 7–41.

Cançado Trindade, A.A., *Derecho Internacional de los Derechos Humanos, Derecho Internacional de los Refugiados y Derecho Internacional Humanitario – Aproximaciones y Convergencias*, Geneva, ICRC, [2000], pp. 1–66.

Cançado Trindade, A.A., *Elementos para un Enfoque de Derechos Humanos del Fenómeno de los Flujos Migratorios Forzados*, Guatemala City, OIM/IIDH, Sept. 2001, pp. 1–57.

Cançado Trindade, A.A., Ferrero Costa, E., and Gómez-Robledo, A., 'Gobernabilidad Democrática y Consolidación Institucional: El Control Internacional y Constitucional de los *Interna Corporis* – Informe de la Comisión de Juristas de la OEA para Nicarágua (Febrero de 1994)', 67 *Boletín de la Academia de Ciencias Políticas y Sociales* – Caracas (2000–2001) n. 137, pp. 593–669.

Council of Europe/Steering Committee for Human Rights, *Final Activity Report on the Protection of Human Rights during Armed Conflict as well as during Internal Disturbances and Tensions*, Strasbourg, C.E. doc. CDDH(2003)026/Add. II, of 26 November 2003.

Council of Europe, *CIA Above the Law? Secret Detentions and Unlawful Inter-State Transfers of Detainees in Europe*, Strasbourg, C.E. Publ., 2008.

Council of Europe, *Guantánamo: Violation of Human Rights under International Law?*, Strasbourg, C.E. Publ., 2007.

Greenwood Arroyo, M., and Ruiz Oporta, R., *Migrantes Irregulares, Estrategias de Sobrevivencia y Derechos Humanos: Un Estudio de Casos*, San José of Costa Rica, IIHR, 1995.

ICC, *Selected Basic Documents Related to the International Criminal Court*, The Hague, ICC, 2009.

IIDH, *Convención CEDAW y Protocolo Facultativo*, 2nd. ed., San José of Costa Rica, IIHR, 2004.

International Institute of Humanitarian Law (IIHL), *Conflict Prevention – The Humanitarian Perspective* (Proceedings, August/September 1994), San Remo, IIHL, 1994, pp. 7–185.

McBride, J., *Study on the Principles Governing the Application of the European Convention on Human Rights during Armed Conflict and Internal Disturbances and Tensions*, Strasbourg, C.E./Steering Committee for Human Rights, doc. DH-DEV(2003)001, of 19 September 2003.

Ruiz de Santiago, J., *El Problema de las Migraciones Forzosas en Nuestro Tiempo*, Mexico, Instituto Mexicano de Doctrina Social Cristiana, 2003, pp. 10–30.

Ruiz de Santiago, J., *Migraciones Forzadas – Derecho Internacional y Doctrina Social de la Iglesia*, Mexico, Instituto Mexicano de Doctrina Social Cristiana, 2004, pp. 9–82.

UNHCR, *The State of the World's Refugees – Fifty Years of Humanitarian Action*, Oxford, UNHCR/Oxford University Press, 2000.

UNHCR, *Memoria del Vigésimo Aniversario de la Declaración de Cartagena sobre los Refugiados (1984–2004)*, Mexico City/San José of Costa Rica, UNHCR, 2005.

IV. ARTICLES

Aldana-Pindell, R., 'An Emerging Universality of Justiciable Victims' Rights in the Criminal Process to Curtail Impunity for State-Sponsored Crimes', 26 *Human Rights Quarterly* (2004), pp. 652–3.

Badawi El-Sheikh, I.A., 'Draft Protocol to the African Charter on Human and Peoples' Rights on the Establishment of an African Court on Human and Peoples' Rights – Introductory Note', 9 *African Journal of International and Comparative Law* (1997), pp. 943–52.

Bassiouni, M.C., 'International Recognition of Victims' Rights', 6 *Human Rights Law Review* (2006), pp. 221–79.

Batchelor, C.A., 'Stateless Persons: Some Gaps in International Protection', 7 *International Journal of Refugee Law* (1995),pp. 232–55.

Bobbio, N., 'Il Preambolo della Convenzione Europea dei Diritti dell'Uomo', 57 *Rivista di Diritto Internazionale* (1974), pp. 437–40.

Borchard, E.M., 'The Access of Individuals to International Courts', 24 *American Journal of International Law* (1930), pp. 359–65.

Buckley, C., 'The European Convention on Human Rights and the Right to Life in Turkey', 1 *Human Rights Law Review* (2001), pp. 35–65.

Cançado Trindade, A.A., 'Vers la consolidation de la capacité juridique internationale des pétitionnaires dans le système interaméricain des droits de la personne', 14 *Revue québécoise de Droit international* (2001), n. 2, pp. 207–39.

Cançado Trindade, A.A., 'Hacia la Consolidación de la Capacidad Jurídica Internacional de los Peticionarios en el Sistema Interamericano de Protección de los Derechos Humanos', 37 *Revista del Instituto Interamericano de Derechos Humanos* (2003), pp. 13–52.

Cançado Trindade, A.A., 'El Derecho de Acceso a la Justicia Internacional y las Condiciones para Su Realización en el Sistema Interamericano de Protección de los Derechos Humanos', 37 *Revista del Instituto Interamericano de Derechos Humanos* (2003), pp. 53–83.

Cançado Trindade, A.A., 'El Nuevo Reglamento de la Corte Interamericana de Derechos Humanos (2000): La Emancipación del Ser Humano como Sujeto del Derecho Internacional de los Derechos Humanos', 30/31 *Revista del Instituto Interamericano de Derechos Humanos* (2001), pp. 45–71.

Cançado Trindade, A.A., 'A Consolidação da Personalidade e da Capacidade Jurídicas do Indivíduo como Sujeito do Direito Internacional', 16 *Anuario del Instituto Hispano-Luso-Americano de Derecho Internacional* – Madrid (2003), pp. 240–47.

Cançado Trindade, A.A., 'Exhaustion of Local Remedies in International Law Experiments Granting Procedural Status to Individuals in the First Half of the Twentieth Century', 24 *Netherlands International Law Review/Nederlands Tijdschrift voor internationaal Recht* (1977), pp. 373–92.

Cançado Trindade, A.A., 'L'interdépendance de tous les droits de l'homme et leur mise-en-oeuvre: obstacles et enjeux', 158 *Revue internationale des sciences sociales* – Paris/UNESCO (1998), pp. 571–82.

Cançado Trindade, A.A., 'A Emancipação do Ser Humano como Sujeito do Direito Internacional e os Limites da Razão de Estado', 6/7 *Revista da Faculdade de Direito da Universidade do Estado do Rio de Janeiro* (1998–1999), pp. 425–34.

Cançado Trindade, A.A., 'Memória da Conferência Mundial de Direitos Humanos (Viena, 1993)', 87/90 *Boletim da Sociedade Brasileira de Direito Internacional* (1993–1994), pp. 9–57.

Cançado Trindade, A.A., 'Exhaustion of Remedies in International Law and the Role of National Courts', 17 *Archiv des Volkerrechts* – Tübingen (1977–1978), pp. 333–70.

Cançado Trindade, A.A., 'The Developing Case-Law of the Inter-American Court of Human Rights', 3 *Human Rights Law Review* (2003), pp. 22–3.

Cançado Trindade, A.A., 'The Evolution of Provisional Measures of Protection under the Case-Law of the Inter-American Court of Human Rights (1987–2002)', 24 *Human Rights Law Journal* – Strasbourg/Kehl (2003), n. 5–8, pp. 162–8.

Cançado Trindade, A.A., 'Les Mesures provisoires de protection dans la jurisprudence de la Cour Interaméricaine des Droits de l'Homme', 4 *Revista do Instituto Brasileiro de Direitos Humanos* (2003), pp. 13–25.

Cançado Trindade, A.A., 'La Humanización del Derecho Internacional y los Límites de la Razón de Estado', 40 *Revista da Faculdade de Direito da Universidade Federal de Minas Gerais* – Belo Horizonte/Brazil (2001), pp. 11–23.

Cançado Trindade, V.F.D., 'Uma Análise das Leis de Auto-Anistia na Evolução Jurisprudencial da Corte Interamericana de Direitos Humanos', 8 *Revista do Instituto Brasileiro de Direitos Humanos* (2008), pp. 281–91.

Cançado Trindade, A.A., 'The Developing Case-Law of the Inter-American Court of Human Rights', 3 *Human Rights Law Review* (2003), pp. 1–25.

Cançado Trindade, A.A., 'The Evolution of Provisional Measures of Protection under the Case-Law of the Inter-American Court of Human Rights (1987–2002)', 24 *Human Rights Law Journal* – Strasbourg/Kehl (2003), n. 5–8, pp. 162–8.

Cançado Trindade, A.A., 'Les Mesures provisoires de protection dans la jurisprudence de la Cour Interaméricaine des Droits de l'Homme', 4 *Revista do Instituto Brasileiro de Direitos Humanos* (2003), pp. 13–25.

Cançado Trindade, A.A., 'The Humanization of Consular Law: The Impact of Advisory Opinion n. 16 (1999) of the Inter-American Court of Human Rights on International Case-Law and Practice', 4 *Chinese Journal of International Law* (2007), pp. 1–16.

Carrillo Salcedo, J.A., 'El Derecho Internacional ante un Nuevo Siglo', 48 *Boletim da Faculdade de Direito da Universidade de Coimbra* (1999–2000), pp. 257–60.

Cassin, R., 'Vingt ans après la Déclaration Universelle', 8 *Revue de la Commission Internationale de Juristes* (1967), n. 2, pp. 9–17.

Cassin, R., 'Quelques souvenirs sur la Déclaration Universelle de 1948', 15 *Revue de droit contemporain* (1968), n. 1, p. 10.

Çelik, A.B., 'Transnationalization of Human Righs Norms and Its Impact on Internally Displaced Kurds', 27 *Human Rights Quarterly* (2005), pp. 969–97.

Cholewinski, R., 'Strasbourg's "Hidden Agenda"?: The Protection of Second-Generation Migrants from Expulsion under Article 8 of the European Convention of Human Rights', 12 *Netherlands Quarterly of Human Rights* (1994), pp. 287–306.

Cleveland, S.H., 'Legal Status and Rights of Undocumented Migrants – Advisory Opinion OC-18/03 [of the] Inter-American Court of Human Rights', 99 *American Journal of International Law* (2005), pp. 460–65.

Cohen-Jonathan, G., 'Cour Européenne des Droits de l'Homme et droit international général (2000)', 46 *Annuaire français de Droit international* (2000), pp. 640–42.

Cohn, M., 'Torture of Prisoners in U.S. Custody', 16 *I Diritti dell'Uomo – Cronache e Battaglie* (2005), pp. 59–62.

Daes, E.-I.A. (rapporteur spécial), *La condition de l'individu et le Droit international contemporain*, U.N. doc. E/CN.4/Sub.2/1988/33, of 18 July 1988, pp. 1–92.

Dubois, O., 'Rwanda's National Criminal Courts and the International Tribunal', 37 *International Review of the Red Cross* (1997), n. 321, pp. 717–31.

Favoreu, L. (coord.), 'Vers un Droit constitutionnel européen – Quel Droit constitutionnel européen? (Actes du Colloque de Strasbourg, 1993)', 7 *Revue universelle des droits de l'homme* (1995), pp. 357–456.

Flauss, J.-F., 'Le droit de recours individuel devant la Cour européenne des droits de l'homme – Le Protocole n. 9 à la Convention Européenne des Droits de l'Homme', 36 *Annuaire français de droit international* (1990), pp. 507–19.

Harvey, C., and Livingstone, S., 'Protecting the Marginalised: The Role of the European Convention on Human Rights', 51 *Northern Ireland Legal Quarterly* (2000), 448–56.

Hennebel, L., 'L'"humanisation" du Droit international des droits de l'homme – Commentaire sur l'Avis Consultatif n. 18 de la Cour Interaméricaine relatif aux droits des travailleurs migrants', 15 *Revue trimestrielle des droits de l'homme* (2004), n. 59, pp. 747–56.

Hune, S., and Niessen, J., 'Ratifying the U.N. Migrant Workers Convention: Current Difficulties and Prospects', 12 *Netherlands Quarterly of Human Rights* (1994), pp. 392–3.

Ingelse, C., 'The Committee against Torture: One Step Forward, One Step Back', 18 *Netherlands Quarterly of Human Rights* (2000), pp. 307–27.

Jescheck, H.-H., 'The General Principles of International Criminal Law Set Out in Nuremberg, as Mirrored in the ICC Statute', 2 *Journal of International Criminal Justice* (2004), pp. 42–3.

Karydis, G., 'L'ordre public dans l'ordre juridique communautaire: un concept à contenu variable', 1 *Revue trimestrielle de droit européen* (2002), pp. 1–25.

Laly-Chevalier, C., Poïan, F. da, and Tigroudja, H., 'Chronique de la jurisprudence de la Cour Interaméricaine des Droits de l'Homme (2002–2004)', 16 *Revue trimestrielle des droits de l'homme* (2005), n. 62, pp. 459–98.

Lambert, H., 'Protection against *Refoulement* from Europe: Human Rights Law Comes to the Rescue', 48 *International and Comparative Law Quarterly* (1999), pp. 515–18.

Mennecke, M., 'Towards the Humanization of the Vienna Convention of Consular Rights – The *LaGrand* Case before the International Court of Justice', 44 *German Yearbook of International Law/Jahrbuch für internationales Recht* (2001), pp. 430–68.

Meron, Th., 'The Humanization of Humanitarian Law', 94 *American Journal of International Law* (2000), pp. 239–78.

Mubiala, M., 'La Cour Africaine des Droits de l'Homme et des Peuples: mimetisme institutionnel ou avancée judiciaire?', 102 *Revue générale de Droit international public* (1998), pp. 765–80.

Mullerson, R.A., 'Human Rights and the Individual as Subject of International Law: A Soviet View', 1 *European Journal of International Law* (1990), pp. 33–43.

Musila, G.M., 'The Right to an Effective Remedy under the African Charter on Human and Peoples' Rights', 6 *African Human Rights Law Journal* (2006), pp. 442–64.

Ortiz Ahlf, L., 'Derechos Humanos de los Migrantes', 35 *Jurídica – Anuario del Departamento de Derecho de la Universidad Iberoamericana* (2005), pp. 14–29.

Paust, J.J., 'Judicial Power to Determine the Status and Rights of Persons Detained without Trial', 44 *Harvard International Law Journal* (2003), n. 2, pp. 503–32.

Philippe, X., 'The Principles of Universal Jurisdiction and Complementarity: How Do the Two Principles Intermesh?', 88 *International Review of the Red Cross* (2006), n. 862, pp. 375–98.

Quilleré-Majzoub, F., 'L'option juridictionnelle de la protection des droits de l'homme en Afrique – Étude comparée autour de la création de la Cour Africaine des Droits de l'Homme et des Peuples', 44 *Revue trimestrielle des droits de l'homme* (2000), pp. 758–9.

Quintana Osuna, K., and Citroni, G., 'I minori d'età di fronte alla Corte Interamericana dei Diritti dell'Uomo', 2 *Pace Diritti Umani* – Università di Padova (2005), pp. 55–101.

Reidy, A., Hampson, F., and Boyle, K., 'Gross Violations of Human Rights: Invoking the European Convention on Human Rights in the Case of Turkey', 15 *Netherlands Quarterly of Human Rights* (1997), pp. 162–72.

Sudre, F., 'Extradition et peine de mort: Arrêt *Soering* de la Cour Européenne des Droits de l'Homme, du 7 juillet 1989', 94 *Revue générale de Droit international public* (1990), pp. 103–21.

Symonides, J., 'UNESCO's Contribution to the Progressive Development of Human Rights', 5 *Max Planck Yearboook of United Nations Law* (2001), pp. 317–40.

Thornberry, P., 'Confronting Racial Discrimination: A CERD Perspective', 5 *Human Rights Law Review* (2005), pp. 239–69.

Weckel, Ph., 'Chronique de jurisprudence internationale', 105 *Revue générale de Droit international public* (2001), pp. 764–70.

Weckel, Ph., Helali, M.S.E., and Sastre, M., 'Chronique de jurisprudence internationale', 104 *Revue générale de Droit international public* (2000), pp. 791–94.

Weiner, M., 'Ethics, National Sovereignty and the Control of Immigration', 30 *International Migration Review* (1996), pp. 171–95.

Yang, L., 'On the Principle of Complementarity in the Rome Statute of the International Criminal Court', 4 *Chinese Journal of International Law* (2005), pp. 122–5.

Zwaak, L., 'The European Court of Human Rights Has the Turkish Security Forces Held Responsible for Violations of Human Rights: The Case of Akdivar and Others', 10 *Leiden Journal of International Law* (1997), pp. 99–110.

Index

19 Tradesmen case, Colombia 180
Abdulaziz, Cabales and Balkandali versus United Kingdom 66, 142–3
Abu Ghraib 181
Accioly, Hildebrando 8
ACHPR *see* African Charter on Human and Peoples' Rights
ACHR *see* American Convention on Human Rights
admissibility 21, 35–6, 50–1, 67, 110–11, 209
AfComHPR *see* African Commission on Human and Peoples' Rights
African Charter on Human and Peoples' Rights 23, 57, 73–4, 85, 163
  Burkina Faso Protocol 46–7
African Commission on Human and Peoples' Rights 46, 57, 73–4, 105–6, 162–3
African Court on Human and Peoples' Rights 32, 46–7
African Institute for Human Rights and Development versus Gambia 107
Airey versus Ireland 60
Akdivar and Others versus Turkey 66, 104, 160
Aksoy versus Turkey 66, 104
Alhassan Abubakar versus Ghana 57
Alikhadzhiyeva versus Russia 31
Alkema, E.A. 69
Almonacid Arellano versus Chile 181–2, 195–6, 200–1
Álvarez, Alejandro 8
American Convention on Human Rights (ACHR) 42–5, 53, 61–7, 85–6, 115–22, 195, 199–201, 206
  displaced persons 159, 169
  effective remedy 51–2, 54–7
  harmonization of domestic legal order 83, 129, 193
  individual petition 17–18, 22–6, 28–9, 130
    see also individual petition
  legal personality 58
  massacres 184–8
  non-refoulement 144–5
  protection 37–9, 43, 157–8
  rule of law 74–5
  street children 152, 155
    see also street children; *Villagrán Morales and Others versus Guatemala*
American Declaration of Human Rights 7, 19
American Declaration on the Rights and Duties of Man 53, 67
Aréchaga, Eduardo Jiménez de 10
Arendt, Hannah 136

armed conflict 133, 136–8, 151–2, 157–62, 176–7, 211
  Africa 73
  Central America 166
  El Salvador 155
  Guatemala 185
  Kosovo 70–1
  Turkey 66–7
asylum 148
atrocities 2, 4, 11, 16, 18, 108, 154, 162, 185, 190–1, 201, 208
Avena and Other Mexican Nationals 165

Baena Ricardo and Others versus Panama 62, 120
Bámaca Velásquez versus Guatemala 65, 119–20, 142
Barbados 45
Barbera, Messegué and Jabardo versus Spain 60
Barberis, J. 10
Barrios Altos case (Peru) 62, 185, 193–6, 200, 212
Basis for a Draft Protocol to the American Convention on Human Rights to Strengthen Its Mechanism of Protection 44
Baysayeva versus Russia 31, 105
Bazorkina versus Russia 28
Beldjoudi versus France 144
Belgian Vagrancy cases 32
Belilos versus Switzerland 92, 114, 119
Benin 106
Bissangou versus Republic of Congo 73, 106
Bitiyeva and X versus Russia 31
Blake versus Guatemala 62, 89
Bodin, J 178
Bourquin, Maurice 8
Bridgetown, Barbados, Assembly of 45
Brothers Gómez Paquiyauri versus Peru 111, 198
Burkina Faso 46
Bynkershoek, Cornelius van 2

Caballero Delgado and Santana versus Colombia 55, 85
Caesar versus Trinidad and Tobago 89, 95, 198
Campbell and Fell versus United Kingdom 172
Cantos versus Argentina 62
Caracazo case, Venezuela 187–8
Cardot versus France 104
Cassin, René 10, 21, 53
Castillo Páez versus Peru 39, 51–2, 61, 64, 103, 206
Castillo Petruzzi and Others versus Peru 13, 39, 50, 62, 115, 130–1

censorship 111, 193
Central American Council of Human Rights
    Ombudsmen 147
Chechnya 25, 105
*Children Yean and Bosico versus Dominican
    Republic* 155
Chile 44, 181, 193–4
Chilean Constitution 193
*Civil Liberties Organisation in Respect of the
    Nigerian Bar Association versus
    Nigeria* 106
Civil Liberties Organisation versus Nigeria 106
Cold War 137
collective guarantee 26, 84, 89–91, 96, 116,
    122, 208
Colombia 52, 157
Commemorative Colloquy of Mexico City 167
Committee on the Protection of the Rights of All
    Migrant Workers and Members of Their
    Families 138
*Communities of Jiguamiandó and
    Curbaradó* 157–8
*Community of Peace of Peace of San José of
    Apartadó versus Colombia* 157–8
compensation 69–70, 171, 190
concentration camps 181
Congo 163
*Constitutional Rights Project (in relation to Akamu,
    Adega et alii) versus Nigeria* 57
Constitutional Tribunal versus Peru 115–16, 211
Convention for the Prevention and Punishment
    of the Crime of Genocide 78, 96
Convention on the Elimination of All Forms of
    Discrimination against Women
    (CEDAW) 27, 92
Convention on the Elimination of All Forms of
    Racial Discrimination 22
Costa Rica 34, 167
Council of Europe 33, 35, 100, 121
    Declaration on the Protection of Human
        Rights during Armed Conflict, Internal
        Disturbances and Tensions 162
    Parliamentary Assembly 181
    Steering Committee for Human Rights 161–2
Covenant on Economic, Social and Cultural
    Rights 27
Cruz Varas and Others versus Sweden 23
Cyprus versus Turkey 170, 176

Declaration and Programme of Action of
    Vienna 27
Declarations of Cartegena on Refugees 165–6
Delcourt versus Belgium 60
*Democratic Republic of Congo versus Burundi,
    Rwanda and Uganda* 162
Deng, F.M. 164
deportation 144
detention 171–3, 182, 185, 198, 203, 211
    see also prisoners

displaced persons 152, 163–71, 177, 186, 211
Domenach, J.-M. 136
Draft Practical Guide on Reservations to
    Treaties 92
Drost, P.N. 19
drug-trafficking 158
Dudgeon versus United Kingdom 128

East African Asians 142
ECHR *see* European Convention on Human
    Rights
ECtHR *see* European Court of Human Rights
Ecuador Supreme Court 130
égalité des armes see procedural equality
El Amparo case 38
El Salvador 155
ethnicity 138
European Commission 23–5, 32
European Commission of Human Rights 32,
    128, 172
European Convention on Human Rights
    (ECHR) 9, 21–8, 66–75, 114–15, 122
    armed conflict 160–1
    displaced persons 170–1
    individual petition 17–18, 30, 36–7, 172
    local remedy provision 54, 99–100, 104
    massacres 183
    migrants 142–4
    potential victim 128–9
    protection 33–7
    right of access to tribunal 60–1
    Switzerland 93
European Court of Human Rights (ECtHR) 5,
    59–75, 114–15, 122–4, 176, 206,
    209–12
    aggravating circumstances 183
    armed conflict 160–1
    detention 172–4
    displaced persons 170–1
    individual petition 22–37
    local remedy provision 100, 104–5
    migrants 143–4
    potential victim 127–9
    Rules of Court 33
European Union (EU) 181
Eustathiades, Constantin 8
exploitation 133, 135, 165, 174–6
expulsion 106, 144

Feinberg, N. 19
First World Conference on Human Rights 80
Five Pensioners versus Peru 40, 43, 62, 121–2
Flauss, J.-F. 73

Gangaram Panday versus Suriname 51, 103
Gaskin versus United Kingdom 60
General Course on Public International Law 11
Geneva Convention 4, 85, 163
Genie Lacayo versus Nicaragua 55

genocide 78, 89, 106, 109, 185
Gentili, Alberico 2
globalization 135–6, 165
Godinez Cruz case 38
Goiburú and Others versus Paraguay 181–2, 185, 187, 191, 199–202
Golder versus United Kingdom 60, 70
Greece 26, 72, 121, 170
Greek-Cypriots 176–7
Greek Orthodox Church 26
Grotius, Hugo 2
Grozny 105
Guantánamo 181
Guatemala 14, 62, 65–6, 89, 119–20, 134, 141, 152, 167, 169, 184
Guatemalan Truth Commission 191
Guggenheim, Paul 8

Hague Academy of International Law 8, 10–11, 42, 127, 198, 204
Haitians and Dominicans of Haitian Origin in the Dominican Republic 141, 144–5
Hegelian outlook 2
Hilaire, Benjamin and Constantine versus Trinidad and Tobago 117, 211
Hilaire, Constantine and Benjamin and Otros versus Trinidad and Tobago 65, 119
Hobbes, Thomas 178
Holy Monasteries versus Greece 26–7
Honduras 37–8, 156
Hornsby versus Greece 72, 121
human rights violations 37, 76–86, 159–63, 173–6, 203, 211
crimes of State 183
displaced persons 168
local remedies 102
migrants 136, 144–6
street children 152–5

I. Gueye et alii versus France 93
I. Ilascu, A. Lesco, A. Ivantoc and T. Petrov-Popa versus Moldova and the Russian Federation 115, 119
Ilascu and Others versus Moldova and Russia 30
Imakayeva versus Russia 31
Indigenous Community Sawhoyamaxa versus Paraguay 169–70
Indigenous Community Yakye Axa versus Paraguay 168, 170
individual petition 7, 13–15, 17–31, 36–40, 43–50, 100–2, 114, 117, 122, 125–31, 171–2, 174, 193, 196
Institut de Droit International 7
Institute of Rehabilitation of Minors versus Paraguay 154–5, 173
Inter-American Commission on Human Rights
potential victim 130
Special Rapporteur 167

Inter-American Commission on Human Rights (IAComHR) 32, 37, 43, 50–1, 147, 185, 187, 193
Inter-American Court of Human Rights (IACtHR) 5, 11–15, 56–9, 61–5, 117–24, 144–9, 193–202, 209–10, 212
armed conflict 157–8, 161
category of victim 187–90
detention 172–4
displaced persons 170
effective remedy 50–52, 55, 206
individual petition 17–18, 27–9
massacres 110, 180–6
migrants 141
potential victim 129–30
protection 37–46
street children 152–6
subsidiarity 110–11
Inter-American Institute of Human Rights 134
International Convention on the Protection of the Rights of All Migrant Workers and Members of Their Families 138, 140
International Court of Justice (ICJ) 96–7, 114–15
International Covenant on Civil and Political Rights 146
International Criminal Court (ICC) 108
Rome Statute 204
Trust Fund for Victims 109, 202
Victims Participation and Reparations Section 202
ad hoc International Criminal Tribunal for Rwanda 5, 108, 201
ad hoc International Criminal Tribunal for the Former Yugoslavia 5, 108, 201
International Human Rights Tribunals 193
International Humanitarian Law 3–4, 73, 79, 85, 158, 162, 164, 167–8, 177
International Labour Organization (ILO) 138, 141, 174
International Law Commission *see* U.N. International Law Commission
International Law of Human Rights 3, 18, 39, 59, 103, 156, 159, 167, 169–70, 197, 203–4
International Organization for Migration (IOM) 137
International Refugee Law 164, 167–8, 170
Isayeva, Yusupova and Bazayeva 105
Issa and Others versus Turkey 159
Italian courts 70
Ivcher Bronstein versus Peru 62, 115–16, 119, 211

Jawara versus Gambia 106
Jelicic versus Bosnia and Herzegovina 72
Jenks, C.W. 174
Jessup, Philip 8
Johnston and Others versus Ireland 128

Juridical Condition and Human Rights of the Child 12, 14, 40, 156
Juridical Condition and Rights of Undocumented Migrants 15, 133, 138, 147–8, 159, 165, 196, 199
juridical personality 8, 12, 14, 40, 50, 58–9
jurisprudence constante 24, 29, 51–2, 60–5, 70, 90, 103–4, 194, 199, 207

Kantian thinking 12
Kenya 142
Khashiyev and Akayeva versus Russia 69, 105
Klass and Others versus Federal Republic of Germany 22, 66, 128
Klyakhin versus Russia 30
Kosovo 70
Kudla versus Poland 68
Kurds 29, 67
Kurt versus Turkey 25, 70, 104, 123

La Cantuta *see University of la Cantuta Versus Peru*
LaGrand case 165
Lamguindaz versus United Kingdom 144
Las Palmeras case (Colombia) 62
Last Temptation of Christ, The (Chile) 111, 193
Lauterpacht, Hersch 8
Lawless versus Ireland 32–3
Lawyers Committee for Human Rights 105
Lawyers for Human Rights versus Swaziland 107
League of Nations 3, 19
legal personality 4, 6–7, 9–10, 12–14, 16, 58, 88, 121–2, 132, 156, 203–4
Les Témoins de Jehovah 105
Loayza Tamayo versus Peru 39, 51, 62, 103, 119, 122–3
Loizidou et alii versus Turkey 25, 114, 206, 211

Malawi 106
Mamatkulov versus Turkey 36
Mandelstam, André 7
Markovic and Others versus Italy 70–1
massacre 110, 133, 141, 162–3, 170, 173, 196, 201, 211
Massacre of Mapiripán, Colombia 64, 170, 180, 185–7
Massacre of Plan de Sánchez 180, 184–5, 187, 191
Massacre of Pueblo Bello versus Colombia 52, 64, 71, 83, 158, 180, 197, 199
Massacres of Barrio Altos 180
Massacres of Ituango, Colombia 180, 186–7
Maya 184–5
Media Rights Agenda and Others versus Nigeria 106
Mentes and Others versus Turkey 67–8
Mertens, Pierre 67
Mexico Declaration and Plan of Action to Strengthen the International Protection of Refugees in Latin America 165–7

migrants 15, 132–50, 152, 165, 167, 175–6, 211
Moiwana Community versus Suriname 141–2, 144–5, 168–70, 186
Montero Aranguren and Others case, Venezuela 180, 182, 188
Moustaquim versus Belgium 144
Myrna Mack Chang versus Guatemala 66, 180

NATO 70–1
Nigeria 106
non-governmental organization (NGO) 5, 22, 26, 47, 130, 147
Norris versus Ireland 24
Northern Ireland 172
Nurmagomedov versus Russia 30

Olmedo Bustos and Others versus Chile 193
Operation Condor 181–2, 185, 191, 199, 201, 203
Optional Protocol to the Covenant on Civil and Political Rights 22
Organization of American States (OAS) 22, 25, 44–5, 71, 130–1, 133–4, 167

P. and A. Marckx versus Belgium 128
Pact of San José 28
Palais des Droits de l'Homme 34, 118
Paniagua Morales and Others versus Guatemala 62
PCIJ *see* Permanent Court of International Justice
people-trafficking 135, 165, 167
Permanent Court of International Justice 113–14
Peru 39, 116–17
Petra versus Romania 171–2
Plattform 'Ärzte für das Leben' versus Austria 60
Poleshchuk versus Russia 31
Popov versus Russia 30
potential victim 22, 78, 125–31
Prison Castro Castro case, Peru 173, 180, 182
Prison 'Urso Branco' case, Brazil 173
prisoners 30, 171–2, 181
see also detention
Prisons of Mendoza case, Argentina 173
procedural equality 40, 42, 64, 146
protection, law of 6–7, 103, 209
protectionism 150
Provisional Measures of Protection 157–8, 172
Public International Law 7, 27, 36, 97
Pufendorf, Samuel 2
Purohit and Another versus Gambia 106

refugees 107, 135–7, 140, 145, 164–8
religion 138, 184
Rencontre Africaine pour la Défense des Droits de l'Homme versus Zambia 57, 106

reparations 1, 109, 118, 131, 188–90
  ACHR 86
  massacres 177, 179–80, 186–8
  migrants 141, 145–6
  notion of victim 126–7
  street children 152–6
  U.N. Commission on Human Rights 81–2
Reuter, Paul 10
Right to Information on Consular Assistance in
  the Framework of the Guarantees of the
  Due Process of Law 11, 64, 138, 144–6,
  165
Röling, B.V.A. 9
Rome Conference 34
Russia 25
Rwanda 106, 163

San José Declaration on Refugees and Displaced
  Persons 165–6
*Sawhoyamaxa Indigenous Community versus
  Paraguay* 58–9
Scelle, Georges 7
Second World Conference on Human Rights
  (1993) 27, 79–80
self-amnesty 193–6
Selmouni versus France 172
Servellón and Others versus Honduras 156
*Shamayev and Others versus Georgia and
  Russia* 31, 70
Sierra Leone 107
Silver and Others versus United Kingdom 66
Sisters Serrano Cruz versus El Salvador 155
*Social and Economic Rights Action Centre
  (SERAC) and Another versus Nigeria* 106
Soering versus United Kingdom 129
street children 14, 132, 176, 188, 211
Street Children case *see Villagrán Morales and
  Others versus Guatemala*
Suárez, Francisco 2
Suárez Rosero versus Ecuador 61, 129
subsidiarity 110–11
Switzerland 92

Tanaka, Kotaro 9
Tanrikuly versus Turkey 29, 104
terrorism 122, 181–2, 198, 201
Th. Lubanga Dyilo 204
Tibi versus Ecuador 198
Togo 106
Tomasi versus France 172
torture 66, 78, 80, 126, 153, 160, 171, 181–8,
  195, 198–9
Trinidad and Tobago 117
Trubnikov versus Russia 31
Trujillo Oroza versus Bolivia 62
Trust Fund for Victims *see* International
  Criminal Court (ICC)
trusteeship system 3
Turkey 25, 29, 66–70, 104, 114, 159–60, 170

Uganda 142, 162
U.N. Basic Principles and Guidelines on the
  Right to a Remedy and Reparation for
  Victims of Gross Violations of
  International Human Rights Law and
  Serious Violations of International
  Humanitarian Law 81, 127
U.N. Centre for Human Rights 138
U.N. Centre for International Crime
  Prevention 189
U.N. Commission on Human Rights 52–3, 81,
  134, 164
U.N. Convention 138–9
  on the Rights of the Child 12
  against Torture 78, 85
U.N. Convention against Torture 22
U.N. Convention on the Rights of the Child 85
U.N. Covenant on Civil and Political Rights 54,
  83–5, 92, 99, 141
  Human Rights Committee 93
U.N. Declaration on Basic Principles of Justice
  for Victims of Crime and Abuse of
  Power 126, 189
U.N. General Assembly 53, 137, 207
  Rule of Law at the National and International
  Levels 207
U.N. Guiding Principles on Internal
  Displacement 169
U.N. Handbook on Justice for Victims 189–90
U.N. High Commission for Human Rights 166
U.N. High Commissioner for Refugees
  (UNHCR) 133, 148
  Committee of Legal Experts 167
U.N. High-Commissioner for Human Rights 79
U.N. International Law Commission (ILC) 92,
  94–5, 180
U.N. Millennium Declaration 150
U.N. Security Council 108
U.N. Special Rapporteurs 134
U.N. World Conferences 5, 149
U.N. World Summit (2005) 207
UNESCO 52, 175
Union Interafricaine des Droits de
  l'Homme 105
Unit of Tatuapé of FEBEM, Brazil 173
United Kingdom 142–3
Universal Declaration of Human Rights
  (UDHR) 5, 7, 10, 19, 21, 52–6, 138, 206
University of La Cantuta versus Peru 185, 196, 200

Vagrancy cases, Belgium 32
Velásquez Rodríguez case 38
Venezuela 38, 173, 180, 182, 187–8
Victim's Declaration *see* U.N. Declaration on
  Basic Principles of Justice for Victims of
  Crime and Abuse of Power
Vienna Conference on Human Rights 80
Vienna Convention on Consular Relations
  139, 146

Vienna Conventions on the Law of Treaties 83,
    89–91, 93–4, 97, 116
Vienna Declaration and Programme of Action 164
*Vietnamese Orphans case (H. Becker versus
    Denmark)* 128–9
*Villagrán Morales and Others versus
    Guatemala* 14, 66, 152–5, 169
Vitoria, Francisco de 1, 11

Weil, Simone 136
Wolff, Christian 2
World Organization against Torture 105

Zaire 105
*Zimbabwe Human Rights NGO Forum versus
    Zimbabwe* 74, 106

Printed in the USA/Agawam, MA
June 4, 2019

704420.001